Integrated Communication:
Synergy of Persuasive Voices

ADVERTISING AND
CONSUMER PSYCHOLOGY
A series sponsored by the Society for
Consumer Psychology

AAKER/BIEL • Brand Equity & Advertising: Advertising's
(1993)   Role in Building Strong Brands

CLARK/BROCK/STEWART • Attention, Attitude, and Affect in
(1994)   Response to Advertising

ENGLIS • Global and Multi-National
(1994)   Advertising

MITCHELL • Advertising Exposure,
(1993)   Memory, and Choice

THORSON/MOORE • Integrated Communication:
(1996)   Synergy of Persuasive Voices

Integrated Communication:
Synergy of Persuasive Voices

Edited by

Esther Thorson
Missouri School of Journalism
University of Missouri-Columbia

Jeri Moore
CCS LTD.

LEA
LAWRENCE ERLBAUM ASSOCIATES, PUBLISHERS
1996   Mahwah, New Jersey

Lawrence Erlbaum Associates, Inc., Publishers
10 Industrial Avenue
Mahwah, New Jersey 07430

Cover design by Jan Melchior

Library of Congress Cataloging-in-Publication Data

Integrated communication: synergy of persuasive voices / edited by
Esther Thorson and Jeri Moore.
      p. cm.
    Papers presented at the 11th Advertising and Consumer Psychology
Conference held at DDB Needham Worldwide, Chicago, Ill., 1992.
    Includes bibliographical references and index.
    ISBN 0-8058-1391-8 (alk. paper)
    1. Communication in marketing — Congresses. 2. Marketing —
Management — Congresses. I. Thorson, Esther. II. Moore, Jeri.
III. Series: Conference on Advertising and Consumer Psychology (11th
: 1992 : Chicago, Ill.)
HF5415.123.I58 1995
658.8 — dc20   95-19673
                                             CIP

Printed in the United States of America
10 9 8 7 6 5 4 3 2

Contents

Preface

This volume is the result of a series of papers presented at the 11th annual Advertising and Consumer Psychology Conference held at DDB Needham Worldwide, Chicago, Illinois, on May 14–15, 1992. The conference was sponsored by DDB Needham Worldwide and the Division of Consumer Psychology of the American Psychological Association. The co-editors of the volume served as chairpersons for the conference.

Special thanks are due to the authors of these chapters. These authors participated in the conference, presenting their papers and engaging in discussions of them. They also reviewed each others' chapters, and then prepared their own papers for publication in this volume.

The editors are enthusiastic supporters of efforts to integrate the various persuasive tools of marketing. They present these papers to the reader with the knowledge that many interesting and challenging ideas are contained in them, and the hope that they will prove interesting and stimulating.

Esther Thorson
Jeri Moore

Introduction

Esther Thorson
University of Missouri-Columbia

Jeri Moore
CCS Ltd.

> Integrated marketing communications are those messages that address multiple consumer and nonconsumer audiences and achieve synergy of messages and timing.

The concept of *integrated marketing communication* (IMC) continues to produce both intense interest (e.g., "Ad Age," 1993) and a violent negative response, generally along the lines of "Why do these people think they've invented something new? We've been doing integrated marketing for years?" (e.g., Duncan & Caywood, chapter 1, this volume). It is true, in fact, that many smaller advertising agencies have been using a variety of persuasive tools to market their clients' brands (Gronstedt & Thorson, 1993), and that there are many examples of brand campaigns that have coordinated to one degree or another a number of persuasive tools. However, many—if not most—marketers that employ advertising, public relations, direct marketing, and promotions companies to produce multiple messages about the same brands do not fully integrate their communications in the sense used in this book.

This brings us to the question of what, precisely, we mean by IMC. For us, IMC is the strategic coordination of multiple communication voices. Its aim is to optimize the impact of persuasive communication on both consumer and nonconsumer (e.g., trade, professional) audiences by coordinating such elements of the marketing mix as advertising, public relations, promotions, direct marketing, and package design. Although there are a number of important publications that have focused on this issue (e.g., Schultz, Tannenbaum, & Lauterborn, 1992; Wang & Petrison, 1991), there is thus far little attempt to discuss or research theory about how the persuasive voices work together.

For us there appear to be at least three important issues that must be addressed within the concept of IMC. A first issue focuses on how the media both within and across voices relate to each other. For example, there have been a small number of studies (e.g., Edell & Keller, 1989, 1993) of how to combine advertising media such as radio, television, newspapers, and so on, for maximum impact. There have been no analogous studies of media combinations in public relations (e.g., press releases, corporate publications, or special events) and in promotions (e.g., sampling, couponing, premiums, and point-of-purchase advertising). For the field to move forward, studies that do examine combinations within each of the persuasive tool areas (advertising, public relations, promotions, direct marketing, and packaging) will be necessary.

A second issue in integrated communications involves point of entry for the integrated campaign. Although persuasive theory is usually driven by the idea that advertising communications lead and dominate, this is clearly not the only model possible. For example, campaigns are now being initiated based on ideas about direct marketing or promotional activities (e.g., Moore, 1993). However, this means that an important question is how to theorize about the impact of campaigns in which the dominant voice is not advertising.

A third issue involves reconceptualizing the importance of various target groups. For example, one can consider a variety of consumer targets as well as sales force personnel, retailers, government officials, and so on. Although conventional communications planning often assumes that the consumer communications should take precedence, there are a number of examples (Moore, 1992) in which highly successful IMC programs were driven either by nonconsumer audiences, or by important (IMC-generated) interactions between consumer and nonconsumer audiences. Again, however, there is little theory available for guiding coordination of messages to a variety of targets.

Before introducing the chapters represented in this volume, therefore, we suggest an overall framework that allows us to consider all three of these aspects of "coordination." We then discuss how each of the chapters herein provide important input to the framework.

A STRATEGIC FRAMEWORK FOR CONSIDERING IMC

One important way to consider IMC is in terms of the planning of the promotional campaign. We believe that only by developing a comprehensive strategy for using the different persuasive tools can we build effective linkages among them.

There are three critical components in an IMC strategic plan. The first is the definition of the essential nature of the brand. The second is definition of the target audience or audiences. The third component is the set of persuasion tools to be employed in linking the communications of the brand essence to the target(s).

Brand Essence

The first task of strategic planning for IMC is to define and understand in detail the brand itself and the "equity" that it possesses.

A brand is basically a name that refers to an exemplar in a particular product category. Of course, a brand includes tangible, or intrinsic, qualities, such as its physical appearance, its performance attributes, its package, and guarantees or warranties that are attached to it. But perhaps more importantly, a brand involves aspects that the consumer attributes to it beyond its tangible ones. These aspects may include attitudes toward the company that produces the product, attitudes toward the brand itself, beliefs about the brand in relationship to self and others, and so on.

Attributes of brands beyond their intrinsic qualities are frequently provided by advertising. In a world filled with parity brands in many product categories, it is often these attributes that determine the success of the brand. We can think of a brand name as "adding value" to a product beyond its intrinsic qualities. We can also think of the brand name as providing critical differentiation between one brand and other brands.

Based on this conception of the brand, *brand equity* can be defined as "everything the consumer walks into the store with" (Farquhar, 1989, p. 24). In other words, equity is the "value added" to the product by the fact that it wears a brand name and has a history in the mind of the consumer.

Thus, the first step in building a strategic plan for IMC is to define and explore extensively the brand's essence—both current and intended. Brand essence, as we have seen, involves many attributes. A brand may be associated with a mood, as, for example, Dr. Pepper is associated with an upbeat mood with an individualistic flavor. A brand may cause emotional response in consumers, as, for example, the name Hallmark Cards does as a result of its long history of poignant commercials.

Brands may be closely associated with their advertising, that is, people may quickly recall ads when someone mentions the brand name. Or, brands may not bring forth much ad memory at all. This attribute is sometimes called *ad cue strength*. Brands may have strong associations with visual images. Usually these are the product itself, or sometimes its packaging. But they may also be images that have been present over the course of many years in the advertising for the brand.

Brands may belong to categories of products that people are highly involved with, or they may belong in low-interest categories. Brand essences may be very extensive and rich. Brands may or may not be associated richly with people's own personal autobiographical histories. And brands may be salient or nonsalient representatives of their product categories. There are probably many other aspects of brand essences, but for the present we concentrate on these.

The Target Market

The second important apex in the strategic planning triangle is, of course, the target market. The target market provides an answer to the question, "To whom will the persuasion be addressed?" Identification of targets often involves examining both the best consumer prospects as well as various influencer or channel audiences. Frequently, multiple targets are used; it is important to understand the potential interactions between these multiple targets. Descriptions of target markets should be personal and precise.

The Persuasion Tools

The five main areas of persuasive tools that can be used include: (a) public relations, (b) direct marketing, (c) promotions, (d) packaging, and (e) advertising. It is important to define each of these terms. First, *public relations* is a management function that evaluates public attitudes, works to achieve effective relationships with various audiences, and plans and executes programs of action to earn public understanding and acceptance. Second, *direct marketing* is a form of mediated communication that establishes a one-to-one relationship with the consumer. The persuasive message may itself go individually and directly to the individual, usually by mail or telephone. Or, the consumer may be enabled to respond directly to the marketer. Such direct marketing opportunities may be provided, then, by broadcast as well as the other media, because the consumer initiates the contact, usually by using a 800 or 900 number. Third, *promotions* are activities or entities aimed to getting the customer to take action. They are usually direct inducements to the consumer and have the primary objective of creating an immediate sale. Fourth, *packaging* is a persuasive tool that operates directly from the package itself—its design, its shape, the information on it, and so on. And finally, *advertising* is paid, professionally designed messages channeled through the media to potential consumers.

With these definitions in mind, we are now ready to look more carefully at the strategic triangle. The job for the marketer is to communicate efficiently and effectively to the target(s) the essence of the brand. Often, of course, the essence that is defined as most important depends on what is expected to appeal to the target(s). Once an essence is identified, however, there are three critical interrelated questions that remain: First, how can the brand essence be best articulated? Second, what audiences must receive the message about the brand in order for the marketing objectives to be achieved? Third, what set of communications vehicles (media) will be best at delivering the brand messages to the various targets? Message delivery itself, of course, is not simple, but involves both the McLuhan (1966) observation that "the medium is the message," and the idea that there is a certain time, place, and condition of the target audience that will optimize response to the persuasive impact.

When we think of "persuasion interfaces," it becomes clear that there are a number of very different kinds of occasions in which interfacing can occur. Message encounters occur when the target is exposed to actual selling articulations. These are generally messages. They often, although not always, contain words and pictures. A second interface occasion involves trial. During this kind of occasion, the target actually consumes the product. The trial can occur either by natural usage events after the brand is purchased, or by trial on a sample that has been provided to the target. A third interface occasion involves an event wherein the brand is associated with something external to and separate from the brand itself. The associated something can be an emotion, a celebrity, a sports event, the reward of learning new information, or virtually anything else that is desired to be added to the essence of the brand.

A fourth interface encounter occurs at the location at which the consumer is making the purchase. Here the main kind of persuasion tool is the point-of-purchase message.

There may be a salesperson present who shows how the brand can be used, provides information about the brand, or simply helps with the acquiring of the brand. At some purchase encounters there may be a celebrity interacting directly with the consumer.

The decision about which persuasion tool to use depends both on which aspect of the brand essence you wish to enhance or create and the kind of interface you hope to make between the brand essence and the target. For example, if you want people to associate your brand with "fun," then you are trying to create an emotional response as part of the brand essence, and it is likely you can use an associational encounter most effectively because you want to associate an emotion with your brand.

Or, you may want to encourage people not just to purchase your brand, but to use it up and purchase more. In this case, you want to enhance the "desire for further purchase." You might concentrate on encounters that offer rewards at the point of trial or usage (e.g., in-pack recipes) or on those that offer rewards at the point of purchase.

These examples of working with both brand essence and influence occasions to choose persuasive tools are purposely simple in order to show clearly how the thinking works. The examples must, however, be pushed to demonstrate how combinations of tools can be selected so as to further enhance the specific desired brand essence.

THE CHAPTERS IN THIS VOLUME AND THEIR RELATIONSHIP TO THE IMC STRATEGIC MODEL

Definitions and Theoretical Foundations

The first two chapters are concerned with defining IMC, both from a theoretical point of view, and from the point of view of how it is defined by marketing professionals. In the Duncan and Caywood chapter, there is an important attempt to trace historically the emergence of IMC in the late 1980s and early 1990s. Duncan and Caywood argue that significant changes in the structure of the market itself have necessitated the movement toward coordinating persuasive efforts. These changes include loss of advertising credibility, increasing promotional expertise of clients, mergers and acquisitions of both client companies and marketing communication agencies, fragmentation of the media, the increase in power of retailers, and the direct competition with advertising of promotions—whose effects are more easily observed. Based on surveys of professionals, Duncan and Caywood hypothesize that the transition to integrated marketing progresses through a series of stages. At each stage, a company essentially redefines its way of conducting business. At the first stage, there is only awareness of the possibility of integrated marketing. At the last stage, the entire management system is organized around integrated marketing. The authors discuss each of the stages in detail. They also give some consideration to the variables that lead companies from one stage to another.

In chapter 2, Lloyd focuses on how advertising agency media directors think about integrated communication. The data reported in the chapter consist of a focus group and five in-depth interviews with marketing communication executives and media managers in New York. Lloyd provides evidence that these professionals perceive the media world as having become increasingly complex. One result has been that media planners are becoming involved earlier in the development of promotional campaigns—and this itself has led toward more and more coordinating of the media early on—that is, toward IMC campaigns. The conceptions of many of these professionals about the importance of considering all interfaces between consumers and promotions is highly consistent with the model presented here.

Psychological Processes and Integrated Communication

The five chapters in this section are concerned with various aspects of individual consumer contact with the messages of integrated campaigns.

Schumann, Dyer, and Petkus (chapter 3) focus on how these messages can, in their interaction, produce negative or "boomerang" effects. One important possibility is that different messages encountered by consumers lead them to counterargue. Another possibility is that consumers will encounter both advertising for a company's brand, and advertising the company is producing for other purposes such as to increase careful use of the brand (e.g., don't drink and drive) or to increase positive views of the company itself. Often these messages can lead to clear inconsistencies for the consumer, and essentially damage brand attitude. The authors of the chapter, then, are concerned with developing theory at the individual level about how consumers integrate in their own cognitive and motivational systems, the various messages they are receiving, and then asking how the integration of those messages can produce negative or problematic consumer responses.

Solomon and Englis (chapter 4) examine the concept of consumption constellations and their relationships to integrated campaigns. Consumption constellations are "clusters of complementary products, specific brands, or consumption activities used to construct, signify, and/or perform a social role." Consumption constellations can be important to integrated campaigns in a number of ways. For example, they can suggest types of promotions that would be most successful, and they can be used to identify the types of events and product placements that will appeal to users of a particular brand. The authors, in addition to pointing out the utility of consumption constellations to integrated communication, also make significant suggestions about what research needs doing in order for more thorough understanding of this link.

The Stern chapter (5) is an interesting approach to the psychology of corporate image. Stern conceptualizes the corporation as having a persona, which is created, presumably in the minds of consumers, by combining the various "voices" with which the corporation speaks. This conception provides an excellent heuristic for thinking about how the various messages of the integrated campaign must relate to each other and to a "whole" which is the persona.

Keller's chapter (6), the final one in this section, is concerned with how integrated communications can be used to build brand equity. The model presented in the chapter suggests that the job for marketers is threefold: to build brand *awareness* and brand *associations;* to create consumer motivation, ability, and opportunity to *process* persuasive messages; and to create consumer motivation, ability and opportunity to *retrieve* brand information from memory when making a brand choice. To accomplish these ends, Keller suggests that marketers integrate across different kinds of persuasive tools (i.e., advertising, promotions, direct marketing, packaging), and across different media.

Managing Integrated Marketing Communication

Moore and Thorson (chapter 7) pursue and develop the idea that the best way to think about integrating campaigns is in terms of strategic planning. Some of the benefits of using a planning system to bring various marketing professionals together are identified, and a suggested framework for developing a plan is elaborated.

Petrison and Wang (chapter 8) also look at IMC from a strategic management point of view. These authors differentiate between coordination of executional communications elements (i.e., consistency of messages) and coordination of the overall plan (i.e., ensuring that each type of persuasive tool is used to its best effect). Both of these forms of coordination are, of course, important, but accomplishing each one provokes differing management challenge. The authors describe and compare these differing challenges and then build a framework for helping companies insure that both forms of coordination are accomplished.

In chapter 9, Prensky, McCarty, and Lucas also focus on the management of IMC. But here the focus is on differing organizational structures for accomplishing that management. The authors present four structures, and then evaluate those structures in terms of some organizing concepts: culture and politics in the company, the role of managers, and the strategic goals of the company. The authors conclude with some recommendations for more effective management of IMC.

Stewart, Frazier, and Martin (chapter 10) are concerned with combining the communication and distribution functions of companies. They point out that although channels of distribution and marketing communications are presently differentiated, they can in an IMC framework now be thought of as having virtually identical functions. Just as the medium can be thought of as the message (McLuhan, 1966), the channel and the messages can be thought of as the medium. A good example of this would be "event marketing," in which a running shoe sponsors a race, or the idea of placing an ad for a telecommunications company on a public telephone. For both of these, the consumption experience is located at the same point as the persuasive message.

The last chapter in the management section of the book (Jones, chapter 11) focuses on the management of the financial resources of the marketer, and is concerned with the relative profitability of advertising and promotions. Jones suggests that, given the much higher costs of promotions, their use in the integrated program must be planned very carefully.

Integrated Campaigns: Case Studies

No analysis of IMC would be complete without significant attention to case studies in which IMC was employed, and chapters 12 and 13 provide in-depth coverage of just such cases.

The Haytko chapter looks at an integrated public service campaign designed to encourage reading. This case is an example of a program in which a number of marketing professionals worked together to conceive and produce an integrated marketing program that had as its point of entry a promotion that was driven by public relations.

The Deighton chapter looks at and compares two more very different cases; one is the Tylenol poisoning situation, and the other concerns the launching of a new brand of disposable contact lenses. Highly consistent with the strategy model introduced here, Deighton emphasizes the idea that integration is a process that must be linked with interfaces that the target group experiences with the brand.

Measuring the Impact of Integrated Campaigns

The two chapters in this section are concerned with evaluating the impact of integrated campaigns. Katz and Lendrevie (chapter 14) define a system for comparing "exposures" regardless of which kind of persuasive tool is being used. Obviously, exposures for traditional advertising media have well-defined measures, but what about public relations, direct marketing, and the other persuasive tools? The authors argue that for these other media, the appropriate coinage is the "impression" (i.e., the opportunity for a single exposure).

Baldinger (chapter 15) suggests that for integrated campaigns to be appropriately evaluated, it is necessary to use multiple indices of their impact. Baldinger's chapter uses two of the persuasive tools most commonly employed by packaged goods marketers — advertising and promotions — as illustrative. He argues that it is important to look at both the in-home impact (for advertising) and the in-store impact (for promotions) and then to integrate the two kinds of measures.

The Role of Public Relations in Integrated Marketing Communication

The two chapters in this section focus on public relations and its relationships to both advertising and the other promotional tools. Gronstedt (chapter 16) posits that what public relations adds to integrated communications is a more sophisticated idea of the target market. Targets are reconceptualized as "stakeholders."

Hallahan (chapter 17) explores the various ways in which product publicity has and could be used to sell products. He compares the kind of impact product publicity and advertising have, looking at the two promotional tools in terms of a number of important marketing models. He concludes that the role of product publicity, both alone and in tandem with advertising, holds considerable promise. He also makes suggestions about possible directions research on product publicity might profitably take.

Theoretical Summary, A Research Agenda, and Conclusions

The final section of the book includes two chapters. In Moriarty (chapter 18), there is an integrated overview of the various orientations that have been introduced throughout the proceeding chapters. The concept of synergy is defined in terms of the memory impact of integrated campaigns, and this definition is then used to bring together issues of planning, media selection, management of campaigns and ways of thinking about the audience. The chapter provides an excellent round-up of the variety of topics that must be examined when integrated communication is the focus.

Chapter 19 provides Lutz an opportunity to look back over the chapters to evaluate where we have progressed, where more work is needed, and to explore the consistent themes that run through the contributions. Not only is the chapter integrative, it suggests what Lutz considers to be the most profitable future directions for IMC research to take.

REFERENCES

Ad age conference to explore effects of integrated marketing. (1993, October 18). *Advertising Age*, p. 2.
Edell, J. A., & Keller, K. L. (1989). The information processing of coordinated media campaigns. *Journal of Marketing Research, 26*(2), 149–163.
Edell, J. A., & Keller, K. L. (1993). *Analyzing media interactions: Print reinforcement of television advertising campaigns* (Working Paper). Durham, NC: Fuqua School of Business, Duke University.
Farquhar, P. H. (1989, September). Managing brand equity. *Marketing Research*, pp. 24–33.
Gronstedt, A., & Thorson, E. (1993, August). *In search of integrative communications excellence: Five organizational structures in advertising agencies*. Paper presented at the annual meeting of the Association for Education in Journalism and Mass Communication, Kansas City, MO.
McLuhan, M. (1966). *Understanding media: The extensions of man*. New York: McGraw-Hill.
Moore, J. (1993). Building brands across markets: Cultural differences in brand relationships within the European Community. In D. Aaker & A. Biel (Eds.), *Brand equity and advertising*. Hillsdale, NJ: Lawrence Erlbaum Associates.
Schultz, D. E., Tannenbaum, S., & Lauterborn, R. F. (1992). *Integrated marketing communications: Pulling it together & making it work*. Chicago: NTC Business Books.
Wang, P., & Petrison, L. (1991, Fall). Integrated marketing communications and its potential effects on media planning. *Journal of Media Planning*, pp. 11–17.

Integrated Marketing Communication: Definitions and Theoretical Foundations

1 The Concept, Process, and Evolution of Integrated Marketing Communication

Tom Duncan
University of Colorado

Clarke Caywood
Northwestern University

Recognizing that the marketplace was changing and that advertising was fast losing its golden halo, ad agencies went on a merger and acquisition binge in the late 1970s and throughout the 1980s in an attempt to offer their clients more than just advertising. Unfortunately, most of these marriages with public relations, sales promotion, and direct response agencies were based on a physical (i.e., financial) attraction, not on love and respect for their new partners' communication skills. The acquisitions were driven by the attempt to not lose the money that clients were transferring out of advertising into the other communication areas. In addition, these agencies had little understanding of the integrated marketing communication concept. They continued to have tunnel vision, responding to most situations with the attitude of "advertising is the answer, now what's the problem." The advertising agencies were either unwilling or unable to fully assimilate their newly acquired communication functions, in most cases allowing the newly acquired agencies to remain independent profit centers. Consequently, ad agency clients, for the most part, saw little benefit in ending their relationships with their current public relations, sales promotion, and direct response agencies. Advertising agencies are still searching for the best way to incorporate the concept and practice of integrated marketing communication (IMC).

Recognizing that IMC was more than a fad, in the late 1980s, the ad agencies, led by the American Association of Advertising Agencies, tried to co-opt the concept by calling it the "new advertising." To say the least, this self-serving term did little to build positive relationships with public relations, sales promotion, and other nonadvertising communication agencies. If anything, the "new advertising" title made some of these increasingly important players feel disenfranchised. Some public relations academics began to refer to IMC as "marketing imperialism." Also, several have pushed hard for changing or dropping the word *marketing* and referring to the concept as "integrated communications." (This latter phrasing actually more accurately describes the advanced stages of IMC, as explained later in this chapter.)

Although the advertising agencies continue to struggle with how to recognize and focus their efforts, more and more clients are taking a hard look at IMC because of the synergistic effect it can provide — giving them a better return on their marketing communication investment, which is extremely important as bottom-line pressures increase. Partially because many advertising agencies' first attempts to use IMC were more for their own benefit than for their clients', the understanding of IMC has been mixed, at best. This understanding is clarified when it is recognized that IMC is both a concept and a process. Although most people agree that it is conceptually a good idea, there is still little agreement about what it truly means and even less agreement about "how to do it." And to make things even more confusing, both the concept and the process continue to evolve.

To help explain this concept and process, we first look at the two "parents" of IMC — changes in the marketplace and the growth in expertise of the various marketing communication functions. This is followed by a discussion of several IMC definitions that show how the focus has expanded from the consumer to all stakeholders. Two U.S. studies that document IMC's perceived value as well as the barriers to using IMC are then presented, followed by a discussion of the various levels of integration.

Some marketing communication practitioners contend that IMC is nothing new. They cite advertising agencies such as Leo Burnett, which has designed Kellogg packaging since the 1950s, put together the Pillsbury Bake-Off in the mid-1960s, and guided Marlboro and Virginia Slims into event sponsorships and direct marketing (e.g., the Marlboro Store) when, after the early 1970s, cigarettes were no longer allowed to be advertised on TV. They also argue that many small- and medium-sized agencies have traditionally handled public relations, sales promotion, and other marketing communications, in addition to advertising, for their clients whose budgets have not justified separate agencies for each communication function.

It is true that some clients have long had their marketing communications centrally planned and executed; however, today's marketing arena has significantly changed since the 1960s and 1970s, requiring, we believe, a similar significant change in the strategic planning and execution of marketing communications. Although having marketing communications centrally controlled is an important element of IMC, this element alone is not enough to provide organizations a competitive advantage in today's marketplace that is being shaped by the following trends.

MARKETPLACE TRENDS THAT HAVE NECESSITATED NEW WAYS OF COMMUNICATING

The following trends and changes have been the primary factors driving organizations to adopt integrated marketing communication.

→ *Decreasing message impact and credibility:* Not only are consumers becoming more callous to commercial messages, the growing number of commercial messages makes it increasingly difficult for a single message to have affect.

→ *Decreasing cost of using databases:* In the mid-1970s, the cost of storing and retrieving a single name and address was about $1.50; today, that cost is less than one cent. This drastic cost reduction, coupled with the increased sophistication of audience segmentation, has provided marketers with a whole new way to more efficiently reach target audiences.

→ *Increasing client expertise:* Gone are the days when only the ad agencies had MBAs and client marketing departments were run by promoted (or demoted) salespeople — clients are now not only pushing their agencies to be more cost effective, but are also no longer accepting the idea that TV advertising should always be the primary medium for reaching consumers. At the same time, many clients are realizing that other stakeholders and publics are often just as important to communicate with as are consumers.

→ *Increasing mergers and acquisitions of marketing communication agencies:* Today, the top 10 public relations firms are owned or merged with an ad agency. At the same time, the 10 largest ad agencies (except Leo Burnett) either own or are partnered with a variety of agencies and firms offering specialized communication functions such as public relations, sales promotion, direct response, event planning, and packaging. Although these mergers have resulted in few clients moving all their communication business under one roof, the mergers have underlined that even advertising agencies recognize that these other forms of marketing communications are important and will comprise an increasing portion in their clients' marketing communication mix.

→ *Increasing "mass" media costs:* While database costs were falling, increases in mass media CPMs, especially television's, far outpaced the consumer price index throughout most of the 1980s.

→ *Increasing media fragmentation:* With the exception of the decreasing number of newspapers, the number of AM, FM, and public radio stations, television stations (especially cable), and magazines in the United States increased between 1980 and 1990, thus increasing the competition for consumers' attention.

→ *Increasing audience fragmentation:* With the help of computers and more sophisticated research methods, companies have increasingly been able to more accurately segment and target specialized audiences such as Asian Americans, teenagers, Hispanics, affluent retirees, and so on. This has, in turn, placed more emphasis on finding media that can efficiently reach these niche markets.

→ *Increasing number of "me-too" products:* With the increased ability to analyze and match successful competitive products, manufacturers have continued to flood retailers with new products that are nearly identical to many already on the shelves. The fact that many of the new products have few if any significant differences means that marketing communication must either create a strong brand image and/or deliver enough commercial messages to gain attention and sales.

→ *Increasing power of the retailer:* The December 21, 1992, cover of *Business Week* summed this up with the headline: "CLOUT! How Giant Retailers Are Revolutionizing the Way Consumer Products Are Bought and Sold." Because of their size and the instant information provided by scanner data, retailers now have both the clout and knowledge to tell suppliers the kind of products and promotions they want and when they want them. Most suppliers cannot afford not to cooperate.

→ *Increasing global marketing:* Nearly every major company is involved in global marketing in some way today. Even if a company is not selling outside its native country, it must be aware that its competitors will increasingly be foreign based. There is also the possibility that equipment and supplies will, to a greater extent, come from outside the United States. These changes underline the increase in competition and the necessity for companies to concentrate on maximum efficiency in all their operations.

→ *Increasing pressure on bottom lines:* Wall Street and the rest of the financial community continue to look at quarterly earnings of public companies, thus driving managements to push marketing to do more with less and give priority to short-term rather than long-term results.

GROWING EXPERTISE OF "OTHER" COMMUNICATION AREAS HAS CREATED COMPETITION FOR AD AGENCIES

Through the mid-1970s, advertising agencies were the gurus of promotion. Clients, both large and small, looked to them for guidance on nearly every aspect of marketing, especially in all areas of communication. This is not to say that there were no sales promotion, public relations, packaging design, or direct response agencies operating during this time, but rather these agencies were generally considered as auxiliary services and used mostly on a per-project basis. It is true that many public relations firms have had long relationships with many of the clients; however, these most frequently have involved corporate counseling in areas other than marketing communications.

In the late 1970s and throughout the 1980s, these relationships significantly changed. The decreased cost of using databases provided direct response agencies with competitive advantage for reaching niche audiences. The increase in media cost and decrease in paid message credibility at the same time opened the marketing door for public relations agencies. In essence, brand managers began discovering the power and cost efficiencies of product publicity. As retailers became more demanding and Wall Street put more pressure on quarterly reports, marketing managers turned more attention and a greater portion of their budgets to sales promotion, an activity that was both more predictable and more short term than traditional advertising. In their drive to do more with less, marketing managers began to discover that often for the cost of producing one TV commercial they could redesign a line of packages and significantly increase sales. This, in turn, gave packaging firms more attention and respect, and soon many packaging firms began offering corporate identity programs and brand positioning strategies.

No longer were advertising agencies the only game in town. Both the clients' attention and marketing communication dollars began to be divided among other communication agencies. With their increased revenues and client involvement, these "other" communication agencies grew in expertise. The result has been that clients now have many alternative ways to solve a communication problem or take advantage of a marketing opportunity.

The new challenge for clients is to find the most effective and efficient way to make use of the "new" marketing communication alternatives. The concept of integrated marketing communication is helping them meet that challenge, allowing them to strategically focus and coordinate their marketing communication programs in a way that will produce a synergistic effect, a result that can also help the bottom line.

Evolving IMC Definitions

One of the first widely discussed definitions of IMC came from the American Association of Advertising Agencies (the 4As) in 1989. This definition, which is presented here, focused on the "process" of using more than just advertising to achieve maximum communication impact. No reference is made to audience(s) or effectiveness other than impact:

[ICM is a] concept of marketing communications planning that recognizes the added value of a comprehensive plan that evaluates the strategic roles of a variety of communication disciplines—general advertising, direct response, sales promotion, and public relation—and combines these disciplines to provide clarity, consistency, and maximum communication impact. (Caywood et al., 1991)

In 1991, Don Schultz and his colleagues in Northwestern University's Integrated Marketing Communication program came up with the following definition of IMC: "The process of managing all sources of information about a product/service to which a customer or prospect is exposed which behaviorally moves the consumer toward a sale and maintains customer loyalty" (Northwestern University's brochure, 1991).

This definition focuses strictly on the customer or prospect and places an implied emphasis on building a relationship between the customer and the brand. For IMC to be successful, according to this definition, there must be a behavioral response from the customer or prospect. By including "all sources of information" to which customers and prospects are exposed, the definition includes a wider variety of communication functions than that suggested by the 4As' definition, even those not originating from the organization or its communication agencies.

Duncan's first definition appeared in *Marketing* in 1992. It viewed IMC as: "The strategic coordination of all messages and media used by an organization to collectively influence its perceived brand value" (Keegan, Moriarty, & Duncan, 1992, p. 631).

Unlike Schultz's definition, Duncan's first definition did not limit the focus to just customers and prospects, but implied that whoever had an interest in the organization/brand was to be taken into consideration. Also unlike Schultz's, this definition limited the message and media focus to those originating from the brand or its agencies. Another difference was the focus on an attitudinal rather than a behavioral change.

Duncan subsequently revised his definition to focus more on relationship building with all stakeholders and added a behavioral response effect (e.g., "create and nourish profitable relationship") and a dialogue element to his attitudinal effect. Also, his revised definition placed more emphasis on the organization, not just its brand(s), stating that IMC is "the process of strategically controlling or influencing all messages and encouraging purposeful dialogue to create and nourish profitable relationships with customers and other stakeholders" (Duncan & Moriarty, 1994).

Not only has the evolution of IMC definitions moved away from the literal integration of major communication functions under direct control of an organization, but it has expanded the concept of audience and placed more emphasis on long-term effects such as brand loyalty and maintaining relationships rather than on just impact. Also, when Duncan added *stakeholders* to the definition, it moved the concept beyond the trade and consumer target audiences to include employees, stockholders, regulators, and all others who have a direct or indirect impact on organizational operations and profitability. These broader definitions open the door for public relations, especially, to play a more important role in IMC. To do this, however, they must be less defensive—no more cries of marketing imperialism—and seize the opportunity to demonstrate their skills in building relationships with a variety of publics or target audiences so that the long-term survival of profitable businesses will be assured.

Studies Show Clients Value the IMC Concept

Two studies of U.S. client organizations' perceptions and uses of IMC were conducted in 1991. The Caywood, Schultz, and Wang (Northwestern University) study, which was done in cooperation with the AAAA and ANA, was based on responses (30%) from 94 corporations that had average sales of $9.6 billion. Its sample was drawn from *Advertising Age*'s 1990 listing of the 100 Leading Advertisers and from *Adweek*'s supplement "American's Top 2,000 Brands." The Duncan and Everett (University of Colorado) study drew its sample from client marketing managers who subscribed to *Advertising Age*. Of its 216 responses (43%), 31% were from companies with sales under $100 million and 46% from companies with sales over $500 million.

Although the two studies asked slightly different questions, the overall findings were fairly consistent except in the area of who should take the leadership in making IMC work. Even though only 59% said they were familiar with the term *integrated marketing communication*, over 4 out of 5, when given a definition of IMC, said it was of value and would increase the effect and impact of their marketing communications efforts.

When asked why and how IMC would add value to their communication programs, there was strong agreement with the following points: it provides greater consistency in marketing communication programs, reduces media waste, and it gives a company a competitive edge. Respondents did not anticipate, however, that IMC would save them meeting time or money. Also, at this time they said it would have little impact on their hiring criteria.

The majority of respondents expected the use of IMC to increase within the next five years. Also, they expected their advertising and other marketing communication agencies to work more closely with each other in the future.

Although respondents said IMC was not inconsistent with their corporate culture, a majority of respondents indicated that the major barriers to using

IMC are turf battle and egos, both internally and with their outside agencies. Also, there was some concern about departmental and agency allocations being reduced if IMC began to be practiced.

It was found that advertising agencies were much more likely to handle multiple marketing communication functions (i.e., public relations, sales promotion, direct response, packaging) than were any of the other communication agencies. This suggests, it seems, that advertising agencies have a head start over the other communication agencies in assuming a major role in a client's effort to integrate its marketing communications.

As mentioned previously, however, what role an outside communication agency should play in IMC was the only major area in which the Duncan and Everett and Caywood et al. findings significantly differed. Caywood et al. found that nearly 9 out of 10 respondents said the client alone should take the leadership and responsibility for making IMC work. Duncan and Everett, however, found that less than a third said "the client alone" should determine communication strategies, and over half said both the client and agency should take the initiative to make IMC successful.

A probable explanation of this difference is the fact that respondents in the Caywood et al. study (which had average sales of $9.6 billion) had much larger and more sophisticated marketing and marketing communications departments than the average respondents in the Duncan and Everett study. Duncan and Everett's sample included more small- and medium-sized companies, the ones less likely to feel confident about handling their marketing communications and certainly more wary of adopting a new approach such as IMC. In a case study on a marketing unit of IBM, Caywood (1992d) chronicled the leadership role of a business unit manager demanding integrated services from smaller agencies while rejecting the "agencies of record."

Entrepreneurial Companies Doing IMC Best

Although there is to date little empirical evidence to prove that IMC is an improved means by which an organization can structure its communications, there are several companies that have been extremely successful and, based on observation, are doing excellent jobs of integrating their communication efforts. Ben & Jerry's, Nike, The Body Shop, Banana Republic, and Apple have been able to quickly establish strong brand images by making sure that each company's communication plan has been an honest and genuine outgrowth of its corporate culture. An example is The Body Shop, which has an image of honest products made by a company that is socially and environmentally concerned. Such an image is not the creation of a copywriter working on the 39th floor of a New York ad agency but, rather, stems from the personality and values of the company's founder,

Anita Roddick. Not only does she obtain ingredients for the products from developing countries whenever possible, but she also requires her employees to spend at least two weeks a year — at company expense — doing some type of humanitarian work. All her products are made from natural ingredients and none of them are tested on animals. The stores and packaging have a consistent look and feel. The result has been the growth of an international chain of very successful retail stores.

It is likely, however, that if Anita Roddick and others in The Body Shop organization were asked about its use of integrated marketing communication, they would probably not understand the question. The fact the company is practicing IMC is more a result of intuition and a very focused set of principles and standards laid down by Roddick.

Most of the other companies that seem to be benefiting from using IMC have been created and driven by strong entrepreneurial individuals or couples. If this analysis is true, it brings up the question of whether IMC can work in a large organization. The answer is probably one of degrees. Without question, it is easier for an organization that has strong leadership and a unique corporate culture to use IMC than a diversified company with two and three tiers of branding. The larger companies and the ones not blessed with an Anita Roddick or Nike's founder, Philip Knight (Chairman, CEO, and past President of Nike Corporation), can use IMC, but the level of benefit depends on to what extent the IMC concept is employed. As explained in the next section, there are different levels of IMC. Some believe that merely using a variety of communication functions is IMC; others that using "one voice" is IMC. What is being discovered, however, is that a ✶ complete conversion to IMC involves much more.

Multiple Levels of IMC

The development of any new field or the logical extension of a field involves an evolving acceptance and definition of the area. The theoretical boundaries of an integrated approach to marketing communications and management are only limited by the imagination of managers and management theoreticians.

This introduction to concepts in integrated marketing communication presents a framework for an applied understanding of the field. Several dimensions of integration identified from two national studies of advertisers cited previously form the basis of the framework. Additional trends and assumptions have been added to the description. The framework is not final; it contains the seeds of discussion, some discontent, and the opportunity to test in practice and research several propositions to document the value of integration to successful corporate and other organizational managements.

Integrated marketing communication begins with awareness and may advance through several stages to a general integration of new ways of conducting business. Visually, the model may be represented as a set of concentric circles moving from the first stage of "awareness" progressively outward to the final stage of "general management integration" (see Fig. 1.1). Although some might arrange the stages of integration into a hierarchical pyramid, the language of the model attempts to reduce the value-laden labels indicating that one stage of integration is superior to another. Each stage of integration may build on the experience of the previous stages, but each organization finds the stage that fits its current management, market, and environmental situation. There may be a progression through the stages, but the learning process of integration and the highly fluid nature of the field demands that each stage contribute to the

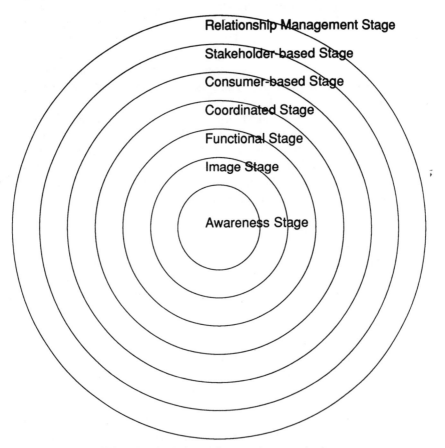

FIG. 1.1   Evolutionary integrated communications.

firm's ability to survive and to meet the challenges of the trends discussed earlier in this chapter and labeled "Awareness Stage" in Fig. 1.1.

A number of research propositions are offered at each stage to suggest the opportunity to test the developmental model. The propositions are stated in a less rigorous form than is a strict research hypothesis, but would permit both qualitative and quantitative research to test them. Systematic research on agencies and corporations using marketing communications and public relations would permit a more refined description of each organization. The level of integration, whether it is a 3-stage or 7-stage model, could be tested for the existence of the traits this conceptual model assumes exist at each stage.

The present framework contains seven stages. Each stage contains the elements of the previous stage and then adds or reinterprets some dimension. The stages recognize that new management systems and processes take time to develop, must be matched to the nature of the resources of the organization, and are themselves adaptive and changing.

The stages are not sacrosanct. The conceptualization of the stages could conceivably include more or less stages. The concept must be reviewed and tested to redefine and refine the ideas. The stages of integration as conceived include:

1. Awareness.
2. Image integration.
3. Functional integration.
4. Coordinated integration.
5. Consumer-based integration.
6. Stakeholder-based integration.
7. Relationship management integration.

At each stage the communications strengths and weaknesses of advertising, promotions marketing, direct response marketing, marketing public relations, and corporate public relations are weighed and balanced to create the best mix. A fully integrated strategy will permit each form of communications to contribute to the success of the corporate mission. Although the process begins with a particular emphasis on the customer and prospective consumer, it expands the range of integrated marketing communications to integrated communications, reaching a wider range of intended and unintended publics and stakeholders.

The greatest degree of integration emerges from the cooperative efforts of the traditionally separate fields of advertising, public relations, promotions marketing, personal selling, and direct marketing. For example, the early evidence of integration in IBM-Midwest has occurred when direct response, promotions, advertising, and marketing public relations focused on targeting new customers and developing long-term relationships with customers (Caywood, 1992d). The full range of corporate public relations (including community relations, employee relations, investor relations, public affairs, philanthropy, etc.) are not often fully integrated into the early marketing efforts. Although it may be ideal for the full range of communications and relationship management to include audiences beyond the customer, marketing is beginning again with the customer. Later stages of marketing integration may show evidence of a fully integrated communications program (Caywood, 1992b).

Stage One Integration — Awareness

Awareness of the changing business, social, technological, political, and cultural environments creates the demand for new business systems to respond to the market. The trends discussed at the beginning of this chapter have contributed to management's recognition that unpredicted changes (discontinuous change) and some predicted changes will force marketing managers to adapt to a new marketplace. Awareness assumes that change will reinforce the opportunity for developing an integrated management and marketing system.

The basic shifts in market power, taste, access, and diversity will demand new organizational strategies and tactics to communicate with the customer and to establish new relationships with customers and other stakeholders. From the trends discussed previously, including decreasing message impact and credibility, decreasing costs of databases, increasing client expertise, increasing mergers, increasing mass media costs, power of the retailer, increasing global marketing, and pressure on profits, some testable propositions can be offered. The research proposals suggest that the greater the degree of change on the existence of specific market pressures, the greater the likelihood that integrated marketing communication will emerge.

The greater the power of the retailer in a market, the greater the likelihood of awareness integration.

The greater the demand for international marketing in the organization, the greater the likelihood of awareness integration.

The less the perceived differences between product brands by consumers, the greater the likelihood for awareness integration.

The greater the degree of competition in a market, the greater the likelihood of awareness integration.

The greater the degree of change in an organization, the greater the likelihood of awareness integration.

Stage Two Integration—Image Integration " One Voice, One Vision "

Stage two integration recognizes the value of having a consistent message, look, and feel from an organization. Efforts to integrate logically focus initially on the appearance of integration or the lack of integration. For many years, IBM has placed enormous effort by communications professionals on the precise representation of the IBM logo. The appearance of the logo in appropriate communications vehicles (brochures, advertising, media stories) was controlled by IBM communications professionals. As the firm expanded its relationships with what it calls "IBM Partners" or business allies, the use of the logo was closely monitored to control the way in which IBM product resellers and service organizations used the logo.

The corporate image reflected in the icons of trademarks and corporate symbols can be an important element of consistency in the look of communications. However, the tone of the message and the quality of the message production across media is also important. Some of the criticism of this stage of integration characterizes it as a relatively superficial level of integration. Again, our objective is to reduce the value-laden labels in this emerging discipline. The issues facing an organization may compel it to examine its communications for conflicting images. Although not all market challenges require a full range of marketing communications, the visual and verbal consistency (if they do not conflict with other goals) may be an important stage of developing internal cooperation among advertising, sales, public relations, and other areas of communications.

The logic of this stage of integration is that it overcomes some of the most evident aspects of an unintegrated effort. Compelling communications and marketing managers to cooperate at the stage of consistent message symbols and message content may prevent unnecessary duplication of work. Radio and television ads that use consistent language may be an example. This stage of integration provides an opportunity to build initial stages of collaboration among the specialty areas of public relations, advertising, promotions, marketing, and direct response marketing. Stage two provides a reasonable set of tasks to begin the process, and two also suggests some testable propositions to define the extent of integration in organizations:

The greater the degree of oral or written message consistency, the greater the likelihood of image integration.

The greater the degree of visual message consistency, the greater the likelihood of image integration.

The greater the number of media used by an organization, the greater the likelihood of image integration.

Stage Three Integration — Functional Integration

Stage three integration moves the process to a greater degree of involvement among the still traditionally separated areas of communications responsibilities. The process of integration at this stage begins with a strategic analysis of the strengths and weaknesses of each of the functional communications areas, including public relations, advertising, sales promotion, and direct marketing.

As an example, public relations permits a product/service or organization to use third-party credibility with careful targeting and placement of newsworthy stories in the media. Advertising allows (with sufficient budget) a message to be repeated. Promotional marketing may capture the consumer at the point of purchase better than other communications, whereas direct marketing permits constant testing of various offers to the consumer.

Strategic exercises may be developed within a cross-functional team to identify in detail the strengths and weaknesses of each area to the specific project to be marketed. Drawing from each functional area allows practitioners to develop tactics to meet the goals of the marketing team.

Traditional models of marketing communications (MARCOM) have suggested to managers that each area should be considered in the promotional mix. The weakness of traditional MARCOM models is the staff role that specialists in public relations, advertising, direct response, and sales promotion play. Instead, integrated marketing communication places these functional areas at the management table with traditional marketers. An understanding of each functional area by the marketing manager (or at least confidence in their agencies) has traditionally allowed the marketing manager to develop a combination of promotional tactics based on the strengths and weaknesses of each.

An outstanding example of this interplay is the large public relations agency Burson-Marsteller, which promotes a model of integrated communications that suggests each functional area of sales promotions, public relations, events, direct marketing, and advertising can permit the company to reach the consumer. The mix will depend on the problem and market opportunity.

At this functional stage, agencies providing public relations, advertising, sales promotions, or direct marketing may implement an integrated program by "cross-selling" services from within their full-service agency or through affiliate agencies. The integration at this stage permits a wider range of services to be offered. Although some large advertising agencies have reported mixed experience with this level of integration, they have also been inconsistent in moving to the next level of integration.

At this stage of integration, the research propositions suggest that in a situation with a decreasing or stable budget for marketing communications, integration is less likely to develop. Unfortunately, this stage of integration carries with the process an assumption by traditional practitioners that marketing communications is a fixed-sum game. For example, the gain of budget for one functional area suggests a loss for another (assuming there is no increase in the total budget).

Barriers to integration suggested by the Northwestern research (Caywood et al., 1991) may include the failure of agencies and managers in corporations to create incentives to provide the customer or client with the best mix of communications. Under traditional budgeting processes in agencies, for example, the advertising team may be penalized for loss of revenue that was assigned to the same agencies' direct marketing or public relations units. Research propositions to test this stage of integration might include:

The greater the likelihood that the communications budget can be increased, the greater the likelihood of functional integration.

Corollary: Fixed sum budgets for marketing communications will decrease the likelihood of functional integration.

The greater the number of marketing communications functions offered within a firm or agency, the greater the likelihood of functional integration.

Stage Four Integration—Coordinated Integration

At the fourth stage of integrated marketing communication, some of the barriers to integration have diminished. All the communications functions are equal in their potential to contribute to the marketing effort. Much of the historical negative or positive status associated with each field has been reduced. The opportunity for advertising, public relations, promotions marketing, or direct marketing to lead the integrated effort exists.

The integration may be directed by the corporate client rather than a full-service agency. In fact, the concept of "agency of record," with one agency providing a continuing array of services and subcontracted services, may be in a stage of decline as the client shops for the agencies most likely to work together on the integrated campaign in an effective manner.

On special marketing projects or continuing campaigns, one of the specialties may "lead." Depending on the marketing goals and objectives, public relations, advertising, promotions, or direct marketing have an equal opportunity to drive the communications effort. Each functional specialty recognizes that it must cooperate in the development of a communications program or risk not participating at all. Shared budgets, shared performance measures, and outcomes rule the process. For example, IBM found the communications agencies (advertising, sales promotions, direct response, public relations, video services) following an all-or-nothing approach to the campaign budget until the corporation redirected the agencies to integrate their plans and tactics before presenting their ideas to the firm's managers.

This stage of the marketing effort reveals a new element in the promotional mix. Personal selling and the sales management process are included in the mix as the connection to the customer, and marketing becomes more direct (Caywood, 1992a). The interpersonal communications aspect of the selling process is included in the integrated plan. In business-to-business marketing and consumer marketing, a key marketing objective is to develop a communications strategy that increases the customer's propensity to buy with several carefully directed communications tactics using the best communications tools.

The consumer buying process is considered linear, because the prospective customer is moved increasingly toward the buying stage. The classic acronym AIDA approach to marketing—attention, interest, desire, and finally action—represents this approach to integration. For example, the Midwest Integrated Marketing Unit of IBM adopted a version of this model to spur its planning process. The process at IBM was used to plan an 18-month marketing campaign around a full mix of marketing communications (Caywood, 1992d). At many points in the process, response mechanisms from the customers and prospects were used to measure the effectiveness of the campaign. Moving the customers along the consumer path was a key objective.

Also evident in this stage may be elements of an emerging database. The database may initially consist of simple and accurate contact information, including names, titles, addresses, and phone and fax numbers. As the database is strengthened through marketing-driven contacts, information about past purchases, competitive purchases, capital expenditures, and services expenses are added. Also included are the details of what forms of communications the customer responds to—be it advertising, a sales call, direct mail, a seminar, or other contacts.

Particularly in business-to-business marketing, the sales force and marketing communications team contribute to identifying, segmenting, and resegmenting the target markets. The use of direct response mechanisms in advertising, telemarketing, and direct mail are crucial to database building and maintenance. Propositions to test at this stage of the process might include:

The greater the degree of sales force involvement with marketing strategy, the greater the likelihood of coordinated integration.

The greater the degree of customer database orientation, the greater the likelihood of coordinated integration.

Corollary: The less the power of communication agencies of record, the greater the likelihood of coordinated integration.

The greater the number of communications tactics used, the greater the likelihood of coordinated integration.

The greater the degree of client management (versus agency) control of the marketing communications process, the greater the likelihood of coordinated integration.

Stage Five Integration — Consumer-Based Integration

"Outside-In"

As each step of integration is mastered and accepted, the elements begin to work together. The original objectives of integration to manage the marketing communications process more efficiently by wasting fewer resources becomes a matter of practicing greater marketing effectiveness. Only the fully targeted consumers are reached with the strongest and most effective media and through the most precise channels of communications. In a more fully developed marketing communications process, the customer and the consumers are rediscovered, as marketing is planned from the outside in. Both customers and prospective customers-consumers are included in the formula.

The lessons learned from earlier stages of integration document the value of a refined customer and prospect database. Experience with the sales and communications information augmented with marketing research permits increasing predictions as to the prospect's readiness to buy. Attitudinal data related to business trends collected through surveys of customers and prospects may add insights to the customer.

The consumer's contact points with the brand and company are carefully uncovered through quantitative and qualitative research (Fortini-Campbell, 1992). Each contact point, whether it be initiated by the customer or the company, is identified. For example, all customer contacts with an airline — from the travel agent to the baggage handler and counter service representative, as well as experience with airport signage, airplane cleanliness, on-time flight, safety, and so on — are considered part of the contact points with the airline. Each point of contact is a message, a form of marketing communications, that reinforces the customer's business opinion of the airline.

Carefully collected behavioral data recording the customer and prospect's response to marketing communications can help the marketer plan. For example, data that suggest a customer is interested in new technology trends in his or her industry and evidence that the customer has asked for information or attended seminars about new technology may be powerful predictors of future actions. Eventually the database may reveal the buying stage or readiness to buy of the prospective customer. In customer goods marketing, scanner data can provide evidence of impact of specific messages in various combinations of media.

The full implications of what marketing has characterized as a consumer orientation can be fulfilled with an integrated strategy that focuses on the communications-stimulated behavior of the customer. In a system that focuses on the target customer, the components of integrated marketing communication become mere tactics. The advertising, public relations, promotions, and direct marketing simply execute in an integrated way the strategy to anticipate and respond to the customer.

In this stage, issues of customer loyalty are examined as firms create a marketing plan that builds and maintains relationships with current customers. Rather than constantly replacing customers, attention is given to holding and building the correct customer base. Increased customer satisfaction and subsequent increased purchases are the goals. Several models of integrated marketing communication, developed as part of the creation of a Department of Integrated Marketing Communications at Northwestern University, describe this stage of integration development (Caywood et al., 1991; Schultz, Tannenbaum, & Lauterborn, 1992). This stage also raises several research propositions:

The greater the consumer (and customer) orientation, the greater the likelihood of consumer-based integration.

The greater the recognition of multiple consumer contact points, the greater the likelihood of consumer-based integration.

The greater the base of loyal customers, the greater the likelihood of consumer-based integration.

The greater the amount of information collected on the customer and the consumer, the greater the likelihood of consumer-based integration.

The greater the available behavioral data on the consumer and customer, the greater the likelihood of consumer-based integration.

Stage Six Integration — Stakeholder-Based Integration

The evolution of integration suggests that the success of each stage may lead to new dimensions in the next stage. Beyond the customer and the consumer are numerous publics and stakeholders that have a stake in the outcome of the success or failure of a firm. They may or may not have a customer or prospective customer relationship with the firm.

At this stage of marketing and business practice, the firm moves to a broader definition of its function as more than a merely profitable promotional and sales-driven one. Integrated marketing communication moves to a more broadly defined integrated communications as it expands the communications to other stakeholders, including employees, the community, government, the press, vendors and suppliers, and others.

As the efficiency and effectiveness of integration are tested and proved, a third element emerges in a more mature integrated program. Although it can be argued that the third value should be embedded from the beginning, the issue of equity is more likely to be considered in a more established and confident business organization. Equity suggests the strongest elements of social responsibility that drive an organization to broaden its communications. Issues of social responsibility related to race, gender, environment, health, and so on compel managers to examine the marketing communications for evidence of exploitation, exclusions, and unintended messages. If these problems affect an organization's marketing plans, they may be characterized as "risk marketing" issues. Publicly owned or highly visible consumer firms may be at greater risk than some business-to-business firms (Caywood, 1992c).

For example, an integrated marketing communication program that includes a message on the recycled packaging of a product may inadvertently fall into a risk marketing situation. McDonald's situation with the clamshell foam packaging of its food products created a public relations crisis with various environmental groups and a potential risk to its marketing objectives. The tobacco and alcohol companies have experienced the same risk with transparent ethnic and racial marketing strategies and marketing communications. For example, Uptown cigarettes and Powermeister beer were both failed efforts against the social and new business pressures reflected by equity issues. Past narrow definitions of marketing, as being only promotional to sell the product to customers and consumers, must be enhanced by a complete strategy of integrated communications and relationship management.

Integrated communications begins with a careful stakeholder identification, with dozens and even hundreds of possible groups and individuals being labeled as important to the future success of the firm. The process demands that managers or staff be "assigned" to each stakeholder group to monitor and track their actions relevant to the firm. For example, in Chicago the outdoor advertising industry must watch closely the statements and activities of Fr. Michael Pfleger and his parishioners. Their crusade against tobacco and alcohol advertising in African-American communities has created a risk to the industry and a need to negotiate with social activists. Similar attention to local governments, opinion leaders, and other stakeholders is a necessary component of a fully integrated communications program.

Although the full role of public relations may have seemingly been limited in the first five stages to the promotional aspects of marketing public relations, the sixth stage demands a fully integrated corporate communications function. Communications at the corporate stage of integration must include employees, the media, community leaders, investors, vendors, suppliers, competitors, government at all stages, and so on.

For example, NCR Corporation, before and after its acquisition by AT&T, in 1991, has operated a Department of Stakeholder Relations directed by an officer with the title of Vice President of Stakeholder Relations. The NCR approach more formally recognized the importance of a full communications strategy targeting all important stakeholders and incorporating them into the business and marketing plan. The work of a national task force of business and university leaders from the academic group, the Association for Education in Journalism and Mass Communications (AEJMC), has developed an approach to integration that can be labeled integrated communication rather than merely integrated marketing communication (Duncan, Caywood, & Newsom, 1993). Propositions raised at this stage include:

The greater the public visibility of the business, the greater the likelihood of stakeholder-based integration.

The greater the degree of marketing risk facing a business, the greater the likelihood of stakeholder-based integration.

The greater the number of stakeholders of the organization, the greater the likelihood of stakeholder-based integration.

Stage Seven — Relationship Management Integration

The development of a fully integrated communications strategy to reach customers and all stakeholders brings communications professionals into direct contact with the full range of management functions in businesses and other complex organizations. The integration of the communications function in advertising, public relations, promotions, direct marketing, and personal selling is not complete if the integration is only among these fields. Integration implies (and a managerial approach to communications demands) that communications be regarded as a strong element in the total management process. The process has become a full range of relationship management, both internally and externally.

Several management processes should converge with a successfully integrated marketing and integrated communications program. The still-developing field of total quality management clearly demands a fully integrative management effort from production, human resources, marketing, finance, and communications. The successful completion of the Malcolm Baldridge National Quality Award requires the complete cooperation of all management functions. An already integrated communications program can assist the company, employees, vendors, customers, and others in meeting the goals of continuous quality improvement.

In the same vein, the development of strategic alliances in more collaborative business relationships can be augmented by an already integrated communications program. As IBM has developed its business partners concept with resellers and software suppliers in the market, the role of a fully integrated communications program can more rapidly contribute to the partnership.

In general, the fully integrative model should place communications professionals at the management table and redefine their roles from staff to management. Each stage of integration contributes to the performance of communications in the management process. As integration is proven both internally and externally to be a logical framework for managing the communications and relationships of an organization, it will prove to be an integral part of the management effort. Propositions to be tested at this stage include:

The greater the commitment to total quality management, the greater the likelihood of relationship management integration.

The greater the participation in strategic alliances, the greater the likelihood of relationship management integration.

CONCLUSION

There is no intended hierarchy of integration. The model of integration discussed here suggests that as organizations begin to integrate they proceed to redefine their strategies and objectives. Each organization examining integration as a new management approach will analyze its situation and the stage of integration that fits its situation. An organization may or may not immediately implement the strategies of other stages of integration. However, each stage of integration provides a useful "value-added' dimension to the process of complete integration. Each stage contributes to the efficiency, effectiveness, and equity of a fully integrated marketing communications plan, a fully integrated communications plan, and a program for total relationship management organization.

A key question for marketing, communications, and other managers based on this process and these stages of integration is: What is your integrated communications saying to past and present employees, future employees, suppliers, community, stockholders, public interest groups, women, minorities, unemployed persons, opinion leaders, political leaders, all stakeholders, others, and, of course, the consumer and customer? And finally, these managers must respond to this question: Is your integrated system efficient, effective, and equitable?

REFERENCES

Caywood, C. L. (1992a). *To integrate or not to integrate* (Communique, pp. 1–2). Chicago: Corporate Communications.

Caywood, C. L. (1992b, November). *How PR will lead IMC.* Paper presented at the Association of Advertising International conference, Denver, CO.

Caywood, C. L. (1992c, February). *What PR needs to know about marketing and vice versa.* Paper presented to the Chicago chapter of the Public Relations Society of America.

Caywood, C. L. (1992d). *Integrated marketing in IBM-Midwest: The distribution market.* Evanston, IL: Northwestern University.

Caywood, C. L., Schultz, D. E., & Wang, P. (1991). *A survey of consumer goods manufacturers.* New York: American Association of Advertising Agencies.

Duncan, T., Caywood, C. L., & Newsom, D. A. (1993). *Task force report on integrated communications.* Armonk, NY: IBM.

Duncan, T. R., & Everett, S. E. (1993). Client perceptions of integrated marketing communications. *Journal of Advertising Research, 33*(3), 30–39.

Duncan, T. R., & Moriarty, S. E. (1994, October). *IMC audit workshop.* Presentation to BBDO Europe, Paris.

Fortini-Campbell, L. (1992). *Hitting the sweetspot: How consumer insights can inspire better marketing and advertising.* Chicago: Copy Workshop.

Keegan, W., Moriarty, S., & Duncan, T. (1992). *Marketing.* Englewood Cliffs, NJ: Prentice-Hall.

Schultz, D. E., Tannenbaum, S., & Lauterborn, R. F. (1992). *Integrated marketing communications: Pulling it together and making it work.* Chicago: NTC Business Books.

2

How Leading Advertising Agency Media Directors View Integrated Communication: A Qualitative Study of Integrated Communications and the Media Planning Process

Carla V. Lloyd
Syracuse University

The days of merely scheduling and placing ads are over. Now it's a whole different media mix. A down economy, client and consumer shifts, and escalating product and media clutter require more than traditional advertising to effectively speak to consumers. Clients, who are under tremendous pressure to perform on a sales, marketing and financial basis (Martin, 1992) are now embracing other forms of communication (Sissors & Bumba, 1993). And there's much more from which to choose. Today, some experts estimate that there are as many as 204 (DDB Needham, 1991) communication options available to media planners and marketers — and the number is still growing.

Evidence shows that professionals are opting to invest more in marketing communications tools, specifically public relations, direct marketing, and sales promotions (Bergstrom, 1992). Advertising, which used to snare 70% to 80% of marketing mix dollars, is now lucky to get 30% ("Integrated Communications," 1992). Instead, clients are spending more on public relations and direct marketing, and getting better results ("Integrated Communications," 1992). Evidence shows that clients are also willing to spend more on sales promotion. Nielsen Marketing Research surveyed 103 companies and found 52% of the typical company's marketing dollar in 1990 went to trade promotion. Twenty-one percent went to consumer promotions. The rest went to advertising ("Trade Budgets," 1992). Therefore, the term *media* has been expanded to include all available marketing communications tools and is hailed as any opportunity to make contact with a consumer (Rice, 1991).

When used, these media alternatives are expected to work in harmony with each other to deliver one cohesive message to consumers. This process is part of a concept known as *integrated marketing communications* (IMC), which has recently been defined as: "Marketing communications planning that recognizes the added value of a comprehensive plan that evaluates the strategic roles of a variety of communications disciplines and combines these disciplines to provide clarity, consistency, and maximum communications impact" (Schultz, 1992).

IMC's full effect on media planners is yet unknown. Some researchers speculate that the media department, more than any ad agency department, is expected to be most drastically affected by the expansion and integration of communications tools (Wang & Petrison, 1991). The expectation is that the media department's role will become more complex and more important as messages become more specialized and media selection becomes more indispensable to the overall success of the marketing plan (Wang & Petrison, 1991). The purpose of this study is to explore the changes that will occur in the media planning process because of integrated marketing and the media explosion.

METHODOLOGY

To begin to understand this question, a two-part qualitative study was conducted: one focus group and five in-depth interviews. To acquire general themes and understanding on media trends as they relate to integrated marketing communications and undergraduate advertising education, a 75-minute focus group with marketing communications executives and media managers was conducted in New York City on February 13, 1992. Practitioners from all four marketing communications disciplines, print and broadcast media buying services, and audience measurement firms attended the session. Those attending included:

Robin Butner
Vice President/Account Supervisor
Development & House Counsel
Lawrence Butner Advertising, Inc.*
New York, NY
*Direct-response advertising agency

Steve Coffey
Vice President of Nielsen Advertising
  Services
Nielsen Marketing Research
New York, NY

John Chasin
Vice President Marketing Development
Advertiser/Agency Services
Arbitron *ScanAmerica*
New York, NY

Chester Elton
National Marketing Manager
Blair Television
New York, NY

Sabrina Gallen
Personnel Assistant/Internship
  Coordinator
Rogers & Cowen Public Relations
New York, NY

John Mennenga
Vice President, Director of Research
  & Marketing
Sawyer-Ferguson-Walker Co.*
New York, NY
*Newspaper representative firm

Keith Reinhard
Chairman/CEO
DDB Needham Worldwide Inc.
New York, NY

Kerry E. Smith
Editor & Publisher
*PROMO: The International Magazine
  for Promotion Marketing*
Wilton, CT

THE MEDIA REVOLUTION AND ADVERTISING FOCUS GROUP FINDINGS

With respect to media, this focus group suggested: (a) Media are significantly affecting advertising evolution toward integrated communications, (b) media are more critical to advertising's success than ever before, and (c) the media explosion is creating an information glut nearly impossible for one media person to keep up with.

These focus group findings produced additional questions about media planning and media planners, specifically: How do media planners integrate general advertising with other marketing communications disciplines? How are media planners contending with the media explosion? And last, how do media planners determine accountable media plans?

In-Depth Interviews

To address these issues raised by the focus group, an open-ended interview schedule was devised. Five in-depth interview with media directors were conducted.

Special care was taken in selecting media directors so that the small sample would reflect a wide range of agencies and corporate philosophies. The purposive sample aimed to include ad agencies that:

1. Were international, national, regional, and local.
2. Included a diversity of clients comprised of service, consumer goods, and retail.
3. Were diverse in advertising approaches, spanning from creative boutiques to full-service multisubsidiary shops.

Additionally, each media director had to be currently working on or have previously devised an *IMC media plan*. Finally, media directors were chosen from agencies with noted or award-winning media departments.

The five media directors selected for this phase of the study encompassed these criteria. With the exception of one, all media directors chose to be identified in the final report and four were interviewed on-site between February and April 1992. Those interviewed included:

John Osborn
V.P. Associate Media Director
BBDO
New York, NY

Steve Kline
Media Director
Kirshenbaum & Bond
New York, NY

Ira Bass
V.P. Media Director
Eric Mower & Associates
Syracuse, NY

Debra Merskin
Former Media Director
Bozell
Tampa, FL

Executive V.P. Media Director
Undisclosed national, image-driven agency
New York, NY

In-Depth Interview Findings

Finding 1. Today's media planning is based on an expanded definition of advertising that includes all marketing communications. Advertising should aim to integrate all of these disciplines in an effort to reach people who can conceivably purchase clients' products.

This study found that today's media planning starts with a clear understanding and acceptance of integrated marketing communications. Even though they are IMC advocates, these agencies have not renamed advertising. Kirshenbaum and Bond's media director Steve Kline brushed the whole notion of semantics aside, suggesting that it is just how his agency goes about doing business.

These professionals mentioned that advertising refers to all marketing communications disciplines including advertising, sales promotions, direct marketing, corporate communications, and public relations. All of these marketing communications tools are considered media. This study also found that *integration* is a primary goal of today's advertising. Eric Mower's executive media director, Ira Bass, supported this claim, saying, "Advertising must find ways to make all of these elements work together as one, unified, solid entity."

According to these media directors, advertising's most fundamental and perhaps most challenging task is trying to reach people who can conceivably purchase a client's product. The difficulty in reaching prospects is blamed on an overly segmented marketplace one-on-one communications, media-savvy consumers and clients, and more fragmented media. Yet, traditional advertising still has its large agency supporters, as BBDO's media director, John Osborn, who supervises the VISA account, defended: "It's fun to play around with these concepts (of IMC), but in the end you have to answer to the economies of scale that traditional advertising brings — balancing between the *efficient* mass broadcast media and one-on-one communications."

Finding 2. The vast influx of change endemic in today's marketplace has generated a radical philosophical swing in media planning. The broad-market approach to media planning is being replaced by a more market-specific concept known as zero-based media planning.

Within the last 15 years, the concept of media planning has gone full spectrum. Briefly stated, this study found that in the mid-1970s, zero-based media planning, a back-to-basics approach to strategic media planning, was preferred by planners. The early 1980s nixed the market-specific, zero-based approach. At this point, many large advertisers preferred broad market coverage over market-by-market penetration. Thus they embraced mass communications and large audience delivery. Now, in the 1990s with the surgence of relationship marketing, the downturn of network TV, and client and audience changes, a major transition has occurred, as one media director described: "We are back to where we were in the mid-70s — building the plan market-by-market, brand-by-brand, where the efficiencies are not driving the plan but the communication and the personal sell are."

Today's zero-based media planning also requires flexibility. To make use of various marketing tools or emerging media, professionals must create plans that can change throughout the year. This requires an open-mindedness on the part of media planners.

Finding 3. Increasingly, media planners are becoming involved at an earlier and more important stage in the overall strategic planning process. Media planners are joining the account services group to assist in preliminary brand analyses.

To create effective IMC media plans, some media directors interviewed believe that their preliminary background reviews should include thorough brand analyses. To capture important brand insights, some media planners are becoming involved at an earlier and more important stage in the overall strategic planning process. Additionally this study shows that media planners often join the account services team to study brands both quantitatively and qualitatively. Faced with increased audience fragmentation and almost unlimited media choice, both forms of analyses appear to help media planners find appropriate ways to deliver messages to potential consumers that both reinforce the brand and avoid waste.

For instance, improvements in sales data reporting has given media planners a source of stronger quantitative information that allows for direct media and regional sales matches. Many clients have developed "incredible sophistication in tracking sales," said one media director. When shared with members of the account team, these data can provide sales on a market-by-market basis. To minimize waste and hopefully maximize sales, media must then parallel that information source for each brand.

At the same time, this study also found that brands are being examined more qualitatively by members of the account team. Kirshenbaum and Bond (K&B) media planners, who view themselves "as keepers of the brand for how the brand speaks," find that a more conceptual analysis of brands often helps isolate when it is appropriate to use particular marketing communications tools.

For instance, at K&B each brand is viewed as having a "volume," which can either be cranked up loud or turned down low. Media planners join the account team to discover the *appropriate* sound level for each brand. This qualitative interpretation in turns tells media planners how intrusive the brand can be in the marketplace. For instance, if a brand is found to have a loud volume then more intrusive communications tools like sales promotions (contests, sweepstakes) can be used.

Regardless of which approach media planners opt for, a complete diagnosis of the brand is essential. As K&B's Kline admonished, "Media planners must be completely enveloped in the brand . . . because brands are very easy to kill."

Finding 4.   Integration has placed even more importance on two specific parts of media strategy. The search for accurate target audience descriptions and budgetary considerations appear to be the most widely affected portions of strategic media decision making.

Finding 4a.   Including highly segmented media in the media mix puts pressure on media planners to do a better job of honing target audience definitions.

Changing audience demographics and lifestyles have created more segmentation (BBDO, 1992; Weaver, 1991). Media and marketing have reacted to these major audience shifts by becoming less national and more regional or local in focus. Because of these changes, media planners are adding highly targeted media into their media mixes more and mass media less

(Bergstrom, 1992; Levin, 1992; Lukovitz, 1992). Planners are moving away from defining target audiences merely demographically. As might be expected, this movement from broadly defined target audiences to more narrowly refined segments is the debate right now. This study found that media planners are looking for answers on how to target better, and the process of deciding who to advertise to is far from resolved. As a matter of fact, Bass said, "It's still evolving."

Media directors interviewed for this study are wrestling with the targeting issue. The goal of today's media mix is much more demanding. It should "aim to find customer involvement," said Merskin.

Referring to his department's corporate brochure, BBDO's Osborn indicated that today's targeting challenge really is "getting the most impactful, need-fulfilling environments with which to deliver the client's message." This can only happen if media planners "have crucial knowledge of . . . the users of client's brands and every brand within the category," said Kline. He feels that media planners should strive to fully understand the users' lifestyles, personalities, psychographics, and even their social and political concerns in order to find effective and compelling ways to reach users. And as he pointed out, this kind of intimate understanding can only occur if planners "are smart and wily enough to dig and find what consumers are out there in the big haystack."

But with these shifts in targeting have come some concerns, complications, and complaints. For instance, one media planner finds "that over-segmenting is personally distressing. I don't want to deal on a 'zip code' level, but I have clients who do. Some want all five zip-code numbers and next the four after that."

Besides personal dissatisfaction, media planners also pointed out some problems that this type of segmenting creates. Some media do not lend themselves to being regionalized or localized. There is a lot of qualitative data, but there isn't enough time to tap into it. As Merskin explained, "buyers are so overworked, planners are too busy . . . and narrowcasting is expensive."

Finding 4b. IMC and the new media have ushered in many new budgetary concerns and challenges.

Integrated marketing communications and the rise of the new media have significantly changed how media planners contend with the media budget. This study found that clients are now more media wise and cost conscious. Likewise, they are becoming more actively involved in media planning. Eric Mower's Bass maintained that clients "are more savvy and more in-tuned to what is necessary from a media point of view. They understand the necessity of making media a more vibrant part of the marketing process."

This involvement is perhaps due to clients' growing concern over one of their biggest expenses: media. Merskin contended that clients see media as an important investment. She added that, "clients—big and small—are quite aware of every penny spent." Bass concurred, saying "For every dollar they spend, clients want to know it had some effect." Additionally, clients are scrutinizing media planning aspects that were previously considered incidental, such as specific day parts and publications.

All the new media that technology and IMC have brought into the marketplace have created "a budgeting nightmare for media planners," said Merskin. Planners are finding that the vast majority of new media are negotiable and becoming increasingly more so. This emphasis on negotiation poses a whole new set of client billing problems for agencies.

An additional effect that IMC and the media explosion are having on media planning is that it is making an already labor-intensive activity even more arduous. Orchestrating one-on-one communications is cited as being particularly costly for ad agency media departments. With the *buy TV mentality* gone and more targeted media being ushered in, one media director said that, "Media planning, which is a detail-oriented business, is now in an even greater detail dump."

To cut costs, BBDO's Osborn reported that large advertising agencies are now in the process of "unbundling and consolidating these expensive services groups." Another cost-cutting measure that regional advertising agencies have instituted is a process of constantly analyzing client estimates and resigning accounts that are not making money. As Bass explained, "They aren't bad accounts . . . they just don't meet the needs of our agency from either profitability, portfolio, or potential."

Budgeting for IMC can also cause turf wars among various marketing communications personnel. Getting all the disciplines to agree on one budget can become a big problem. Public relations, direct response, sales promotion, and advertising personnel must be willing to split the budget to accomplish the marketing objectives without becoming territorial. Bass said that advertising people's reaction to IMC can be "Oh, there goes my budget . . . PR can't have half of the budget. Budgeting for IMC programs requires all marketing communications professionals to be committed to the marketing objectives and not their own departmental interests."

Finding 5. The growing number of alternative media are creating a greater demand for accountability.

Today's media planners can choose from a greater variety of communications tools than ever before. "It's any means possible to *appropriately* communicate a brand's message to that particular targeted consumer," said Kline. However, with all of these choices come formidable challenges. Dealing with all of the new niche forms appears to be one of the most critical questions of the 1990s.

Media directors interviewed have taken up the challenge and are learning how to evaluate the effectiveness of the alternative media. Additionally, they are finding ways to make comparisons between the disparate voices that can speak on behalf of a brand. And most importantly, they have made *accountability* the rule behind all of their IMC media decisions so that their recommendations will enhance a brand's positioning, protect clients' dollars, and hopefully generate favorable responses.

At this point, evaluating IMC media planning is, at times, "still at the gut-level of measuring performance," said Bass. To get beyond this subjective evaluation and move toward making concrete comparisons among the emerging media, a media department's first step is to harness all of the new media information that bombards the agency.

BBDO and Kirshenbaum & Bond have adopted a practice of compiling books on all of the emerging communications tools. BBDO has also hired a media coordinator who puts out a monthly report that analyzes all of the new media. These reports are compiled in the "new media book" at BBDO. The value of this organizational process is that it provides the department with a resource that planners can readily access and, thus, begin to make intermedia comparisons.

When hiring a media coordinator to analyze the new media is out of the question, then the existing media staff assumes the added responsibility. "What Bozell was doing was creating *medium specialists*," recalled former media director Merskin. In theory this made sense, but in practice it fell short, because people who are already overworked many times become the specialists.

Criteria that media directors use to evaluate the new media are varied. Sometimes testing is the only way to discover a new medium's accountability. But should it be an ad agency's job to test a new communication tool? One media director objected to the practice altogether saying, "We are not about to fund a new media idea. If we do test, we will do it without them. I would never steal their idea, but why should I pay them to sell me something?"

This study found that when an agency chooses not to test, then a new media form's accountability can be evaluated by its ability to deliver a *specialized audience,* its capacity to be validated or measured, its track record of ethical practices, its degree of intrusiveness, and cost effectiveness.

K&B's Kline underscored advertising's responsibility to function ethically in today's cluttered media marketplace. In other words, accountability means using promotions and overt media responsibility so that communications activity does not become irritating or unlawful. Before adding a new communication tool to an existing mix, media planners should ask themselves several questions: Is this media environmentally and ethically sound?

How does it affect the environment? Is it so intrusive that it violates personal space and air space?

Cost efficiency remains an important way of measuring a media plan's accountability. When new media are identified, one media director recommended that their cost efficiency be evaluated several ways. For instance, can a new media deliver a client exclusivity within the product's category? Can it also offer franchises, merchandising opportunities, marketing partnerships, and point-of-purchase impact? Cost considerations are also a factor. For one media director, accountability can be measured by asking specific cost questions: "Are the new media's prices negotiable? What are the out-of-pocket costs? Will the new media form require new creative? How will the budget be affected by adding this new media form? Will this addition be handled as an incremental to the budget or will it yank funds away from the existing 'big idea' of my plan?"

IMC has made media planning more accountable because certain promotional tools can deliver measurable results. For instance, a media plan that starts with a database and incorporates a direct response ad, a sales coupon, an ad campaign, and PR messages was viewed by Bass as "having four or five guns working at the same time. It just means . . . more targeted marketing. Clients can see actual results," he said.

Finding 6.   IMC has made significant changes in how the media department interacts with clients. IMC has given media planners more client contact and a greater consulting role.

Faced with a fragmented marketplace and a greater variety of communication tools, today's clients are now relying on media planners more than ever before for expert advice on delivering messages to potential purchasers. Thus, client contact has increased significantly for media planners. "More than any other time in media's history we are seeing media people being account people . . . in terms of client contact," observed Bass. Given this added responsibility, today's media planners are expected to forge relationships with clients that engender trust.

Identifying clients willing to incorporate IMC along with their media plans is not a formal process. Rather, agencies search for opportunities to practice IMC-driven media planning. Planners must know which of their clients are willing to be pioneers. Account managers can help media planners with this. Directly working with account people is one way of identifying receptive clients who are open to experimentation.

After receptive clients are identified, agencies must then convincingly demonstrate their IMC capabilities. IMC success stories are important at this point. They help convince clients that agencies are capable of handling this kind of multiple-level approach to marketing. Regional ad agencies need a minimum of two IMC success stories to persuade clients to give up some of their marketing responsibility, Merskin suggested.

Media planners can bolster an ad agency's perceived IMC capability by being as well versed in the IMC disciplines as the traditional advertising media. This familiarity serves two purposes. First, media planners can readily recommend other marketing communications tools as options to more progressive clients. Second, media planners who do their homework can educate more traditional clients on new options and the alternative ways to get the word out.

IMC has affected media professionals in yet another way. The communications boom has given media planners a larger advisory role among the various agency departments. Most notably, the walls that have traditionally separated the creative department from the media department are dissolving. Increasingly, media and creatives are sitting in the same room, according to Merskin. Planners alert creatives about new communications opportunities and feasibilities.

Finding 7.   The role of media planners is evolving in three ways, all of which are transforming media planners into more well-rounded communications advisers.

As media planning embraces a wider variety of marketing communications tools, the challenge is to coordinate all marketing efforts into a single, unified plan that communicates one cohesive message to consumers no matter what tool delivers the message (Sissors & Bumba, 1993). What scares media planners is trying to speak to consumers in one voice when many communications tools are involved. Media planners fear that five different disciplines "will go off on their own directions," said Bass. To avoid this, today's multidisciplinary media planning demands three requirements from media planners.

First, media planners must know how each of the marketing communications disciplines can be combined. Media people have to be more and more aware of what other disciplines are and how they can work together.

Second, if planners are not experienced in specific marketing communications areas, such as sales promotions, direct marketing, and the like, they are expected to get help. They should work directly with the subsidiaries. The media landscape has gotten so big and varied that increasingly media planners are relying on marketing communications experts or specialists. Associate media directors, then, are generalists. They are "point guards for the client and when something is needed they pull it in," said Osborn. As such, individual marketing communications specialists execute necessary components of the media plan.

Third, media planners, when implementing an IMC media plan, need to systematically phase in each marketing communications discipline and subsequently scrutinize the plan in order to guarantee unified message delivery.

Finding 8.   Media planners must still be grounded in media fundamentals.

Media planners should acquire a thorough knowledge of media fundamentals. Known for his "guerilla media" philosophy, Kline has created media plans that are equally as courageous and outrageous as they are effective. For instance, for client Bamboo lingerie, Kline turned to New York's West Side sidewalks to deliver advertising messages. He had the pavement spray painted with the unabashed message: "From here, it looks like you could use some new underwear." Responding to this creative media effort, Kline said media fundamentals are the driving force behind "all that wacky stuff—it doesn't just come out of wacky heads." He said that it "comes out of a bunch of numbers nerds who believe in media fundamentals."

Finding 9.   Creative media planning is part of the integrated process. Creative media planning is not a new concept. As a matter of fact, professionals have spent the last 5 to 7 years in an ongoing debate searching for a more concrete definition for this somewhat illusive subject. But as IMC advances and garners continued acceptance among advertisers, how will creative media planning be factored into the integration process? Will creative media planning ultimately help or hinder integration?

The media directors interviewed suggest that creative media planning starts by putting something big, exciting, and different into media plans in order to break through clutter. Increasingly, these media professionals are putting more variety and creativity into their plans, but they are not leaving integration out. The media directors interviewed help clients and the account services department blend a wide variety of unrelated communications messages into comprehensive media packages that deliver one basic idea to consumers.

Today's creative media plans are bold and daring, but by no means frivolous or disjointed. They aim for "seamless" communications (Sissors & Bumba, 1993) by adhering to the stated objectives and strategies. Advertising budgets are responsibly spent so as to build the client's business.

After analyzing five different media plans that the five professionals interviewed referred to as creative, several commonalities surfaced. To summarize the chief characteristics of these integrated and creative media plans: They start with a willing, entrepreneurial client. They are built from the ground up using zero-based media planning. They contain demanding communications objectives; thus, various marketing tools are added to media mixes to deliver sales results. Media mixes include a wide variety of unconventional media forms that work in unison to solicit participation or action from the consumer. Traditional media tend to be used as a building block of the plan and at times are leveraged to increase the added value of the plan. Partnerships or marriages are created with clients' promotions departments, account services groups, retailers, and media suppliers to develop comprehensive IMC programs.

CONCLUSION

My research begins to evaluate how advertising agency media departments are coping with a vast and more complicated communications landscape. At the same time, my work starts to explore the effects that integrated marketing communications is having on the media planning process and media planners.

First, my interviews with media professionals support earlier speculations and predictions posited by Wang and Petrison's (1991) study, which suggested that integrated marketing communications could eventually have a profound effect on the media department, the media planning process, and media planners.

As media have become increasingly more complex, specialized and prolific, clients have become more discerning and involved in the media planning process. In turn, the media department has become a more prominent and important fixture at advertising agencies. Increasingly, media departments are being enlisted into the account team. Media planners are becoming involved at an earlier stage and to a greater degree in the overall strategic planning process. Yet, IMC and the enlarged media world have left media departments grappling with a whole new set of issues. Targeting goals require more precision and consumer involvement. More intricate and multidisciplinary media plans have created complex billing problems. The flood of new media information that pours into agencies daily has left media departments grasping for more effective ways to manage data and device methods to make effective intermedia comparisons. The crowd of new media have made media departments more labor intensive. For some media departments, this translates to a greater division of labor to get the job done. Media generalists, specialists, and subsidiary specialists are common at larger shops, which can make media departments more expensive to run. From an organizational perspective, media departments are becoming more integrated with other agency departments, which has created newfound turf wars.

This study also challenges the traditionally held viewpoint of media planning in which advertising time and space were relied on to deliver messages to consumers (Barban, Cristol, & Kopec, 1993). The professionals have expanded media mixes to include any possible contact with potential consumers. And after a 15-year hiatus, zero-based media planning has returned. Media plans are expected to be creative, but have all the disparate forms of communications speaking in one voice. More creative and varied media mixes demand more accountability from media plans.

Finally, these interviews found that the more complicated and fragmented media environment has elevated media planners to assume greater advisory and consulting roles. As such, they are being asked to learn more about marketing disciplines and how to apply, evaluate, and integrate them. Whereas in the past media planners were valued for their quantitative and analytical prowess, increasingly they are also prized for their strong conceptual, entrepreneurial, and creative skills.

REFERENCES

BBDO Media Department. (1992). *BBDO media credentials & capabilities.* (Corporate Report). New York: Author.

Barban, A. M., Cristol, S. M., & Kopec, F. J. (1993). *Essentials of media planning: A marketing viewpoint.* Chicago: NTC Business Books.

Bergstrom, K. (1992, May). Integrated marketing intensifies. *Sales and Marketing Strategies & News,* pp. 1, 59, 62.

DDB Needham Worldwide/Chicago Office. (1991). *Inte-comm** [Registered integrated communications program]. Chicago: Author.

Integrated communications proposes blending PR with advertising & direct marketing: Opportunity for one clear voice for users? or danger of de-emphasizing field's highest value? (1992, May 4). *PR Reporter,* pp. 1–2.

Lukovitz, K. (1992). Get ready for one-on-one marketing. *Folio,* pp. 54–56, 58–70.

Levin, G. (1992, November 2). Media ads blasted for loss of impact. *Advertising Age,* p. 14.

Martin, D. (1992, November 2). When times get tough, marketing gets tougher. *Mediaweek,* p. 10.

Rice, F. (1991, December). A cure for what ails advertising? *Fortune,* pp. 199–222.

Schultz, D. E. (1993, January 3). Integrated marketing communications: Maybe definition in the point-of-view. *Marketing News TM,* p. 17.

Sissors, J. A., & Bumba, L. (1993). Integrated marketing communications, database marketing, and media planning. In J. Z. Sissors & L. Bumba (Eds.), *Advertising media planning* (4th ed., pp. 21–34). Chicago: NTC Business Books.

Wang, P., & Petrison, L. (1991, Fall). Integrated marketing communications and its potential effect on media planning. *Journal of Media Planning,* 11–18.

Weaver, J. (1991, October 21). Will media matter more? *Mediaweek,* pp. 16, 18, 22.

II Psychological Processes and Integrated Communication

3

The Vulnerability of Integrated Marketing Communication: The Potential for Boomerang Effects

David W. Schumann
University of Tennessee

Barbara Dyer
Ohio University

Ed Petkus, Jr.
Boise State University

The 1990s may well become the decade of Integrated Marketing Communication (IMC) (Foster, 1990; Novelli, 1989–1990). As evidence, *Public Relations Quarterly* devoted an entire issue to IMC. The American Association of Advertising Agencies (AAAA) has established a task force to examine and initiate it. A number of major universities have created graduate programs that combine traditionally separate elements of the promotional mix, presaging an IMC mandate (Caywood & Ewing, 1991). It seems that both practitioners and academics alike are beating a path to the perceived future of marketing communication — IMC.

Yet, how does IMC differ from traditional marketing communication efforts? IMC adds up to marketing communications that (a) set an overarching public relations goal, (b) integrate and coordinate all functional areas involved in communication, (c) transmit the right message to the right group via the right medium, and (d) evoke the desired response from consumers or other targeted publics. This integrated approach to marketing communication represents a fresh sensitivity to four major factors impacting the communication process. First, IMC approaches must consider the multivariate nature of marketing communication itself — the multiple variables attached to source, message, media, and receiver (McGuire, 1985). Second, these approaches must deal with the "disconnect" between the "functional silos," whose jobs are to carry out the different parts of the marketing communication plan (Sullivan, 1986). Third, because consumer sophistication has grown, these approaches must handle information transmitted through experience and media exposure, and achieve consistency across a host of promotional efforts. Finally, in response to slowing economic growth and increasing promotional costs, IMC must generate more powerful communication strategies and greater cost efficiencies.

As might be expected, many companies see IMC as a way to implement a total quality element in their marketing communication. Through an integrated communication effort that focused on customer wants and needs, IMC promises a "bigger bang for the buck"—higher quality and lower costs simultaneously. Thus, IMC appears to be a most positive, comprehensive, and integrative form of marketing communication. This seemingly ideal communication concept, however, has a downside—what can happen to companies if they fail to successfully integrate their message and their marketing communication efforts thus *boomerang* on them. This chapter addresses the downside and presents the danger of IMC boomerang effects.

AN INTEGRATED MARKETING COMMUNICATION MODEL

The traditional model of marketing communication can be represented as an extension of a basic communication model (Assael, 1990). This model starts with the marketing communication message that the company wishes to send the consumer (see Fig. 3.1A). The message is encoded by the firm and then transmitted through the classic marketing media—a promotional mix of advertising, sales promotions, public relations, and personal selling. In response to the message being sent, the consumer then decodes the message and evaluates it for use in personal choice/purchase decisions. A feedback loop from evaluation to the company message provides the opportunity for information to be considered by the company in their next marketing communication effort. The traditional model represents roughly how marketers have thought of their communication process until recently.

A number of key points need to be made about the nature of the traditional model. First, it is not incidental that the model is substantially linear. Most marketers have tended to see their message decisions as the starting point, often driven by technology, product improvements, and firm capability, with only a nod to customer wants and needs. Second, the feedback loop in the model is weak and certainly secondary to the message communication component of the model. Third, the receiver of the traditional model is the individual consumer. Finally, and most significantly, the focus of the model is unquestionably the company message.

This last point is especially critical to understanding the new IMC model (see Fig. 3.1B). Traditionally, in communication research (e.g., advertising, persuasion, and information processing research), the emphasis has been on

A. Traditional Model of Marketing Communication

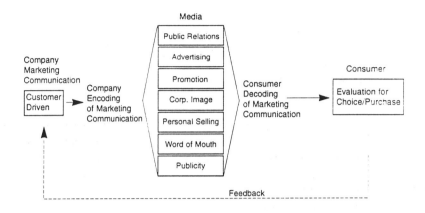

B. Model of Integrated Marketing Communication

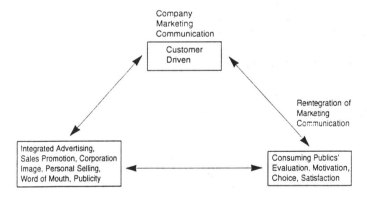

FIG. 3.1.   Models of marketing communication.

the source, the message, or the media (Cushing & Douglas-Tate, 1985). Receiver issues have less often been the focus of analysis. The IMC model reveals a strong interest in how the receiver—the consumer, the government, or any other relevant public—figures into the communication process. This represents not so much a change in perspective as an enriched view of the communication process.

It should be pointed out that the new IMC model is interactive. There is no weak feedback loop because there is no specific starting point. Rather, there is constant exchange between consumer and company. Marketing communication efforts are no longer separate efforts carried out by different functions of the firm, but a single integrated effort. The consumer becomes consuming publics, recognizing that the consumer can be the individual, other firms, the government, associations, and so on. Most important, the model recognizes the significance of the reintegration of the marketing communication message by the receiver. In essence, the IMC model is an implementation of the basic ideas found within the marketing concept—incorporation of customer wants and needs, companywide support, and an agreed-on goal within the firm.

BOOMERANG EFFECTS = when the message backfires

The IMC model focuses attention on the importance of receiver response. If the receiver's integration process results in a perception of consistency, then, happily, the outcome is actualization of the intended communication goal and possible positive affect. If, however, the perception of the receiver is that there is inconsistency, the outcome is goal failure, confusion, and possible undesired negative affect. Positive and negative evaluations often feed back to the firm and may influence subsequent IMC efforts. In the case of strong negative affect, a boomerang effect may occur, posing a potentially serious problem for the company.

A Cognitive Response Approach

The concept of boomerang effects grows out of a cognitive response approach. Cognitive responses have long been recognized as critical mediators of persuasion (Petty, Ostrom, & Brock, 1981). By definition, boomerang effects are antagonistic cognitive responses that persuade more than the received communication message sent out by the firm. As a result, the receiver comes away from the communication encounter with an attitude opposite to the one desired by the source of the communication.

Cognitive responses represent the units of information generated when stimulation by an object or an issue leads to cognitive processing (Cacioppo, Harkins, & Petty, 1981). That is to say, a cognitive response is the result of the processing and structuring activities in which we mentally engage when stimulated by a communication (e.g., an advertisement). We perceive, judge, elaborate, rehearse, and recall information from our memories, resulting in a variety of mental responses. We experience recognition, association, elaborations, images, and thoughts. These responses run the gamut from simple identification of sounds making up the message, to complex message comprehension, to elaboration of that message (e.g., imbuing it with meaning, implications, and values).

The cognitive response approach poses that self-generated thoughts can be as consequential as the stimuli triggering them. In a marketing communication context, the degree to which these self-generated thoughts support the communication stimulus should be reflected in the degree to which the receiver is inclined to support or agree with the source (Haas, 1981). Similarly, the degree to which these self-generated thoughts do not support the communication stimulus should be reflected in the degree to which the receiver is inclined to disagree with the source. Boomerang effects—the changing from a positive attitudinal position to a negative one (or the changing from a negative attitude to a positive one)—result from the latter.

The usefulness of the cognitive response approach stems from illustrating that persuasion can be highly affected by our own self-generated thoughts, as well as by the marketing communication messages initiated by firms. It also helps explicate the cognitive processes, revealing the complex, differentiated nature of those processes. Under this scenario, the need for cognitive integration as experienced by consumers and other relevant publics becomes clear.

Integration Theory

Although boomerang effects result from certain types of cognitive responses, it helps to understand more about how these responses arise from exposure to marketing communication. Anderson's (1971) work on information integration theory provides a link to tie cognitive responses as an information source in the persuasion process to integration issues in marketing communication. How do we go about integrating perceived external marketing stimuli and our internal cognitive responses to them? Information integration theory rests on the concept of multiple causation. From this perspective substantially all thought and behavior spring from multiple causes interacting with one another. In addition, integration theory dictates that information must be considered in terms of the meaning and value that it has for the individual. This integration process is thought to be cognitively carried out via simple algebraic models (Anderson, 1971). Externally, we receive marketing communication stimuli in the form of public relations information, advertising campaigns, sales promotions, direct marketing efforts, and other marketing communication tactics. Receivers must deal with a barrage of messages sent their way and integrate or "input interweave" them. This input interweaving is the process of weaving mental fabrics from foraged facts. The implications for IMC are apparent. Marketers should integrate all communication efforts to ensure realistic messages consistent with all functions, consistent among long-term goals such as corporate image, and consistent with short-term goals such as specific campaign objectives.

Information integration is necessary from an internal perspective as well. The differentiation of cognitive tasks implies that as receivers of marketing communication, we ultimately integrate all separate cognitive responses in order to facilitate the decision process. This integrative process is complicated, because we experience three different levels of cognitive response (Anderson, 1981). On one level, we cognitively process the communication message. On another we process the implications of the perceived message. On the third level, we process the value those implications hold for us as individuals. We must integrate the differentiated responses, and, finally, we must integrate the external sources of information with the internal levels of response. Again, the implications for IMC are apparent. Marketing communicators must anticipate and plan for the possible negative cognitive responses that their messages elicit.

Negative Cognitive Response and Counterarguing

One interesting action that contributes to negative cognitive response, and its resultant boomerang effects, is argumentation by the audience against the position taken by a communication source. Counterarguments have been thought to serve a number of functions, all typically involving the rejection of an advocated position. Thus, the act of counterarguing is the employment of memory information to justify one's own position and to reject the arguments that support a counterattitudinal position.

Two examples of counterarguing positions taken in advertising can be seen in protocol analyses recently conducted by Schumann and his colleagues (Schumann, Boone, Linsky, & Smith, 1992; Schumann, Thorson, & Dyer, 1992). In two unrelated studies asking subjects to provide their thoughts while viewing ads, examples of boomerang effects were apparent. In the first study (Schumann, Thorson, & Dyer, 1992), subjects saw, among a number of ads, a commercial for a well-known fast food company that depicted the company as health conscious, employing only the finest ingredients for their food. Although the company presented a quality/ health image in the ad, some subjects had difficulty integrating the quality/health message with their personal experience and knowledge of fast food. Table 3.1 provides a listing of actual examples from the subjects who appeared to counterargue. Over 30% of the sample recorded some form of negative cognitive response.

In the second study, Schumann, Boone, Linsky, and Smith (1992) tested fear appeal ads for drinking and driving and employed a source manipulation. Subjects viewed one of four different fear appeal commercials embedded with several filler ads. Half the subjects viewed a fear appeal ad sponsored by SADD (Students Against Drunk Driving), whereas the other half viewed an ad sponsored by a well-known beer company. The ads sponsored by the beer company generated a number of negative reactions (see Table 3.2). When comparing those that viewed the beer ads and generated negative cognitive responses with those who saw beer-sponsored ads and had

TABLE 3.1
Cognitive Responses Reacting to Fast Food Commercial

"It tried to show how health conscious _____ is. I thought this was really
stupid because everyone knows that all _____ serves is fried foods."
"All I think about is _____ greasy burgers and soaked, heavy fries. Even
with this commercial."
"Good commercial but it's so obvious that _____ isn't healthy.
"I just don't associate _____ as using as good quality food as the stuff in
the commercial. The hamburger beef, for example, looked really good, like something
your Mom would have at home. _____ hamburgers are definitely not like
ones Mom would cook."
I thought—what a joke. To see a fresh product [meats and vegetables] go into the bag and
to see the unhealthy processed item come out [i.e., apple pie, hamburger].
"They might purchase all those natural fresh food/dairy products to make their foods, but
they are too unhealthy to eat by the time the finished product comes out. All I picture is
grease and fat."
"I felt it was somewhat misleading. Yes—all the products shown are good for you, but are
they good for you in _____ form?"
"I think _____ tries very hard to send a message to consumers that they use
the freshest, best possible ingredients. In my opinion, fast food is fast food. I do
enjoy _____ on occasion, however fried food is simply not good for you."
"For a minute I actually felt like their food was fresh, then I remembered the last
hamburger I had. It will take more than a few well-designed commercials for me to believe that their food is 'fresh of the farm.'"
"It made me think of how stupid _____ must think its customers are because
nothing in their food is fresh. They don't have fresh meat. It was insulting to my intelligence. It makes me not want to ever eat at _____ again."

TABLE 3.2
Cognitive Responses Reacting to Drinking and Driving Commercial

"I laughed and almost thought the whole thing was a mockery since so many of their other
commercials have beers and cars—or have beer and people doing reckless things. The
main thing I remember was thinking that _____ had some nerve."
Who are they trying to fool?"
"The company is trying to promote their name."
"_____ is probably doing this as a PR effort."
"Does _____ really mean what they say?"
"There is a conflict between this commercial and other commercials sponsored by
_____."
"They're just trying to make themselves look good [ethically]."
"Good idea but bad sponsor."
"Seemed to be doing it out of obligation instead of concern."
"_____ throwing their name in for publicity."
"For beer industry to sponsor this is the height of hypocrisy!"
"I'm sure _____ does not want people to drink and drive, but I'm sure that
_____ wants people to drink themselves silly with their beer."
"_____ to me is a beer seller, not a promoter of responsible drinking."

neutral or positive response, the boomerang effects become apparent. The negative responders were more likely to recall the sponsor, less likely to want to change their drinking behavior, less likely to believe the company was interested in promoting responsible behavior, and less persuaded by the message.

THE VULNERABILITY OF IMC

Today's consumers and other publics, the receivers of our marketing communication, are a sophisticated lot. People are exposed to a vast array of information from early childhood on. This information represents a combination of personal product/service experience, sales promotion effort, word-of-mouth information, and hefty helpings of multiple media advertising. After customers/consumers graze these informational pastures, they engage in input interweaving as predicted by integration theory. As they weave mental fabrics from their foraged facts, they become aware of any breaks in the consistency of those fabrics. These inconsistencies disrupt cognitive integration and signal a threat to IMC.

Common Threats

The fundamental ground rules of marketing communication have shifted in recent times due to the information revolution (Schlossberg, 1992). Yet, awareness of the shift lags. Thus, probably the most common threat to IMC is simple oversight. Marketers have long considered the response of customers/consumers to products and services, but perhaps have been less sensitive to their responses in the marketing communication area. To complicate matters, due to the differentiation of task and function within firms and the farming out of functions to agencies, firms have often failed to view their total communication package from the point of view of the receiver of those communications. One hand (in marketing communication, e.g., public relations, advertising, personal selling) has often not known what the other was doing.

Two additional situations also threaten the successful implementation of IMC. The first is very basic. Successful IMC results in powerful, impactful communication if, and only if, the communication is perceived as being based on reality (Foster, 1990). In other words, the customer/consumer must see the communicated message and intended image as being consistent with his or her perceived reality of product/service and corporate image, or else a threat to IMC exists. The second situation suggests that with the recent emphasis of "green" and other "conscience" products, firms must carefully integrate and present their efforts in these social marketing arenas or such communication may be perceived by the receiver as too self-serving (Niederquell, 1991).

Message and Source Factors

Boomerang effects can strike unbeknownst to the marketing communicator. The vast potential for such effects looms large when one considers all possible message and source factors in the study of persuasion. The fast food example mentioned previously reflects a counterarguing of message content. Other researchers have found such negative results related to other aspects of message, including clarity (McCroskey & Mehrley, 1969), forcefulness of message delivery (see Bowers, 1963; Carmichael & Cronkhite, 1965; Robinson & McArthur, 1982), timing of the message position delivered and ordering of confirming arguments (Anderson, 1959), repetition of weak messages (Cacioppo & Petty, 1984), and extravagant claims (Bochner & Insko, 1966; White, 1975). The beer-sponsored ad described earlier generated a number of negative responses concerning the motives of the source. Aspects of source credibility of this type have been investigated by others and include advocacy of extreme positions (Sternthal, Phillips, & Dholakia, 1978), remoteness from expert sources (Huston, 1973), source involvement and resultant loss of objectivity (Harmon & Coney, 1982), forewarning (McGuire, 1961, 1964, 1969), and increasing the number of sources when the arguments are weak (Harkins & Petty, 1981).

IMC STRATEGIES

In simplest terms the receiver of marketing communication, having completed all input interweaving from a given company's marketing communication efforts, develops an image of that company. Commonly, firms interested in proactively establishing, or reestablishing, such an image pursue two basic strategies. These strategies, image positioning or image rectification, must incorporate an IMC effort if they are to be successful. An image positioning strategy involves the development of a positively perceived image by consumers and other relevant publics. This strategy can apply to either a particular company or to an industry as a whole. For example, McDonald's, in promoting its switch from styrofoam to paper packaging, may position itself as the "environmentally responsible" fast food company. Further, the aluminum industry may develop an environmentally responsible image by promoting its involvement in recycling.

Image rectification involves using IMC to change an adverse or otherwise unwanted image. Again, this strategy can apply to either a particular company or to an industry as a whole. Johnson and Johnson's efforts to ameliorate the Tylenol tampering fiasco would fall into this category. Industry examples include similar efforts by the chemical and forest products industries to counteract negative publicity associated with waste disposal or deforestation.

There are numerous contexts in which image positioning or image rectification strategies might be undertaken. These include economic patriotism (i.e., "buy American"), social patriotism (e.g., Olympic sponsorship), and socially beneficial sponsorship (e.g., support for AIDS or cancer research, literacy programs, United Negro College Fund, etc.). Indeed, any context involving the potential for a positively perceived corporate or industry image would be appropriate. Which one is used would, of course, depend on the nature of the company's or industry's current perceived image.

Unfortunately for IMC, both of the aforementioned strategies are vulnerable to boomerang effects. These effects can be driven by inconsistency between the image that is being presented in the communication and the audience perception of that image. Three different types of inconsistencies can be described: motivational inconsistency, circumstantial inconsistency, and negligent inconsistency.

Motivational inconsistency involves audience perception that the IMC strategy used by the company/industry is motivated exclusively by performance (e.g., profitability, sales, etc.) rather than by actual concern for the relevant social issue. For example, boomerang effects could occur if people perceive that a company's Olympic sponsorship is just a scheme to make them look good, or some similar negative impression. Motivational inconsistency is especially likely if the communication is perceived as merely jumping on the bandwagon. For that reason, a proactive IMC strategy is less vulnerable than a reactive strategy.

The other two types of inconsistency involve contraindicative information—information to which the audience is exposed that indicates some inconsistency in the IMC strategy. Circumstantial inconsistency results when contraindicative information arises, but the transgression is perceived by the audience to be unintentional and unavoidable. In contrast, negligent inconsistency results when contraindicative information arises, and the transgression is perceived by the audience to be intentional or due to abject carelessness.

As an illustration, assume a company has implemented an image positioning strategy, promoting itself as the only company that uses a certain pollution-reducing chemical in its production processes. Contraindicative information relevant to the situation could arise (e.g., further testing may show that the pollution-reducing chemical actually harms other aspects of the environment). Boomerang effects could occur as people react negatively to the company's environmentally responsible marketing communication efforts. If this situation is perceived by the public to be unintentional, the boomerang effects would be due to circumstantial inconsistency. If it is perceived to be intentional (i.e., it is perceived that the company/industry purposefully promoted the image despite having knowledge of the contraindicative information), the boomerang effects would be due to negligent inconsistency.

Although all three types of perceived inconsistency can generate boomerang effects, negligent inconsistency would most likely result in the strongest effects because of the perceived intention. Motivational inconsistency should have the second strongest effect because, although the "profit motive" is perceived as intentional, it would most likely be perceived to be more acceptable than outright negligence. Circumstantial inconsistency would most likely generate the weakest boomerang effect because it is perceived as unintentional.

DELAYED IMC BOOMERANG EFFECTS

The vulnerability of IMC does not end with the consumer's prepurchase and purchase input interweaving; it lingers on into the postpurchase product/ service experience. A number of studies in the consumer satisfaction literature have suggested that individuals employ standards to make judgments about products during use (see Woodruff, Clemons, Schumann, Gardial, & Burns, 1991; Woodruff, Schumann, & Clemons, 1990). These individually generated standards (e.g., desires, ideals, equity, and norms) and a number of communicated standards are also potentially influential in generating boomerang effects. Examples might include comparative brand advertising, promotion claims, and salesperson promises.

If, for instance, an IMC effort touts certain attributes of a product that fail to perform up to expectations in actual use, then the potential for a delayed boomerang effect exists. It is not enough for a fast food company to claim its product is made of quality ingredients and, therefore, imply that fast food is healthy food. The process by which the product is made and the consumer's personal knowledge of fast food will be scrutinized by consumers for consistency with a quality/health theme. It is interesting to note that in some product arenas an effort to diffuse the possibility of such delayed negative effects is taking place. Some companies have started to require that customers sign agreements reflecting customer understanding of appropriate product expectations and limitations.

SUMMARY

This chapter presents the potential for and problems associated with the downside of Integrated Marketing Communication (IMC). If, for example, a promotional message is perceived by the receiver as inconsistent with his or her own thoughts, of if supposedly integrated marketing messages conflict in the mind of the receiver, then the probability of a boomerang effect increases. Such a boomerang effect, to the detriment of the firm, engenders the opposite response from the consuming public than was intended by the marketing communication effort.

It is clear that IMC can provide substantial benefits to the marketer, such as increased power in marketing communication and the concomitant lowering of costs. It is also clear that the firm's consuming publics can gain from IMC via a much improved understanding of products, services, and corporate images. It should not be forgotten, however, that potential costs are also inherent in such an effort. Marketers need to consider the complexity and the outcome of their IMC efforts, employing an especially critical and objective eye, or else their enthusiasm for IMC may blind them to the subtleties and strengths of the cognitive responses generated by consuming publics.

Caveat emptor, or buyer beware, enjoys a long history and acceptance in common law and marketing. Today, however, given the litany of possible opportunities for IMC to go awry, *caveat venditor*, or seller beware, may be a more appropriate maxim as firms approach their future marketing communication efforts. After all, it may be better to read about boomerang effects in a book than to experience them.

REFERENCES

Anderson, N. H. (1959). Test of a model of opinion change. *Journal of Abnormal Social Psychology, 59*, 371–381.

Anderson, N. H. (1971). Integration theory and attitude and change. *Psychological Review, 78*(3), 171–206.

Anderson, N. H. (1981). Integration theory applied to cognitive responses and attitudes. In R. E. Petty, T. M. Ostrom, & T. C. Brock (Eds.), *Cognitive responses in persuasion* (pp. 361–397). Hillsdale, NJ: Lawrence Erlbaum Associates.

Assael, H. (1990). *Marketing principles and strategy.* Chicago: Dryden Press.

Bochner, S., & Insko, C. A. (1966). Communicator discrepancy, source credibility, and opinion change. *Journal of Personality and Social Psychology, 4*, 614–621.

Bowers, J. W. (1963). Language intensity, social introversion and attitude change. *Speech Monographs, 30*, 345–352.

Cacioppo, J. T., Harkins, S. G., & Petty, R. E. (1981). The nature of attitudes and cognitive responses and their relationships to behavior. In R. E. Petty, T. M. Ostrom, & T. C. Brock (Eds.), *Cognitive responses in persuasion* (pp. 31–54). Hillsdale, NJ: Lawrence Erlbaum Associates.

Cacioppo, J. T., & Petty, R. E. (1984). Central and peripheral routes to persuasion: The role of message repetition. In L. Alwitt & A. Mitchell (Eds.), *Psychological processes and advertising effects* (pp. 91–112). Hillsdale, NJ: Lawrence Erlbaum Associates.

Carmichael, C. W., & Cronkhite, G. L. (1965). Frustration and language intensity. *Speech Monographs, 32*, 107–111.

Caywood, C., & Ewing, R. (1991). Integrated marketing communications: A new master's degree concept. *Public Relations Review, 17*(3), 237–244.

Cushing, P., & Douglas-Tate, M. (1985). The effect of people/product relationships on advertising processing. In L. Alwitt & A. Mitchell (Eds.), *Psychological processes and advertising effects* (pp. 241–259). Hillsdale, NJ: Lawrence Erlbaum Associates.

Foster, J. (1990). Working together. *Public Relations Journal, 46*(9), 18–24.

Greenwald, A. G., & Albert, R. D. (1968). Acceptance and recall of improvised arguments. *Journal of Personality and Social Psychology, 8,* 31–34.

Harkins, S. G., & Petty, R. E. (1981). Effect of source magnification of cognitive effort on attitudes: An information-processing view. *Journal of Personality and Social Psychology, 40,* 410–413.

Harmon, R. R., & Coney, K. A. (1982). The persuasive effects of source credibility in buy and lease situations. *Journal of Marketing Research, 19,* 255–260.

Hass, R. G. (1981). Effects of source characteristics on cognitive responses and persuasion. In R. E. Petty, T. M. Ostrom, & T. C. Brock (Eds.), *Cognitive responses in persuasion* (pp. 141–172). Hillsdale, NJ: Lawrence Erlbaum Associates.

Huston, T. L. (1973). Ambiguity of acceptance, social desirability, and dating choice. *Journal of Experimental Social Psychology, 9,* 32–42.

McCroskey, J. C., & Mehrley, R. S. (1969). The effects of disorganization and nonfluency on attitude change and source credibility. *Speech Monographs, 36,* 13–21.

McGuire, W. J. (1961). Resistance to persuasion conferred by active and passive prior refutation of the same and alternative counterarguments. *Journal of Abnormal Social Psychology, 63,* 326–332.

McGuire, W. J. (1964). Inducing resistance to persuasion. In L. Berkowitz (Ed.), *Advances on experimental social psychology* (Vol. 1, pp. 191–229). New York: Academic.

McGuire, W. J. (1969). The nature of attitudes and attitude change. In G. Lindzey & E. Aronson (Eds.), *Handbook of social psychology* (2nd ed., Vol. 3, pp. 136–314). Reading, MA: Addison-Wesley.

McGuire, W. J. (1985). Attitudes and attitude change. In G. Lindzey & E. Aronson (Eds.), *Handbook of social psychology* (Vol. II, pp. 233–349). New York: Random House.

Niederquell, M. O. (1991). Integrating the strategic benefits of public relations into the marketing mix. *Public Relations Quarterly, 36*(1), 23–24.

Novelli, W. D. (1989-1990). One-stop shopping: Some thoughts on integrated marketing communications. *Public Relations Quarterly, 34*(4), 7–9.

Petty, R. E. Ostrom, T. M., & Brock, T. C. (1981). Historical foundations of the cognitive response approach to attitudes and persuasion. In R. E. Petty, T. M. Ostrom, & T. C. Brock (Eds.), *Cognitive responses in persuasion* (pp. 5–29). Hillsdale, NJ: Lawrence Erlbaum Associates.

Robinson, J., & McArthur, L. Z. (1982). Impact of salient vocal qualities on causal attribution for a speaker's behavior. *Journal of Personality and Social Psychology, 43,* 236–247.

Schlossberg, H. (1992). Data base is "nerve center" of integrated marketing plan. *Marketing News, 26*(3), 5.

Schumann, D. W., Boone, D., Linsky, A., & Smith, M. (1992). *The role of receiver perceived fear and message source on fear appeal effectiveness* (Working paper). Knoxville: University of Tennessee College of Business.

Schumann, D. W., Thorson, E., & Dyer, B. (1992). *The differential impact of situational relevance and executional involvement in television advertising* (Working paper). Knoxville: University of Tennessee College of Business.

Sternthal, B., Phillips, L. W., & Dholakia, R. (1978). The persuasive effect of source credibility: A situational analysis. *Public Opinion Quarterly, 42,* 285–314.

Sullivan, L. P. (1986). The seven stages in company-wide quality control. *Quality Progress, 19*(5), 77–83.

White, G. W. (1975). Contextual determinants of opinion judgements: Field experimental probes of judgemental relativity boundary conditions. *Journal of Personality and Social Psychology, 32,* 1047-1054.

Woodruff, R. B., Clemons, D. S., Schumann, D. W., Gardial, S. F., & Burns, M. J. (1992). The standards issue in CS/D research: A historical perspective. *Journal of Consumer Satisfaction/Dissatisfaction & Complaint Behavior, 4,* 103-109.

Woodruff, R. B., Schumann, D. W., & Clemons, D. S. (1990). Consumer's reactions to product use experiences: A study of meaning of satisfaction and dissatisfaction. In M. P. Gardner (Ed.), *Proceedings of the Society for Consumer Psychology* (pp. 26-30). Newark, DE: Department of Marketing and the Society for Consumer Psychology.

4 Consumption Constellations: Implications for Integrated Communication Strategies

Michael R. Solomon
Basil G. Englis
Rutgers University

A surge of interest by marketers in integrated communications strategies, by which promotional messages are coordinated among advertising, public relations, and sales promotions efforts, brings with it the implicit acknowledgment that people assimilate consumption data from many sources (cf. Schultz, 1990). Information about desirable and undesirable products is sifted from magazine ads, television commercials, movies, store displays, observation of peers and celebrities, MTV, and so on (cf. Faber & O'Guinn, 1988). These messages, in turn, are assimilated by consumers as they construct a lifestyle representing their unique interpretations of the consumption ideals prevalent in popular culture.

Although most conventional promotional perspectives focus on only one communications category at a time, the consumer is busily incorporating consumption imagery from many sources. Similarly, most product marketing perspectives focus on only one product category at a time, when in fact consumers' choices often reflect cross-category considerations. Consumption imagery emanates from many channels, and this imagery impacts product choices as consumers choose from a "menu" of products, services, and activities that collectively define a desired lifestyle. This chapter emphasizes the strategic importance of combining holistic views of both communications and consumption—a broad perspective that permits marketers to paint a more comprehensive picture of the complex and multidimensional consumption environment.

Old and New Media Strategies

Because product information is transmitted in so many ways, marketing strategists must coordinate the messages they hope to convey about their

65

products by expanding their scope to include both conventional and innovative media vehicles. These new formats, which blur the traditional distinction between advertising and editorial sources, include (but are not limited to) infomercials, product placement, collaborative marketing, and lifestyle merchandising (cf. Elliott, 1991; Leinster, 1987; Magrath, 1991).[1]

Consumers acquire information regarding the consumption patterns associated with desirable and undesirable lifestyle categories through direct exposure, as well as through media depictions of social types. These depictions are often influenced by marketers, who strive to create images of attractive lifestyles to foster identification between consumer and product.

Accordingly, we believe that a goal of integrated marketing strategies should be to present coordinated, consistent, and alluring lifestyle images to consumers in a variety of communications formats. This chapter thus first addresses the issue of lifestyle construction through multicategory product choices, and then delineates some of the communications formats that serve as vehicles to transmit the consumption ideals embodied by collections of disparate, expressive products and services.

THE FOREST OR THE TREES: CONSUMPTION CONSTELLATIONS

A basic assumption of our perspective is that consumers organize information about product–person associations in ways that resemble other types of cognitive categorization, in which an object's symbolic or functional features are used by the perceiver to assign it to a category (cf. Cantor & Mischel, 1979; Solomon, 1988). Information about social categories (e.g., Linville & Jones, 1980) and products (Ward & Loken, 1986) is organized in a similar manner. Products associated with distinct social categories acquire symbolic utility, however, only to the extent that consumers agree that certain products seem to "go together," and thus mutually define a lifestyle category.

For example, Ralph Lauren's campaigns have succeeded in creating a moneyed fantasy world; his mass media images of affluence and sophistication, in turn, become ideals for those who aspire to this quasi-mythical lifestyle (cf. "A Dream World," 1989). Similarly, the sets used in such sitcoms as *All in the Family*, *Roseanne*, and *The Cosby Show*, are also emblematic of prototypical lifestyles—although the desirability of the

---

[1]A timely corroboration of this emphasis on innovative media was provided in a recent report by Myers Marketing and Research, which compiled suggestions to improve communications effectiveness from major advertisers. One of the report's major recommendations was to "recognize product placement in movies as a new medium" (cf. Elliott, 1992).

lifestyles depicted will surely vary among market segments. In each case, however, the stage for the depiction of a lifestyle is set with groups of products assumed to be emblematic of a pattern of consumption intimately associated with that lifestyle (cf. Solomon & Greenberg, 1993). The set "works" to the extent that the audience agrees with the intended connotation.

From the Brand to the Assortment

Marketing theory has generally been slow to acknowledge cross-category relationships, although isolated studies of product interdependencies have been reported (cf. Green, Wind, & Jain, 1972, on "commodity bundles" and Holbrook & Lehmann, 1981, on complementarity among preferences for discretionary leisure time activities). The notion that marketing exchanges involve sets of products rather than goods in isolation can be traced to Wroe Alderson, who argued that exchanges occur because the utility of a product assortment held by A can be improved by the addition of a product held by B (Alderson, 1957). Twenty years later, Wind (1977) observed that researchers' neglect of product interdependencies may partially account for the relatively disappointing results often obtained in the prediction of single brand choice behavior.

The consumption constellation construct has been developed to describe such symbolic interdependencies (cf. Englis & Solomon, 1995; Solomon, 1988; Solomon & Assael, 1987; Solomon & Buchanan, 1991). It is defined as a cluster of complementary products, specific brands, and/or consumption activities used to construct, signify, and/or perform a social role. Because they tend to span many diverse consumption categories, elements of a constellation often display symbolic rather than functional complementarity. Thus, although consumers might easily associate, say, Tony Lama cowboy boots with a Ford pick-up or Gucci loafers with a BMW, the manufacturers and advertisers of these products do not generally take advantage of these symbolic linkages.

These complementary relationships can be traced to each product's common signification of an underlying cultural category (cf. McCracken, 1986). The categories in this case are reference groups—aggregated social ideals employed by consumers to compare and orient their self-definitions. In a global sense, these social benchmarks are assumed to exert potent effects on consumer choice processes (cf. Bearden & Etzel, 1982; Cocanougher & Bruce, 1971; Stafford, 1966), although the specific dynamics of reference group influences have received surprisingly little empirical attention (Englis & Solomon, 1995).

By choosing distinctive products laden with symbolic meaning, consumers communicate their affiliation with a desired reference group (either actual or ideal) and its attendant values. Conversely, they may at the same time eschew other products because of their association with avoidance groups.

In effect, such products may possess stigmatizing properties due to their symbolic association with a negatively valued group. Our perspective seeks to anchor reference group effects more firmly by empirically identifying clusters of products associated with specific positive and negative reference groups. We then consider the effects of these product–group associations on consumers' knowledge and evaluation of expressive products found in these constellations.

CONSTELLATIONS: DISTORTED STEREOTYPES OR ACCURATE REFLECTIONS?

The correspondence of constellations to actual consumption patterns is an interesting empirical question. One study employing Simmons data provided tentative support for the notion that at least one stereotypical constellation corresponds to the purchase patterns of consumers who fall into that category (Solomon & Buchanan, 1991).[2]

A well-publicized social type at the time was the "yuppie," a media creation that appeared to dominate the consumption ethos of the 1980s. The researchers began by defining the yuppie role in broad demographic terms (i.e., consumers aged 25–44 making more than $20,00 a year who live in cities with populations greater than 100,000).[3] Based on media reports prevalent at the time (i.e., the late 1980s), a diverse set of products stereotypically associated with the yuppie was identified. Employing a Bayesian probability approach, the researchers calculated consumption probabilities for these products within the demographic subgroup of interest, and compared these to the Simmons database as a whole.

As is shown in Table 4.1, in each case the probability of purchase for the subgroup exceeded the general population probability. Thus, the constellation of products associated with yuppies by mass media vehicles were reflected in the actual consumption patterns of this group. Next, conditional purchase probabilities for consumers within the demographic subgroup were calculated (thus controlling for income, etc.). This analysis demonstrated that the joint purchase probability of products stereotypically

---

[2]The Simmons Market Research Bureau database monitors the consumption patterns of a statistically representative sample of approximately 20,000 American consumers.

[3]This definition was deliberately constructed to be very broad, because the intent in this exploratory study was to capture the strong aspirational quality of the yuppie role. This rough demarcation yielded a subgroup of approximately 1,200 consumers within the Simmons database.

TABLE 4.1
Joint Occurrences of Consumables

Conditional consumption probabilities are computed within category against total sample.
Consumption probabilities are higher within target group than for general population.

Consumables	Probability [i]	Probability [i/R]
Foreign cars	0.165	0.282
Imported wines	0.190	0.312
Magazines	0.373	0.624
Credit cards	0.310	0.459
Urban sports	0.188	0.303
Ice cream	0.062	0.114
Television	0.762	0.860
Appliances	0.475	0.535

Source: Data adapted from "A Role-Theoretic Approach to Product Symbolism: Mapping a Consumption Constellation," by M. R. Solomon and B. Buchanan, 1991, *Journal of Business Research*, *22*, p. 101. Copyright 1991 by Elsevier Science Publishing Co., Inc. Adapted with permission.

associated with the yuppie lifestyle in fact exceeded each product's individual probability of purchase by consumers demographically included in the yuppie category. For example, a person in this subgroup who buys imported wine is more likely to also buy gourmet ice cream—over and above the individual consumption probabilities for each product within the demographic cohort (and thus controlling for gross socioeconomic effects on purchase probabilities). Because both products belong to the same consumption constellation, their joint consumption is apparently meaningful to consumers who belong to (or aspire to) that lifestyle.

Lifestyles as Prototypes

The exploratory study described previously implies that perceptions of at least some constellations are to some degree grounded in reality. Ironically, however, in a sense this issue is a moot point: As social psychologists well know, people often react to their assumptions about reality rather than to some objective "truth" (cf. Hastorf & Cantril, 1954). Thus, it is important to examine how consumers subjectively perceive constellation content, and how these perceptions translate into product evaluations. To do so, our analysis adapts the large body of work on social cognition to better understand how consumers integrate the consumption imagery they perceive through both vicarious experience and personal observation.

The social cognition literature suggests that individuals "code people and their behavior in terms of . . . a few simple cognitive categories [to simplify] what one needs to know and look for in particular people" (Cantor & Mischel, 1979, p. 6; cf. also Cohen, 1981; Wyer & Srull, 1981), and this approach has also been applied in studies of stereotyping (cf.

Broverman, Broverman, Clarkson, Rosenkrantz, & Vogel, 1970; Park & Hastie, 1987).

We extend this perspective to consumption behavior: A consumption constellation in essence constitutes a prototypical set of products associated with a social category. As a result, those products that are firmly embedded as category prototypes should also be more easily retrieved from memory, and consumers' evaluations of them should be more polarized (positively or negatively).

Some empirical evidence supports the notion that persons, or person categories, are employed as a form of cognitive organization. The essential features of people who belong to these categories form stereotypes representing an integrated image. "So for example, if you know somebody wears tweed, drives a small cheap foreign car, and is introverted, forgetful and smart, those facts tend to go together because they fit your professor stereotype" (Fiske, 1982, p. 6). As Fiske's example illustrates, the contents of these categories include diverse products and consumption behaviors, as well as personality traits and other interpersonal data.

The methodologies used to study object categorization have thus far been adapted to several exploratory examinations of constellation processing. Consistent with past prototype research (cf. Cantor & Mischel, 1979; Rosch, 1978; Ward & Loken, 1986), these studies employ a free-response format. Subjects are given a prompt (in this case, a social or occupational label), and are then asked to provide a list of products and/or specific brands they associate with that prompt. This approach has been widely used in attempts to study subjective cultural associations (cf. Hirschman, 1980; Szalay & Deese, 1978; Triandis, 1972). In order to code responses at both the product and brand levels, a hierarchical coding scheme was developed that assigned specific numbers to brands within subcategories (e.g., domestic beer, sports magazines, etc.). An index of agreement across subjects was then computed that permitted a comparison of free-response data in which the number of responses per subject is not constrained.[4]

Mediators of Cognitive Representation

Of course, the clarity and content of a constellation is not constant across consumers. Differences in cognitive representation of lifestyle stereotypes are important insofar as the nature of a consumer's internalized consumption ideal will influence his or her set of positively and negatively valued products, as well as the particular reference groups he or she is motivated to emulate or avoid.

Just as the degree of consensus and polarization in person prototypes is

---

[4]The first study of this genre by Solomon (1988) adapted the Gini index, a measure used in industrial economics. In subsequent work by Englis and Solomon (1995), a different index was devised that permits more precise, individual-level statistical comparisons.

dependent in part on the relationship between the observer's own social role and the social role in question (Linville & Jones, 1980), similar findings have been obtained for consumption constellations. For example, familiarity with an occupational role has been shown to mediate the degree of consensus among perceivers who are asked to generate the consumption constellation associated with that role (Solomon, 1988).

Group members tend to be capable of finer or more articulated discriminations within that group, while nonmembers tend to see members as being relatively similar (Markus, Moreland, & Smith, 1985; Taylor, Fiske, Etcoff, & Ruderman, 1978; Walker, Celsi, & Olson, 1987). By extension, this difference may result in more idiosyncratic associations by group members due to the greater flexibility of members' knowledge structures (cf. Walker, Celsi, & Olson, 1987). For example, academics may disagree that all or even most of their colleagues wear tweed sportcoats with elbow patches, drive cheap foreign cars, and so on.

On the other hand, out-group members may be more likely to rely on a few prototypical product symbols of a role for their sign value, and attach more importance to ownership of these exemplars. Related phenomena have in fact been observed in work on anticipatory role acquisition, cultural assimilation, and compensatory symbolism. Newcomers to a role tend to purchase more stereotypical products, and to be brand loyal to market leaders as a way to speed acculturation (e.g., Solomon & Douglas, 1987; Wicklund & Gollwitzer, 1982; Zaltman & Wallendorf, 1979).

Ironically, this suggests that consumers less involved with a social role may actually exhibit greater agreement in their product associations. Their assumptions about the products used by role occupants would reflect the relatively homogeneous stereotypes depicted in popular culture (cf. Solomon, 1988). Thus, the contents of a product constellation, and consensus regarding its composition, may be affected by the perceiver's relative degree of role knowledge and/or role aspiration.

Indeed, Solomon (1988) found that subjects with relatively lower desire to occupy a social role exhibited greater agreement regarding products associated with the role. A median split was performed based on responses to a scale measuring aspiration to the occupational roles included in the study, and a mean index value for subjects below the median were compared with those above. Subjects with relatively lower desire to occupy a social role exhibited significantly greater agreement (i.e., the index value was greater) regarding products associated with the role.

Reference Groups and Constellations

A more recent study explicitly examined the relationship between the appeal of reference groups and consumers' cognitive representations of the constellations associated with those groups (Englis & Solomon, 1995). In order to ground the study in actual consumption data, the PRIZM system (a geodemographic clustering system developed by Claritas, Inc.) was used. This system classifies every U.S. zip code into one of 40 categories, ranging from "Blue-Blood Estates" to "Public Assistance" (cf. Weiss, 1988). Each of the 40 clusters is defined by detailed demographic, lifestyle, and consumption information, often including brand level data.

For example, the "Shotguns and Pickups" cluster is defined, in part, by the following consumption preferences and dislikes: high usage of chain saws, snuff, canning jars, AMC Eagles, frozen potato products, and whipped toppings. Cluster members are exceptionally low users of car rental services, country clubs, *Gourmet* magazine, and Irish whiskey. In contrast, "Furs and Station Wagons" cluster members are likely to have a second mortgage, buy wine by the case, read *Architectural Digest*, drive BMW 5-series cars, eat natural cold cereal and pumpernickel bread, and watch *The Tonight Show*. Members of this cluster are unlikely to chew tobacco, hunt, drive a Chevy Chevette, use nondairy creamers, eat canned stews, or watch *Wheel of Fortune*.

The clusters defined by systems such as PRIZM are empirically derived, and are then labeled to elicit stereotypical images (e.g., "Norma Rae-ville," "Bohemian Mix"). One or more of these marketer-constructed stereotypes is then selected by clients who wish to reach just the types of consumers described. The correspondence of these clusters to the categories used by everyday consumers is an interesting empirical question: Would a consumer placed in the Norma Rae-ville cluster necessarily agree that he or she is especially likely to use the set of products identified by PRIZM (e.g., consume chewing tobacco, eat canned spaghetti, watch professional wrestling)? Moreover, would that consumer be able to generate accurately the list of products associated with another cluster, particularly one to which he or she either aspires or is motivated to avoid (e.g., possibly "God's Country" or "Hard Scrabble," which are, respectively, affluent versus poor rural clusters)?

In this study, we first empirically characterized lifestyle clusters derived from the PRIZM scheme into one of four reference groups that had been pretested to apply specifically to our sample of consumers (undergraduate business majors). We identified those lifestyle clusters that—for these particular students—represented an aspirational or desirable reference group, an avoidance or rejected reference group, an occupied or current group, and an irrelevant group.

Next, subjects were provided with a demographic description of each group and asked to generate (again, in a free-elicitation format) a list of products spanning four categories that they would expect each group to own or use. Consumption information from PRIZM was used to define the four clusters selected in pretesting to correspond to reference groups (see Table 4.2).

TABLE 4.2
Consumption Information Presented to Respondents for Each Lifestyle

Lifestyle Cluster (Reference Group)	High Usage Products*	Low Usage Products*
Money & brains (aspirational group)	These people are especially likely to use, buy, or do: Travel/entertainment cards Aperitif/specialty wines Classical records Valid passports These people are especially likely to eat: Natural cold cereal Whole-wheat bread These people are especially likely to watch: "At the Movies" "Murder, She Wrote"	These people are especially unlikely to use, buy, or do: Hunting Pick-up trucks CB radios Watch roller derby These people are especially unlikely to eat: Presweetened cold cereal Canned stews These people are especially unlikely to watch: "Super Password" "As the World Turns"
Smalltown downtown (avoidance group)	These people are especially likely to use, buy, or do: Salt-water fishing rods Watch pro wrestling Cafeterias Gospel records/tapes These people are especially likely to eat: Canned meat spreads Packaged instant potatoes These people are especially likely to watch: "Scrabble" "The Today Show"	These people are especially unlikely to use, buy, or do: Money-market funds Racquetball Travel/entertainment cards Chewing tobacco These people are especially unlikely to eat: Natural cold cereal Mexican foods These people are especially unlikely to watch: "The Tonight Show" "Late Night with David Letterman"
Young suburbia (occupied group)	These people are especially likely to use, buy, or do: Rental cars Swimming pools Mutual funds Health clubs These people are especially likely to eat: Cheese spreads Pretzels These people are especially likely to watch: "Cheers" "Night Court"	These people are especially unlikely to use, buy, or do: Snuff Watch pro wrestling Soul records/tapes Civic clubs These people are especially unlikely to eat: Powdered fruit drinks Canned stews These people are especially unlikely to watch: "Friday Night Videos" "The Young and the Restless"

(Continued)

TABLE 4.2 (Continued)

Lifestyle Cluster (Reference Group)	High Usage Products*	Low Usage Products*
Middle America (irrelevant group)	These people are especially likely to use, buy, or do:	These people are especially unlikely to use, buy, or do:
	Domestic air charters	Travel by bus
	Christmas/Chanukah clubs	Depilatories
	Pipe tobacco	Burglar alarm systems
	Electric drills	Foreign tour packages
	These people are especially likely to eat:	These people are especially unlikely to eat:
	Pizza mixes	Canned meat spreads
	Canned tea	Liquid nutritional supplements
	These people are especially likely to watch:	These people are especially unlikely to watch:
	"The Facts of Life"	"Loving"
	"Simon & Simon"	"Friday Night Videos"

* Consumption data are taken from *The Clustering of America*, by M. J. Weiss, 1988, New York: Harper & Row.

Source: Table adapted from "To Be *and* Not to Be: Lifestyle Imagery, Reference Groups and *The Clustering of America*," by B. G. Englis and M. R. Solomon, 1995. *Journal of Advertising, 24*, 27–28.

We then examined accuracy—the degree to which empirically derived PRIZM data correspond to consumers' perceptions of what people in different PRIZM clusters are likely to consume, and consensus—the extent to which lifestyle stereotypes (regardless of their veridicality) are shared by consumers in a given segment. Details regarding the occupied and irrelevant groups are provided elsewhere (Englis & Solomon, 1995). In the following section we discuss some of the findings obtained for aspirational and avoidance groups.

Based on previous findings in the field of social cognition, a number of predictions were advanced. For example, although group familiarity usually yields greater category accuracy, it is also associated with more fine-grained knowledge about acceptable idiosyncrasy, whereas increased social distance is associated with greater stereotypy (cf. Linville & Jones, 1980; Solomon, 1988).

Therefore, it was hypothesized that consensus will be lowest when consumers describe the consumption constellations associated with a group to which they currently belong, whereas the highest levels of stereotyping, and hence consensus, should be obtained among consumers who are describing the constellations associated with a group they wish to avoid. Furthermore, it was predicted that those categories that consumers are motivated to approach or avoid are more likely to be marked by greater consensus and/or accuracy. As described in the next section, the overlooked notion of avoidance products was of particular interest in this investigation.

Stigmatized Products

One of the most interesting outcomes of this research is the finding that some products and activities may acquire stigmatizing properties owing to their association with avoidance groups. Some of the products and media most closely associated with the avoidance group for this sample were pick-up trucks, wrestling and fishing magazines, Budweiser beer, Jack Daniels whiskey, Brut cologne, and Mennen Speed Stick.

As expected, a lifestyle that represents an avoidance role is perceived in a highly stereotyped manner: Consumers possess little information about that role, the information that is in memory is very inaccurate, and yet there is a high level of agreement with others for whom the lifestyle also represents an avoidance group.

This pattern of results suggests that some consumption constellations may acquire stigmatizing properties owing to their perceived association with avoidance groups. Consumers will eschew purchase, ownership, and use of such products and activities owing to their disinclination to be affiliated with an avoidance group.

Coveted Products

The pattern obtained for the avoidance group was in striking contrast with that obtained for the aspirational role. As expected, accuracy and extent of knowledge about the aspirational group were both high, and consensus was relatively low. Owing to their motivation to affiliate with and emulate members of an aspirational group, consumers learn about the actual consumption activities of the group and as a consequence accuracy is high. However, consumers also learn to make fine-grained distinctions regarding acceptable consumption activities, and knowledge of these nuances of variation lowers the degree of consensus across consumers. This interactive relationship is diagrammed in Fig. 4.1. One ramification of this pattern is that communications should perhaps be focused on consumers' cognitive representations of desired lifestyle prototypes, rather than on the actual consumption patterns anchored to their current demographic cohort.

MEDIA PORTRAYALS OF LIFESTYLES

In general, these results suggest that the meaning of a lifestyle group (or other marketer-defined category) needs to be understood in relation to

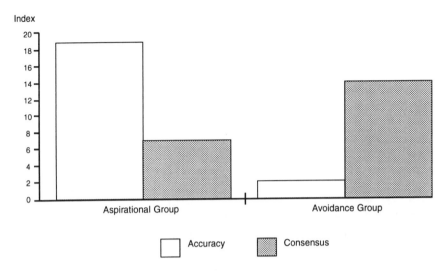

FIG. 4.1.   Interaction between reference group and accuracy versus consensus.

specific groups of consumers. The social meaning of a lifestyle group influences consumers' knowledge and appraisal structures. This further implies that the definition of a brand's social identity must go beyond the simple mapping of a target product vis-á-vis competitors. Rather, we argue that products should be positioned as part of a relevant consumption constellation. The consumption constellation should be defined by its specific association with a desirable reference group for that target market segment. Although other positioning strategists (e.g., Aaker & Shansby, 1982) argue in favor of approaches that seek to position products by their association with particular lifestyle profiles, we maintain that information about aspirational as well as avoidance lifestyle groups is pertinent. A product can be thought of as positioned with an aspirational group's consumption constellation and against an avoidance group's consumption constellation: In effect, "one person's meat is another person's poison."

We now consider the varied communications formats in which such constellation information can be or is currently imparted. In addition to conventional media such as radio, television, magazines, and newspapers, we consider any environment in which consumption information is available (and in which the "reality" depicted is subject to editing by marketers) to be a viable communications format. The increasing immersion of the consumer in an all-encompassing marketing environment has been a catalyst for the evolution of new, hybrid forms of communications. This section briefly delineates some of the traditional and emerging communications formats available to strategists, and emphasizes the potential of these multiple formats in transmitting appropriate constellation imagery.

Advertising: Traditional Approaches

One's lifestyle is a statement about who one is in society, as well as who one is not. Group identities, whether of hobbyists, athletes, or drug users, gel around forms of expressive symbolism. The self-definitions of group members are derived from the common symbol system to which the group is dedicated. Such self-definitions have been described in various ways, including lifestyle, taste public, consumer group, symbolic community, and status culture (Peterson, 1979).

Lifestyle advertising is predicated on the notion that people sort themselves into groups on the basis of the things they like to do, how they like to spend their leisure time, and how they choose to spend their disposable income (Zablocki & Kantor, 1976). These choices, in turn, create opportunities for market segmentation strategies that recognize the potency of a consumer's chosen lifestyle in determining both the types of products purchased and the specific brands likely to appeal to a designated lifestyle segment. Lifestyle advertising goes well beyond creating a brand personality; it depicts a whole way of life (Moore, 1988).

Because a goal of lifestyle marketing is to allow consumers to express their social identities, a key aspect of this strategy is to focus on product usage in social situations. The goal of associating a product with a social situation is a long-standing one for advertisers, whether the product is included in a round of golf, a family barbecue, or a night at a glamorous club surrounded by "jetsetters" (Leiss, Kline, & Jhally, 1986).

Thus, people, products, and settings are combined to express a certain (often idealized) consumption style. Because the context of lifestyle advertising (sets, characters, etc.) plays such a vital role in the creation of meaning, some marketers are beginning to acknowledge the overlooked role that the environment depicted in an ad can play in determining perceptions and/or social desirability of the focal product.

Executional Elements and Lifestyle Inferences

Because the goal of lifestyle advertising is to place a product in an environmental context that will resonate with the viewer, the executional options available to creatives take on added importance. The setting of an ad is more than an attractive background for a focal product; it speaks volumes about the consumption patterns the marketer hopes to link to that product.

When a more holistic perspective on advertising is adopted, it becomes apparent that — much like a play — the characters, props, costumes, and other "dramatic" elements in an ad should be more rigorously conceived and deployed. Although many of these decisions are made intuitively (and at times quite successfully) by creatives, we propose that an ad's context may be a ripe area for more systematic research. Although we respect the value of freewheeling artistic expression, there is a need for greater coordination of lifestyle messages across both product categories and communications formats. Creative framing may be better informed by more systematic attempts to identify and include important constellation elements in construction of ad settings.

Set Design. A commercial set consists of a physical location and collateral objects that are naturally present, plus those that have been deliberately placed to aid in the creation of a setting, which (with such other elements as lighting effects, costumes, the protagonist's occupation, etc.) dramatically represents the qualities of the characters (cf. Holman, 1980; Stern, 1992). These factors are especially critical to the staging of commercials that parallel the format of realistic drama, in which elements (e.g., plot, characters, dialogue, etc.) are intended to portray everyday life (Abrams, 1988).

In contrast to the meticulous attention paid to minute aspects of the focal product in terms of package design, copy effectiveness, media placement, consumer psychographics, and so on, the surroundings in which the product is embedded appear to be left largely to intuition.[5] These perceptions may be influenced both by product or brand usage (e.g., an actor is shown wearing a suit versus overalls); by more subtle, stylistic variations (e.g., a full-cut Armani suit versus a conservative Brooks Brothers pinstripe); as well as by the pace and timing of an ad (e.g., Pavelchak, Gardner, & Broach, 1991); and even the physical attractiveness of spokespeople within it (cf. Joseph, 1982).

Endorsements and characterizations. Media can create an illusion of personal contact, what Horton and Wohl (1956) termed "intimacy at a distance." Thus, the people or characters portrayed in advertising dramas can themselves make lifestyle statements that will moderate the meaning of the focal product.

Actors, for example, often appear in ad campaigns as characters they play, and as a result are likely to evoke the lifestyle connotations connoted by their roles. Tim Allen, the star of the sitcom *Home Improvement*, is slated to appear in ads for Builders Square, a chain of home-improvement

---

[5]Research on the production of media and/or advertising has largely been limited to differences in production values across television genres (e.g., Barbatsis & Guy, 1991; Barker, 1985, for studies on aesthetic intensification as related to the verisimilitude of soap operas and sitcoms), biases in the depiction of reality in the selection and representation of news (cf. Tuchman, 1978), or nonempirical explorations of the creative process in advertising (cf. Arlen, 1980; Hirschman, 1989; McCracken, 1986).

stores. Gertrude Berg, who played Molly Goldberg on radio and Television, sold S.O.S. soap pads in character in the 1960s, and *M*A*S*H* characters extolled the virtues of IBM products (cf. Elliott, 1992). The character's attributes (it is hoped) will transfer to the product (cf. McCracken, 1989).

Similarly, celebrities associated with certain lifestyles or taste cultures frequently are used to create or modify a brand image, whether it be Cher for Jack Lalanne, Paula Abdul for L.A. Gear, or Martha Raye for Polident. Character actors and celebrity endorsers often are selected in terms of specific lifestyle connotations as well as overall popularity and/or recognition, but the failure of some campaigns featuring well-known endorsers implies that a figure representing an inappropriate constellation was employed (cf. McCracken, 1989, for numerous examples).

A New Weapon: Collaborative Advertising

Although reference is sometimes made to the use of several products in a single advertisement or campaign, this is an underutilized strategy (e.g., Magrath, 1991). However, there are notable examples of such collaborative marketing and advertising strategies. Several years ago, Eastern Airlines and Disney advertised together in a campaign that stressed the advantages of flying to Disney World. In this case there is a clear associative link between air travel and vacationing at a resort. More recently, an ad for Weber grills prominently featured a Corvette in the background as a way to make a carefully crafted lifestyle statement. A TV spot for the NASDAQ exchange (created by Messner Vetere Berger Carey Schmetterer) showcases MCI Telecommunications, a company for which NASDAQ helped to attract investment dollars. Most viewers probably did not realize, however, that MCI is also a Messner Vetere client ("Synergy 'R Us," 1992a).

The role of consumption constellations as part of lifestyle prototypes suggests other areas in which collaborative marketing of this sort may be effective. For example, sports products that are tied together not because they are needed for a single sport but due to the lifestyle of their users could be advertised together. Another application might involve associating a particular line of clothing with a watch and shoe line—such as Cole–Hahn with Burberry and Movado, or Guess clothes with Swatch and Nike. Again, the selection of a particular group of products is predicated on their association with a desirable lifestyle for the target of the advertising.

Public Relations: Traditional Approaches

A variety of public relations efforts also have strong relationships to the creation, perpetuation, and/or depiction of desirable lifestyles. Almost by definition, these efforts involve the attempt to position a client's product or service in the context of naturally occurring activities. For example, a popcorn manufacturer might wish to depict the product (albeit without butter) as being congruent with a healthy, light lifestyle by arranging for this product to be mentioned in feature stories about modern diets and snack alternatives. Many disparate routes are available to garner publicity, but all involve to some degree the separation between the source and the message. This disassociation makes it more likely that the consumer will readily integrate available consumption imagery into his or her cognitive representation of a constellation — without the counterarguing that often impedes the acceptance of advertising messages.

Sponsored Events

The first sponsored events were in the 1920s, when Standard Oil and Firestone sponsored car racing, and the sports event market is now a $1.4 billion a year industry (Rosen, 1990). The attempt to create linkages between a specific product and a lifestyle component as exemplified by an athletic contest is of course quite prevalent, even when common constellation membership is dubious (e.g., the occasional criticism voiced of such events as the Virginia Slims Tennis Tournament, where an unhealthy product is tied to a vigorous activity). More recently, other (perhaps ethically questionable) opportunities have arisen to insert a product into a lifestyle context, as so-called "ambush marketers" run advertising that implies they are sponsors of an event when in fact this "honor" has gone to a competitor (e.g., as occurred in the Olympics).

Media Plugs

Public relations efforts also help to determine the use of "plugs," where brand mentions are made in the context of news shows or other programming. One study, which monitored the frequency of plugs over a 24-hour period, found 360 occurrences during news programs alone, and a total of 818 free plugs during that period (cf. *Advertising Age*, 1990).[6] Marketing sometimes seem to exert a self-fulfilling prophecy on popular culture. As commercial influences on popular culture increase, marketer-created symbols are incorporated into cultural products to a greater degree. Historical analyses of Broadway plays, bestselling novels, and the lyrics of hit songs, for example, clearly show large increases in the use of brand names included

---

[6]A more recent study of free publicity for food products, counted the number of times certain food companies, brands, and/or brand icons were mentioned in consumer publications in 1991 (cf. "Free Ink," 1992). Some of the prominent corporate beneficiaries included Quaker Oats (1,419 mentions) and General Mills (1,402 mentions), whereas some widely mentioned specific brands were Tropicana (480 mentions), Coke (5,436 mentions), and Pepsi (4,090 mentions).

in these artistic vehicles over time (Friedman, 1985, 1986). As a consequence, the inclusion of branded consumption imagery in aesthetic media can only be expected to increase.

A New Weapon: Product Placement

In many cases the appearance of specific products or the use of brand names in scripts is no accident. More than 30 companies in the United States specialize in product placement. Their job is to get exposure for a product by inserting it into a movie or a television show. The movie *Rocky IV* clearly showed products by Panasonic, Sony, and Lamborghini, whereas *Ghostbusters* featured Coca-Cola and *Desperately Seeking Susan* highlighted Polaroid. Perhaps the greatest success story was achieved by Reese's Pieces, where sales jumped by 65% after the candy appeared in the film *E.T.* (Cole, 1985).

Product placement has become so common that 20% of consumers report they actively look for brands in movies (Sharkey, 1988). In fact, a 1992 report that culled viewpoints from major advertisers recommended that the industry "recognize product placement in movies as a new medium" (cf. Elliott, 1992). When justifying its payment of a fee to have a drill featured in *Die Hard 2*, Black & Decker cited research indicating that this medium yielded 2½ times better recall than normal TV advertising (Colford, 1990).[7] Similarly, about 40 game shows give away prizes with the help of placement agencies. These shows sell exposure ("fee-spots") for about $60,000 — and anywhere from 500 to 2,000 such spots are sold per year (Rosen, 1990).

CONSUMERS LOOK FOR CONSTELLATIONS — ADVERTISERS SHOULD TOO

This Chapter has attempted to make the case for a holistic perspective on consumption, to be accompanied by an equally holistic perspective on communications strategy. Just as consumers do not necessarily make individual purchase decisions in a vacuum, advertisers must coordinate media decisions to permit the simultaneous transmission of lifestyle imagery in diverse media, whether traditional or newly emergent forms. This holistic model is depicted schematically in Fig. 4.2.

This more comprehensive view of strategic communications brings with it a host of unresolved issues that need to be addressed by researchers. One

---

[7]Unfortunately, the company later sued 20th Century-Fox because the scene was cut out of the movie's final version.

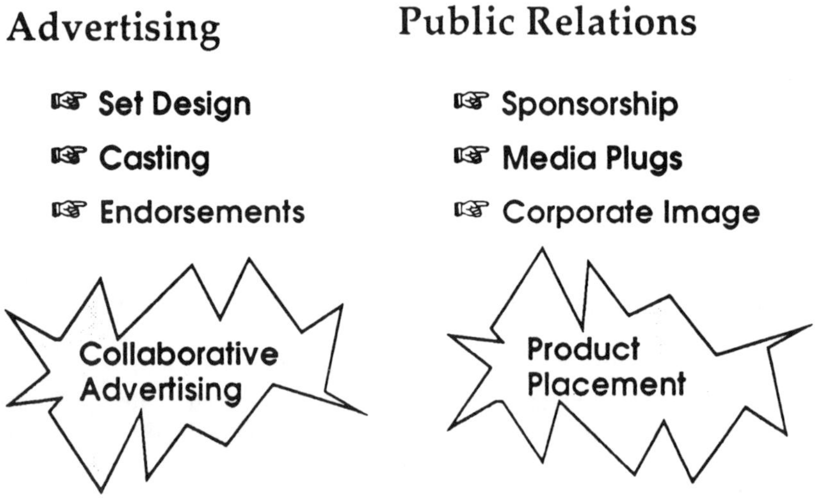

Advertising

☞ Set Design

☞ Casting

☞ Endorsements

Public Relations

☞ Sponsorship

☞ Media Plugs

☞ Corporate Image

Collaborative
Advertising

Product
Placement

FIG. 4.2.   Integrated communications: A strategic gestalt.

issue is raised by the conventional media environment, which has become so saturated that new forms of advertising are continually being invented to break through the clutter. These range from the creation of new advertising media ranging from infomercials, MTV, promotional tie-ins with cultural and art products, and licensing agreements, to intrusive formats such as "junk FAXes," video networks for health clubs and medical offices, or even advertising placards in public bathrooms.[8]

In particular, the proliferation of distribution outlets available to consumers has resulted in increasing recognition among marketers of the lifestyle statements that can be made by purchase environments. Sophisticated approaches to the design of retail atmospherics and the constellation possibilities created by strategic cross-merchandising result in an even greater need to take into account appropriate product constellations, whether for stores or for direct mail catalogs that have come to resemble lifestyle advertisements (e.g., Victoria's Secret, Banana Republic, Land's End, etc.).

Another important issue is the lack of research on the origins of constellations and how their contents are transmitted to consumers. In any

---

[8]For example, companies ranging from McDonalds to Harley-Davidson have authorized the use of their names on products ranging from clothing to chocolates and cologne. After conducting extensive research, for example, the Murjani clothing company licensed the Coca-Cola name. As one Murjani executive observed: "Because of the advertising Coke had done over the years, it turned out that people had a picture in their minds of what the clothes would look like" (Sherman, 1986).

setting, real or contrived, social information is communicated on verbal and nonverbal channels. Although the contexts of advertising depictions are certainly not determined in a random or capricious manner, researchers have yet to explore the ways in which these rich cues may influence the meanings (desired or not) communicated by ad executions. More work is needed to determine the effect of contextual variables on such issues as audience involvement, attitude toward the ad, and halo effects that may influence perceptions of the focal product's "personality."

In addition, even less is known about the dynamics of the encoding process whereby consumption symbolism is selected by those cultural specialists who create advertising "worlds" (cf. Solomon, 1988; Solomon & Greenberg, 1993). These gatekeepers appear to follow cultural formulae when designing sets for slice-of-life depictions; personal intuition or taste appears to be based on a common *Zeitgeist* regarding what artifacts are associated with a particular type of person and his or her lifestyle. Even those involved in the selection process are not necessarily aware of the common threads of symbolism each uses to weave his or her social tapestry, yet these choices reverberate throughout popular culture.

Given the complexity of inferences made by consumers when exposed to advertisements, further exploration of advertising context may hold important clues to increasing advertising effectiveness. In particular, more needs to be known about the role of props in allowing viewers to identify with a brand. This identification process, so desired by advertising strategists, may ironically be influenced as much or more by the intuitive choices of set designers and other production personnel than by the careful attention paid to nuances of package design, casting of actors, and so on. The need to explore encoding processes is especially important in an era in which commercial sets increasingly are designed by creatives with backgrounds in music videos, movies, or theater (cf. Miller, 1990).

A particularly crucial issue is the extent to which the meanings shared by these creatives are congruent with those held by viewers. For example, is an ad's effectiveness reduced if its props or settings clash with viewers' expectations or aspirations? Can a new product's attractiveness to a target audience be enhanced by allowing it to bask in the limelight by carefully embedding it in a context of styles and settings that correspond to specific social meanings desired by potential users? Is it possible (or desirable) to construct a semiotic glossary of props, codified to permit more systematic selection of desired artifacts by creatives?

The ability of the media (and of advertisers) to significantly shape the landscape of social reality underscores the need for research on the processes by which this reality is created and tangibilized. In order to better understand what viewers take away from advertising, we must further explore what creatives put in — and the vast array of communications modes now available to transmit constellations. More knowledge of this complex process will allow practitioners of integrated communications strategies to truly speak with one voice when talking to consumers.

REFERENCES

A dream world labeled Lauren. (1989, June). *Marketing Insights*, p. 9.

Aaker, D., & Shansby, J. G. (1982, May/June). Positioning your product. *Business Horizons*, pp. 36–62.

Abrams, M. H. (1988). *A glossary of literary terms* (5th ed.). New York: Holt, Rinehart and Winston.

Alderson, W. (1957). *Marketing behavior and executive action: A functionalist approach to marketing theory*. Homewood, IL: Irwin.

Arlen, M. J. (1980). *Thirty seconds*. New York: Farrar, Straus and Giroux.

Barbatsis, G., & Guy, Y. (1991). Analyzing meaning in form: Soap opera's compositional construction of "realness." *Journal of Broadcasting & Electronic Media 35*, 59–74.

Barker, D. (1985). Television production techniques as communication. *Critical Studies in Mass Communication*, 2, 234–246.

Bearden, W. O., & Etzel, M. J. (1982). Reference group influence on product and brand purchase decisions. *Journal of Consumer Research*, 9(2), 183–194.

Broverman, I. K., Broverman, D. M., Clarkson, F. E., Rosenkrantz, P. S., & Vogel, S. R. (1970). Sex-role stereotypes and clinical judgments of mental health. *Journal of Consulting and Clinical Psychology, 34*, 1–7.

Cantor, N., & Mischel, W. (1979). Prototypes in person perception. In L. Berkowitz (Ed.), *Advances in experimental social psychology* (Vol. 12, pp. 4–52). New York: Academic.

Cocanougher, A. B., & Bruce, G. D. (1971). Socially distant reference groups and consumer aspirations. *Journal of Marketing Research*, 8, 79–81.

Cohen, C. E. (1981). Person categories and social perception: Testing some boundaries of the processing effects of prior knowledge. *Journal of Personality and Social Psychology, 40*(3), 441–452.

Cole, B. M. (1985, March 5). Products that want to be in pictures. *Los Angeles Herald Examiner*, p. 36.

Colford, S. W. (1990, December 3). Lawsuit drills Fox, Cato. *Advertising Age*, p. 3ff.

Elliott, S. (1991, July 5). Marketers favor tales of 2 brands. *New York Times*, p. D1ff.

Elliott, S. (1992, January 9). Presenting "15 best ideas" for ads that work better. *The New York Times*, p. D22.

Englis, B. G., & Solomon, M. R. (1995). "To be *and* not to be: Lifestyle imagery, reference groups, and *The Clustering of America*." *Journal of Advertising, 24*, 13–28.

Faber, R. J., & O'Guinn, T. C. (1988). Expanding the view of consumer socialization: A nonutilitarian mass-mediated perspective. In E. C. Hirschman & J. N. Sheth (Eds.), *Research in consumer behavior* (Vol. 3, pp. 49–78).

Fiske, S. T. (1982). *Stereotypes or piecemeal: Two modes of reacting to others*. Paper presented at the Midwestern Psychological Association, Minneapolis, MN.

Free ink: A battle of the brands. (1992, March 9). *Adweek*, p. 11. *Advertising Age*. (1990, January 29), p. 6.

Friedman, M. (1985). The changing language of a consumer society: Brand name usage in popular American novels in the postwar era. *Journal of Consumer Research, 11* 927–937.

Friedman, M. (1986). Commercial influences in the lyrics of popular American music of the postwar era. *Journal of Consumer Affairs, 20* 193ff.

Green, P. E., Wind, Y., & Jain, A. K. (1972). Benefit bundle analysis. *Journal of Advertising Research, 12*(2), 31–36.

Hastorf, A. H., & Cantril, H. (1954). They saw a game: A case study. *Journal of Abnormal and Social Psychology, 49*, 129–134.

Hirschman, E. C. (1980). Commonality and idiosyncracy in popular culture: An empirical examination of the "layers of meaning" concept. In E. C. Hirschman & M. B. Holbrook (Eds.), *Symbolic consumer behavior* (pp. 29–35). Ann Arbor, MI: Association for Consumer Research.

Hirschman, E. C. (1989). Role based models of advertising creation and production. *Journal of Advertising, 18*(4), 42–53.

Holbrook, M. B., & Lehmann, D. R. (1981). Allocating discretionary time: Complementarity among activities. *Journal of Consumer Research, 7* 395–406.

Holman, C. H. (1980). *A handbook to literature* (4th ed.). Indianapolis, IN: Bobbs-Merrill.

Horton, D. & Wohl, R. R. (1956); Mass communication and para-social interaction. In J. Combs & M. Mansfield (Eds.), *Drama in life: The uses of Communication in Society* (pp. 212–278). New York: Hastings House.

Joseph, W. B. (1982). The credibility of physically attractive communicators: A review. *Journal of Advertising, 11*(3), 15–24.

Leinster, C. (1987, September 28). A tale of mice and lens. *Fortune,*

Leiss, W., Kline, S., & Jhally, S. (1986). *Social communication in advertising.* Toronto: Methuen.

Linville, P. W., & Jones, E. E. (1980). Polarized appraisal of out-group members. *Journal of Personality anp n Social Psychology, 38*(5), 689–703.

Magrath, A. J. (1991 September). Collaborative marketing comes of age again. *Sales & Marketing Management*, pp. 61–64.

Markus, H., Moreland, R. L., & Smith, J. (1985). Role of the self-concept in the perception of others. *Journal of Personality and Social Psychology, 49*(6), 1494–1512.

McCracken, G. D. (1986). Culture and consumption: A theoretical account of the structure and movement of the cultural meaning of consumer goods. *Journal of Consumer Research, 13*, 71–84.

McCracken, G. (1989). Who is the celebrity endorser? Cultural foundations of the endorsement process. *Journal of Consumer Research, 16*, 310–321.

Miller, J. (1990). Set pieces: Set stories. *Advertising Age, 61*, 20–22.

Moore, S. (1988). Insider trading: Inner selves for sale. *New Statesman, 115*, 14.

Park, B., & Hastie, R. (1987). Perception of variability in category development: Instance-versus abstraction-based stereotypes. *Journal of Personality and Social Psychology, 53*, 621–635.

Pavelchak, M. A., Gardner, M. P, & Broach, V. C. (1991). Effect of ad pacing and optimal level of arousal on attitude toward the ad. In R. H. Holman & M. R. Solomon (Eds.), *Advances in consumer research* (Vol. 18, pp. 94–99). Provo, UT: Association for Consumer Research.

Peterson, R. A. (1979). Revitalizing the culture concept. *Annual Review of Sociology, 5*, 137–166.

Rosch, E. (1978). Principles of categorization. In E. Rosch & B. B. Lloyd (Eds.), *Cognition and categorization* Hillsdale, NJ: Lawrence Erlbaum Associates.

Rosen, M. D. (1990, December). Big-time plugs on small-company budgets. *Sales & Marketing Management*, pp. 48–55.

Schultz, D. E. (1990). *Strategic advertising campaigns* (3rd ed.). Lincolnwood, IL: NTC Business Books.

Sharkey, B. (1988, August 29). Moviegoer study finds 20% look for brand names. *Adweek's Marketing Week*, p. 27.

Sherman, B. (1986, June 9). Coca-Cola finds murjani clothes are it. *Advertising Age*, p. S-4.

Solomon, M. R. (1988). Mapping product constellations: A social categorization approach to symbolic consumption. *Psychology & Marketing, 5*(3), 233–258.

Solomon, M. R., & Assael, H. (1987). The forest or the trees?: A gestalt approach to symbolic consumption. In J. Umiker-Sebeok (Ed.), *Marketing and semiotics: New directions in the study of signs for sale,* (pp. 189–218). Berlin: Mouton de Gruyter.

Solomon, M. R., & Buchanan, B. (1991). A role-theoretic approach to product symbolism: Mapping a consumption constellation. *Journal of Business Research, 22,* 95–110.

Solomon, M. R., & Douglas, S. P. (1987). Diversity in product symbolism: The case of female executive clothing. *Psychology & Marketing, 4,* 189–212.

Solomon, M. R., & Greenberg, L. (1993). Setting the stage: Collective selection in the creation of environments depicted in advertising. *Journal of Advertising, 22,* 11–24.

Stafford, J. E. (1966). Effects of group influences on consumer brand preferences. *Journal of Marketing Research, 3,* 68–75.

Stern, B. B. (1992). The drama of realism: Classical principles and contemporary "slice of life" advertising. *Proceedings of the American Academy of Advertising.*

Synergy 'r us: One spot, two clients. (1992, February 17). *Adweek,* p. 12.

Szalay, L., & Deese, J. (1978). *Subjective meaning and culture.* Hillsdale, NJ: Lawrence Erlbaum Associates.

Taylor, S. E., Fiske, S. T., Etcoff, N. L., & Ruderman, A. J. (1978). Categorical and contextual bases of person memory and stereotyping. *Journal of Personality and Social Psychology, 36*(7), 778–793.

Triandis, H. C. (1972). *The analysis of subjective culture.* New York: Wiley.

Tuchman, G. (1978). *Making news.* New York: The Free Press.

Walker, B., Celsi, R., & Olson, J. (1987). Exploring the structural characteristics of consumers' knowledge. In M. Wallendorf & P. F. Anderson (Eds.), *Advances in consumer research* (Vol. 14, pp. 17–21). Ann Arbor, MI: Association for Consumer Research.

Ward, J., & Loken, B. (1986). The quintessential snack food: Measurement of product prototypes. In R. L. Lutz (Ed.), *Advances in consumer research* (Vol. 13, pp. 126–131). Provo, UT: Association for Consumer Research.

Weiss, M. J. (1988). *The clustering of America.* New York: Harper & Row.

Wicklund, R. A., & Gollwitzer, P. M. (1982). *Symbolic self completion.* Hillsdale, NJ: Lawrence Erlbaum Associates.

Wind, J. (1977). Toward a change in the focus of marketing analysis: From a single brand to an assortment. *Journal of Marketing, 12,* 143.

Wyer, R. S., & Srull, T. K. (1981). Category accessibility: Some theoretical and empirical issues concerning the processing of social stimulus information. In E. T. Higgins, C. P. Herman, & M. P. Zanna (Eds.), *Social cognition: The Ontario symposium* (Vol. 1, pp. 161–197). Hillsdale, NJ: Lawrence Erlbaum Associates.

Zablocki, B., & Kanter, R.M. (1976). The differentiation of life styles. *Annual Review of Sociology,* 269–297.

Zaltman, G., & Wallendorf, M. (1979). *Consumer behavior: Basic findings and management implications.* New York: Wiley. end[te

5 Integrated Communication: The Company "Voice" and the Advertising Persona

Barbara Stern
Rutgers, the State University of New Jersey-Newark

> Try to give each advertiser a becoming style. To create the
> right individuality is a supreme accomplishment. (Claude
> Hopkins, in Ogilvy, 1985, p. 204)

The purpose of this chapter is to examine the way a firm communicates the
"right individuality" when its voice is projected to the consuming public by
means of selection, maintenance, and revision of advertising personas. The
paper introduces the concept of the persona to distinguish between "voice"
in the singular and "voices" in the plural, at present used interchangeably
and somewhat confusingly to refer to company or brand personality,
image, or tone (Ogilvy, 1985). The distinction adapts the definition of *voice*
in modern literary criticism (McConkey, 1958) as the one "distinctive
authorial presence" (Abrams, 1988, p. 137) behind the many personas —
voices or characters — that an author creates. In this analogy, the firm's
communication voice — Lasswell's marketing "who" (1948) — is viewed as the
authorial company voice parallel to that of a literary author. By reconceptualizing a singular company voice as the repository of the firm's essence
that multiple personas can publicize, advertising managers can extend a
firm's controllables with the addition of another *p* to the marketing mix.

Literary criticism (Stern, 1989b), notably the body of research on
narrative (Martin, 1986), is the conduit for introducing the *p* of persona
into marketing communication. This theory evolved (see R. C. Elliott,
1982) to clarify the relationship between an author as a historical person
and the characters the author creates. Its relevance rests on the parallel
between the firm's authorial voice and the characters or personas (R. C.

Elliott, 1982; McCracken, 1989; Stern, 1989a) who express the firm's voice in a variety of vehicles (public relations releases, annual reports, promotional messages, direct marketing campaigns) to a variety of publics (the government, shareholders, employees, suppliers, retailers, etc.). A company persona — like a literary one — speaks for a firm or any other sponsoring institution (Booth, 1983) that offers its values, beliefs, and moral vision as evidence to persuade the public that it is worthy of attention, respect, and belief.

This chapter focuses on the study of the advertising persona in particular as the most prominent manifestation of the company voice. It first provides a brief background discussion of the persona, and next discusses three general characteristics — createdness, distinctiveness, and adaptiveness to change. It then examines issues relevant to the ongoing process of managing communication — media choice and consumer credibility — and suggests questions for future research. Greater awareness of the properties of the advertising persona can be generalized to other communication activities, enabling firms to make the most informed choices in selecting, maintaining, and changing personas over time.

VOICE AND PERSONA THEORY: BACKGROUND

One reason that the concepts of voice and persona are so intertwined and complex is that they have been studied by many disciplines, including but not limited to literary criticism (R. C. Elliott, 1982). The same terms are found in philosophy, psychology, communications, and other fields, although not necessarily with the same meaning. Some source disiplines for the multidisciplinary ideas that have entered marketing and consumer behavior research (Deighton, 1985; Deighton, Romer, & McQueen, 1989) are psychology (Allport, 1937; Hall & Nordby, 1973), philosophy and speech act theory (Austin, 1978; Pratt, 1977; Searle, 1969, 1979), speech communication (Fisher, 1984), social psychology (McCracken, 1989), and semiotics (Mick, 1986). Although the application of terms varies from one field to another, this paper accepts voice in the rhetorical sense (see Booth, 1983) as the ethos or soul of a company, expressing itself in advertising through a created persona designed to persuade.

Aristotle's *Rhetoric* provides the theoretical link between an advertising persona's persuasive role and the literature of persuasion, for it is the best-known source of the concept (see Prince, 1982). Aristotle's ethos, first described in reference to political oratory, is the origin of the equivalent voice in rhetoric (Nichols, 1963). It is defined as the "pervasive presence, determinate intelligence, and moral sensibility, which has selected, ordered, rendered and expressed" the materials in a specific work (Abrams, 1988, p.

136), including the persona who appears in that work. An author is said to project his or her ethos by creating a personal character—usually a narrator—who functions as the agent of persuasion. That is, what the author stands for is made manifest by means of his or her created persona, whose purpose is to propound the authorial point of view. The parallel in advertising exists in that the firm is the voice behind the persona, whose goal is to persuade the consumer to purchase the firm's offering.

The concept of the persona allows disentanglement of the abstraction of a company voice from that of the physical qualities of an advertising spokesperson (see Reynolds & Gutman, 1984). Such separation is necessary, for although all firms have a voice, not all firms choose spokespersons to reveal that voice. Even when there is no first-person spokesperson who speaks as "I" or "we" (Abrams, 1988), a company is nonetheless presumed to be responsible for the communication text. This assumption derives from the underlying communication assumption that audiences (viewers, auditors, readers) impute a source to messages—a message sender in the standard model (Grice, 1989)—whether or not the sender is seen.

This assumption is fundamental to advertising as well as to literary communication, for researchers have pointed out that "presenter effects are present, to a greater or lesser degree, in *all* advertising messages" (Rossiter & Percy, 1987, p. 288)—including those with an implied presenter (Haas, 1981). The distinction between voice and persona has not been much discussed in prior research, perhaps because earlier studies of advertising that dealt with brand personality or image focused mainly on the visible presenter, often a celebrity (see McCracken, 1989). However, since only about one third of television ads and one fourth of print ads (Rossiter & Percy, 1987) employ celebrity spokespersons, the question of how a firm communicates personality when it does not use a recognizable spokesperson must also be addressed. To do so, we turn to the concept of the persona as a created entity whose capacity for representing the firm's ethos derives from characteristics inherited from literary forebears.

CHARACTERISTICS OF THE PERSONA: CREATED, DISTINCTIVE, CHANGEABLE

Advertising personas, like literary ones, share three general characteristics—they are created, distinctive, and changeable. Createdness is the root of the others, for this allows the persona to borrow from the real world of marketing actuality as well as from the fictional world of literary art. This double derivation empowers distinctiveness, for a persona partakes of both human and artistic uniqueness. In turn, adaptiveness to change relates to the balance of change and consistency necessary to modify a persona over time while still retaining its unique qualities. The following discussion provides more detailed examination of these characteristics in advertising examples.

Createdness: Fact and Fiction

The first and most important characteristic of the persona is that it is a created entity indebted to both the world of fact and that of fiction—it is a fictional invention emanating from a factual institution. *Fictional* is used here to mean "made" and "made up" (Kenney, 1988, p. 97), qualities that a persona possesses as an invention devised by a firm to particularize its voice in an advertisement. *Factual* is used to refer to the reality of the firm—an actual company at some historical juncture in the external world. The two qualities fuse in the persona, for although it is not identical to the real-world firm itself, nonetheless, its function is to represent that firm within an advertisement. As such, it is a "creation of the words on the printed page" (Brower, 1951, p. 19), a fictional mimesis or imitation (not a derogatory term) of something that the real firm wants to convey to consumers.

The fictionality/facticity of a persona raises the issue of sincerity (Booth, 1983; Trilling, 1972). Just as readers of literature want to know what an author's values are in relation to those of his or her created characters, so too in advertising are consumers presumed to take an interest in the real firm's values in relation to those expressed by an advertising persona. In this view, although the fictional persona is not identical to the real firm because it exists on a different plane of reality, it is, nevertheless, the vehicle for transmitting those values and beliefs that the firm wants consumers to accept as sincere and authentic.

The persona is created as a blend of fact and fiction out of details of speech, thought, and action selected by the sponsoring firm, usually working through advertising creatives. These copywriters (and others in the process) make the decision to use a few words (out of an infinity of possibilities) best able to express the firm's voice. Among the verbal devices used to create the persona are familiar poetic elements such as imagery (metaphor, symbol, and other tropes), harmonious sounds (rhythm and rhyme), and felicitous tone (proper matching of form to content and speaker to audience). Advertising personas are built up not simply out of the message content—what is said—but also out of its form—how it is said (see Stern, 1988a, 1989a).

One example of a persona that illustrates the way that fact and fiction can be commingled by verbal art alone is a New York Hair Laboratories advertisement (New York Hair Laboratories, 1987). Here, sounds, symbols, and structural details evoke a medical authority as speaker, using only words in an all-print magazine advertisement. The headline reads, "Medical Breakthrough! We Can Grow Hair." The copy continues:

> At the New York Hair *Laboratories*, our *doctors'* advanced *formulation* of Minoxidil Plus can help you regrow your own natural hair. In addition, our *formulation* can also keep you from losing further hair.
>
> Our unique *formulation* contains special enhancers which increase the effectiveness and results of our proven hair growing *medication*. The success rate for treatment has been *remarkably high* and *surprisingly quick*.
>
> Our exclusive *medical* program is available only at the New York Hair *Laboratories*. So if you are one of the millions of men and women experiencing hair loss—even if you are now bald—call us to arrange your personal appointment. (p. 118; emphasis added)

Despite the lack of a within-ad spokesperson—there is neither a dialogue, a picture, nor a character—a persona is created by means of the verbal details (R. C. Elliott, 1982). The persona resolves a dialectical opposition in the real world between belief in the miraculous and in the scientific. This tension is embodied in the conflict between the hyperbole of the headline and the understatement of the copy, not resolved until the last line. Although the headline promises a near-miraculous reversal of the unidirectional flow of time (it claims to be able to regrow lost hair), the copy itself relies on medical verbiage ("laboratories," "doctors," "medical," and the triple repetition of "formulation") to emphasize the power of science. In the final sentence, the persona transcends the opposition by offering a fiction— "personal" attention—to resolve the miracle–science clash. This resolution provides the persuasive close, in which potential consumers are told to call a prominently displayed telephone number to arrange for an appointment.

The sentence is noteworthy as a departure from the structure of the previous sentences, all of which begin as statements in the first-person plural ("we" and "our"). The reversal from a "we" opening to a "you" opening diverts attention from what the persona claims to be able to do— a confounding of the medical and the miraculous—to what the persona can actually do—provide empathy with the experience of hair loss. The promise of personal attention is the benefit emphasized in the significant last copy position, where nurturant caring is put forth as a synthesizer to resolve the miracle–science opposition. This synthesis offers a fiction as the persuasive benefit, because everything else in the advertisement is hedged in such a way that there are no factual claims at all.

The persona makes no factual claims and uses hyperbolic phrases ("remarkably high" and "surprisingly quick") that are probably unprovable modifiers of the benefit (the treatments' success rate). What is being sold is a verbal concoction that implies medical efficacy by innuendo, in which the firm, like a poet, aims at cultivating "an air of truth with such success that the context markers are ignored and [its] poetic statements made captive to the truth of a foolish world" (R. C. Elliott, 1982, p. 77). The use of the first-person persona presents a particularly tangled rhetorical situation, for it is an instance in which the relation between the real author and the invented character raises an obvious question of truth claims. When a persona uses "I," are his or her words to be given greater weight as factual truths coming from the author? The answer in literary criticism is "no," for the first-person narrator in a novel or poem is a fictional construct (R. C. Elliott, 1982), and his or her revelation is considered a form of fiction. However, readers of literature tend to assume that the first-person narrator who talks about him- or herself is revealing something true (Stern, 1991). In advertisements such as this one, danger lies in the mimesis of fictional verisimilitude used as a cover for the absence of factual content in the form of externally verifiable claims.

Insofar as a first-person persona blurs the boundaries between fiction and fact, selection of this mode of narration may represent a legitimate issue for research on deceptive advertising. An autobiographical persona who purports to tell the truth in what Sartre claimed was the only possible way—through fiction (R. C. Elliott, 1982)—may be especially likely to deceive consumers because they may be prone to accept the "I" or "we" as a narrator expressing truths about him- or herself. To this extent, advertising that is mimetic of personal dialogue ("I" or "we" talking to "you") may be likely to be interpreted as genuinely revelatory, to the consumer's detriment. The interplay between the fictional and the factual aspects of a first-persona persona requires closer examination to determine under what circumstances the amalgam moves from being an effective creation to a deceptive one.

Distinctiveness: The "Right Individuality"

The blend of fact and fiction characteristic of the created persona gives rise to its distinctiveness, another quality that affects persuasion. The persona's distinctiveness flows from two sources that combine synergistically. On the one hand, a persona resembles a human being in that it displays a unique bundle of traits. No two humans are identical, nor are any two personas. On the other hand, a persona also resembles an artistic object, in that it is an original creation in its own right. Thus, the persona derives individuality from its twin ancestry in human personality and in creative art—it is individualized as a result of matter (substance) and manner (style). Such distinctiveness is especially useful for competitive differentiation of products viewed by the public as nearly generic, for here the persona can be used strategically to make a product identifiable in a sea of competitors (Stern, 1988b, 1990).

One current persona whose history exemplifies distinctiveness in a generic market is the Energizer bunny (Kanner, 1991) — a persona who differentiates Eveready from other batteries by associating the product with the bunny's fictionalized and humanized traits. Eveready introduced the bunny in response to the 1988 successes of its main competitor and market leader — Duracell (Foltz, 1989). By the end of 1988, Eveready had lost share in the total battery market, declining to about 47% from 52% in 1986, when Purina bought the company (Erickson, 1989c). Eveready's first response was to fall back on traditional segmentation strategy. Like most of its packaged goods competitors, it relied on the standard grocery product marketing model, with new products and line extensions (Erickson, 1989c). Eveready developed new products such as colored batteries (GiftMates) and ones designed specifically for audio equipment (Conductor). These were not successful, however, because consumer excitement about new batteries was difficult to stir up, and trade support for innovations with no demonstrable technological superiority was not forthcoming. Thus, Eveready decided on another strategy: going head to head with Duracell by rebuilding an existing line, and "growing" the Energizer brand into a market leader. Its tactic was to create an "Energizer image" (Erickson, 1989c), a unique persona designed to sell more of an old brand by giving it a distinctive new personality.

Distinctiveness, however, is difficult to convey in this market, for alkaline batteries are "classical parity products" (Garfield, 1989, p. 120) that all last about the same number of hours. Nevertheless, although there is little new that can be said about batteries, it can be said in a new way. Eveready humanized its brand (Blyth, 1989) by means of the fictional device of allegory — the bunny is an allegorical persona (Stern, 1988b, 1990) who vivifies the abstract trait of longevity (Kanner, 1991) inherent in the Energizer name. The bunny is energetic, demonstrating the traits of strength, persistence, and long-livedness that the firm wants the consumer to associate with the brand. In this way, the bunny is readily identifiable in a market in which product competition is not based on personality.

Although all of Eveready's competitors claimed longevity, their campaigns were not focused on the batteries themselves (a secondary product). Rather, the manufacturers differentiated brands by associating them with their function in use situations with battery-operated products. Kodak showed photography items with its tagline "Depend on us"; Rayovac featured flashlights and testimonial letters; and Duracell showed toys in need of a power source. Eveready's persona was unique in turning away from use situations, in which battery-operated products were the focus of advertising, to the battery itself as a humanized character, showing long life along with continued strength in action. The Eveready bunny's distinctiveness is such that it has been called "advertising's hottest star" (Erickson,

1989a), recognizable even outside Eveready advertisements. It has marched through television shows (Johnny Carson) (Erickson, 1989b), has appeared in an *Advertising Age* cartoon (April 6, 1992), and has been featured in a movie trailer for a mock foreign film, *Dance With Your Feet* (Kanner, 1991).

This distinctiveness facilitated integration across the marketing mix by enabling transference from one element of the mix (advertising) to others (promotion, coupons, direct marketing, publicity, etc.) Eveready engaged in strategic integration of its marketing mix by leveraging the bunny across other forms of communication ranging from sales promotions (Blyth, 1989) and consumer promotions to point-of-purchase materials (Erickson, 1989a). Since 1989, Eveready has used the bunny to improve relations with retailers, offering small stuffed bunnies as promotional giveaways and sponsoring Sunday supplement coupons tying in the purchase of bunnies by mail with proof-of-purchase of batteries. When the bunny moved from television to print advertising, the form of the advertisement changed. The print campaign for general interest magazines such as *Newsweek* did not continue the parody of unrelated spots; instead, the bunny was shown marching through scenic areas such as Utah's Monument Valley. However, the context was still parodic, for according to the company spokesperson, the print advertisements were spoofs of the "genre of travel postcards" (S. Elliott, 1992).

Although the change from television to print advertising apparently did not detract from viewer comprehension, when the parent company tried to overintegrate across products, confusion was the result. This occurred after Ralston Purina, the parent company, attempted to make the bunny the representative of the total company voice rather than a persona representing one brand. Because the bunny had gained so much attention, Ralston Purina decided to use it to advertise its own unrelated product lines— Purina Cat Chow, Hostess Twinkies, and Chex cereal. In this melding, previously multiple communication voices were collapsed into a single persona. The broadening misfired, for consumers became confused as to which Ralston Purina products were "real" in the external supermarket world and which were made-up mock products in the world within the advertisement.

The possibility of overintegration suggests that although the essence of a persona is its distinctiveness, its value as a spokesperson for one brand may be diluted by trying to make it do double duty for a family of brands. In Eveready's case, the networks took a literal view of the advertising goal— they wanted double payment for advertising two products (Leisse, 1991). Consumers, however, did not interpret the doubled spots as advertisements for two products. Instead, they viewed them as extensions of a campaign featuring only one real product (the batteries) marching through a host of fake ones. Thus, efforts to enlarge the scope of a persona into a more global advertising voice were not successful. However, much additional research will be necessary to determine whether the Eveready bunny represents an isolated case or a general phenomenon. The issue of a distinctive persona's potential for integration across a family of brands versus its limitation to the marketing mix for a particular brand is worth investigating, because strategic planning can be made more accurate if more is known about the limits as well as the capabilities of a persona over time.

Adaptiveness to Change

The characteristic of the persona that reflects its passage through time is adaptiveness to change. Adaptiveness flows from the coexistence of both a core identity and a capacity for change, because although a persona requires core consistency to convey stability, it is also able to develop chronologically. Because the persona is a fictional entity with human characteristics, the balance between stability and progress can be calibrated by the firm to adapt to developments in the external environment. An adaptive persona is needed to keep pace with changes in consumer values and tastes, movement through the product life cycle, and new societal trends. Alterations are often required to respond to changing sociocultural values, because openness to change is approved in our culture as a sign of a flexible and responsive personality.

One example of an adaptive persona is Betty Crocker, a fictional character who embodies (Lee, 1989) baked-goods quality and expertise. Her skills in the kitchen and her ability to impart them to consumers are constant, but her looks, attire, and media appearances are regularly updated by General Mills. Her portrait and signature have made her a distinctive persona since 1921, but she did not appear on a cake box until 1936. Her hair has always been brown and her dress or suit red, but she has undergone regular makeovers as needed—in 1955, 1965, 1972, 1980, and 1987—to reflect "the changing life-style of America's consumers" (Bovee & Arens, 1989, p. 306).

However, the full flexibility of an advertising character allows for more than mere cosmetic alterations. Betty's alterations over the past 70 years demonstrate her adaptiveness to changes in media habits stemming from changing consumer values—she has been transposed from pictures to words and from electronic to print media, to keep up with what consumers want. In the first transformation, Betty underwent development from a static pictorial representation of the product (a portrait on the package) to a dynamic verbal one (a radio hostess). Her portrait remains a constant media placement, for she continues to appear on the package, but her other media appearances have changed in recent times. She has now become "America's newest newspaper columnist," offering a weekly advice column ("Dear Betty Crocker") targeted primarily to readers of smaller local newspapers (Austin, 1987). This is a change from her original media role as hostess of the "Cooking School of the Air," the first radio food service program, begun in 1924 and continued until 1948.

The reason for this change lies in a shift in consumer media habits. Since the post-World War II years, the market segment of women consumers likely to buy packaged mixes no longer provides a mass daytime radio audience for food advice (Strasser, 1982). Now, specialized local print media — including weekly "shoppers" — are a better way to reach the geographically fragmented and time-pressured target market of women interested in cooking tips. Radio has been supplanted by print, for consumers no longer have the time or inclination to write down recipes broadcast over the air. However, they do clip out and save recipes and cooking hints from print media. Betty's media change illustrates the adaptiveness of the persona, because although she has retained the core traits and the physical attributes that have made her recognizable for three fourths of a century, she has been repositioned in the media to meet the needs of the changing consumer.

Managing Advertising Communication: Media Choice and Consumer Credibility

Managing the communication process involves dealing with issues such as media choice and consumer credibility. Management of the persona over time can proceed on a more informed basis when managers begin the process with awareness of the expressive strengths of different media and the relationship between persona type and consumer credibility. The view of the persona as a created entity for whom the firm takes responsibility suggests a new perspective on control over media selection and consumer propensity to believe.

Media Choices: Words and Pictures

The characteristics of a persona that advertising creatives borrow from the world of fiction have implications for media choice rooted in theory-based media differences. Narratology theory is the branch of literary criticism that addresses the different expressive strengths of each media (Chatman, 1980), because its object of study is the way that the same set of events (also called the "story") can be represented by different modes of expression (also called the "discourse"). Although technically any story can be translated into any medium — narrative events can be actualized in written stories, spoken words, filmed movements, pictures, dance, and even music — each medium does some things better than others. Important media differences center on the peculiar power of words, pictures, and films to present time and to activate perceiver imaginative responses. These differences endow the print persona, the pictorial one, and the filmed one with advantages and disadvantages germane to media choices.

To begin, the most salient difference between written words, printed pictures, and films lies in their respective capacities to treat time. The spatial representation of static time—no action at all—is the forte of pictorial art in print media. Although this kind of representation can occur in filmed works by means of freeze-frames, close-ups, and establishing shots, cinematic stopped time interrupts the dynamic flow of narrative that is the special strength of the cinematic mode. In contrast, the special attribute of pictures in nonelectronic media—magazines, catalogs, newspapers, outdoor billboards, transportation advertisements, and so forth—is the ability to capture frozen moments of time in a "tableau vivant" (Chatman, 1980). In this regard, Marchand (1985) pointed out that "consumption tableaux" are characteristic of print advertising, which features moments of time that have been stopped so that the reader can contemplate some aspect of consumption. Thus, in contrast to the static nature of print advertising, television is the medium best suited to show passage of time as well as movement in space. This strength is evident in the rhetorical structure of many television commercials according to patterns of chronological progression, notably problem–solution, symptom–resolution, before–after, and cause–effect.

All-print media—words alone—can represent both static and moving time, for temporal indicators such as verb tenses, transitional words, and time denoters can be used to indicate nearly any desired chronological phenomenon. However, the great limitation on verbal media is that they can only describe or "tell" a temporal event, not "show" it happening (Wells, 1989). Thus, although a verbal persona can describe either moving or stopped time, a pictorial one in print advertisements can best show stopped time, and a cinematic one in television commercials can best show moving time.

The different time representing capabilities of media also have implications for activating perceiver effects. Purely verbal media describe events in words alone, presenting abstract symbols that differ in kind from the "constructions imaged by the reader out of words" (Chatman, 1980, p. 129). That is, words on a page are not iconic visual images, but merely evocative of images that occur in the reader's mind. However, when the descriptions in verbal narrative elicit visual elaboration in the reader's mind, each reader provides exactly the right mental image to match his or her notion of what the words describe. That is, although the words on a page are limited to describing something that is only potentially able to activate a mental image on the part of readers, when readers respond, they fill in their own imaginative picture of what has been described. In contrast, pictorial and cinematic representations are iconic, better able to depict whatever in real life is being imitated, but doing so in such a way that the viewer has less imaginative work to do (Chatman, 1980). What the artist or film director aims at is "the audience's agreement to the justice of the visual clues" (Chatman, 1980, p. 130).

This contrast suggests that the verbal media—print and radio—may have special power to stimulate visual elaboration or imaging in the reader's mind, because words can provoke each reader to supply the mental image that best suits his or her interpretation of the verbal text. Pictorial media, on the other hand, may have special power to present the viewer with the preselected choice of a ready-made image as a visual representation of some product attribute or benefit. In this sense, words force a reader to do some imaginative work, whereas pictures and films provide mimetic verisimilitude.

Media choice thus depends on what the advertising goal for the persona is as much as pragmatic matters such as cost, efficiency, reach, frequency, timing, and so forth. The New York Hair Laboratories (NYHL) advertisement is a good example of the use of words alone as a strategy for manipulating chronological time to encourage reader imaging. What is not in the advertisement is as important as what is. The headline—"Medical Breakthrough! We Can Grow Hair"—begins the time manipulation (a promise of future action) that is extended in the first copy sentence ("can help you regrow"). The verbs confound past, present, and future in a mixed chronological scheme, where "regrow" describes a future time (hair will grow again), but one that looks backward to the reader's past, when he or she first lost hair. The chronological sequence in the advertisement—its "discourse"—moves from the future ("regrow") to the past (having hair) to the present (losing hair) and again to the future (stoppage of hair loss). The final sentence begins with present action ("if you are experiencing hair loss"), stops the action by shifting to a state of being that fuses past and present ("even if you are now bald"), and then moves to the future ("call us" for an appointment).

This advertisement illustrates the flexibility of a verbal persona to represent the multiple aspects of time, for it can move back and forth in the past, present, and future as well as describe both static and dynamic situations. Instead of showing before and after pictures—a common device in advertisements for hair growth products that shows visual proof in chronological demensions—the NYHL advertisement avoids temporal sequencing and visual representation. The persona thus evades the necessity of natural temporal progression as well as that of visual evidence that something has happened in the course of this progression. The chronology is so jumbled that the natural order of life events is suspended, encouraging consumers to believe that they can return to the past in the future. The lack of pictures further encourages readers to fill in a personally relevant image of their ideal selves based on a recollected mental image from the past. The rationale for the fragmentation of time order seems to be the advertising goal of stimulating readers to fill in their own picture of an ideal self (with regrown hair). This verbal persona in a print advertisement is so abstract a representation of the product benefit that the media choice seems designed to encourage readers' subjective beliefs by allowing them to specify the image. Objective claims are thus avoided.

Credibility and "Suspension of Disbelief"

Reader belief raises the issue of the credibility of different persona types as vehicles through which the firm's communication voice is projected. Although credibility has usually been viewed as a characteristic of a spokesperson (see discussion earlier in the chapter), that is too limited an approach, for not only need a persona not be a physically visible speaker, it need not even be human. Instead, it can be an allegorically humanized character from the world of animals (Charlie the Tuna), vegetables (Regina wine vinegars), insects (the Raid Roachettes), minerals (Vanish's dancing toilet bowls), or anything else that a creative mind thinks up.

An important consequence of treating the credibility of a persona apart from the physical spokesperson is that the impact of a variety of fictional forms on the likelihood of consumer belief can be investigated. Consumer belief in fictional personas is an aspect of what Coleridge termed "suspension of disbelief" — an audience's acceptance of fictional creations as representations of reality. In drama, for example, audiences accept the stage as Scotland, an actor as Macbeth, a staged murder as a real death, and so forth. Imputed audience relationships to different types of fictional personas are said to be embedded in "codes" or conventions of narrativity (see Barthes, 1974) that program responses to a persona. That is, audiences within a culture become accustomed to attribute different kinds of meaning (McCracken, 1989) to different presenters because the forms of narration are culturally encoded in association with typical subjects, themes, and types of narration (Frye, 1973).

For example, a 1992 D'Arcy Manius Benton & Bowles television commercial for Blend-A-Med toothpaste in Hungary presents a persona designed to be credible to audiences in newly emergent noncommunist countries, but one who would be incredible (as well as illegal) in this country. The Blend-A-Med persona is an actor dressed as a dentist, who avoids any quantitative measure of the toothpaste's effectiveness or any indication of its popularity. The reason is that the use of percentages in advertisements (e.g., reduction of cavities) is not viewed as a credible message strategy because consumers in communist countries associate percentages with government-imposed quotas in planned economies (S. Elliott, 1992) and dismiss them as fabrications. In addition, consumer dislike of authority figures affected the agency's selection of the actor to play the dentist — they chose "someone who was very warm" (S. Elliott, 1992, p. D-9) because consumers are wary of aggressive sales types. Nonetheless, Hungarian consumers were found likely to accept the actor-as-expert as credible, although this kind of persona — a staple of 1950s American advertising — has not been used since the practice was ruled deceptive in the 1970s.

Future research on persona types is necessary to develop a taxonomy that will allow consideration of credibility in reference to two questions: First, what is the distinction in credibility between fictional (Madge the Manicurist) and real personas (Lee Iacocca, Frank Perdue)? And second, what are the distinctions among various persona types within each category? One way of conceptualizing credibility that may assist the advertiser in making decisions about trade-offs in the choice of a persona is to lay it out as as a continuum, with a real-life spokesperson anchoring one end point and a fictional character anchoring the other. More sophisticated analysis of both types can enrich future research on the relationship between a persona type and its ability to generate consumer belief. Some questions are: Does a fictional presenter who is an actor playing the role of a character (Clara Peller for Wendy's) engender more consumer belief than a fictional presenter who is a cartoon character (McDonald's Moon Man)? Similarly, does a fictional character who talks about a product (Mr. Whipple for Charmin toilet tissue) stimulate consumer belief in a product attribute or benefit more than an allegorical representation who demonstrates the attribute (Mr. Clean, Mr. Goodwrench)? Recognition of distinctions not only between fictional versus real-life personas, but also among different categories of the latter may help advertisers to understand the nature of credibility by reformulating it to include the truth of fiction as well as that of fact.

CONCLUSION

In sum, the firm's selection, maintenance, and control over its personas — advertising's "who" — is essential if it is to achieve coordinated and effective communication (Lasswell, 1948/1971). Literary criticism provides a framework for analyzing the persona's characteristics as well as for suggesting implications that affect advertising management. Integration of persona theory into current research on communication can lead to more informed creation and management of presenter types. Ongoing research interest in communication content, media, audience, and effect analysis (what is said, in which channel, to which groups, and with what effect) requires the addition of what Lasswell called (1948/1971 p. 84) "control analysis" — examination of the advertising voice — to understand integrated communication fully.

REFERENCES

Abrams, M. H. (1988). *A glossary of literary terms* (5th ed.). New York: Holt, Rinehart and Winston.

Allport, G. W. (1937). *Personality: A psychological interpretation.* New York: Henry Holt.

Austin, B. (1987, September 7). Betty Crocker column to offer range of advice. *Advertising Age, 58,* 8.

Austin, J. L. (1978). *How to do things with words* (2nd ed.). Cambridge, MA: Harvard University Press.

Barthes, R. (1974). *S/Z* (R. Miller, Trans.). New York: Hill & Wang.

Blyth, J. S. (1989, December 4). Animated characters making not-so-surprising comeback. *Marketing News,* p. 16.

Booth, W. (1983). *The rhetoric of fiction* (2nd ed.). Chicago: University of Chicago Press.

Bovee, C. L., & Arens, W. F. (1989). *Contemporary advertising* (3rd ed.). Homewood, IL: Irwin.

Chatman, S. (1980). What novels can do that films can't (and vice versa). *Critical Inquiry 7*(1), 121–133.

Deighton, J. (1985). Rhetorical strategies in advertising. In M. B. Holbrook & E. C. Hirschman (Eds.), *Advances in consumer research* (Vol. 12, pp. 432–436). Ann Arbor, MI: Association for Consumer Research.

Deighton, J., Romer, D., & McQueen, J. (1989). Using drama to persuade. *Journal of Consumer Research, 16,* 335–343.

Elliott, R. C. (1982). *The literary persona.* Chicago: University of Chicago Press.

Elliott, S. (1992, January 10). Building a consumer economy amid communism's ruins. *The New York Times,* p. D-9.

Erickson, J. L. (1989a October 23). Energizer bunny gets the jump. *Advertising Age, 60,* 4.

Erickson, J. L. (1989b, November 20). Energizer bunny beats on. *Advertising Age, 60,* 2.

Erickson, J. L. (1989c, November 27). Ralston lesson: Batteries aren't groceries. *Advertising Age, 60,* 114.

Fisher, W. R. (1984). Narration as a human communication paradigm: The case of public moral argument. *Communication Monographs, 51,* 1–22.

Foltz, K. (1989, October 23). Amid TV's ad clutter, a rabbit runs wild. *The New York Times,* p. D-11.

Frye, N. (1973). *Anatomy of criticism: Four essays.* Princeton, NJ: Princeton University Press.

Garfield, B. (1989, October 23). Ad review: Energizer's parody campaign is one bunny of a concept. *Advertising Age, 60,* 120.

Grice, H. P. (1989). *Studies in the way of words.* Cambridge, MA: Harvard University Press.

Haas, R. G. (1981). Effects of source characteristics on cognitive responses and persuasion. In R. E. Petty, M. Ostrom, & T. C. Brock (Eds.), *Cognitive responses in persuasion* (pp. 141–172). Hillsdale, NJ: Lawrence Erlbaum Associates.

Hall, C. S., & Nordby, V. J. (1973). *A primer of Jungian psychology.* New York: New American Library.

Kanner, B. (1991, March 4). Grand allusions: Borrowed interest in advertising. *New York Magazine,* pp. 14–15.

Kenney, W. (1988). *How to read and write about fiction* (2nd ed.). New York: Simon & Schuster.

Lasswell, H. D. (1971). The structure and function of communication in society. In W. Schramm & D. F. Brooks (Eds.), *The process and effects of mass communication* (pp. 84–99). Urbana: University of Illinois Press. (Original work published 1948)

Lee, L. (1989, February 15). Getting to know you: Brownies tell their tales. *The New York Times,* pp. C1, C6.

Liesse, J. (1991, April 8). How the bunny charged Eveready. *Advertising Age,* pp. 20, 55.

Marchand, R. (1985). *Advertising the American dream: Making way for modernity, 1920–1940.* Berkeley: University of California Press.

Martin, W. (1986). *Recent theories of narrative.* Ithaca, NY: Cornell University Press.

McConkey, J. (1958). The voice of the writer. *The University of Kansas Review, 25,* 86–87.

McCracken, G. (1989). Who is the celebrity endorser? Cultural foundations of the endorsement process. *Journal of Consumer Research, 16,* 310–321.

Mick, D. G. (1986). Consumer research and semiotics: Exploring the morphology of signs, symbols, and significance. *Journal of Consumer Research, 13,* 196–213.

New York Hair Laboratories. (1987, October 5). *New York Magazine,* p. 118.

Nichols, M. H. (1963). *Rhetoric and criticism.* Baton Rouge: Louisiana State University Press.

Ogilvy, D. (1985). *Ogilvy on advertising.* New York: Vintage Books.

Pratt, M. L. (1977). *Toward a speech act theory of literary discourse.* Bloomington: Indiana University Press.

Prince, G. (1981). *Narratology: The form and function of narrative.* Berlin: Mouton.

Reynolds, T. J., & Gutman, J. (1984). Advertising is image management. *Journal of Advertising Research, 24,* 27–37.

Rossiter, J., & Percy, L. (1987). *Advertising and promotion management.* New York: McGraw-Hill.

Searle, J. R. (1969). *Speech acts: An essay in the philosophy of language.* London: Cambridge University Press.

Searle, J. R. (1979). The logical status of fictional discourse. In J. R. Searle (Ed.), *Expression and meaning: Studies in the theory of speech acts* (pp. 58–75). Cambridge, England: Cambridge University Press.

Stern, B. B. (1988a). How does an ad mean? Language in services advertising. *Journal of Advertising, 17,* 3–14.

Stern, B. B. (1988b). Medieval allegory: Roots of advertising strategy for the mass market. *Journal of Marketing, 52,* 84–94.

Stern, B. B. (1989a). Literary analysis of the company *persona*: A speaker schema. In J. H. Leigh & C. R. Martin, Jr. (Eds.), *Current issues and research in advertising 1988* (Vol. 11, pp. 3–19). Ann Arbor: The University of Michigan.

Stern, B. B. (1989b). Literary criticism and consumer research: Overview and analysis. *Journal of Consumer Research, 16,* 322–334.

Stern, B. B. (1990). *Otherspeak*: Classical allegory and contemporary advertising. *Journal of Advertising, 19* (3), 14–26.

Stern, B. B. (1991). Who talks advertising? Literary theory and narrative "point of view." *Journal of Advertising, 20,* 9–22.

Strasser, S. (1982). *Never done: A history of American housework.* New York: Pantheon.

Trilling, L. (1972). *Sincerity and authenticity.* Cambridge, MA: Harvard University Press.

Wells, W. (1989). Lectures and dramas. In P. Cafferata & A. M. Tybout (Eds.), *Cognitive and affective responses to advertising* (pp. 13–20). Lexington, MA: Lexington Books.

6 Brand Equity and Integrated Communication

Kevin Lane Keller
Stanford University

INTRODUCTION

In the past few decades, a number of alternative media and promotion options have emerged by which marketers can communicate to consumers. A modern marketing communications program might consist of television, radio, magazine, and newspaper advertising; consumer and trade promotions; direct response, point-of-purchase, sponsorship, and public relation activities; as well as a number of other nontraditional media. Although these options provide much flexibility in targeting customers and communicating messages, they also differ on a number of dimensions, making it difficult for managers to appreciate how they can and should be used when developing brand strategies. Despite this fact, and the reality that the vast majority of an advertising campaign budget goes to media and promotion expenses, research has provided little guidance on how to evaluate different combinations of marketing communication elements.

The purpose of this chapter is to provide an information processing perspective on how to enhance brand equity through the integration of marketing communications. The brand equity concept has attained much importance with marketers because it provides guidance as to how marketing programs can effectively contribute to the value of a brand, as well as how the value created for a brand can be advantageously exploited. By focusing on how an individual consumer processes the various elements of a marketing communication program, a number of strategies to assist managers in brand-building activities will be put forth. Toward this objective, the first section outlines a conceptual framework for brand equity based on Keller (1993a). This framework defines *customer-based brand equity* as the differential effect that brand knowledge has on consumer response to the marketing of that brand. Brand knowledge is conceptualized in terms of two components: brand awareness (i.e., the ability of the consumer to recognize or recall the brand) and brand image (i.e., a set of brand associations). According to this view, customer-based brand equity occurs when the consumer is aware of the brand and holds some strong, favorable, and unique brand associations in memory.

The second section uses some basic principles of memory processes and structure to provide a simple conceptual model of marketing communication effects. This section asserts that marketing communication effectiveness depends on consumer motivation, ability, and opportunity to process the information contained in a communication element (i.e., in an ad, promotion, sponsorship, etc.) and consumer motivation, ability, and opportunity to retrieve this information from memory later when making a brand evaluation or choice. The third section builds on these conceptual notions to consider how brand awareness can be established and how associations can become strongly linked to the brand in memory. Two key implications emerge from this discussion: multiple marketing communication options should be considered, and the marketing communication elements chosen should be explicitly linked to allow for the interactions to occur that can help to create a positive brand image and build brand equity.

The remainder of the chapter examines these two implications in more detail. The fourth section considers the appropriate range of marketing communication options that can be employed to build brand equity and the proper role of alternative or nontraditional media. The following three sections describe three different approaches for explicitly integrating marketing communications to build brand equity. Specifically, the fifth section considers issues in integrating across communication elements. In particular, emphasis is placed on how advertising messages can be reinforced by nonadvertising media such as product packaging. The sixth section considers issues in integrating across advertising media. This section reviews Edell and Keller (1989, 1993) to present empirical evidence and provide some guidelines based on information processing theory as to one approach to coordinate television, radio, and print advertising. The seventh section considers several issues in integrating within an advertising medium. This section considers how 15-second versions can be created to cue longer 30- and 60-second television ads, how television campaigns that use a pool of ads can improve consumer learning by creating an umbrella ad that explicitly links the various individual ad executions, and how ad campaigns can be cued over time to leverage brand associations created by past ad campaigns. The chapter concludes in the eighth section by summarizing the guidelines for integrating marketing communications to build brand equity that emerge from these applications.

A CONCEPTUAL MODEL OF BRAND EQUITY

A *brand* can be defined as a name, symbol, logo, trademark, and so forth that identifies and differentiates a product or service. Brand equity can be defined in terms of the marketing effects uniquely attributable to the brand — for example, when different outcomes result from the marketing of a product or service because of its brand name than would have otherwise occurred if the same product or service had a different name. Keller (1993a) built a conceptual model of brand equity that incorporates recent theoretical advances in conceptualizing consumer knowledge and memory structures (Alba & Hutchinson, 1987; Alba, Hutchinson, & Lynch, 1991). Specifically, Keller defined *customer-based brand equity* as the differential effect that brand knowledge has on consumer response to the marketing of that brand. A brand is said to have positive (negative) customer-based brand equity if consumers react more (less) favorably to an element of the marketing mix for the brand, as compared to when the same marketing mix element is attributed to a fictitiously named or unnamed version of the product or service. Consumer response to marketing is defined in terms of consumer perceptions, preferences, and behavior arising from marketing mix activity (e.g., brand choice, recall of copy points from an ad, actions in response to a sales promotion, or evaluations of a proposed brand extension).

According to this view, brand knowledge is the foundation for the creation of brand equity. Brand knowledge is conceptualized according to an associative network memory model (Anderson, 1983; Wyer & Srull, 1989) as consisting of a brand node in memory with a variety of associations linked to it. The strength and organization of these brand associations are important determinants of the information that can be recalled about the brand and that can influence consumer response and product or service decisions (Keller, 1987; Lynch & Srull, 1982).

Brand knowledge is characterized in terms of two components: Brand awareness and brand image. *Brand awareness* is related to the strength of the brand node or trace in memory, as reflected by consumers' ability to identify the brand under different conditions (Rossiter & Percy, 1987). Brand awareness consists of brand recognition (reflecting the ability of consumers to confirm prior exposure to the brand) and brand recall (reflecting the ability of consumers to retrieve the brand when given the product or service category, the needs fulfilled by the category, or some other type of probe as a cue). *Brand image* is defined as consumer perceptions about a brand as reflected by the brand associations held in consumers' memory. *Brand associations* are the informational nodes linked to the brand node in memory and contain the meaning of the brand for consumers.

Positive customer-based brand equity occurs when the consumer is aware of the brand and holds some strong, favorable, and unique brand associations in memory. In some cases, differential consumer response results from brand awareness alone, for example, in low involvement decision settings. In other cases, the favorability, strength, and uniqueness of the brand associations play a critical role in determining this differential response. If the brand is perceived by consumers to be the same as a representative brand or abstract version of the product or service in the category, then consumer response should not vary from when the marketing is attributed to a fictitiously named or unnamed product or service. If the brand has some salient, unique associations, then consumer response should differ. The actual nature of how that response differs will depend on how favorably consumers evaluate these associations, as well as the particular marketing mix element under consideration. Brand awareness (in terms of brand recognition and recall) and a positive brand image (i.e., strong, favorable, and unique brand associations) might lead consumers to be more accepting of a new brand extension, less sensitive to price increases and withdrawal of advertising support, and more willing to seek the brand in a new distribution channel.

In the next two sections, a memory-based model of how marketing communications can affect brand equity is highlighted and then the implications of some basic memory principles for creating brand knowledge structures to build brand equity are examined.

A CONCEPTUAL MODEL OF MARKETING COMMUNICATION EFFECTS

The role of marketing communications is to contribute to brand equity by establishing the brand in memory and linking strong, favorable, and unique associations to it. The challenge in achieving that goal is to break through competitive clutter and consumer indifference to teach consumers about the brand. For marketing communications to successfully convey brand information that consumers will use in their product or service decisions, two steps must occur. First, consumers must initially encode the relevant brand information and store it correctly in memory. Second, consumers must later retrieve the relevant brand information from memory when making a product or service decision. In other words, for marketing communications to work, the appropriate brand information has to get into memory and be retained over time so that it can later get out of memory to affect consumer decision making.

A number of factors make successful encoding and retrieval difficult. One problem is that either when initially exposed to a marketing communication or when making later product or service decisions, consumers may lack one or more of three key factors necessary for successful encoding or retrieval (Batra & Ray, 1986; MacInnis & Jaworski, 1989; MacInnis, Moorman, & Jaworski, 1991; Petty & Cacioppo, 1986; Roberts & Maccoby, 1973; Wright, 1981). First, for successful encoding to occur, consumers must have motivation to process and be willing and interested in devoting the mental resources or capacity and expending the mental effort to process information from an ad. Second, consumers must have the ability to process and actually possess the mental resources or capacities necessary to comprehend the intended effects of the ad. Third, consumers must have the opportunity to process and be exposed to the ad in an environment conducive for processing and free from distracting external conditions.

A person's motivation, ability, and opportunity to process an ad will determine, in turn, the intensity and direction of encoding processes during ad exposure (Bettman, 1979; Mitchell, 1981). *Processing intensity* is defined as the amount of mental resources or capacity devoted to encoding information. *Processing direction* refers to the focus of processing in terms of the particular stimuli or information that receive these mental resources or capacity. The amount of elaboration or processing intensity at encoding and the nature or processing direction of that elaboration determine the resulting content, strength, and organization of brand associations and knowledge in memory. Greater intensity of processing from more elaboration and more connections formed to prior information in memory produces stronger brand associations and more durable memory effects. Thus, for successful encoding to occur, a consumer must be motivated, able, and have the opportunity to process a communication with sufficient intensity and proper direction so that the desired communication effects become properly stored in memory.

Successful encoding is a necessary but not sufficient condition for marketing communications to contribute to brand equity. It must also be the case that the communication effects that are stored in memory must be successfully retrieved and used as inputs into consumer decisions (Keller 1993b). *Communication effects* are what consumers saw, heard, learned, thought, felt, and so on while exposed to a communication. The antecedents of how information is retrieved or accessed from memory can be similarly characterized in terms of retrieval motivation, that is, consumers' willingness and desire to allocate mental resources to attempt to retrieve information from memory; retrieval ability, that is, consumers' capabilities to access information if attempting to do so through internal and external retrieval cues; and retrieval opportunity, that is, the extent to which external conditions are present that are conducive for retrieval. Similarly, actual retrieval processes can be thought of in terms of retrieval intensity, that is, the amount of cognitive effort used to retrieve information from memory; and retrieval direction, that is, the particular information in memory that receives this retrieval effort as a result of the entry points in the memory network that arise from internally generated or externally provided retrieval cues. Thus, for successful retrieval to occur, a consumer must be motivated, able, and have the opportunity to retrieve stored communication effects with sufficient effort and proper retrieval cues so that the desired communication effects become accessible during product or service evaluations and choices.

To summarize, successful recall of communication effects will occur only with successful encoding and successful retrieval. The conceptual framework presented here suggests that a marketing communications program that effectively builds brand equity is one that: (a) at encoding, motivates consumers to elaborate on and process fully the communication, recognizes consumers' prior knowledge and abilities when designing the communication, and presents the communication in an environment conducive for processing; and (b) at retrieval, motivates consumers to consider relevant communication effects, recognizes how communication effects are organized in the brand knowledge structure, and encourages product or service decisions in an environment conducive for retrieval of communication effects.

HOW MARKETING COMMUNICATIONS CAN BUILD BRAND EQUITY

Establishing brand awareness and a positive brand image in consumer memory produces the knowledge structures that can affect consumer response and generate different types of customer-based brand equity.

Establishing Brand Awareness

In general, brand awareness is created by increasing the familiarity of the brand through repeated exposure (Alba & Hutchinson, 1987), although this is generally more effective for brand recognition than for brand recall, which is a much more demanding memory task. That is, although brand repetition increases the strength of the brand in memory and thus its recognizability, improving recall of the brand requires linkages in memory to the appropriate cues such as the product or service category. Pairing the brand with its corresponding product or service category through sponsorship, advertising, promotion, and so on can help to establish these links and facilitate brand recall. It should be noted that the manner by which the brand and its corresponding category are paired (e.g., as with an advertising slogan) will also be influential in determining the strength of product category links.

Creating Favorable and Unique Brand Associations

A positive brand image is created by marketing programs that link strong, favorable, and unique associations to the brand in memory. Choosing which favorable and unique associations to link to the brand requires careful analysis of the consumer and competition to determine the optimal positioning for the brand. In the most basic sense, favorable brand associations are created by convincing consumers that the brand possesses relevant attributes and benefits that satisfy their needs and wants. Thus, favorable associations for a brand are those associations that are desirable to consumers and are successfully conveyed by the supporting marketing program for the brand. Favorable brand associations come in a variety of forms. Although they are primarily determined by product-related ingredients and specifications or service-related requirements, they may also be determined by abstract imagery related to typical users or usage situations for the brand. Not all brand associations will be deemed important and viewed favorably by consumers, nor will they be equally valued across different purchase or consumption situations.

To create the differential response that leads to customer-based brand equity, it is important that some of the favorable associations for a brand are also unique. Unique brand associations are distinct associations not shared with competing brands. Beliefs about unique brand attributes and benefits that consumers value more favorably than for competitive brands can, according to a multiattribute attitude model (Ajzen & Fishbein, 1980; Wilkie & Pessemier, 1973), lead to more favorable brand evaluations and a greater likelihood of choice. Thus, it is important to associate unique, meaningful points of difference to the brand to provide a competitive advantage and a reason why consumers should buy it. For some brand associations, however, consumers only need to view them at least as favorably as competitors. That is, for some brand associations, it may be sufficient that they are seen as equally favorable with competing brand associations so that they function as points of parity and negate potential points of difference for competitors. Assuming that other brand associations are evident as points of difference, more favorable brand evaluations and a greater likelihood of choice should then result.

Creating Strong Brand Associations

By implementing the chosen positioning, a marketing communications program helps to build brand equity by creating or enhancing favorable and unique brand associations in memory. Given the brand positioning, however, how can strong brand associations be created by advertising or other marketing communication options? Prior research has shown that a number of factors affect the accessibility of information from memory and the ability of consumers to recall or retrieve communication effects and brand associations (Anderson, 1983). Here we briefly highlight some of those factors (see Alba, Hutchinson, & Lynch, 1991; Lynch & Srull, 1982, for additional discussion).

First, several factors affect the way information is encoded and the strength of a new brand association. A key determinant of the strength of a newly formed association will be the content, organization, and strength of existing brand knowledge in memory. All else equal, it will be easier for consumers to create an association to new information when an extensive, relevant knowledge structure already exists in memory. In addition to congruency or consistency with existing knowledge, the ease with which new information can be integrated into established knowledge structures clearly depends on the nature of that information, in terms of characteristics such as its inherent simplicity, vividness, concreteness, and so on. Repeated exposures to information provide greater opportunity for processing and, thus, the potential for stronger associations. Recent advertising research in a field setting, however, suggests that the manner or style of processing of information in any one ad exposure is generally more important than the cumulative number of ad exposures per se (Lubetkin, 1992). Finally, the time since exposure to information at encoding affects the strength of a new association—the longer the time delay, the weaker the association. The time elapsed since the last exposure opportunity, however, has been shown generally to only produce gradual decay (Loftus & Loftus, 1980).

Successful recall of information does not depend only on the associative strength of that information in memory but also on other retrieval factors. Two such factors are particularly important. First, the presence of other information in memory can produce interference effects and reduce the accessibility of communication effects (Postman & Underwood, 1973). The presence of other information in memory may cause the target information to be either inaccessible or confused with this other information. Second, the number and type of external retrieval cues that are available will be key factors affecting memory accessibility. That is, information may be available in memory (i.e., potentially recallable) but inaccessible (i.e., unable to be recalled) without the proper retrieval cues or reminders.

Summary

Positioning decisions determine which associations are to be linked to the brand as well as their intended favorability and uniqueness. To contribute to brand equity, these associations must also become strongly linked to the brand so that they are recalled when product or service decisions are being made. The particular associations that are recalled and salient depend on the strength of information in memory, which is a function of the amount or quantity of initial processing the information receives and the nature or quality of that processing, as well as the context in which the brand is considered and the retrieval cues that are present. In particular, the strength of brand associations and accessibility of communication effects depend on a number of specific factors, including processing intensity (elaboration), existing brand knowledge in memory, repetition, recency or time since last exposure, competing associations, and retrieval cues. Consequently, a marketing communications program can contribute to the creation of strong brand associations and recalled communication effects through the use of creative communications that cause consumers to elaborate on brand-related information and relate it appropriately to existing knowledge. These communications would be shown or evident repeatedly over time and many strong retrieval cues would be present as reminders.

The following sections consider some implications of these conceptual notions in terms of the optimal range of marketing communication options and the desired relationship among those communication options to build brand equity.

MIXING AND MATCHING COMMUNICATION OPTIONS

One implication of the conceptualization of customer-based brand equity is that the manner in which brand associations are formed does not matter — only the resulting favorability, strength, and uniqueness of brand associations that, in turn, produce the differential effect in consumer response that is at the heart of customer-based brand equity. Thus, from the perspective of customer-based brand equity, the "medium is the message" interpretation of communication effects is only valid if different types of media create additional associations or differentially affect the favorability, strength, and uniqueness of existing associations in some way. In other words, if a consumer has an equally favorable brand association from Rolaids antacids to the concept "relief" because of exposure to a television ad that concludes with a tag line "Rolaids spells relief" or because of knowledge of the fact that Rolaids sponsors the "Relief Pitcher of the Year" award for major league baseball, the impact in terms of customer-based brand equity should be identical unless additional associations are created (e.g., "advertised on television") or existing associations are affected in some way (e.g., "speed or potency of effects"). Thus, from the perspective of customer-based brand equity, marketers should evaluate all possible communication options available to create knowledge structures according to effectiveness criteria as well as cost considerations.

This broad view of brand building activities is especially relevant when considering marketing communication strategies to improve brand awareness. Brand awareness is closely related to brand familiarity and can be viewed as a function of the number of product-related experiences that have been accumulated by the consumer (Alba & Hutchinson, 1987). Thus, anything that causes the consumer to notice and pay attention to the brand can increase brand awareness, at least in terms of brand recognition. Obviously, the visibility of the brand in many sponsorship activities suggests that these activities may be especially valuable for enhancing brand recognition. To enhance brand recall, however, more intense and elaborate processing of the brand may be necessary so that stronger brand links to the product or service category are established to improve memory performance. Similarly, because brand associations can be created in an abstract sense in many different ways, all possible marketing communication options should be considered to create the desired brand image and knowledge structures. As noted previously, television, radio, magazine, and newspaper advertising; consumer and trade promotions; direct response, point-of-purchase, sponsorship and public relation activities; as well as a number of other nontraditional media can all be employed to create strong, favorable, and unique brand associations.

Regardless of which options are chosen, the entire marketing program should be coordinated to create a consistent and cohesive brand image, that is, where brand associations share content and meaning. The consistency and cohesiveness of the brand image is important because it determines how easily existing associations can be recalled and how easily additional associations can become linked to the brand in memory. In general, information that is consistent in meaning is more easily learned and recalled than unrelated information − although the unexpectedness of information inconsistent in meaning with the brand sometimes can lead to more elaborate processing and stronger associations than even consistent information (Heckler & Childers, 1992; Houston, Childers, & Heckler, 1987; Srull & Wyer, 1989). With inconsistent associations and a diffuse brand image, consumers may overlook some associations or, because they are confused about the meaning of the brand, form less strong and favorable new associations. Therefore, in the long run, different communication elements should be designed and combined so that they work effectively together to create a consistent and cohesive brand image.

Note also that there may actually be memory advantages to using multiple communication options to create positive brand images. The encoding variability principle argues that presenting information in varied contexts causes information to be encoded in slightly different ways. As a result, multiple retrieval routes are formed in memory — each converging on the to-be-remembered information — thereby enhancing recall (Melton, 1970; Young & Belleza, 1982). In other words, multiple ways to learn information provide multiple cues to recall information, thereby improving memory performance. Thus, the encoding variability principle suggests that an integrated marketing communications program, by employing multiple communication elements, may be an effective way to create, maintain, or strengthen brand associations in memory.

One approach to integrating marketing communications is to literally take information from one communication element and use it in some fashion in another communication element. The rationale behind such a strategy is that this information can cue or serve as a reminder to related information and facilitate learning by enhancing consumer motivation, ability, or opportunity to process or retrieve brand-related information. The next sections consider strategies related to three different forms of such direct reinforcement: across communication elements, across advertising media, and within advertising media.

INTEGRATING ACROSS COMMUNICATION ELEMENTS

Marketing Communication Challenges

As noted previously, many different types of marketing communication options can help to build brand equity. In this section, we consider how one problem common with television advertising — weak brand links to communication effects stored in memory as a result of ad processing — can be effectively addressed by strategically employing other, nontelevision communication options as well.

Because consumers generally cannot make purchase decisions about a brand or product immediately after ad exposure, advertising effectiveness often depends on the memory performance of consumers. A number of factors can result in weak links from communication effects created by advertising to the brand (Keller, 1993b). Most important, competing ads in the category can create "interference" and consumer confusion as to which ad goes with which brand (Burke & Srull, 1988; Keller, 1987, 1991a; Kent,

1993). Numerous instances can be found where consumers mix up competing ads and brands. For example, Eveready introduced a clever ad campaign in 1989 for their Energizer batteries that featured a pink bunny toy that kept on "going . . . and going . . . and going." Unfortunately, consumer research by Video Storyboard uncovered that of the people in their annual survey who named the popular commercial as their favorite of the year, 40% mistakenly attributed it to Eveready's main competitor, Duracell, and only 60% correctly identified it as an Energizer ad. To exacerbate this interference problem, it is often the case that competing ads often appear in the same media vehicle because they typically target the same consumers. For example, an analysis of one recent week of prime time television advertising (*Advertising Age*, October 14–20, 1991) found that of the 57 commercials that ran in an average hour, 24, or 42%, faced at least one competitor running an ad during that same time period.

In addition to competitive advertising, factors related to the content and structure of the ad itself can result in weak links from the brand to communication effects created by ad exposure. For example, advertisers have a vast range of creative strategies and techniques at their disposal to improve consumer motivation and lead to greater involvement and enhanced ad processing on their part. These "borrowed interest" tactics — such as the presence of cute babies, frisky puppies, popular music, well-liked celebrities, provocative sex appeals, or fear-inducing threats — may effectively grab consumers' attention for an ad. Unfortunately, although intensity of processing may be raised as a result, this processing may be directed in a manner that does not create strong brand associations. Moreover, when these attention-getting tactics are employed, the position and prominence of the brand in the ad is often downplayed. Delaying brand identification or providing few brand mentions may also raise processing intensity but result in processing directed away from thinking about the brand. Furthermore, limited brand exposure time in the ad allows little opportunity for elaboration of existing brand knowledge, also contributing to weak brand links.

Finally, in certain circumstances consumers may not have any inherent interest in the product or service category or may lack knowledge of the specific brand (e.g., in the case of a low share brand, a new market entry, etc.). The resulting decrease in consumer motivation and ability to process also translates to weaker brand links. Similarly, a change in advertising strategy to target a new market segment or add a new attribute, benefit, or usage association to the brand image may also fail to produce strong brand links because consumers lack the ability to easily relate this new advertising information to existing brand knowledge.

Thus, for a variety of reasons, consumers may fail to correctly identify advertising with the advertised brand or, even worse, incorrectly attribute advertising to a competing brand. In these cases, advertising worked in the sense that communication effects — ad claims and executional information, as well as cognitive and affective responses by consumers to that information — were stored in memory. Yet advertising failed in the sense that these communication effects were not accessible when critical brand-related decisions were made.

To address this problem, one common tactic marketers employ to achieve ad and point-of-purchase congruence and improve ad recall is to make the brand name and package information prominent in the ad. Unfortunately, this increase in brand emphasis means that communication effects and brand associations that can potentially affect brand evaluations are less likely to be able to be created by the ad and stored in consumer memory. In other words, although consumers are better able to recall the advertised brand with this tactic, there is less other information about the brand to actually recall. A potentially more effective tactic to improve consumers' motivation and ability to retrieve communication effects when making a brand-related decision is advertising retrieval cues, discussed next.

Advertising Retrieval Cues

Advertising retrieval cues are visual or verbal information uniquely identified with an ad that are evident when consumers are making a product or service decision. Their purpose is to maximize the probability that consumers who have seen or heard the cued ad retrieve from long-term memory the communication effects that were stored from earlier processing of that ad. Ad retrieval cues may consist of a key visual, a catchy slogan, or any unique advertising element that serves as an effective reminder to consumers. For example, in an attempt to remedy the problem they had with mistaken attributions, Eveready featured a picture of the pink bunny on the packages for their Energizer batteries. Ad retrieval cues can be placed in the store (e.g., on the package or as part of a shelf talker or some other point-of-purchase device), combined with a promotion (e.g., with a FSI coupon), included as part of a Yellow Pages directory listing, or embedded in any marketing communication option where recall of communication effects can be advantageous to marketers.

By using ad retrieval cues, greater emphasis can be placed in the ad on supplying persuasive information and creating positive associations so consumers have a reason why they should purchase the brand. Ad retrieval cues allow for creative freedom in ad execution because the brand and package need not be the centerpiece of the ad. The effectiveness of ad retrieval cues depends on how many communication effects are potentially retrievable and how likely these communication effects are to be retrieved from memory with only the brand as a cue, as compared to the executional information making up the ad retrieval cue. An ad retrieval cue is most effective when many communication effects are stored in memory but are only weakly associated to the brand because of one or more of the various factors noted previously.

Keller (1993b) summarized the results of three major studies investigating this technique (Keller, 1987, 1991a, 1991b). This research program yielded a number of conclusions concerning the effectiveness of ad retrieval cues and memory factors in advertising, which are only briefly highlighted here. First, all the studies showed that an ad retrieval cue can increase recall of communication effects and, assuming the ad was well received, produce higher brand evaluations. Evidently, without the ad retrieval cue consumers were unable or unwilling to access or consider communication effects from the ad when making product decisions. Second, although a higher level of competitive advertising can decrease recall of communication effects and produce lower evaluations for well-regarded brands, these effects can be offset by the use of an ad retrieval cue. Thus, one strategy to offset the detrimental effects of competitive advertising is the use of point-of-purchase cues. Third, an ad retrieval cue can affect brand evaluations even when there is no or little competing advertising in the product or service category. In this case, an ad retrieval cue does not necessarily improve consumers' ability to retrieve communication effects as much as it affects consumers' motivation to retrieve, encouraging more extensive retrieval than would have otherwise occurred.

The first three findings provide evidence on the effectiveness of ad retrieval cues. Additional findings provide greater insight into how ad retrieval cues actually operate. The fourth conclusion that emerged from these studies was that the effectiveness of an ad retrieval cue depends on how consumers process an ad during exposure. The cue compatibility principle maintains that successful recall of communication effects from memory is most likely to occur when the type of information contained in retrieval cues is compatible or congruent with the type of information stored previously during encoding. The most effective type of ad retrieval cues are ones that are easily recognized by consumers and that are encoded uniquely with the to-be-remembered information. Fifth, an ad retrieval cue is particularly effective at improving recall of communication effects related to the creative strategy of the ad execution (e.g., positive or negative thoughts or feelings that consumers have concerning how claims are made in the ad). Moreover, an ad retrieval cue also affects the salience or weight given to communication effects recalled from memory in brand evaluations. In other words, not only do cues affect what information can be recalled from memory, they also affect the importance this information plays in consumer decisions. Finally, although an ad retrieval cue facilitates recall of strongly associated information, it can also inhibit recall of other, less strongly associated information in memory. In other words, by reminding consumers of certain information that they may have been otherwise overlooked or ignored, other information not suggested by the cue may instead be overlooked or ignored.

Summary

Advertising retrieval cues — key visuals or distinctive slogans evident at the point-of-purchase or any place where consumers are making product or service decisions — are powerful tools that advertisers can employ to better leverage the effects of their advertising. Ad retrieval cues may be particularly useful when much competitive advertising interference exists or when, for any other reason, the ad campaign results in positive communication effects that are only weakly associated to the brand. The rationale behind ad retrieval cues is that, by strategically adapting other communication options to directly reinforce the ad campaign for the brand, available but inaccessible or overlooked communication effects can be effectively leveraged to impact product or service decisions. In other words, explicitly integrating across elements of a marketing communications program in this manner capitalizes on the strengths and weaknesses of advertising and other communication options to facilitate brand learning and the creation of brand knowledge structures to contribute to brand equity.

Two related points deserve discussion here. First, the main purpose of ad retrieval cues is to enhance recall of communication effects to improve brand evaluations and choice. Many advertising researchers have dismissed recall as an appropriate criteria or measure of ad effectiveness (e.g., Gibson, 1983). These opinions would seem to be the result of a narrow view of the meaning of ad recall. In particular, these researchers fail to fully recognize the multi-dimensional and dynamic nature of memory. Memory is multidimensional in that many different types of information can be stored and thus recalled as a result of ad exposure. For example, advertising effectiveness depends not only on recall of ad information but also on recall of consumers' own personal reactions to that information. Memory is dynamic because different types of information can be recalled depending on the retrieval cues or reminders provided. Dismissing ad recall as a diagnostic tool for improving ad effectiveness ignores the potentially valuable insights that arise from a more complete view of consumer memory structures and processes, for example, as with the antecedents and consequences of ad retrieval cues.

The second point to note concerns the optimal strategy for employing marketing communications at the point of purchase. Recognizing that consumers make many decisions at the point of purchase, advertisers recently have placed greater importance on packaging and in-store marketing programs. Such efforts clearly can pay off by influencing consumers when they are making product or service decisions. It is important to recognize, however, the context in which these communications are received. In many shopping situations, consumers may lack either motivation, ability, or opportunity to process any type of message because of the time constraints that arise from having to make numerous product or service decisions. Moreover, the nature of many in-store communication media (e.g., shelf talkers) limit creative possibilities and the potential power to persuade. Rather than attempt to create persuasive communications at the point of purchase under such difficult processing conditions, a more effective strategy might be to attempt to create communication effects outside the store through more conventional advertising and promotion means and then cue those effects inside the store through judiciously chosen ad retrieval cues.

INTEGRATING ACROSS ADVERTISING MEDIA

Because of its richness in sensory dimensions and extensive reach, television is often the primary medium of national ad campaigns. Despite its potential power in persuasion, the great expense of advertising on television has led to increased consideration of complementary media by marketers. Although advertising in other media can be designed to reach and persuade target markets that are not exposed to television advertising, advertising in secondary media can also be designed to reinforce or complement television advertising. Thus, as more marketing dollars move into multiple media, the question arises of how advertising campaigns should be coordinated across media, if at all, to build brand equity.

One possible strategy to coordinate a multiple media ad campaign would be to retain some parts of the ad as it moves from one medium to another. For example, advertisers have been known to take the audio track from a TV ad and run it, with some adjustment, on the radio as an ad. Similarly, a key scene from a TV ad has been used as the visual component of a print ad. To the extent that audience overlap exists with these different media, advertising can "cue itself" across media. In this section, we consider how both strategies can lead to stronger brand associations and, thus, build brand equity.

Radio Reinforcement

A coordinated TV-radio strategy implicitly assumes that when consumers are exposed to the audio from the TV ad on the radio it serves as a reminder or retrieval cue to the associated communication effects in memory. In particular, the audio should cue or remind consumers of the corresponding video so that, ideally, the effects from radio exposure can closely approximate those from additional television exposures.

Edell and Keller (1989) developed a general conceptual model of media interactions to provide an information processing perspective of a coordinated media campaign employing television and radio. They defined *radio replay* to be the situation in which a consumer views a TV ad and later hears the audio track from the TV ad as a radio ad. Based on their conceptual model, Edell and Keller argued that the outcomes from radio replay depend on the relative extent of comprehension, elaboration, and retrieval processes that consumers undertake during the reinforcing radio ad exposure. In other words, when consumers hear the radio ad with the TV audio, the ad may serve as a retrieval cue for the stored memory trace, a second encoding opportunity, or as an opportunity to elaborate on and have cognitive or affective reactions to either the currently playing ad, the ad memory trace, or both. Given that consumers are often characterized as having low involvement during ad exposure such that little processing effort would be normally forthcoming, it would be unlikely that all three processes would occur concurrently. Thus, the trade-offs among these competing processing activities were expected to determine the outcomes from radio replay.

The results of their laboratory study showed that when consumers heard a radio replay, they did very little critical, evaluative processing. Rather, consumers appeared to replay mentally the video from the TV ad while listening to the radio ad. Thus, less effortful comprehension and retrieval processes appeared to be predominate with radio replay. Nevertheless, the outcomes of interest to advertisers — recall of brand claims, attitude toward the ad or brand, and purchase intentions — were very similar with radio replay as compared to when the second exposure was to the TV ad again. Thus, the study findings suggest that radio replay can be a cost-effective way to extend and reinforce a television campaign.

Because advertisers may not always be able to control the order of consumer exposure to the radio and television versions of the ad, the Edell and Keller study also examined the reverse sequence when consumers heard the radio ad first and then saw the TV ad. Interestingly, when the linked radio ad appeared before the TV ad, more elaborative processing of the TV ad occurred than if the radio ad had not appeared at all. This enhanced processing was especially evident when the audio from the TV ad that made up the radio ad was only generally related to the TV video. A number of factors may have contributed to this greater processing. When consumers heard the radio ad, they might have imagined what the people accompanying the voices looked like. To the extent that the radio ad evoked such imagery in consumers' minds, they might have been curious during the later TV ad exposure to see what the video looked like, how characters were portrayed, and so on, perhaps comparing it to what they had imagined while processing the earlier radio ad version. Because these were most likely different images, additional processing may have then been devoted to resolving the inconsistencies. For these reasons, consumers may have been more motivated to process the TV ad such that they engaged in more extensive processing.

An industry field study sponsored by ABC, American Urban, CBS, Westwood One, and Unistar radio networks (the 1993 Imagery Transfer Study) provides further evidence concerning radio replay. Specifically, a national sample was surveyed to explore if consumers could identify the visual images of a previously viewed TV ad when they heard a radio commercial made up of the audio of the TV ad. Respondents were exposed to 20- and 30-second excerpts from two television commercials for a long-distance service, fast food restaurant, or automobile. Seventy-five percent of the sample were reported as being able to correctly describe the prime visual elements in the TV commercials after hearing only the audio, reinforcing the conclusion that closely related audio as a radio ad can serve as an effective retrieval cue to the corresponding video from a TV ad.

A number of factors will determine the success of a coordinated TV-radio campaign. The effectiveness of the audio track on the radio clearly depends on how strongly the audio is associated with the video and other communication effects stored in memory from the TV ad exposure. This association, in turn, should be a function of the relationship between the audio and video tracks of the TV ad. There must be substantial overlap in audiences of the two media, and, ideally, the radio ad would stand alone so that it could achieve the campaign objectives even for those consumers who would not be exposed to the corresponding TV ad campaign. Thus, the television audio must be meaningful enough and of high enough quality to air effectively on the radio.

Print Reinforcement

Another possible way to reinforce a TV ad is with magazine or newspaper ads. A number of industry studies over the years have considered the effects of combined television and print ad campaigns (see Consterdine, 1990; Smith, 1990, for examples and reviews). One of the most comprehensive studies was a recently completed joint research project completed by Magazine Publishers of America and J. Walter Thompson (Confer, 1991). As part of this project, relevant research studies from Great Britain, Canada, Italy, South Africa, the Netherlands, West Germany, and the United States were reviewed. The conclusion of the review was that print advertising, when used in combination with television, can enhance the depth and breadth of the communication that an advertiser achieves. The project also reported the results of a new, more controlled experiment that examined the effects of integrated print and TV media advertising for three brands (Kraft Miracle Whip, Reynolds Crystal Colored Plastic Wrap, and Warner-Lambert's early pregnancy test, e.p.t.). Although the results were not uniformly positive, they were able to generally corroborate the findings of other mixed media studies. They concluded that:

> The most effective advertising campaigns are those which use both print and television in an integrated manner. That is, the proper way to start to plan a campaign is to assume from the beginning that both print and television will be used and to develop the creative strategies and executions accordingly and in coordination. . . . The days when print is tacked onto a television campaign as an afterthought if sufficient money is available, and if there is any time left to put together some creative executions, should be left behind. With all the weight of evidence now available, we are reaching a position where the challenge for the 1990s should be to seek a greater understanding of the best ways, creatively, to exploit the potential for media synergy. (Confer, 1991, pp. RC9-10)

Toward this goal of a greater understanding of the strategic implications of a coordinated media campaign employing TV and print, Edell and Keller (1993) provided an information processing perspective of a print reinforcement strategy. Print reinforcement involves taking a key visual from the TV ad and/or some of its audio copy and including it as the visual and/or verbal elements of a print ad. The basic premise of the Edell and Keller study was that print reinforcement can be a particularly useful way to: capture consumers' attention when they are reading a magazine, encourage more evaluative processing of the brand information in the ad, and facilitate the formation of strong brand associations to the resulting communication effects. The following scenario illustrates how print reinforcement can build brand equity.

Consumer processing of a TV ad is frequently fairly passive in that few brand evaluations occur, and any thoughts or feelings that do arise are usually directed toward ad execution information. As a result, relatively weak brand associations are formed. Consumer processing of a print ad is also often characterized by a fairly low level of involvement and, because of its unintrusive nature, a print ad can be easily "tuned out" and ignored. With print reinforcement, however, assuming reactions to the TV ad are generally favorable and some salient cue from the TV ad is present in the print ad execution, consumers would be expected to pay greater attention to and more carefully consider the brand claims of a print ad than if they had not been motivated from the prior TV ad exposure. Moreover, the self-paced nature of print ad processing would allow consumers the opportunity to consider the ad and brand in more detail, increasing the likelihood that overall evaluations are formed and strengthening the association of the brand with whatever communication effects are created by the print and TV ad exposures. In short, print ad reinforcement can contribute to brand equity by increasing consumer motivation, ability, and opportunity to process a print ad and thus produce stronger brand associations.

A laboratory study was conducted that found some support for these notions, although, as with the radio-TV study, much stronger effects on brand evaluations were evident when the print ad preceded the TV ad. In any case, the findings of all of the studies reported here imply that one potentially effective integrated media strategy is to create a clever, attention-getting TV ad that consumers like and then take a key visual from the TV ad, place it in a print ad, and include additional product or service information to further elaborate on the relevant brand claims or promise. Such a strategy would capitalize on the unique strengths of each media to compensate for the respective weaknesses of the other media: The limited amount of information that can be conveyed in a TV ad can be overcome by an explicitly linked print ad that has detailed supporting information, and the limited attention-getting properties of a print ad can be overcome by an explicitly linked TV ad that is favorably evaluated and, therefore, interest arousing. Under these circumstances, the communication effects and brand associations resulting from print reinforcement should be stronger and more favorable than if one medium is used alone or if both media are used but not coordinated in the manner described.

Summary

Combined, the Edell and Keller coordinated media studies show how cueing a TV ad with an explicitly linked radio or print ad can create similar or even enhanced processing outcomes that can substitute for additional TV ad exposures. Moreover, the findings indicate that a potentially useful, although rarely employed, media strategy is to run explicitly linked print or radio ads prior to the accompanying TV ad. The print and radio ads in this case act as a teaser and increase consumer motivation to process the more complete TV ad consisting of both audio and video components.

Although the principle of cueing across media was illustrated with radio and print reinforcement of TV ads, other strategies are possible. Another obvious approach is out-of-home or outdoor reinforcement where a key visual from a TV ad and/or some of its audio copy is included as the visual and/or verbal elements of a print ad. As with print reinforcement, outdoor reinforcement is a cost-effective way to cue communication effects from TV ad exposure and build brand equity. Although the opportunity to process in any one exposure may not be as great with outdoor media as compared to print, the repetition in exposures may afford greater opportunities to encode the brand and form stronger links to communication effects.

INTEGRATING WITHIN ADVERTISING MEDIA

Finally, we consider three different ways that advertising can be integrated within an advertising medium to build brand equity, again concentrating on television advertising.

Cueing with 15-Second TV Ads

Starting in 1984, the three major American television networks permitted the use of shorter 15-second commercials as compared to conventional 30- and 60-second commercials. Because of their lower cost, 15-second commercials were quickly adopted and rose to make up roughly a third of all commercials on television. Unfortunately, as many advertisers discovered, it is very difficult to communicate new information to consumers and be persuasive in such a short period of time.

Because 15-second commercials provide consumers with limited opportunity to process, a more effective use of them might be in more of a reminder function. For example, one such strategy would be to create traditional 30- and 60-second television commercials at the start of a campaign but to edit these ads down into 15-second versions later in the campaign. These shorter ads could serve as a reminder to communication effects stored from prior exposure to the longer versions. This strategy would seem most appropriate when consumers already know a lot about the brand and current ad campaign such that favorable associations exist, but, because of competitive advertising or some other reason, the strength of those associations are weakening over time.

Cueing Multiple TV Ads With An Umbrella Ad

Many ad campaigns do not use a single ad execution but rather multiple ad executions. Different ads may be used to target different market segments. Alternatively, different ads may be used to convey different types of information to the same target market. Schumann, Petty, and Clemons (1990) made a distinction between cosmetic differences (e.g., ad execution information) and substantive differences (e.g., brand claim and attribute information) across a pool of ads. These two differences arise from very different motivations on the part of the advertiser. Cosmetic differences arise from the need to vary creative strategies to capture consumer attention or to convey appropriate user or usage imagery. Contextual ad execution information varied across a pool of ads can, according to the encoding variability principle, enhance memory performance (Edell, 1993). Substantive differences across a pool of ads would appear to be less common — most ad campaigns are reasonably single-minded and tend to emphasize one or two main product or service benefits. Even if multiple attributes were to be advertised, they often can be communicated within one ad. Nevertheless, there are various reasons why an advertiser may need to vary brand claims or attribute information across a pool of ads. For example, the consumer decision process in the product or service category may be complex enough to require advertising multiple attributes or benefits, but, at the same time, the individual attributes or benefits involved may need a fair amount of elaboration or support to be fully understood and appreciated by consumers.

Regardless of the particular motivation, one potentially useful strategy to build brand equity when advertisers employ an ad campaign consisting of multiple ad executions is to create a single umbrella ad consisting of excerpts or highlights from the individual ad executions. Such an ad could be scheduled to run later in the history of the ad campaign when consumers would have already been exposed to the individual ad executions. As a result, the excerpts or highlights making up the umbrella ad would serve as cues to the more extensive communication effects stored in memory.

The rationale behind an umbrella ad is that consumers would never consider the broader meaning of an ad campaign unless the full nature of that campaign was brought to their attention. Consumers are often literal in how they process any one ad. Cueing the individual ad executions within one umbrella ad may clarify to consumers the implicit message being conveyed by the pool of ads. In other words, an umbrella ad can facilitate a more abstract understanding of the product meaning and higher order learning by consumers. The more abstractly a single attribute or benefit is made across a pool of ads, the more likely it is that an umbrella ad is necessary for consumers to be able to fully comprehend the desired message conveyed by the ad campaign.

Another benefit of an umbrella ad is that it may increase the likelihood that an overall attitude is formed toward the ad campaign as a whole and linked to the brand. Much prior research has shown that consumer reactions to the creative strategy of an ad itself — in terms of the likability, believability, convincingness, and so on of the ad execution — can influence their evaluations of the advertised brand (see Brown & Stayman, 1992, for a summary). Much of the research examining "attitude toward the ad" effects has been done in experimental settings that made it easy for ad attitudes to be formed and ad attitudes to be used as inputs into brand evaluations. In practice, both steps may be difficult to achieve. Because of the combination of brief excerpts in one umbrella ad, consumers should be more aware of their reactions to individual ads and, thus, more likely to form evaluations of the campaign as a whole. The use of ad retrieval cues, as noted previously, is a way to ensure that the second step happens and that ad attitudes are in fact able to be recalled and influence brand evaluations. Besides facilitating the formation of ad attitudes, an umbrella ad may facilitate the formation of brand attitudes based on the full range of product information when the pool of ads vary on product-related dimensions due to different attributes or benefits.

Cueing Past Advertising Campaigns

Finally, we can expand the scope of advertising cueing to consider the effects of ad campaigns over time. For many brands, it is tempting to change advertising as a way to rejuvenate sales. No ad, no matter how popular, can run forever. As the cumulative number of exposures to an ad campaign increases, so does the risk that consumers tune out the ad from boredom or, even worse, become irritated and actually begin to actively dislike the ad. If the effects of an ad appear to begin to wear out, some changes in the communication strategy may be necessary. Changes in advertising or message strategy for a brand can be characterized as creative changes, in which the brand positioning remains the same but the creative strategy changes in some way, or positioning changes, in which the brand is repositioned and a new creative strategy may also be introduced at the same time.

One way to establish continuity with past advertising is to use some salient element of a past ad campaign as part of the current ad campaign. This approach could take a number of different forms. One strategy would be to rerun past advertising on a limited basis, for example, as part of a holiday or special event. This strategy would be particularly useful if the current ad campaign failed to address some key brand associations that made up the brand's heritage and were an important part of its image. Running past advertising on a limited basis would help to reinforce the original positioning while at the same time making it less likely to disrupt the communication goals of the current ad campaign.

Another approach to establish continuity with past advertising would be to embed an identifiable element or symbol of the past advertising in some manner in the current ad. This may take the form of a musical jingle, a key tag line, or some unique visual image. For example, Victor Kiam, the chairman and CEO of Remington razors, was used as a spokesperson in ads for years where he claimed "he liked the product so much he bought the company." Subsequent ad campaigns that developed different themes still used him as a sign off. Similarly, even though Michelin's current U.S. ad campaign is based on a safety theme represented in part by a creative strategy of visual images of babies playfully intertwined with tires, they still use their well-known tire character from old ad campaigns at the end of their ads.

Summary

This section considered three different strategies designed to improve the contribution of television advertising to brand equity. The basic rationale for these strategies is that TV ads should not be considered as discrete units that are created for a particular ad campaign and, therefore, run for a certain length of time before being replaced by a new ad campaign. Rather, TV ads should be thought of more broadly as consisting of different ingredients or pieces of information that advertisers might choose to combine in different ways over time. The most important ingredients are those identifiable visual scenes, characters, symbols, and verbal phrases or slogans that can serve as cues or reminders to communication effects created by a single TV ad, an ad campaign with multiple TV ads, or a previous ad campaign.

Combining these ingredients to leverage communication effects over time offers several potential benefits. First, it can help to maintain the strength of unique and favorable brand associations. In particular, without such reminders, the heritage of a brand and its original associations may become weakened because the ad campaign is not being currently aired or a new ad campaign is using different appeals or creative strategies to reposition or modernize the brand. Second, it can facilitate the formation of favorable attitudes by consumers toward the advertising and brand. In other words, consumers may be likely to say, "I like the ads for that brand." As noted previously, these attitudes toward the ad can favorably impact brand evaluations, especially for low-involvement consumer decisions.

Note that an implicit issue in this discussion is the optimal continuity to have with advertising and communication campaigns over time. Congruity theory would suggest that a moderate amount of change is appropriate (Mandler, 1982; Myers-Levy & Tybout, 1989). Too little change may not be noticed by consumers and, thus, have no effect. On the other hand, more dramatic changes in brand positioning may confuse consumers and result in them still continuing to think of the brand in the old way. Because of strong associations already in memory, consumers may either fail to incorporate new ad information into their brand knowledge structures or fail to retrieve new ad information when making later product or service decisions. In many cases, a moderate change in creative, for example, retaining the current positioning but communicating it with a new creative, may be the most effective way to maintain or enhance the strength of brand associations. If the favorability or uniqueness of brand associations are deficient in some way, however, then a more severe change in positioning emphasizing different points of parity or points of difference may be necessary.

SUMMARY AND CONCLUSIONS

The purpose of this chapter was to provide conceptual frameworks and managerial guidelines as to how marketing communications can be integrated to enhance brand equity (see Table 6.1 for a summary). The chapter addressed this issue from the perspective of customer-based brand equity (Keller, 1993a), which maintains that brand equity is fundamentally determined by the brand knowledge created in consumers' minds by the supporting marketing program. Specifically, *customer-based brand equity* was defined as the differential effect that brand knowledge has on consumer response to the marketing of a particular product or service. Brand knowledge was conceptualized in terms of an associative memory model as consisting of a set of associations linked to the brand. Customer-based brand equity occurs when consumers are aware of the brand and hold strong, favorable, and unique brand associations in memory.

Basic principles about memory structures and processes were outlined to provide some general guidelines as to how marketing communications can build brand knowledge and contribute to customer-based brand equity. To create or affect brand associations in memory, consumers must have motivation, ability, and opportunity to process or encode marketing communication information. Motivation, ability, and opportunity affect the intensity and direction of processing and the resulting strength of brand associations. A number of factors can affect consumer motivation, ability, and opportunity to process an ad (e.g., the form, content, and context of the ad, the number of previous ad exposures, as well as various characteristics of the consumer such as existing brand knowledge). For brand associations to be recallable from memory and affect consumer product and service decisions, consumers also must have motivation, ability, and opportunity to later retrieve that information. A number of factors beside the strength of association will affect consumer motivation, ability, and opportunity to recall information (e.g., recency or time since last exposure, competing advertising or brand associations, and retrieval cues or reminders).

Two key implications emerged from these conceptual frameworks. First, all possible communication options should be evaluated in terms of their ability to affect brand equity. In particular, the customer-based brand equity concept provides a common denominator by which the effects of different communication options can be evaluated: Each communication

TABLE 6.1
Managerial Guidelines for Integrating Marketing Communications to Build
Brand Equity

- The role of marketing communications is to contribute to brand equity by establishing the brand in memory and linking favorable, strong, and unique associations to it.
- A marketing communications program that effectively builds brand equity is one that: (a) at encoding, motivates consumers to elaborate on and fully process the communication, recognizes consumers' prior knowledge and abilities when designing the communication, and presents the communication in an environment conducive for processing; and (b) at retrieval, motivates consumers to consider relevant communication effects (i.e., what consumers saw, heard, learned, thought, felt, and so on while exposed to the communication), recognizes how communication effects are organized in the brand knowledge structure, and encourages product or service decisions in an environment conducive for retrieval of communication effects.
- A marketing communications program can contribute to the creation of strong brand associations and recalled communication effects through the use of creative communications that cause consumers to elaborate on brand-related information and relate it appropriately to existing knowledge. These communications should be shown or evident repeatedly over time and many strong retrieval cues should be present as reminders.
- From the perspective of customer-based brand equity, marketers should evaluate all possible communication options available to create knowledge structures according to effectiveness criteria as well as cost considerations.
- Regardless of which options are chosen, the entire marketing program should be coordinated to create a consistent and cohesive brand image, that is, where brand associations share content and meaning.
- Advertising retrieval cues — key visuals or distinctive slogans evident at the point of purchase or any other place where consumers are making product or service decision — are powerful tools that advertisers can employ to better leverage the effects of their advertising. Ad retrieval cues may be particularly useful when much competitive advertising interference exists or when, for any other reason, the ad campaign results in positive communication effects that are only weakly associated to the brand.
- Cueing a TV ad with an explicitly linked radio or print ad can create similar or even enhanced processing outcomes that can substitute for additional TV ad exposures. Moreover, a potentially useful, although rarely, employed media strategy is to run explicitly linked print or radio ads prior to the accompanying TV ad. The print and radio ads in this case function as a teaser and increase consumer motivation to process the more complete TV ad, consisting of both audio and video components.
- TV ads should not be considered as discrete units that are created for a particular ad campaign and, therefore, run for a certain length of time before being replaced by a new ad campaign. Rather, TV ads should be thought of more broadly as consisting of different ingredients or pieces of information that advertisers might choose to combine in different ways over time. The most important ingredients are those identifiable visual scenes, characters, symbols, and verbal phrases or slogans that can serve as cues or reminders to communication effects created by a single TV ad, an ad campaign with multiple TV ads, or a previous ad campaign.

---

option can be judged in terms of the effectiveness and efficiency by which it affects brand awareness and by which it creates, maintains, or strengthens favorable and unique brand associations. The second important insight that emerges from the conceptual framework is that marketing communications often must be explicitly linked (i.e., cued) to allow for the necessary interactions to create a positive brand image. Specifically, the key assertion of the chapter is that marketers often should integrate marketing communications by literally taking visual or verbal information from one communication element and using it in different ways in another communication element. The rationale is that this information can cue or serve as a reminder to related information. By enhancing consumer motivation, ability, and opportunity to process and retrieve brand-related information, these cues can facilitate the formation of strong, favorable, and unique brand associations. Explictly integrating media in this manner also increases the likelihood that brand knowledge is used in consumer product and service decisions. In these ways, explicitly integrated media can contribute to brand equity.

Issues associated with strategies related to three general forms of such direct media reinforcement were described. First, ad retrieval cues—by which a key visual or distinctive slogan is evident at the point of purchase or any place where consumers are making product or service decisions—were identified as a way to integrate across communication elements. These reminders are necessary because one of the major difficulties facing advertisers is often not in creating any communication effects in consumer memory during ad exposure but in making sure that whatever the consumer saw, heard, learned, thought, or felt can be successfully retrieved after ad exposure (e.g., when purchase decisions are later made in the store). Ad retrieval cues help to strengthen the identification of a brand with its communication effects during those moments when product or service decisions are being made. Second, print and radio reinforcement of TV ads—in which the video and audio components of a TV ad serve as the basis for the respective type of ads—were identified as a way to integrate across advertising media. Print and radio reinforcement can be an effective means to leverage existing communication effects from TV ad exposure and more strongly link them to the brand. Third, different combinations of TV ad excerpts within a campaign (e.g., 15-second spots consisting of highlights from longer 30- or 60-second spots for those campaigns characterized by only one dominant ad or umbrella ads consisting of highlights from a pool of ads for those campaigns consisting of multiple ad executions) and across campaigns over time (e.g., including key elements from past ad campaigns that are strongly identified with the brand as part of the current ad campaign) were identified as ways to integrate within an advertising media. These strategies may be particularly helpful for strengthening dormant associations and facilitating the formation of consumer evaluations of and reactions to the ads as well as their linkage to the brand.

In closing, the basic message of this chapter is simple: Advertisers need to evaluate marketing communication options strategically to determine how they can contribute to brand equity. To do so, advertisers need some theoretical and managerial guidelines by which they can determine the

effectiveness and efficiency of various communication options both singu-
larly and in combination with other communication options. An important
goal for future research is to identify measurement techniques that assist in
these evaluations based on conceptual frameworks such as the ones
presented here.

ACKNOWLEDGMENTS

Helpful comments from Jennifer Aaker and Margaret Campbell are gratefully
acknowledged. Financial support for studies reported in this chapter from the
Marketing Science Institute and faculty fellowships at Stanford University's Graduate School of Business provided through the generosity of James and Doris
McNamara and the Fletcher Jones foundation is greatly appreciated.

REFERENCES

Ajzen, E., & Fishbein, M. (1980). *Understanding attitudes and predicting social behavior.*
Englewood Cliffs, NJ: Prentice-Hall.
Alba, J. W., & Hutchinson, J. W. (1987). Dimensions of consumer expertise. *Journal of
Consumer Research, 13,* 411–453.
Alba, J. W., Hutchinson, J. W., & Lynch, J. G. (1991). Memory and decision making. In T.
S. Robinson & H. H. Kassarjian (Eds.), *Handbook of consumer behavior* (pp. 1–49).
Englewood Cliffs, NJ: Prentice-Hall.
Anderson, J. R. (1983). *The architecture of cognition.* Cambridge, MA: Harvard University
Press.
Batra, R., & Ray, M. L. (1986). Situational effects of advertising repetition: The moderating
influence of motivation, ability, and opportunity to respond. *Journal of Consumer
Research, 12,* 432–445.
Bettman, J. R. (1979). *An informational processing theory of consumer choice.* Reading, MA:
Addison-Wesley.
Brown, S. P., & Stayman, D. M. (1992). Antecedants and consequences of attitude toward the
ad: A meta-analysis. *Journal of Consumer Research, 19,* 34–51.
Burke, R. R., & Srull, T. K. (1988). Competitive interference and consumer memory for
advertising. *Journal of Consumer Research, 15,* 55–68.
Confer, M. G. (1991). The media multiplier: Nine studies conducted in seven countries.
Journal of Advertising Research, 31(1), RC4-RC10.
Consterdine, G. J. (1990, May). How print and TV interact: "The media multiplier." *ADMAP,*
pp. 41–45.
Edell, J. A. (1993). Advertising interactions: A route to understanding brand equity. In A. A.
Mitchell (Ed.), *Advertising exposure, memory, and choice.* Hillsdale, NJ: Lawrence
Erlbaum Associates.
Edell, J. A., & Keller, K. L. (1989). The information processing of coordinated media
campaigns. *Journal of Marketing Research, 26*(2), 149–163.
Edell, J. A., & Keller, K. L. (1993). *Analyzing media interactions: Print reinforcement of
television advertising campaigns* (Working paper). Durham, NC: Fuqua School of Business,
Duke University.

Gibson, L. D. (1983). "Not recall." *Journal of Advertising Research*, pp. 39–46.

Heckler, S. E., & Childers, T. L. (1992). The role of expectancy and relevancy in memory for verbal and visual information: What is incongruency? *Journal of Consumer Research, 18,* 475–492.

Houston, M. J., Childers, T. L., & Heckler, S. E. (1987). Picture-word consistency and the elaborative processing of advertisements. *Journal of Marketing Research, 24,* 359–369.

Keller, K. L. (1987). Memory factors in advertising: The effect of advertising cues on brand evaluations. *Journal of Consumer Research, 14,* 316–333.

Keller, K. L. (1991a). Memory and evaluation effects in competitive advertising environments. *Journal of Consumer Research, 16,* 463–576.

Keller, K. L. (1991b). Cue compatibility and framing in advertising. *Journal of Marketing Research, 28,* 42–57.

Keller, K. L. (1993a). Conceptualizing, measuring, and managing customer-based brand equity. *Journal of Marketing, 57,* 1–22.

Keller, K. L. (1993b). Memory retrieval factors and advertising effectiveness. In A. A. Mitchell (Ed.), *Advertising, exposure, memory, and choice* (pp. 11–48). Hillsdale, NJ: Lawrence Erlbaum Associates.

Kent, R. J. (1993, March/April). Competitive versus noncompetitive clutter in television advertising. *Journal of Advertising Research,* pp. 40–46.

Loftus, E. F., & Loftus, G. R. (1980). On the permanence of stored information in the human brain. *American Psychologist, 35,* 409–420.

Lubetkin, B. (1992). *An overview of the "How Advertising Works" study: A landmark analysis of advertising effectiveness* (Working paper). Chicago: Information Resources.

Lynch, J. G., Jr., & Srull, T. K. (1982). Memory and attentional factors in consumer choice: Concepts and research methods. *Journal of Consumer Research, 9,* 18–36.

MacInnis, D. J., & Jaworski, B. J. (1989). Information processing from advertisements: Towards an integrative framework. *Journal of Marketing, 53,* 1–23.

MacInnis, D. J., Moorman, C., & Jaworski, B. J. (1991). Enhancing and measuring consumers' motivation opportunity and ability to process brand information from ads. *Journal of Marketing, 55,* 32–53.

Mandler, G. (1982). The structure of value: Accounting for taste. In M. S. Clark & S. T. Fiske (Eds.), *Affect and cognition: The 17th Annual Carnegie Symposium* (pp. 3–36). Hillsdale, NJ: Lawrence Erlbaum Associates.

Melton, A. W. (1970). The situation with respect to the spacing of repetitions and memory. *Journal of Verbal Learning and Verbal Memory, 9,* 596–606.

Mitchell, A. A. (1981). The dimensions of advertising involvement. In J. C. Olson (Ed.), *Advances in consumer research* (Vol. 7, pp. 25–30). Ann Arbor, MI: Association for Consumer Research.

Myers-Levy, J. & Tybout, A. M. (1989). Schema congruity as a basis for product evaluation. *Journal of Consumer Research, 16,* 39–54.

Petty, R. E., & Cacioppo, J. T. (1986). *Communication and persuasion.* New York: Springer-Verlag.

Postman, L., & Underwood, B. J. (1973). Critical issues in interference theory. *Memory and Cognition, 1,* 19–40.

Roberts, D. F., & Macoby, N. (1973). Information processing and persuasion: Counterarguing behavior. In P. Clarke (Ed.), *New models for communication research* (pp. 269–307). Beverly Hills, CA: Sage.

Rossiter, J. R., & Percy, L. (1987). *Advertising and promotion management.* New York: McGraw-Hill.

Schumann, D. W., Petty, R. E., & Clemons, D. S. (1990). Predicting the effectiveness of different strategies of advertising variation: A test of repetition-variation hypotheses. *Journal of Consumer Research, 17*(3), 192–207.

Smith, A. (1990, May). Three ways of examining the effectiveness of combined print and television campaigns. *ADMAP,* pp. 46–49.

Srull, T. K., & Wyer, R. S., Jr. (1989). Person memory and judgment. *Psychological Review, 96*(1), 58–83.

Wilkie, W. L., & Pessemier, E. A. (1973, November). Issues in marketing's use of multi-attribute attitude models. *Journal of Marketing Research,* pp. 428–441.

Wright, P. L. (1981). Cognitive responses to mass media advocacy. In R. E. Petty, T. M. Ostrom, & T. C. Brock (Eds.), *Cognitive responses in persuasion* (pp. 263–282). Hillsdale, NJ: Lawrence Erlbaum Associates.

Young, D. R., & Belleza, F. S. (1982). Encoding variablity, memory organization, and the repetition effect. *Journal of Experimental Psychology: Learning, Memory & Cognition, 8*(6), 545–559.

Managing Integrated
Marketing Communication

7
Strategic Planning for Integrated Marketing Communications Programs: An Approach to Moving From Chaotic Toward Systematic

Jeri Moore
CCS LTD.

Esther Thorson
University of Missouri–Columbia

During the 1970s and early 1980s, a battle was fought inside many advertising agencies over the issue of whether the use of strategic discipline was a good idea or, instead, a hindrance to "creativity." Today, most advertising people agree that strategy is not the ruination of good advertising; rather, strategy is seen as a necessary first step in the creation of campaigns that will be effective in achieving their sponsors' objectives. Strategy is recognized as the compass that provides the direction to keep the creators of advertising on course amid a sea of possible advertising messages.

One reason that advertising strategy has been embraced by many advertising practitioners is that the competitive environment for most products is crowded with numerous brands that are quite similar in terms of attributes and tangible benefits provided; in most categories, it is not at all obvious what message will most effectively sell a particular brand. Indeed, it is is often not even clear to whom the brand should be sold. The careful attention to what to say, and to whom, is a necessary first step to developing successful advertising in such challenging situations.

A second reason that advertising strategy has been recognized as a useful tool is that the advertiser — the client of the agency — usually has enough involvement in his or her own market and marketing process that he or she has opinions about what the advertising should say. If the agency and client don't reach explicit agreement — before the agency begins creative development — on the general direction the campaign is to take, the agency will often find itself redoing campaign after campaign, as the client rejects many proposed creative approaches. Consensus on a campaign is unlikely until there is recognition that the advertiser's objection is to the strategy behind the proposed advertising. Starting with agreement on advertising strategy can, therefore, improve the efficiency with which the advertising agency functions.

Hence, both advertisers and their agencies benefit from the early investment of time and attention to advertising strategy. The principle benefits are that advertising is more likely to be effective, because it is based on thorough analysis of the marketplace, and the process is likely to be more efficient, because it is predicated on early agreement on the message to be conveyed by the advertising.

A typical advertising strategy usually identifies and describes the target audience for the campaign, often including a consumer problem that the brand (presumably) can solve. Then, the strategy states the benefit that is to be the focus of message communication, along with the attributes or other support that will be used to convince consumers that they will receive the stated benefit if they buy, use, or otherwise consume the product. Often, advertising strategies include descriptions of competitive offerings. Statements of the intended tone or personality are also common.

Although most advertisers and advertising agencies have by now adopted the practice of developing a strategy before creating advertising campaigns, there has been less acceptance—thus far—of using a comprehensive strategic approach to the development of integrated marketing communications programs. In our experience, many marketers use much less analytic approaches for their overall IMC programs than they do for advertising campaigns, often relying on the advertising strategy as a surrogate for an IMC strategy.

Although most advertising strategy development systems do address many of the issues that are important in the creation of an IMC strategy, advertising strategies differ from IMC strategies in at least two important regards:

- Most practitioners agree that advertising, to be most effective, should generally involve singleminded focus. The typical advertising strategy identifies a single target audience, and one particular benefit that this audience is to be promised.

  Many IMC programs, however, are characterized by their coordination of the messages to be sent to, and indeed the interactions among, a number of target audiences. For example, an IMC program for an automobile could include communications that speak to people in the market for a new car, current owners of the automobile brand, writers for automotive magazines, dealers and salespersons who sell the car, and even the service department of the auto dealerships.

Using an advertising strategy development system to plan for such a program is like using a blueprint for a single-story house to build a high-rise apartment building—it provides better guidance than no blueprint at all, but is much harder to work from than if the builder had invested in the development of a new blueprint for a high-rise apartment building.

- Advertising strategies make implicit assumptions about the media to be used (generally, these assumptions are based on the size of the advertising budget and the breadth of the target audience—large budgets and broad audiences suggest television-dominated plans, whereas smaller budgets and narrower targets suggest the use of magazines as primary medium). There is little examination, within the course of a typical advertising strategy development process, of other communications options from either a strategic or an efficiency standpoint.

In IMC programs, the available communications channels are far more diverse. In fact, many of the ways that communications can occur between the marketer and the audience work from different sets of assumptions than are true for advertising. For example, the communications that occur when a consumer calls an 800-number are far more interactive than the much more passive receipt and processing of the content of a 30-second commercial.

The plan for an IMC program must, therefore, take into account a much wider range of forms of communication, and must provide a means by which the planner can evaluate and select communications vehicles.

Most marketers do not have available to them the type of comprehensive IMC planning procedure that would turn the planning for IMC into a systematic process. The approaches to planning for IMC that appear most common among marketers of consumer products in the United States are as follows:

The Mandated "One Look" Approach.   As suggested by Duncan and Caywood (see chap. 1, this volume), companies that are in a fairly early stage of understanding and implementation of IMC focus on the importance of having common colors, graphics, and logo treatments throughout the company's communications materials. Within those companies that define IMC to mean a common look, the approach to planning for IMC is really quite simple: Some centralized or corporate group develops guidelines, and the makers of all communications materials are asked to develop their materials accordingly. Sometimes, particularly in consumer products companies, the "one look" emanates from an advertising campaign involving a visual approach developed by the advertising agency. In this regard, the mandated one-look system is a strategic precursor to the following approach.

The Themelines on Matchbooks Approach. This method is used by some marketers who think in terms of the consumer advertising being the central communications element, and is often the result of an advertising agency's encouragement. Given a particular advertising campaign, the idea is to make sure that consumers are reminded of the advertising through the use of the other IMC vehicles. Often, the advertising theme line is the element that is carried over. In the best cases, the theme line or other executional element is transferred onto IMC vehicles that have some thematic tie with the line and are likely to effectively reach the target audience. Example of this would be the use of the Coppertone line, "Tan, don't burn . . ." in skywriting over beaches during the summer, or the premium developed by a cat food marketer: A cat food dish with the theme line on it, so the cat owner would see the line whenever it was time to feed the cat. In other cases, the goal of achieving broad exposure for the theme line strays from the idea of strategic focus, and theme lines are placed on communications vehicles based on nonstrategic considerations (e.g., cost, the personal preferences of senior management, etc.). For example, the maker of a brand of house paint defended its sponsorship of Indy 500 race cars on the basis that it enabled exposure of the brand's theme line in a venue that matched the paint's upscale positioning as, "It [the Indy 500] is unique, and we're unique."

Supply-Side Planning. In supply-side planning, a package of communication vehicles is assembled based on what the supplier has to sell. The supplier might be an advertising agency that has divisions that provide other communication services, or—as part of a recently growing trend—the supplier might be a media conglomerate. These media conglomerates are companies that once were active in a single medium, such as television or magazines. Over the past decade, a number of the more successful media companies have diversified into other media, entertainment and promotional companies. These companies approach advertisers with packages that include media advertising, direct marketing using tailored segments of the supplier's subscription list, sweepstakes and contests, special event sponsorship, and even the production of sales training films in the supplier's studios. To the advertiser, these packages can seem quite appealing, based on very attractive pricing and the appearance of complete integration. The disadvantage, of course, is that a program made up of only what the supplier has to sell will not necessarily be comprised of the elements that are optimal from the buyer's standpoint.

Ad Hoc Approaches.   A number of marketers who understand the value of IMC programs and have organizations that can be mobilized to integrate their communications attempt to create such programs through a combination of market analysis and meetings of the groups involved. Typically, an individual within the marketing organization will lead this effort, and will involve internal departments (such as the public relations (PR) department), the advertising agency, and other outside suppliers—the direct marketing agency, promotional agency, and public relations firm. This process has the potential to result in effective programs. The case described by Haytko (see chapter 12, this volume) seems to be a good example of a team coming together and working out an IMC program that proved to be well integrated and effective. Success stories notwithstanding, there are two principle drawbacks to ad hoc approaches: First, the process often isn't efficient—much time is generally wasted in the development of a program, because the participants do not know where to start, or how best to proceed. The second drawback is that the outcome may or may not be a well-balanced program, depending on the skills of the group leader and differences in persuasion skills of the advocates of individual disciplines (e.g., a particularly aggressive proponent of advertising or direct marketing may effectively lobby that the program should be dominated by his or her discipline, even when a more rigorous analysis would suggest that this is not in the best interests of the marketer).

In contrast to any of these approaches, using a strategy planning system for IMC avoids the pitfalls of:

- Implementing only superficially integrated communications, such as a program that shares only common graphics and logo treatments.
- Using the tools of IMC to build consumer preference (a common function of consumer advertising) instead of using each tool to accomplish other tasks necessary to complete the selling cycle.
- Developing a program that allocates resources across IMC tools for the wrong reasons—such as the pressures from suppliers or organizational politics.

In fact, on a more general level, the advantages to using a planning system to develop IMC programs are similar to those that marketers and their advertising agencies have experienced in using advertising strategy planning approaches. Specifically:

- Using a disciplined approach to planning marketing communications is far more likely to result in effective communications than a more intuitive process, particularly as the competitive market for the product becomes more cluttered, and unique selling points are less obvious.

• The program development becomes more efficient. Although some time is invested at the beginning to create the strategy, fewer false starts should result in reduced program development time.

The use of a strategic system is particularly effective in large organizations, in which it is important for many individuals and groups—with different perspectives and different roles to play—to reach consensus on the program before implementation begins. The development of the plan, if done in a manner that includes all key group members, enables all members to contribute. The structure of the planning system helps to make the process orderly and logical, and ensures that the outcome is a program that is both synergistic and balanced.

Although the advantages of efficiency and effectiveness should be compelling enough to motivate marketers and their agencies to adopt a strategic approach to the development of IMC programs, this has—for the most part—not yet happened.

This is understandable, in that the strategic system that would aid in the planning of an IMC program requires a more complex set of interrelated considerations and decisions than does a system in which a single audience and message are identified.

Specifically, an IMC planning system, if it is truly comprehensive, must first take into account:

• Various consumer groups with differing levels of involvement with the category or brand (e.g., purchasers and users, mothers and children).
• Multiple nonconsumer audiences (e.g., retailers, recommenders, company employees).
• Opportunities to reach consumers at numerous points during the decision process (e.g., deciding to include the brand on the list; in the store, dealership or showroom at the point of purchase).

The system must provide a way of examining each of these targets, both as a potential recipient of the marketer's message and as a potential voice for the marketer—as someone who, as a recommender, for example, could influence other members of other targets. The IMC planning system also must provide the basis for evaluating an extremely wide range of communications vehicles (the program tools) that could be used in various combinations to reach the targets identified as relevant to the marketing objective. And, finally, the ideal IMC planning system would help the planners with the difficult issues involved in resource allocation; given all of the target audiences and all of the communications tools that could be used, what combination of elements will best accomplish the marketer's objectives at the most efficient cost?

The balance of this chapter presents an overview of a planning system that could be used by marketers and their marketing partners to plan IMC programs. Two key assumptions that underlie this planning system are:

- The effective marketing of a product or service requires the activities and interactions among several different audiences. Because of the importance of the consumer to the marketing concept, and because—we believe—of the importance of consumer advertising (notably TV advertising) as a budget expense, many marketing communications programs of recent decades have focused on the consumer, to the virtual exclusion of other audiences. Although some attention has been paid to the trade as an audience—particularly with the growth of trade promotion in the marketing of packaged goods products—this attention has been superficial at best. Little thought has been given by the majority of marketers to the roles of other audiences or to the interactions between audiences. (The public relations discipline, with its broader focus on a company's stakeholders, provides a useful precedent in the examination of all potential audiences for a marketing program.)
- The consumer audience, no matter how narrowly targeted from a demographic or lifestyle perspective, must be further segmented based on position in the purchase cycle for this particular brand. If a marketer hopes to speak to the consumer in a manner that implies an understanding of the individual's concerns and motivations, this segmentation is critical. For example, a consumer considering trading up to a German luxury car will be quite different than a current owner deciding whether to purchase the same make again. As well, both will differ from a third individual who owned that make in the distant past, switched based on dissatisfaction, but may reconsider newer models of the car.

We advocate a planning system that is both market based and consumer based. The focus on the market is necessary if the marketer is to take into account all of the potential audiences for communications, and to determine the best allocation of resources among these audiences. The consumer focus is important, as in the development of any communications, to ensure that the message is relevant and motivating to each individual for whom it is intended.

The steps involved in the development of a comprehensive IMC plan, based on the system that we advocate, are as follows:

1. First, we use a broad, market-level analysis to determine all of the audiences that are important to the achievement of the marketer's objectives.
2. The next stage of the plan is developed using a consumer-centric purchase decision process, employing appropriate models of consumer behavior to identify the various stages of the purchase process and to isolate discrete target groups based on their stage in this process.
3. At this point, we delve further into the issues of the consumer (or other audience), at the individual level, seeking to understand the issues and motivations that drive individuals at that particular stage of the purchase process. This analysis results in the identification of those messages and communications vehicles that we believe will be most successful at motivating members of the target to take the action we are attempting to motivate.
4. Finally, we revert back to the market level to determine the best allocation of resources, given the marketing objectives, the targets, and the tools available to reach these targets.

These steps are detailed in Fig. 7.1.

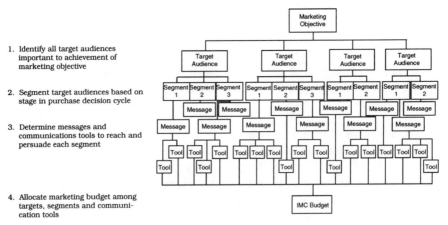

1. Identify all target audiences important to achievement of marketing objective

2. Segment target audiences based on stage in purchase decision cycle

3. Determine messages and communications tools to reach and persuade each segment

4. Allocate marketing budget among targets, segments and communication tools

FIG. 7.1.   A strategic planning approach for IMC program development.

STEP ONE: AUDIENCE IDENTIFICATION

Advertisers are accustomed to identifying a target audience for the advertising campaign. Generally, this involves narrowing down the entire universe of consumers to a single identifiable group comprised of individuals who are most likely to buy the product.

In the development of an IMC program, the marketer must also determine the most likely consumer for the product. Because IMC programs are more comprehensive, the marketer should also identify those other audiences that play a role in the product sale, either directly or indirectly. These audiences will often include channel members such as the sales force and the retail trade, and influencer audiences such as editors and writers of specialized media as well as other experts such as doctors, pharmacists, and nutritionists.

The identification of all potential audiences usually involves examination of the distribution or sales process for the product or service. The strategist should make sure to include those audiences that represent weak links in the current marketing chain. For example, if the marketer has not been able to achieve good retail distribution for the product, those groups that can influence retail distribution should be included as potential marketing targets. In the sales of travel products, perhaps sales are being lost at the booking stage because travel agents are not motivated to book the marketer's product, or, if repeat purchases are a problem in a service business, perhaps employee communications should be considered.

Other influencer audiences that are not directly involved in the distribution or sale of the product can be identified through examination of the consumer purchase process. For example, if consumers frequently ask their doctors before buying a new brand in a particular product category, this suggests that doctors should be considered as a target for marketing communications. (This examination typically occurs during the next stage of the development of the IMC plan; planners are encouraged to think of the creation of the plan not as linear, but as a series of interconnected issues. Therefore, influencer or recommender audiences might be added to an initial list later, as they emerge in the course of the consumer analysis.)

In addition to these nonconsumer audiences, there may be more than one consumer group that represents a potential source of business. Although implementation of a broad-based advertising campaign generally requires that the advertiser choose just one consumer target, the availability of targeted communications vehicles often enables the IMC marketer to pursue multiple prospective purchasers. For example, a food brand that is targeted primarily at female heads of household might also be profitably sold to the teen market. Assuming that the product has teen appeal and can be sold through outlets in which teens buy, a specialized communications program might be developed that targets teens, separate from the communications that reach adults.

Evian, a brand of bottled water, represents a specific example of this type of niche marketing. The primary target for Evian water is active, health-conscious adults. The brand is also marketed to new mothers as a pure water to feed to their babies. The new mother target is reached through parent magazines and via coupons distributed in maternity wards.

When considering niche targets, the strategic planner must address issues of brand equity diffusion (will the message that this target finds motivating be compatible with the brand's position in the minds of consumers) and issues of resource allocation (would the money be spent more profitably against the main target, or against this niche group).

At the conclusion of this stage of the planning process, the planner will have a list that includes a number of potential consumer and nonconsumer audiences. Although some potential targets may already have been eliminated, the more rigorous examination of the best use of marketing resources comes later. The important work of this stage of the process is to identify all potential audiences, including those that might not have been addressed by the marketer in the past.

Step Two: Segmenting Consumer Audiences Based on Stage of Purchase Cycle

Advertisers usually think in terms of the consumer target as a relatively homogeneous group, defined by demographic, psychographic, or lifestyle variables. Only occasionally do advertisers make any explicit statement of the stage of the purchase cycle in which the advertising is intended to reach the consumer. When this is done, the target may be generalized as those consumers who are in the process of deciding among various brands, because advertising is frequently intended to create preference. In other cases, the target may be specifically defined as those who don't now use the brand, or — when the objective is to increase frequency — the target may be current customers.

Because an IMC program can include many different communications elements designed to reach consumers at different times and places, an IMC program can effectively reach consumers at various stages of the purchase process. In order to take full advantage of this, a complete examination of the purchase process is useful.

A number of researchers have identified the typical stages through which an individual consumer proceeds when buying a product (see Fig. 7.2). Generally, these begin with awareness of a need or of the brand and proceed through comprehension and acceptance of the brand's benefits, preference,

FIG. 7.2. Typical consumer product purchase decision process.

search, purchase, usage, and confirmation or alteration of beliefs and preference.

In our experience, although these general models provide a useful starting point, it is usually advantageous to create a custom model for a particular product or service when developing an IMC strategy. The strategist will often discover that the model that best represents a given purchase process will vary in important ways from a general model. Using a general model often implies certain types of IMC tools and techniques; creating a custom model will frequently aid in identifying opportunities for tools and techniques that are uniquely suited to the marketer's brand.

For example, the purchase of a car—although starting at the same point—typically includes the creation of a list of acceptable makes and models; after assembling this list, the consumer conducts some informal research to narrow the list to a few makes and models, and then visits these dealerships. Fig. 7.3 illustrates this process.

The marketer can influence the consumer using a variety of means at each of these stages. For example, informal research may involve reading automotive magazines, responding to offers for marketer-supplied information, or talking to current owners of a particular make of car. The IMC program could include public relations directed to automotive magazines with the goal of receiving favorable editorial coverage; videotapes or other informational offerings; and direct mail to current owners intended to reinforce the purchase decision, keep the owner informed of new models, and perhaps even offer incentives for recommending the car to others. In the dealership, displays might reinforce learning to which the consumer was exposed in earlier stages, such as by featuring favorable press reports in dealership display materials.

The need to create custom models applies to packaged goods, as well, even though most general purchase process models were developed with packaged goods in mind. For example, the purchase process for a particular household cleaning product, drain opener, might proceed as shown Fig. 7.4. At least two possible IMC program tactics are suggested by unique

FIG. 7.3. Consumer purchase decision process for automobiles.

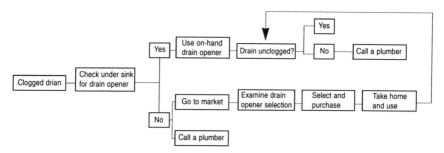

FIG. 7.4. Consumer purchase decision process for drain opener.

aspects of this purchase decision process: first, the benefit (to the marketer and the consumer) of having the drain opener already on hand implies communications that would encourage consumers to prestock the brand. Second, the point at which the consumer decides whether to go to the store or call a plumber is a critical one; if the marketer can intercept the consumer at this point (or communicate messages that the consumer will recall at this point), it might be possible to influence some consumers to go to the store instead of calling a plumber. (Of course, the decision at the store is critical as well, and calls for communications at point of sale. However, these types of communications are not as unique to drain openers, and would likely be considered even if a more standard process were assumed.)

The strategist at this point will have identified a number of different audiences for the communications, defined based on their stage in the purchase cycle. Ideally, not only will the stages have been identified, but there will be some estimates of the size of each of these groups. This information will be helpful later, when decisions about resource allocation must be made.

STEP THREE: IDENTIFYING MESSAGES AND COMMUNICATIONS VEHICLES FOR EACH TARGET

Here, the strategist must delve into the mind of the consumer and examine beliefs, attitudes and motivations. This examination is not unlike that undertaken in the course of developing advertising strategies. The principle differences with IMC strategy development are that many separate targets must be analyzed, as already identified in Steps one and two, and not only should messages be identified, but the strategist has the challenge (or should we say "opportunity"?) of selecting among many communications vehicles those that are best able to reach and persuade the target.

In considering communications vehicles, many factors will come into play. As in the selection of advertising media, the percentage of target audience individuals who are reached by the vehicle and the cost efficiency associated with this reach will be among the principle considerations.

The extent to which each vehicle reaches the target audience during those times at which they are likely to be most receptive to the message may increase the likelihood of their attending to the message. The concept of "apertures of opportunity," (DDB Needham Media Bulletin, 1990; DDB Needham Worldwide Manual, 1991), deals with the idea that consumers will be most receptive to messages that reach them when they are in situations in which they have a need for the benefit provided by the brand or in a frame of mind in which that benefit will appeal to them: "The carefully orchestrated coming together of receptive consumers, of vehicles which have places in those consumers' lifestyles, and of messages those consumers find relevant, attention-grabbing and persuasive translates to effectiveness" (DDB Needham Worldwide Manual, 1991, p. 9).

White and Thompson gave many examples of media vehicles and media buys that are more effective in reaching certain apertures than would be a traditional media plan that seeks only cost efficiencies in reaching the target, without regard for time, place, or frame of mind.

This concept applies equally well to the consideration of communications vehicles in an IMC program. In fact, there are far more opportunities to reach audiences "in aperture" when considering all of the communication vehicles beyond traditional media. For example, in-store displays are a good way to reach shoppers who are making last-minute decisions on what to cook for dinner; messages on litter receptacles can be effective as part of a recycling campaign.

The challenge for the strategist is to identify—from an almost over-whelming array of options—those vehicles best suited to the strategic tasks implied by the stage of the purchase process and the intended message. To help strategists address this challenge the authors developed, for DDB Needham, a database containing detailed descriptions of over 200 communication tools. These tools include available communications vehicles from the disciplines of advertising, direct marketing, promotion, public relations, and package design. Each tool is categorized based on a series of dimensions, including:

- The stage in the purchase process for which the communications tool is best suited (e.g., outdoor advertising creates awareness; sampling encourages trial; direct mail to current customers can be used to encourage repeat purchases).
- In what type of locations the target is reached by the tool (e.g., at home, at work, at the market, etc.).

- What types of activities the target is likely to be engaged in when reached by the tool (e.g., relaxing, exercising, working, parenting, shopping, etc.).
- Types of target audiences that can be reached using the tool (e.g., demographic groups, product usage groups, lifestyle groups, etc.).
- Whether it reaches broad or narrow audiences.
- The amount of information, or level of detail, that can be effectively communicated.
- The types of creative elements from an IMC program that can be carried by the tool (e.g., logos, theme lines, music, celebrity spokespeople, animated characters, etc.).

This database can be used by strategists who know what they want to accomplish and are searching for communications tools that might be appropriate for the task. Strategists who don't have such a database can, nonetheless, use similar strategic dimensions to evaluate communications vehicles to determine their appropriateness for certain types of targets and messages.

STEP FOUR: RESOURCE ALLOCATION

Anyone who has made it to this stage of the plan has learned that the problem is not a dearth of potential targets, messages, or communications vehicles by which those messages might be sent to those targets. In fact, the problem at this stage of the planning process is to determine how to allocate the available resources across a set of options far too broad to be covered with the existing resources.

Typically, marketers who embark on IMC plans have previously allocated resources according to broad disciplines such as advertising and direct marketing. Because we advocate assigning resources to targets, and to specific communications tools that will reach those targets (rather than to the classic marketing disciplines, per se), we suggest a zero-based budgeting approach, at least for the first year of the IMC program.

Unfortunately, budget allocation, like so much of marketing communications field, is an inexact science. The strategist will rarely be able to anticipate precisely the rate of return of investing more money in a certain vehicle to the exclusion of another. In their book, *The Logic of Priorities*, Saaty and Vargus (1982) described the "analytic hierarchy process," a system by which complex allocations of resources can be made, even when the exact outcomes of spending in any one area are uncertain. The basic framework of this model, applied to resource allocation for IMC programs, suggests a series of inquiries such as the following:

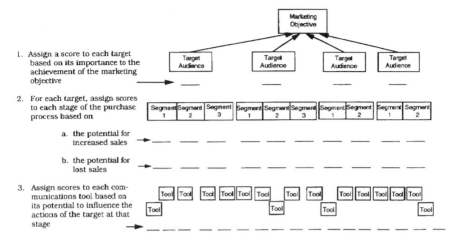

1. Assign a score to each target based on its importance to the achievement of the marketing objective

2. For each target, assign scores to each stage of the purchase process based on

    a. the potential for increased sales

    b. the potential for lost sales

3. Assign scores to each communications tool based on its potential to influence the actions of the target at that stage

FIG. 7.5.   Resource allocation model.

1. Given the marketing objective, what is the relative importance of each target audience segment (consumer and nonconsumer)?
2. For each target audience:
   a. What is the relative importance of each stage of the purchase process in terms of potential increased sales?
   b. What is the relative importance of each stage in terms of potential lost sales?
3. For each stage of the purchase process, what is the relative likelihood that each communications tool under consideration will effectively reach and persuade target audience individuals?

At this point, every potential communications tool can be assigned a value, as shown in Fig. 7.5. Then the cost efficiencies of each tool are considered, along with potential synergies, to arrive at an overall budget allocation.

Of course, budget allocation is never this simple. This framework, however, can provide some general guidance to the strategist who must, working with extremely incomplete information, arrive at recommendations as to how to spend the available marketing resources.

EVALUATING PROGRAM EFFECTIVENESS

To manage the IMC planning process most effectively, the strategist needs feedback on the effectiveness of the programs that are implemented. When it comes to obtaining evaluations of IMC programs, most marketers rely on one or more of the following:

- Overall sales results.
- Tracking studies, which measure brand awareness, consumer attitudes, and so on, but generally on an overall, market-level basis.
- Individual evaluations of some program elements (such as direct mail and promotions), but not others.

Few have found ways to measure the results of the program overall (separate from other marketplace influences) and to also isolate the effects of individual program elements. There are research techniques that can, to some greater or lesser degree, provide these types of information. For example, continuous tracking systems can determine the effectiveness of an advertising campaign in achieving awareness and attitude shift; Communicus evaluations can quantify and isolate the effect of advertising and other major program components. Neither of these approaches has, to date, achieved widespread usage in the evaluation of IMC programs.

Both of these methodologies can be applied to specific IMC programs in market; neither claims to offer general rules to guide the marketer in advance of the development of a program. However, marketers who are serious about developing a body of knowledge about the effectiveness of their own IMC programs and those of their competitors can conduct custom research to learn what works in a particular category and with a particular program.

THE CREATIVE COMPONENT

Some of the most visible successes in IMC have been programs that were based on a highly creative idea that was then "exploded" out into a complete program, reaching several target audiences, at varying purchase process stages, and with a great number of communications tools.

In fact, the strategic approach described earlier should not limit the creation of novel ideas for IMC programs. Sometimes, during the process of strategy development, someone will have an idea that will influence the rest of the plan. Other times, a new idea that emerges during the executional phase—after the strategic development is complete—may suggest, for example, new influencer targets or new communications tools. When this occurs, the planners should be willing to reopen the strategic examination and, if warranted, make changes in the plan and in the resource allocations.

SUMMARY

A strategic plan for IMC can be of great value for the marketer, in that it can improve the effectiveness of the program, and the efficiency with which the program gets developed. Such a plan can ensure that all of the communications tools utilized have a clear role to play in the achievement of the marketing objective, and that the resources are allocated based on their likely ability to contribute, instead of on historical or political factors.

Although the creation of an IMC plan is not easy, and requires a great deal of thought and analysis, it can be useful in the communication and consensus that emerges among the groups involved in the development of the plan.

An overview of one approach to the strategic development suggests that such a plan can be created through:

Market analysis: Examination of all of the audiences and factors that contribute to the success of the brand.

Consumer behavior analysis: A multi-audience analysis, similar to what advertising strategists are accustomed to carrying out for a single audience, to determine the best ways to motivate individual consumers and other audience members.

A combination quantitative and judgmental approach to resource allocation.

Much of the research and study that has, in the past, been devoted to consumer behavior and advertising communications effects can be applied to IMC program development. However, three areas in which IMC strategists have little relevant research to guide them are:

The selection of tools, from a wide array of available options, that will best suit different audiences and communications objectives.

Quantitative comparisons of different tools, based on reach, communications effectiveness, and cost efficiency.

Feedback mechanisms that can be implemented by the marketer to determine the contributions of individual program elements to the success of an overall IMC program.

Until strategists have better research in these areas, the final stages of the development of IMC plans will remain solidly in the venue of "art"; ultimately, the tool selection and resource allocation phases of IMC planning should be part art, part science.

Although a great deal of work remains before systematic IMC planning processes are accepted and used by the majority of IMC marketers, we hope that the framework that we have described can play some small part in the evolution of the planning process from chaotic to systematic.

REFERENCES

DDB Needham Media Bulletin. (1990, May). Opening up aperture: A study of commercial environment. Chicago: Media Research Department, DDB Needham.

DDB Needham Worldwide Manual. (1991, April). New York: DDB Needham.

Saaty, T. L., & Vargus, L. G. (1982). *The logic of priorities: Application in business, health, and transportation*. Boston: Kluwer-Nijhoff.

8 Integrated Marketing Communication: Examining Planning and Executional Considerations

Lisa A. Petrison
Paul Wang
Northwestern University

INTRODUCTION

Integrated marketing — or the idea that all the marketing activities conducted by a particular company should be consistent or coordinated — is hardly a new concept. The issue has been a recurring theme in the marketing industry for at least 25 years, and last became of particular interest in the mid-1970s, when the theory of some practitioners was that rather than sticking with only one activity (such as advertising or direct marketing), maximum effectiveness could be obtained by combining a variety of approaches (4).

The issue of integration has reemerged during the past few years, at least in part because the decline in marketing dollars being spent on advertising has left many professionals in that area scrambling for ways to maintain business. For example, a number of major advertising agencies have committed to integration, and have begun to explore ways to offer services like sales promotion, direct marketing, and public relations to existing or potential clients (26, 30). Northwestern University's Advertising Department changed its name to the Integrated Advertising/Marketing Communications Department (21, 33). Stories in the trade press and conferences for marketing professionals also have dealt extensively with the subject (6, 7, 14, 19).

Despite all the sound and fury over integrated marketing, however, few companies have done much to change the way they actually do business. Most of the newly "integrated" advertising agencies have stated that they have received little new business from clients wanting to take advantage of all these services. In addition, although a few corporations have reported

153

success in getting marketing areas to work together better, most major corporations are still organized and run basically the same as they have been for years, with brand managers supervising some of the promotional activities, and with specialists in direct marketing, public relations, sales promotion, personal selling, and advertising continuing to handle their own functions (3, 12, 15).

This chapter looks at some of the reasons why marketers have been relatively slow to implement integrated marketing, and examines the true usefulness of integrated marketing for today's businesses.

INTEGRATED MARKETING: PLANNING OR EXECUTIONAL?

Although integrated marketing is often assumed to refer to one basic concept, it actually refers to two very distinct ideas. The first interpretation—which might be called *executional integration*—stresses consistency between communications messages. According to this view, because the customer does not distinguish among advertising, sales promotion, direct mail, public relations, personal selling, and packaging, delivering different messages to consumers through different channels can become confusing and, thereby, dilute effectiveness. Executional (or message) integration is typically achieved by using the same benefit, tone, characters, themeline, logo, or other executional elements in all consumer communications (9, 28).

An alternate view—which might be called *planning integration*—suggests that in order to maximize efficiency and effectiveness, marketers need to use each type of communications tool to its best advantage. This type of "thinking" integration suggests that at many companies, functions like public relations and advertising have become too isolated from one another, and that this isolation may result in overall marketing programs that are not as effective as they could be. Planning integration, therefore, proposes that all marketing activities for a product need to be coordinated in order to ensure that they are in line with the overall strategy for the product (18).

Executional integration and planning integration are, therefore, extremely dissimilar concepts—so much so that companies may very easily do one but not the other. For example, it is quite possible that a company could require that all communications use the same logo or themeline, even if all of its communications departments are isolated from one another and work very little on joint strategies. On the other hand, a company in which all customer communications conform to an overall strategic plan may produce executions that end up looking very different from one another—perhaps, for example, in order to target different types of customers.

The American Association of Advertising Agencies (4As) attempts to cover both of these concepts in its definition of integrated marketing. According to the 4As, integrated marketing is:

> A concept of marketing communications planning [planning integration] that recognizes the added value of a comprehensive plan [planning integration] that evaluates the strategic roles of a variety of communications disciplines [planning integration] — for example, general advertising, direct response, sales promotion and public relations — and combines these disciplines to provide clarity [executional integration], consistency [executional integration] and maximum communications impact [planning or executional integration].

Although this definition is a composite of the two views on integration, authors and speakers on the subject have generally focused on only one or the other of the two ideas. It is very important to distinguish between the two, however, because each type has its own advantages, disadvantages, and implementation barriers for companies considering making it a reality.

EXECUTIONAL INTEGRATION AND CONFLICTING TRENDS

On the surface, the concept of executional integration appears to make sense. Maintaining a consistent, nonconfusing image should help companies to stand out in today's cluttered marketing environment, and should help consumers to better understand exactly what they can expect from a particular product.

Because the notion is so simple, therefore, it may be seen as surprising that more companies haven't fully integrated their executions. Most of the academics and practitioners who have addressed this issue have suggested that companies do not integrate executionally either because they don't understand the value of doing so, or because communications functions are so decentralized that specialists are unwilling or unable to reach agreement.

However, another reason that executional integration has been slow to catch on is because it conflicts with a number of major marketing trends, including the following.

Micromarketing.   Most marketers today understand that not everyone in the United States can be sold on the same product with the same message. Consumers in different regions of the country or different types of neighborhoods often have different needs and wants, as well as different prior knowledge about the product (1). For example, a popular dish in Cincinnati is "Chili Five Ways," an unusual chili flavored with cinnamon and chocolate and served with spaghetti, beans, onions, and cheese. Vendor

Skyline promotes the product with commercials showing Cincinnati land-
marks and reminding consumers that Skyline is part of the city's heritage.
When Skyline opened restaurants in other cities, however, it advertised the
product differently, as a change of pace from other fast food. Obviously,
these executions were not integrated, but they did help Skyline to achieve
successful growth.

Database or Relationship Marketing.   One often-cited advantage of
database marketing is that consumers may be targeted with different
communications messages, based on their individual needs and wants. For
example, Mercedes might inform parents of young children of their cars'
safety record, while promoting the power and prestigious image of the cars
to young single men. Through the use of these nonintegrated messages,
therefore, different types of prospects may be sold on the exact same car,
when one message never would have convinced all of them.

Niche Marketing.   Thirty or forty years ago, U.S. consumers were
relatively homogeneous — they looked alike, acted alike, and purchased
alike. Today, however, consumers are much more individualistic, and may
look for different attributes in the same product category. This has resulted
in product proliferation — with each entry appealing to a specific niche — but
it also means that products may be promoted in different ways to appeal to
different kinds of consumers. A marketer like McDonald's, which must
appeal to a broad range of consumers to be successful, may well find itself
creating a great variety of communications efforts, all of which look very
different from one another.

Globalization.   After a few tries at "global marketing," in which one
advertising campaign was used for a variety of countries, most marketers
realized that different approaches are often needed to market products
overseas. This means that U.S. consumers traveling abroad are likely to
encounter messages for products that are much different than the ones they
see at home.

Decentralization.   In recent years, marketing responsibilities at many
companies have shifted from general product managers to regional or
segment managers, to better target niche groups of consumers. However, as
responsibilities become decentralized, the likelihood that all messages will
be consistent goes down considerably.

Image Changing.   Some brands are able to maintain a remarkably
consistent image over time. Others, however, pursue a new image or
strategic direction every year, often accompanied by a switch to a new

advertising agency. An image that changes over time can be just as confusing to the consumer as different slogans or logos in advertising or sales promotion and, therefore, may negate any positive effects generated by integration at a specific point in time.

Behavioral Mapping. Sophisticated marketers understand that consumers go through different stages in their decisions to purchase products — for example, awareness, knowledge, purchase, trial, evaluation, and acceptance or rejection. They also realize that different promotional devices work best on different stages of that process, and may use mapping techniques to allow them to use appropriate tools to address each stage (32, 35). For example, McDonald's relied on public relations to create awareness of its McLean sandwich, and then used advertising to reinforce the message of good taste (2). Eight years ago, Apple Computer launched its new Macintosh computer during the Superbowl with the memorable "1984" commercial, which addressed only awareness and didn't show the product at all. The Superbowl ads were preceded by detailed product demonstrations to industry leaders, and followed with a lengthy spread in news magazines that increased knowledge by supplying detailed knowledge about the product. Obviously, these messages weren't exactly alike, but they were used intelligently to accomplish important goals needed to sell the product.

Corporate Diversification. Corporations are getting bigger and more geographically dispersed than ever before. Many of these large companies — such as IBM or Kraft — sell many products to different customers under the same brand name. Although messages about these varied products can be united to some degree with a graphic or visual identity, the different and, perhaps, contradictory goals of these varied products can make total executional integration impossible.

The presence of these kinds of trends will inevitably make executional integration more difficult for many corporations. The result is that, rather than viewing integration as an all-or-nothing proposition, most companies will have to evaluate how much to integrate on an individualistic basis.

EXECUTIONAL INTEGRATION: HOW MUCH IS RIGHT

Despite the often-cited advantages of executional integration, insisting that all messages delivered by a particular company be 100% alike is not always possible, or even desirable. The barriers cited in the previous section obviously may make it more difficult for some companies to integrate successfully. In addition, if all messages are completely integrated, a loss of flexibility can result. Total integration means that a company will be less able to target different messages to different customers, and to react quickly to competitive pressures. Also, "insistent" integration may prevent marketers from using each medium to its fullest. Even within advertising, media such as TV and radio may require vastly different approaches to be used effectively. Different types of communications tools — such as public relations, advertising, and sales promotion — work even more differently. Companies, therefore, need to determine how much to integrate on an individual basis. They may begin by answering some of the following questions:

How Diversified Are My Customers and My Customers' Need and Wants?   Integration of all messages makes sense when the product has one clear-cut benefit that appeals to a broad spectrum of consumers — for example, in the case of Pepsi-Cola, good taste. It also can be useful in the case of niche brands — for example, a cereal like Lucky Charms can achieve success by appealing to only a small fraction of all consumers. Some companies, however, must by definition sell to a wide range of customers with varying needs and wants in order to be successful. For instance, Kentucky Fried Chicken (now called KFC) must appeal to lovers of greasy fried chicken as well as to health-conscious consumers if it is to reverse share declines. A single message may not be able to do that.

How Many Products Are Sold Under My Brand Name?   A brand that has just one product, like Absolut Vodka, usually has little problem maintaining a consistent image. It's harder, however, for a company like Citicorp, which markets to corporate and retail customers a wide variety of products and services, from checking accounts to mergers and acquisitions advice to small-business loans. A diversified customer base may well mean that messages need to be more varied.

How High Is Consumer Involvement in My Product?   For a low-involvement product, such as chewing gum, it may be necessary to deliver one clear, consistent message throughout all communication. However, for products that prompt higher involvement, the consumer may be willing to understand a more complicated message. Therefore, it may be possible to get across different points through different channels and still have a product that makes sense to the consumer.

How Well Do Consumers Know My Product Already?   New products — or products that consumers don't think about much, or that have a limited communications budget — are probably best off conveying one consistent image across all communications channels. However, some products' benefits are so well known that it's possible to get across a new message without compromising the old one. For instance, McDonald's already has a strong reputation as a restaurant that is clean and provides fast service. Therefore, the company may also be able to emphasize its commitment to the environment through some promotion channels while still maintaining its existing image with consumers.

How Complicated Is the Buying Process? Especially with major purchases, it may be necessary to tell the product story little by little, over time, using each communications message to its fullest. For instance, in the case of Apple's Macintosh, awareness was developed first, followed by knowledge building. Whether or not they try to be integrated, companies may often find that they can generate the most effective results by communicating different messages to consumers at different times in their decision and purchase cycles.

How Can I Use Each Communications Tool to Its Best Advantage? Each of the promotional functions is generally seen to have its own key advantages. A common view, for example, is that advertising builds image; public relations affects credibility; sales promotion influences short-term behavior; direct marketing delivers a complex, targeted message; and personal selling allows for two-way communication. However each function is described, each accomplishes things differently, and is better than others at certain aspects of the communications process. Forcing each of the functions to look the same and to convey exactly the same message can, therefore, result in an overall loss of effectiveness, explaining part of the reason why some professionals in the fields of sales promotion, public relations, or direct marketing have sometimes been resistant to the idea of integrated marketing (8, 10, 13, 17, 23, 24, 27).

The point of these types of questions is to suggest that executional integration is more complicated than just using the same typeface or the same logo or the same shade of blue in all marketing communications. Instead, integration can have a strong effect on the strategic components of the brand, and should, therefore, be approached cautiously rather than blindly.

Intelligent marketers will, of course, make certain that their answers to these types of questions do not lead them to create contradictory images for their products — such as when Cadillac says it's a luxury car through some communications channels and then trumpets price discounts through other channels. However, marketers should realize that products can have a variety of benefits, consumers can have a variety of needs, and communications channels can have a variety of strengths. Using each type of communication to its best advantage may lead to a campaign that doesn't look completely integrated, but nonetheless is effective.

OVERCOMING THE BARRIERS
TO INTEGRATED PLANNING

Although companies may decide that total executional integration isn't always beneficial, most managers do recognize the advantages of integrated planning, which suggests that all parts of the communications mix be coordinated to work together to form an effective, cohesive whole. Integrated planning is important because it allows the organization to maximize its potential and be as effective as possible in its marketing operations. A fully integrated planning operation may also have the advantage of allowing managers to determine more easily how much executional integration is necessary, and of allowing consistent communications to be more easily developed.

At many smaller companies and at firms with one core product line, managers may even claim that they have been doing this kind of integrated marketing all along. At other companies, however, the inherent structure of the organization has created roadblocks to making integrated planning a reality. At many companies, for example, communications responsibilities are scattered throughout the organization and, therefore, it can be difficult to ensure that everyone is attuned to the same goals and game plan.

Therefore, companies that are decentralized often need to begin by taking a top-down approach to developing an integrated marketing plan. This is generally most successful when top management sets the marketing and communications objectives for the company as a whole, and then works with functional managers on ways to use various communications tools to accomplish those objectives. What is most important is not that a variety of different types of vehicles are used, but that they are being used appropriately to meet the company's objectives (5).

In addition, it can also be helpful to have one person, or one team of people, coordinating the whole effort, from personal selling to direct marketing to public relations. It is not always necessary that this person or team have all communications staff reporting to them—that is likely to be infeasible at many companies, especially at those in which functions like direct marketing or public relations serve as a resource for many different brands. However, it can help if team leaders are present to develop and coordinate a plan that uses all of the available tools effectively.

This kind of responsibility is often seen as belonging to the brand manager. However, brand managers at many companies complete only brief sales training and know relatively little about areas such as direct marketing or public relations. Therefore, they are not always qualified to develop a comprehensive campaign that uses each of these disciplines to its fullest (29, 31).

If this is to change, marketing managers will have to become more familiar with all aspects of the communications mix. Although adding specialty courses to MBA programs may help, it may also be useful for companies to encourage marketing managers to divert from the brand management fast track to gain more hands-on experience in a variety of disciplines (25).

Another major issue is compensation. Many agencies or communications departments tend to be rewarded heavily on the amount and type of work that they handle themselves, and thus balk at sharing their customers or responsibilities with other subsidiaries or departments. If integration is to work, people must be rewarded for working well with other areas, and for sharing business with them.

Another problem is integrating communications within the organization. At companies in which reorganization is not possible or desirable, it is important for disparate areas to work together and to share ideas and information on a consistent basis.

This sharing of information, incidentally, would be one of the key advantages of using an integrated agency for advertising, sales promotion, direct marketing, and public relations—if that agency were organized to promote easy communications. However, many full-service agencies operate their various subsidiaries as totally separate organizations in order to be able to service competing clients, and personnel from their various subsidiaries rarely talk to one another except when absolutely necessary. Agency subsidiaries may also have internal rivalries over which section gets which fees, and may not have much respect for one another's intelligence or importance. Therefore, until these problems are resolved, it seems that the big question for clients is not whether to consolidate all their business into one agency, but rather whether all of their agencies can work together to develop a coordinated campaign (16, 22, 34).

It is also important to remember that the communication of the company's mission and message should flow throughout the entire organization, not just through the communications departments. The sales force, the department store clerk, the customer service representative, the flight attendant, or the gas station cashier is just as important—and, in many cases, more important—than advertising or direct marketing in forming customer perceptions of the company. Communications managers not only need to influence representatives to reinforce the company's communications messages, but also need to be certain that these people are capable of carrying out the image being conveyed.

EMPLOYEE RESISTANCE TO INTEGRATED PLANNING

Despite all the arguments in favor of integrated planning, many companies have had a difficult time effectively implementing the concept. One of the main problems is often employee resistance, which may be prompted by a number of key concerns, including the following

Will My Manager Understand My Specialty? Just as few marketing professionals would be enthusiastic about reporting to a manager who knows only finance, functional specialists usually don't want to be controlled by a person who doesn't understand or fully appreciate their area of expertise. This factor is often largely responsible for clashes between different agency subsidiaries, especially when advertising executives attempt to take the lead in integrated marketing programs. In order to make integration work, managers need to have at least a working knowledge of the communications areas they will supervise or coordinate, and need to establish good relationships with specialists from each area.

Will the Integrated Team Share My Goals and Culture? Different communications functions tend to have different personalities and outlooks—for example, the long-term focus of public relations versus the short-term orientation of sales promotion. Again, to circumvent problems, managers need to understand and accept the strengths and weaknesses of each discipline, and to avoid forcing all areas to conform.

Will Integration Slow Down the Process? Specialists may justifiably worry that integration may mean more layers and, therefore, lead to slower reaction times and projects that are compromised because everyone wants to make changes. For example, this may be a special concern of public relations staff, which often works on time-sensitive crisis management projects. Thus, many managers may need to strike a balance between total integration and getting projects done quickly.

What Will Happen to My Budget? Specialists who do not perceive that their managers will fully understand their functional area may worry about having their budgets unjustly slashed. Advertising and public relations departments may have additional fears that budgets will be sacrificed in favor of more short-term projects. These fears may have to be confronted before cooperation can be obtained.

Will My Job Become Less Important—or Disappear? Again, a manager who might not understand a particular field or who might be disposed against it is likely to be regarded with suspicion by experts in the field who are concerned about their own careers. Managers attempting to integrate may, therefore, have to deal with these types of fears.

Solving these kinds of people problems is never easy, and so it should not be surprising that the implementation of integrated marketing efforts has been slow in coming at many companies (11, 20). In order for progress to be made, these kinds of issues cannot be ignored, but instead must be recognized and confronted in an appropriate manner on an individual basis.

SUMMARY

Whether integrated marketing is viewed at the planning stage or the executional stage, it should not be seen as a panacea, nor as a static, concrete concept that can be applied easily and indiscriminately to all companies. Instead, it is an individualistic and often painful process that every company must explore and implement for itself.

This means that the growth of integration is likely to continue to move slowly. However, as managers begin to realize the issues involved in integration and to think about how what they're doing relates to everything else that the consumer sees, hears, and experiences about the product, they should gradually be able to implement the concepts of executional and planning integration in ways that will make a real difference to their businesses.

MANAGERIAL IMPLICATIONS

Managers who are considering pursuing integrated marketing within their own organizations need to think carefully about what they hope to achieve before they act. Managers interested in achieving message integration need to determine what other factors occurring in their organization and in the marketplace may make integration difficult, and what, if anything, will be sacrificed by the achievement of successful integration. Armed with that knowledge, managers can go about establishing the appropriate amount of integration for their particular company.

Managers who would like to achieve more planning integration also need to determine what kinds of organizational or motivational stumbling blocks are likely to present themselves. Managers should be aware that achieving more strategic integration may require major changes in the organization, such as restructuring or cross-training of personnel.

Whatever integration does occur, however, management needs to accept the responsibility for adapting the concepts of integration to their own organization, for it is only then that true benefits are likely to be obtained.

REFERENCES

(1) Aceino, M. (1991, November 19). *Case study: Kraft's micro-merchandising program — the future marketing environment today*. Presentation at Integrated Marketing Conference, Institute for International Research, Chicago.

(2) Bergold, R. (1991, June 19). *Integrating marketing communications: McDonald's*

McLean Deluxe. First Annual Symposium on Integrated Marketing Communications, Northwestern University, Evanston, IL.

(3) Caywood, C., Schultz, D., & Wang, P. (1991). *Integrated marketing communications: A survey of national consumer goods advertisers*. Unpublished paper, Northwestern University, Evanston, IL.

(4) Christian, R. C. (1978, April 9). *Professors and practitioners—partners in progress*. Presentation at 20th Annual Conference, American Academy of Advertising, Columbia, SC.

(5) Duffy, M. (1991, November 19). *Integrating new measurement tools & techniques: Building targeted marketing programs*. Presentation at Integrated Marketing Conference, Institute for International Research, Chicago.

(6) Eisenhart, T. (1990, December). Going the integrated route. *Business Marketing*, pp. 24–32.

(7) Five opinions on integrated marketing. (1991, April). *Target Marketing*, pp. 21–22.

(8) Harris, T. L. (1991, August 8). *The integration of marketing, advertising and public relations: "P's" in a pod or just a shell game*? Annual Conference, Association for Education in Journalism and Mass Communications, Boston.

(9) Integrating the execution. (1991, February). *Promo*, pp. 28–31, 41, 47.

(10) Integration and reality. (1991, March). *Promo*, pp. 6–7, 24.

(11) Juleen, G. (1991, November 19). *Case study: How declining spirits sales have integrated marketing strategies and reversed the trend*. Integrated Marketing Conference, Institute for International Research, Chicago.

(12) Koelle, M. (1991, June 19). *Integrated marketing communications: Barriers to the dream*. First Annual Symposium on Integrated Marketing Communications, Northwestern University, Evanston, IL.

(13) Lewis, H. G. (1988, November). Let them integrate with us! *Direct Marketing*, pp. 52–55, 110.

(14) Lukovitz, K. (1991, October). Get ready for one-on-one marketing. *Folio*, pp. 64–70.

(15) MacClaren, R. C. (1991, July). Clients take the lead on integration. *Promo*, pp. 1,57.

(16) Much, M. (1991, April). Can agencies deliver? *Direct*, pp. 17–18.

(17) Much, M. (1991, October). Not-so-civil war stories. *Direct*, pp. 1, 29–30.

(18) Myers, J. (1991, June 19). *What integrated marketing communications is/is not/could be*. First Annual Symposium on Integrated Marketing Communications, Northwestern University, Evanston, IL.

(19) Nash, E. L. (1983, January). Interdynamic marketing: The wave of the future in direct response. *ZIP*, pp. 4–5.

(20) Neavill, M. (1991, June 19). *Communications from the real customer's viewpoint*. First Annual Symposium on Integrated Marketing Communications, Northwestern University, Evanston, IL.

(21) Northwestern integrating ideas with new graduate program. (1991, March 1–15). *Chicago Advertising and Media*, pp. 1, 8.

(22) O'Brien, R. (1991, June 19). *Can agencies deliver integrated marketing communications*. First Annual Symposium on Integrated Marketing Communications, Northwestern University, Evanston, IL.

(23) Rapp, S. (1988, December). Beware of "integration." *Direct Marketing*, pp. 92–94.

(24) Rapp, S. (1991, July). Integrated communications: Panacea or public relations? *Direct*, p. 68.

(25) Reilly, J. (1991, Fall). The role of integrated marketing communications in brand management. *A.N.A./The Advertiser*, pp. 32–38.

(26) Reitman, J. (1991, June 19). *Integrated communications: Fantasy or the future*? First Annual Symposium on Integrated Marketing Communications, Northwestern University, Evanston, IL.

(27) Robinson, W. A. (1991, March). How to integrate media advertising and promotion. *Potentials in Marketing*, pp. 30–31.
(28) Schneider, G. J. (1991, November 19). *Case study: NEC provides a striking example of effective, integrated marketing communications.* Integrated Marketing Conference, Institute for International Research, Chicago.
(29) Schultz, D. E. (1990). *Integrating marketing communications in an age of specialization: Can it work in the U.S.A.?* Unpublished paper, Northwestern University, Evanston, IL.
(30) Schultz, D. E. (1991, November 19). *The relationship between marketers, their agencies and the media.* Integrated Marketing Conference, Institute for International Research, Chicago.
(31) Schultz, D. E., & Badger, W. (1991, June 19). *The status of integrated marketing communications in client organizations.* First Annual Symposium on Integrated Marketing Communications, Northwestern University, Evanston, IL.
(32) Stephenson, B. Y. (1991, November 19). *Data base: The foundation of an integrated marketing strategy.* Integrated Marketing Conference, Institute for International Research, Chicago.
(33) University to offer "integration" degree. (1991, March). *Promo*, p. 8.
(34) Wang, P., Nelson, H., & Bace, J. (1991, Spring). Integrated media-planning and marketing communication strategies. *Journal of Media Planning*, pp. 38–46.
(35) Wang, P., & Petrison, L. (1991, Fall). Integrated marketing and its potential effects on media planning. *Journal of Media Planning*, pp. 11–18.

9 Integrated Marketing Communication: An Organizational Perspective

David Prensky
Trenton State College

John A. McCarty
American University

James Lucas
Frankel and Company

The fields of marketing and advertising will experience some very dramatic changes in the 1990s. To a great extent, these changes relate to a shift in emphasis from mass media advertising to other forms of marketing communications, such as sales promotions, event marketing, and direct marketing. Although these other promotional activities have been a part of marketing for some time, their use has increased dramatically in recent years. Furthermore, in the past, the strategy and execution of these promotional efforts were generally considered separately from the mass media advertising efforts. Recently, however, the use of these other forms of promotion has increased to the level where it seems reasonable for there to be coordination among the marketing communications across the various channels. Therefore, the notion of integrated marketing communications has been proposed. The essence of integrated marketing communications is that a firm should make an effort to speak in one voice to consumers through the various communication channels.

The success of an integrated communications effort will ultimately depend on many things; clearly, two important areas will be the extent to which the different elements of the communication mix can indeed be designed to achieve a successful communication effort and the extent to which the marketing organizations involved in the effort can work together and efficiently to achieve this integration. A distinction, therefore, can be made between the content of integrated communications and the process of this integration.

The content of integrated communications refers to actual communication efforts, for example, how marketers develop communications across the several channels that will successfully work together and appear integrated to the consumer. These issues are unquestionably important and relate to the very heart of the matter: the ability of the marketing firm to successfully communicate to the consumer in one consistent voice.

The process of integrated communications refers to the actual coordination effort within a marketing firm or among the several marketing firms involved in the coordination. Process addresses the organizational and managerial issues that will ultimately relate to likely success of the integrated communications effort. Process is not only the question of the organizational structure, but the issues of organizational culture, power, and manager's decision processes. It is these process issues that are addressed in this chapter. Our major point is that the changing dynamics of major consumer target markets may indeed dictate an integrated approach to marketing communications, but the strategic response of much of the marketing communications industry is determined by existing organizational constraints. We provide a framework for considering the organizational issues that arise in integrated communications. Only by combining the content of integrated marketing communications with the organizational issues inherent in the integrated communications process itself can a truly integrated communication strategy be achieved. Prior to a discussion of these process issues, we provide a brief history of the factors that have led to a need for integrated marketing communications.

THE EVOLUTION OF MARKETING ORGANIZATIONS, CONSUMERS, AND COMMUNICATIONS

Marketing organizations, like other kinds of organizations, have had to adapt to be competitive in an changing environment (Tedlow, 1990). During the early stages of the industrial revolution, output was limited while efforts were concentrated on physical distribution of goods. This fragmentation era was a period in which firms could sell all that they could produce and there was no need for marketing. As firms began to maximize their production capabilities, they entered a period that Tedlow referred to as the unification era. They hired sales forces to help sell these goods to the mass market across a much wider area. The goal at that time was to shape consumer desires to fit the attributes of the product. As competition among firms developed, it became necessary for firms to concentrate on specific segments of the market. This segmentation era represented the maturing of the marketing concept. Major decisions were made only after a consideration of relevant "consumer input." In essence, the marketing firms had to have a clearer picture of who it was that was buying their products, and firms realized that it would be necessary to tailor their goods to consumer needs in order to continue to attract customers. Over time, therefore, the firm has become increasingly integrated around the marketing function.

Parallel to, although not independent of, the changes in the orientation of marketing firms, there has been a change or evolution of the consumer. There are many indications of this evolution: major shifts in demographics and lifestyles, changes in television viewing patterns, and significant changes in buying and shopping patterns (Rapp & Collins, 1992). For example, there is a greater percentage of adult women in the work force compared to 40 years ago. A majority of women in the United States are now part of the labor force, 57% of total women in 1990 (U.S. Bureau of the Census, 1991). Given this, women cannot be reached as easily as when most were at home and watching daytime television. Furthermore, as Rapp and Collins pointed out, because women as well as the men in the family are now holding full-time jobs, it can no longer be assumed that women are necessarily doing the shopping for the family.

The constitution of the household has changed as well. In the past the typical household was a married couple with children. Over the past few decades there has been an increase in the percentage of single-person households and a decline in families with more than four household members (U.S. Bureau of the Census, 1991). Therefore, it can no longer be assumed that the consumers for the majority of products are married, necessarily women, and at home during daytime television programming. These two changes in consumers, as well as other changes, have made it generally more difficult to identify the consumers of a product and successfully communicate with them.

Changes in the orientation of the marketing firms and changes in the demographics and lifestyles of consumers have coincided with variations in how marketers have communicated with consumers. There has been a proliferation of communication channels over the past several years; during that same period some of the traditional communication channels have been used less. The increases in channels relate to technological advances as well as the apparent difficulty in reaching consumers via traditional approaches.

There has been a decline in the use of network television advertising over the past several decades; cable television and syndicated television advertising has increased over that same period. Technological advances have led to the building of databases by many marketing firms. A recent survey (Donnelley Marketing Inc., 1992) indicated that over half the firms surveyed are currently building databases of consumers. Given this, direct marketing is beginning to be used by a wide variety of marketers.

One of the most significant changes that has occurred in recent years is the increase in the importance of trade promotions and consumer promotions relative to media advertising. The percentage of the promotional dollar spent on advertising declined from 44% to 28% from 1981 to 1990, whereas trade promotions increased from 34% of the promotional dollar to 48% of promotions over that same period of time (Donnelley Marketing Inc., 1992). There was a slight increase in the use of sales promotions over the 10-year period.

One may be quick to assume that the increase in the use of sales promotions, particularly that of trade promotions, has eroded the expenditures on advertising. That is, promotions have grown at the expense of advertising. The available data do not indicate that this is the case. Although the importance of trade promotions has grown relative to media advertising, advertising as a percentage of the gross national product has remained roughly the same over the past 30 years, ranging between 1.8% of the GNP to 2.4% over that period (Coen, 1992; U.S. Bureau of the Census, 1991). This ratio was roughly the same in 1960 as it was in 1990.

Therefore, although there have been changes in how marketers have chosen to communicate with consumers, mass media advertising is still an important part of the picture. Moreover, the nature of the changes have been more subtle than the common misperceptions suggest. Beliefs in the extremity of the shifts in promotional activity, however, have raised fears in the communications industry and, thus, helped develop the interest in integrated marketing communications. Therefore, although the changes are subtle, they have prompted a move toward the idea of integrated communications, a concept that may have value regardless of the relative weight given to mass media advertising, sales promotion, direct marketing, and so on.

INTEGRATED MARKETING COMMUNICATION

The evolution of the marketing firm, consumers, and communications has brought about the need for an integrated communications effort. Because the efforts of many firms are integrated around the marketing function, it seems reasonable that the communication efforts should also be integrated and coordinated. Given the proliferation of choices and communications facing today's consumer, it is crucial to present the proper brand image in a coherent and consistent manner. The move to integrated marketing communication can be considered as an adaptation on the part of the marketing firms to a changing environment, the environmental changes being related to the evolution of the consumer and to advances in technology that have increased the attractiveness of diverse promotional activities. Although it may be very clear that a concept such as integrated marketing communication is necessary and makes good sense, its implementation may be a very difficult matter. This may be particularly true now, because the environment has changed very rapidly and dramatically. In the past, the changes in the marketing environment were slow and marketing firms could react over time to these changes. Presently, marketing firms are faced with rapidly changing environments and organizational structures are typically slow to react to changes. Therefore, although the need for integrated communications is clearly present, many marketing firms are hampered by existing organizational structures. For better or worse, integrated marketing communications will be coordinated through these existing organizational structures for the near future.

Within the marketing industry, there are differing points of view as to how it integrated marketing communications might best be accomplished. At a basic level, most would agree that integrated communications involves coordinating all of the communication efforts for a particular brand. That is, it would involve speaking with consumers in one voice through the different marketing communication channels.

Although there may be agreement on what the basic goal of integrated communications is, there are numerous organizational approaches that are possible to achieve this end. A study of marketing managers of client organizations conducted by Duncan (1991) clearly indicated differences in opinion about how integration should be achieved. Among respondents who were familiar with the term *integrated marketing communication* (59% of the total), 7% believed that integrating the communications was a matter of first the client determining the communication strategies, and then each of the communication functions would be executed by a different firm (advertising agency, direct marketing company, etc.). Twenty-one percent believed that the client would work with one agency, collectively setting the strategies, and then this agency would execute all of the communication functions. Thirty-five percent of the respondents believed that the client and all of its agencies would collectively set the strategies, and then the individual functions would be executed by the specific agencies. Finally, 24% believed that the client alone would determine the communication strategies, then assign specific functions to individual agencies to execute, and expect these agencies to communicate with one another during the execution of the strategy.

We build on the four different methods of organization that Duncan identified by briefly describing the relationships that will be required of the communications firms under each method, and then discuss the impact of these relationships on the strategic goals of these communications firms. The four integrated communications methods suggest very different intraorganizational and interorganizational relationships. The first approach will likely affect relationships within the client organization, but the various agencies will conduct their business in a similar fashion as in the past. The task of integrating the communications is within the client organization and the client would develop the marketing communication strategy, decide on the mix of promotional activities, then simply contract with various agencies to accomplish the communication tasks. As indicated, the second possibility maintains a traditional primary relationship between the client and one agency (in the past this has typically been the advertising agency); however, the agency is expected to engage in a much wider range of promotional activities than has customarily been true in the past. Currently, many agencies are beginning to provide these services either by acquisition or developing the expertise from within. This concept of implementing integrated marketing communications calls for major organizational changes within the agency and a different way of thinking about the different types of communications. For example, marketing professionals in advertising agencies have traditionally considered sales promotions, direct marketing, and so on to be in a subordinate position to mass media advertising. Both the third and fourth methods of implementing integrated marketing communications suggest a level of communication among various agencies that has typically not occurred in the past. The third method suggests that agencies involved in different forms of communications activity will be involved in developing strategy. In the fourth method, the agencies may not interact at the level of strategy, but they are expected to communicate with one another as the strategy is carried out.

Regardless of which of these methods is utilized by a firm, it is clear that the integrated communications effort will be coordinated by organizations that presently exist. Firms are in the process of changing to accommodate the emerging need of integrated communications. There has been a consolidation of marketing communication firms, both within and among types. Within the various types of communications providers, mergers have resulted in increasing size and scale of the leaders within advertising, public relations, promotions, direct marketing, corporate image, and design. Among the types, mergers have resulted in integrated marketing service conglomerates, with the largest firms merging firms from different specialties in order to offer "one-stop shopping." The traditional boundaries among providers of each of these communication mix elements is blurring, with examples of ad agencies developing promotional programs, public relation firms developing corporate ad campaigns, and Michael Ovitz and his Creative Artists Agency producing Coca-Cola advertising in the place of its traditional advertising agency doing so.

Although marketing communication firms clearly recognize that the content of marketing communications must become more integrated, how does the process of developing and implementing integrated communications affect its content? We adopt the view that the process of developing integrated communications has a significant impact on the content. In many instances, the characteristics of the firm's organizational structure, culture, and politics dictate the content of the integrated communications that it produces. Against the backdrop of the firm's own strategic goals, these organizational characteristics will have a significant impact on how the firm's managers think about integrated marketing communications. Therefore, the characteristics will have important consequences on the content of the integrated communication strategies that such managers develop. We discuss the firm's goals, its structure, culture, and politics, and how its managers think about integrated communications in some detail before concluding with the implications for the development of successful integrated communications programs.

THE FIRM'S OWN STRATEGIC GOALS

Marketing communications firms are in business both to serve their clients and to further their own business interests. All such firms, whether in advertising, sales promotion, public relations, direct marketing, corporate image, or package design, must work both to satisfy the client and to achieve a level of profit sufficient to maintain their own operations. In this context, both the interorganizational relationships among communications firms and the organizational characteristics of the individual firm will have a significant impact on the content of integrated communications strategies. For a firm that must work together with other firms to provide needed integrated communications, these interorganizational relationships with the other communications providers will be of great importance. Organizational characteristics will be most important to a firm that seeks to provide the full range of different communication functions internally.

The goal of maintaining profitability and stability will influence the firm's interorganizational relationships with other firms that work to provide different forms of communications for a client. Each firm, although considering the most effective communications method to achieve the client goals, will clearly be motivated to emphasize whatever form of communication they are able to provide. We would expect, for example, that an advertising agency would emphasize consumer advertising to achieve brand awareness and long-term positive attitudes toward a product. At the same time, a sales promotion agency would stress the importance of promotional methods to gain trial and thus influence long-term behavior directly. Such motivation stems both from the intimate knowledge of the familiar form of communication and from self-interest.

A firm will try to maintain its own profitability and stability in the face of conflict with other communications providers and changes in revenue as the communications mix changes. As we discussed earlier, there have been significant changes in the relative importance of various communications channels as new channels have risen to prominence. Organizationally, these changes have required more interorganizational coordination to satisfy clients' complete communications needs. The typical marketing communications program now requires that each firm maintain relationships with a number of other types of firms. Those interorganizational relationships must be managed carefully to ensure that they do not deteriorate into potentially destructive conflicts.

Many communications firms try to avoid such conflicts and capture all of the communications business of their clients. To do so, they provide a number of the communications functions necessary for an integrated communications strategy. There are two major alternative approaches that will support greater integration of communications. One is in-house development of functional groups to provide the wide variety of communications services that the client needs. Firms that specialize in a particular form of communication have created internal groups to provide other required communication services. For example, an advertising agency can develop its own expertise in direct marketing, or a sales promotion firm can create a unit to provide traditional advertising services. The second approach is growth through mergers with providers of other types of communications services. Examples of such mergers have usually been advertising agencies buying other providers and integrating them, or agency holding companies buying other providers and putting them under the corporate umbrella. Both of these alternative approaches will help achieve higher profit or greater financial stability, but the benefits to the client may not be the motivation for such actions.

Advertising agencies that acquire sales promotions firms or develop their own in-house promotional groups are instructive examples. The development of the promotional function represents the agency's attempt to maintain profitability and power by maintaining its share of total communication spending in the face of proportional shifts from advertising to promotion. Although the promised integration between advertising and promotion may also benefit the client, the relative importance of the two motives is unclear.

This motivation to achieve their own strategic business goals provides the context for our examination of the effects of the firm's interorganizational and organizational structure, culture, and politics on its managers' cognitive decision processes. Whether we are considering a firm that specializes in a particular communications form or one that offers several forms to its clients, these issues have a tremendous impact on the content of the integrated communications that the firm produces. The nature of the interorganizational relationships, including formal arrangements, cultural traditions, and political battles; as well as the firm's internal structure, culture, and politics, have a powerful effect on how managers think. How managers think, both the way that they view their world and the heuristics that they employ for decision making, strongly affect the communications strategies that they produce. We now outline these issues and their impact as a way of summarizing the argument of our chapter.

STRUCTURE, CULTURE, AND POLITICS

Interorganizational and organizational structural arrangements, organizational culture, and political power applied in the context of interorganizational and intraorganizational struggles will all have a significant impact on the development of the content of the integrated communications program. Although structure, culture, and politics may be analytically distinct, they are strongly interrelated in actual marketing communications work. These factors have much of their effect on content by influencing how managers think about the development and implementation of marketing communications.

Structure

Interorganizational structure will have its effect through the flows of resources and information that occur among the firms that are providing the communications services. The role of the client and the working arrangements that they mandate will provide much of the structure. The integration of work flows among the various firms will significantly influence the effectiveness and efficiency with which the communications program is created.

Within a firm, standard operating procedures; the centralization, formalization, and complexity of relationships in the firm (Fredrickson, 1986; Ruekert, Walker, & Roering, 1985); and the nature of the compensation system (Jaworski, 1988) will all be important. Relationships within the firm provide some of the best anecdotal evidence of the successful integration of various forms of communications. Many communications professionals have had the experience of meeting fellow employees from different communications specialties for the first time at a client meeting. This certainly does little to demonstrate to clients the coordination necessary for true integrated communications. Obviously, compensation will also affect the nature of communications integration. For example, advertising managers will emphasize advertising, not sales promotion or public relations, if their compensation is based solely on media spending and not linked to fees earned by other specialties in the firm.

Culture

The differences in organizational culture will obviously affect the interrelationships among firms of various types as they collaborate on a communications program. Such differences will operate similarly on the various functions within a firm. Much of the effect of differing cultures will operate through the different cognitive processes employed by the managers working on the program. Culture influences underlying assumptions and actions of managers (Harris, 1989; Pitre & Sims, 1986) as well as affecting the decision-making process itself (Sapienza, 1985). Such cultural influences are powerful, resulting both from distinct training and work experiences as well as the interrelated structural and political differences.

Cultural influences are best illustrated by recalling the criteria used to evaluate the work experience of prospective new employees. Many advertising firms seek to hire managers with experience at Leo Burnett, J. Walter Thompson, or DDB Needham, for example, in order to gain access to some of the strengths of such firms. The assumption is that a former employee of those firms has somehow integrated the social milieu and skills that have made those firms successful into his or her own cultural background. Personal characteristics and abilities, as well as individual goals, do allow for variation in the individual manager's experience. Firm influences do not completely determine each individual manager's experience, but they have a significant impact on its development. Of course, an interesting question is whether the new employee maintains the culture from past experiences or adapts it to the new structure, culture, and politics.

Much of the management literature defines the guiding principles and standard operating procedures of the firm as part of its organizational culture (Martin & Meyerson, 1988; Schein, 1984, 1985). This highlights the difficulty in classifying some aspects of the organization as structure or culture, but this difficulty does not diminish the importance of the phenomena. Deshpande and Webster (1989) provided a review of the theoretical approaches that apply the organizational culture concept to marketing issues. The theoretical approaches view culture either as a variable that influences action in the firm or as a metaphor for organizational cognition, symbolism, or psychological processes.

Politics

From an interorganizational perspective, political struggle will occur as firms try to gain a larger share of the communications budget and increased power over the strategic direction of the communications program. The result is the same whether we view the struggle as self-interest or the commitment to a particular form of communications engendered by the procedural framework. Stern and Reve (1980) and Childers and Ruekert (1982) discussed interorganizational conflict among marketing organizations. Political conflict among functions in a firm has the same genesis. Different functions will attempt to gain reward and power, both for reasons of self-interest and genuine belief in their view. Low and Mohr (1991) discussed the budget allocation between advertising and sales promotion, whereas Piercy (1987) addressed the political nature of the general budgeting process in marketing.

HOW MANAGERS THINK: THE PROCEDURAL FRAMEWORK

Managers make important decisions in a complex and uncertain environment by employing a procedural framework that provides them with the perspective through which they view their world, a way of categorizing events that occur, a list of alternative courses of action, and a guide for choosing among the alternatives. The procedural framework is the collection of cognitive heuristics that are applied to the marketing communications decisions made by managers for their clients. It is the "way we do things at this agency," the obvious truths shared by the managers in any firm. These frameworks have been discussed as frames of reference (Shrivastava & Mitroff, 1984; Shrivastava & Schneider, 1984), schema (Lord & Foti, 1986), scripts (Gioia & Manz, 1985; Gioia & Poole, 1984), cognitive maps (Axelrod, 1976), and cause maps (Weick & Bougon, 1986).

The procedural framework is itself influenced by the firm's structure, culture, and politics. This influence stems both from the firm's need to control the decision making process of its individual managers and from the managers' desires to simplify the complexity and uncertainty of decision making and to develop a well-rewarded career in the firm (Jaworski, 1988; Prensky, 1992). For example, account managers in an advertising agency will make decisions that are consistent with the agency's perspective of the primacy of consumer advertising because they want to ensure that the agency will reward their performance.

Such procedural frameworks reinforce the segregation among the various forms of communications. We are all familiar with the idea of an advertising, promotions, or public relations firm developing and implementing a marketing communications strategy; the approach tends to emphasize the world view of the particular kind of organization developing the strategy (Gordon, 1991). For example, managers in sales promotions organizations are likely to perceive consumers as more price sensitive and less brand loyal than managers in advertising agencies do. That framework will naturally foster a preference for the form of communications with which the manager is most accustomed, a production mentality that emphasizes what the firm knows and does best.

The "garbage can" models of decision making (Cohen, March, & Olsen, 1972) say that much organizational decision making is the application of available solutions to any relevant, and perhaps even irrelevant, problems. Thus, advertising managers will view advertising as the solution for any communication problem and, perhaps, any marketing problem. Kantrow (1987) discussed the same process by describing the constraints of corporate tradition. Barabba and Zaltman (1991) pointed out that the frames of reference that managers use determine what they see and their choice of actions, and then discussed the vital importance of "hearing the voice of the market."

Ignoring the effects of the firm's naked self-interest, a manager views the marketing world and chooses communications strategies on the basis of his or her procedural framework. Managers representing different forms of communications, whether working in different functional groups within a communications conglomerate or in different firms, will have different views of an integrated communications program and the role of specific communication channels. Their different procedural frameworks will affect how they organize their perceptions of the environment (Dutton & Jackson, 1987; Lenz & Engledow, 1986; Porac & Thomas, 1990), recognize problems (Cowan, 1986), gather information (Saunders & Jones, 1990), and observe the results of decisions (Bowen, 1987). It is inevitable that these differences in process will affect the content of the communications program.

IMPLICATIONS AND CONSIDERATIONS FOR THE FUTURE

Divergence in manager's procedural frameworks reinforces segregation among the communications channels, instead of fostering integration. Managers with backgrounds in different forms of marketing communications have divergent procedural frameworks that are indelibly marked by their different backgrounds. Each of these divergent frameworks creates a distinct production mentality that encourages a marketing myopia among the managers in that communications form (Levitt, 1960). Managers in advertising agencies see themselves in the advertising business, not in the communications business. The same is true of managers in the other communications specialties. Their firm's organizational structure, culture, and politics foster a distinct procedural framework that segregates them from practitioners of other communications forms, encouraging a myopic view of marketing communications that divides the content of integrated communications efforts.

The implications of such organizational and managerial myopia are profound for communications firms in such rapidly changing consumer and communications environments. Given the environmental changes that require integrated marketing communications and the client demands that communications firms take those changes seriously, every marketing communications firm must devise its own short- and long-term business strategies. In the short term, the firm must recognize and capitalize on its competitive advantages by identifying its fundamental competencies and capabilities (Hamel & Prahalad, 1990; Stalk, Evans, & Shulman, 1992). Every firm must examine its strengths and weaknesses in producing communications content in light of its existing organizational processes in order to identify what it does best. The firm must consider both the form of communications, whether advertising, public relations, sales promotion, direct marketing, corporate image, or design; as well as the functional area, whether research, strategy, message creation or delivery; and then decide on both which and how many of these tasks it will focus.

Some firms will focus on the creative portion of one form, such as the stereotypical creative boutique in advertising, whereas others will try to provide the fully integrated "one-stop shopping" that demands complete internal integration. Whichever short term strategy is chosen, the firm must remake its organizational structure, culture, and politics in order to ensure its long-term viability. The recognition of competitive advantage will offer some short-term opportunity to communications firms, but long-term viability is dependent on adaptation to the fluid nature of the marketing, communications, and consumer environments. Such adaptation will require changes in the content of integrated marketing communications and, therefore, how managers think must change also.

As is apparent from our discussions, consumers have changed and communicating with them has changed and will continue to evolve. Managers trained in different forms of marketing communications will need to reconsider the assumptions that they make about the nature of the marketing communications process and the role that different forms of communications play. It is important, therefore, to question the most basic beliefs, a process that we recognize will be extremely difficult. As we have mentioned, the procedural frameworks of managers provide them with a set of heuristics to approach problems. Such heuristics are can be useful when similar problems as in the past are encountered. The problems that will be confronted in the future, however, are different, and the answers to old problems will not suffice. Reperceiving the future (Schwartz 1991; Wack 1985) is essentially a matter of recognizing that the problems are new and the tried and true heuristics are no longer useful. It is only after this realization that new solutions can be developed and evaluated.

As an example, consider the basic beliefs regarding the roles of different marketing communication channels. There are long-standing beliefs in the marketing industry that mass media advertising builds brand equity, whereas sales promotions efforts provide short-term sales. If a particular situation suggests that the importance of the brand needs to be established, then advertising is the typical response. On the other hand, if sales are down and short-run profits are desired, then a coupon drop is the answer. Such responses were perhaps the appropriate answers to the marketing environment in the past. In the marketing environment of the future, however, when an integrated approach to communications is desired, the old assumptions about the effects of the different communication approaches may not necessarily be valid. It may well be the case that when a coupon is used in conjunction with advertising and a pamphlet sent to consumers, the resulting influence of each aspect (the advertising, coupon, and pamphlet) may be very different from what would be the case if they were executed separately. The meaning of each aspect of the integrated communications effort may be different in the context of the other parts. Therefore, in the setting of integrated marketing communications, managers must question their basic assumptions about how the different communication efforts work.

The changing marketing environment also suggests a need for rethinking the roles played by different marketing organizations. What happens if advertising agencies are compensated on a basis other than media placement? (The rise of media buying services and in-house media buying among clients point in this direction.) What if advertising agencies become "communications consultants" specializing in message (content of communications) or in a particular area of expertise (e.g., package goods, retail, medical, food service)?

The issues mentioned, by no means exhaustive, are likely to determine the success or failure of individual marketing organizations, as well as the structure and relationships of marketing organizations in the future. These issues are indicative of the changes that can rapidly shift the ground beneath even the best-known and most respected firms. Schumpeter (1950) described this rapid change as capitalism's "creative destruction." The propensity for continual change is one of capitalism and marketing's greatest virtues. Marketing organizations must consider these issues when planning their future in the rapidly developing world of integrated marketing communications.

SUMMARY

Changes in marketing firms, consumer lifestyles, patterns of media consumption, and marketing communications have all brought about a need for integrated marketing communications. This need has come about so abruptly that, at present, marketing organizations are behind in developing the content of communication programs and the process of coordinating such programs. It is our contention that the current structure, culture, and politics of marketing firms and communication agencies may hamper the ability to effectively integrate marketing communications. Although the content of marketing communications should dictate the process, it is all too often the case that process inhibits changes in content. Marketing professionals must "reperceive the future" and recognize that the common answers to problems may not successfully solve the new problems that are likely to be faced.

REFERENCES

Axelrod, R. (1976). *Structure of decision: The cognitive maps of political elites*. Princeton, NJ: Princeton University Press.

Barabba, V. P., & Zaltman, G. (1991). *Hearing the voice of the market*. Boston: Harvard Business School Press.

Bowen, M. G. (1987). The escalation phenomenon reconsidered: Decision dilemmas or decision errors? *Academy of Management Review, 12*, 52–66.

Childers, T., & Ruekert, R. (1982). The meaning and determinants of cooperation within an interorganizational marketing network. In R. F. Bush & S. D. Hunt (Eds.), *Marketing theory: Philosophy of science perspectives* (pp. 116–119). Chicago: American Marketing Association.

Coen, R. (1992). [Expenditures on different types of advertising]. Unpublished raw data.

Cohen, M. D., March, J. G., & Olsen, J. P. (1972). A garbage can model of organizational choice. *Administrative Science Quarterly, 17*, 1–25.

Cowan, D. A. (1986). Developing a process model of problem recognition. *Academy of Management Review, 11*, 763–776.

Deshpande, R., & Webster, F. E., Jr. (1989). Organizational culture and marketing: Defining the research agenda. *Journal of Marketing, 53*(1), 3–15.

Donnelley Marketing Inc. (1992). *14th annual survey of promotional practices*. Stamford, CT: Author.

Duncan, T. R. (1991). *Topline results of the University of Colorado's integrated marketing communications study*. Unpublished report, University of Colorado at Boulder.

Dutton, J. E., & Jackson, S. E. (1987). Categorizing strategic issues: Links to organizational action. *Academy of Management Review, 12*, 76–90.

Fredrickson, J. W. (1986). The strategic decision process and organizational structure. *Academy of Management Review, 11*, 280–297.

Gioia, D. A., & Manz, C. C. (1985). Linking cognition and behavior: A script processing interpretation of vicarious learning. *Academy of Management Review, 10*, 527–539.

Gioia, D. A., & Poole, P. P. (1984). Scripts in organizational behavior. *Academy of Management Review, 9*, 449–459.

Gordon, G. G. (1991). Industry determinants of organizational culture. *Academy of Management Review, 16*, 396–415.

Hamel, G., & Prahalad, C. K. (1990). The core competence of the corporation. *Harvard Business Review, 68*(3), 79–91.

Harris, S. G. (1989). A schema-based perspective on organizational culture. In F. Hoy (Ed.),

Academy of Management best papers proceedings (pp. 178-182). Ada, OH: Academy of Management.

Jaworski, B. J. (1988). Toward a theory of marketing control: Environmental context, control types, and consequences. *Journal of Marketing, 52*(3), 23-39.

Kantrow, A. M. (1987). *The constraints of corporate tradition.* New York: Harper and Row.

Lenz, R. T., & Engledow, J. L. (1986). Environmental analysis: The applicability of current theory. *Strategic Management Journal, 7*, 329-346.

Levitt, T. (1960). Marketing myopia. *Harvard Business Review, 38*(4), 45-56.

Lord, R. G., & Foti, R. J. (1986). Schema theories, information processing, and organizational behavior. In H. P. Sims, Jr. & D. A. Gioia (Eds.), *The thinking organization: Dynamics of organizational social cognition* (pp. 20-48). San Francisco: Jossey-Bass.

Low, G. S., & Mohr, J. J. (1991). The budget allocation between advertising and sales promotion: Understanding the decision process. In M. C. Gilly, F. R. Dwyer, T. W. Leigh, A. J. Dubinski, M. L. Richins, D. Curry, A. Venkatesh, M. Kotabe, R. R. Dholakia, & G. E. Hills (Eds.), *Enhancing knowledge development in marketing* (Vol. 2, p. 448-457). Chicago: American Marketing Association.

Martin, J., & Meyerson, D. (1988). Organizational cultures and the denial, channeling, and acknowledgment of ambiguity. In L. R. Pondy, B. J. Boland, Jr., & H. Thomas (Eds.), *Managing ambiguity and change* (pp. 93-125). New York: Wiley.

Piercy, N. F. (1987). The marketing budgeting process: Marketing management implications. *Journal of Marketing, 51*(4), 45-59.

Pitre, E., & Sims, Jr., H. P. (1987). The thinking organization: How patterns of thought determine organizational culture. *National Productivity Review, 6*, 340-347.

Porac, J. F., & Thomas, H. (1990). Taxonomic mental models in competitor definition. *Academy of Management Review, 15*, 224-240.

Prensky, D. (1992). Control and cognition in decision making: Implications for the role of information in marketing strategy. In R. Leone & V. Kumar (Eds.), *Enhancing knowledge development in marketing* (Vol. 3, p. 385-386). Chicago: American Marketing Association.

Rapp, S., & Collins, T. (1992). *The great marketing turnaround.* New York: Plume.

Ruekert, R. W., Walker, O. C., Jr., & Roering, K. J. (1985). The organization of marketing activities: A contingency theory of structure and performance. *Journal of Marketing, 49*(1), 13-25.

Sapienza, A. M. (1985). Believing is seeing: How culture influences the decisions top managers make. In R. H. Kilmann, M. J. Saxton, & R. Serpa (Eds.), *Gaining control of the corporate culture* (pp. 66-83). San Francisco: Jossey-Bass.

Saunders, C., & Jones, J. W. (1990). Temporal sequences in information acquisition for decision making: A focus on source and medium. *Academy of Management Review, 15*, 29-46.

Schein, E. H. 1984). Coming to a new awareness of organizational culture. *Sloan Management Review, 25*, 3-16.

Schein, E. H. (1985). *Organizational culture and leadership.* San Francisco: Jossey-Bass.

Schumpeter, J. (1950). *Capitalism, socialism and democracy* (3rd ed.). New York: Harper and Row.

Schwartz, P. (1991). *The art of the long view: Planning for the future in an uncertain world.* New York: Doubleday.

Shrivastava, P., & Mitroff, I. I. (1984). Enhancing organizational research utilization: The role of decision makers' assumptions. *Academy of Management Review, 9*, 18-26.

Shrivastava, P., & Schneider, S. (1984). Organizational frames of reference. *Human Relations, 37*, 795-809.

Stalk, G., Evans, P., & Shulman, L. (1992). Competing on capabilities: The new roles of corporate strategy. *Harvard Business Review, 70*(2), 57-69.

Stern, L. W., & Reve, T. (1980). Distribution channels as political economies; A framework for comparative analysis. *Journal of Marketing, 44*(3), 52-64.

Tedlow, R. S. (1990). *New and improved: The story of mass marketing in America*. New York: Basic Books.

U.S. Bureau of the Census (1991). *Statistical abstract of the United States* (111th ed.). Washington, DC: Author.

Wack, P. (1985). Scenarios: Shooting the rapids. *Harvard Business Review, 63*(6), 139-150.

Weick, K., & Bougon, M. G. (1986). Organizations as cognitive maps: Charting ways to success and failure. In H. P. Sims, Jr. & D. A. Gioia (Eds.), *The thinking organization: Dynamics of organizational social cognition* (pp. 102-135). San Francisco: Jossey-Bass.

10

Integrated Channel Management: Merging the Communication and Distribution Functions of the Firm

David W. Stewart
Gary L. Frazier
Ingrid Martin
University of Southern California

The need for integrating all elements of the marketing mix is axiomatic in the marketing literature. The importance of integration is frequently embodied within the very definition of the marketing mix, for example, "Marketing mix is the set of controllable marketing variables that the firm blends to produce the response it wants in the target market" (Kotler, 1986, p. 43).

Recently, several scholars have argued that the increasing availability of information, and the sophistication of the technology for obtaining, processing, and analyzing this information, are blurring the boundaries of the several elements of the marketing mix (Glazer, 1989; Ray, 1985). There have also been calls for changes in the organization of both the marketing function and the firm itself to accommodate this blurring of the traditional functional lines within marketing and between marketing and other functional disciplines within and external to the firm (Glazer, 1989; Webster, 1989).

It is certainly well recognized that the "product" presented to the market by the firm consists of more than just the tangible offering. Price has long been recognized as a product attribute, albeit a special one, and marketing communications is a critical component in defining the purpose, potential users, and relevant atributes of a given product or service. Likewise, the channel of distribution has also been recognized as a contributor to the utility of a product, and more recently, the time and mode of product delivery have taken on greater significance as value-added components of the product (Stalk & Hout, 1990).

The concept of blending all of the elements of the marketing mix into a

185

unified product offering represents one facet of the integration of the marketing mix. It is also the facet of integration that has received the greatest attention from marketing scholars. There are, however, other facets of an integrated marketing mix that have received less attention. The purpose of this chapter is to discuss one of these other facets — the blurring of the lines between the distribution function and the marketing communication function within the firm. The chapter suggests that channels of marketing communication and channels of distribution have become virtually indistinguishable from one another. Although in most firms they are managed separately, integration is needed as quickly as possible. No doubt, this change has implications for marketing practice within the firm and for the types of information required to manage this new integrated entity.

This change also suggests the need for a reconceptualization of channels of distribution and channels of communication. This reconceptualization, which we will call integrated channel management, reflects the current blurring of the boundaries of the communication and distribution functions, as well as the need for management practices and organizations that facilitate simultaneous consideration of both the costs and benefits of the communication and distribution functions.[1]

First of all, we examine the principal factors that are responsible for the growing interdependency and inseparability of the communications and distribution functions, and introduce the concept of integrated channel management. Following this discussion, some examples of integrated channels are provided. We then consider the implications of integrated channel management for marketing practice and research by focusing on media and the media environment. Differences across media, the mediating role of self-selection, the unreliability of media quality judgments, and the need for media indicators are all emphasized. This is followed by a discussion of the role of traditional channels and what channels are supposed to accomplish. Finally, general implications for marketing research and practice are offered.

THE INTEGRATED CHANNEL

Of all of the elements of the marketing mix, channels of distribution and marketing communications have traditionally been the most independent functional marketing responsibilities within most large firms. The channel

---

[1]The term integrated channel(s) has, on occasion, been used to refer to vertical distribution systems owned by the firm. It has also been used to refer to integrated communication programs across different media vehicles. We use the term to encompass both distribution and communication channels that may or may not be owned by the firm.

of distribution has been typically looked on as the pipeline or conduit through which products and services are made available to the firm's customers, whereas the channel of communication has been viewed as a mechanism through which a firm provides information on its products or services to its customers and prospective customers.

Historically, the relative independence of distribution and communication management has been a functional response to the realities of the marketplace. Different skills were required for managing these two functions, and the relative emphasis on these two functions often reflected very real differences of the purchasing behavior of customers. Firms frequently made decisions about whether they would pursue a "push" strategy, which emphasized the role of the channel of distribution in stimulating demand, or a "pull" strategy, which emphasized the use of marketing communications directed at the end user (Frazier & Summers, 1985).

The traditional functions of channels of distribution were different from those of marketing communication, both in terms of specific marketing activities and the target of those activities. Traditionally, the channel of distribution has involved three general types of activities. First, it was involved in buying and selling, that is, activities associated with bringing about changes in ownership. These buying and selling activities not only provide value but also may stimulate demand through promotional activities. Second, channels of distribution performed the task of physical distribution, that is, activities that facilitate the availability of the product. Finally, channels often provided important facilitating activities that supported the other activities, such as information gathering, financing, and holding of inventories. The ultimate purpose of the the channel of distribution was to provide time, place, possession, and form utilities for the firm's customers.

The traditional activities of marketing communication on the other hand, have revolved around direct and indirect persuasion based on information about product benefits or incentives. These activities have included creating awareness of the product, its attributes and benefits, and, subsequently, beliefs, attitudes, and feelings about the product. Marketing communication also facilitated customer decision making by identifying points of difference among competing products and by suggesting decision rules the consumer might use when choosing among alternatives. In addition, marketing communications strengthened purchase behavior after the sale by providing further product information and by reinforcing the wisdom of the decision. Finally, the marketing communications function was often responsible for offering incentives (promotions) that encouraged purchase.

This dichotomy of the distribution channel and communication functions has always been artificial, however. There has always been some overlap of the activities of these two elements of the marketing mix. Channels of distribution almost always have some role in communicating to consumers something about a branded product or its manufacturer.[2] Marketing communications almost always play a role in the distribution of a product, even if that role is only to create awareness of the product. A certain amount of advertising and consumer promotion is often necessary to convince channel members that they should stock a particular product.

In some cases, the distribution channel and the communication channel are one and the same, example, direct response marketing through any of a variety of media and the use of a direct sales force. Thus, from a functional perspective, it is not likely to be useful to consider distribution decisions as independent of marketing communication decisions and vice versa. To a large extent the historical independence of communication management and distribution management has been associated more with the targets of these activities than the activities themselves.

Perhaps the most fundamental force driving the need for integrated channels management is the fact that the channels themselves are becoming increasingly integrated. Evidence of this increasing integration is found in both the changes occurring within traditional channels of distribution and communication and in the rise of new channels that combine the communications and distribution functions. The increasing use of direct response marketing (i.e, products sold through various media channels such as catalogs, direct mail, broadcast, telephone, magazines, newspapers, and the like), which communicates product information, provides a means for the customer to order, and provides for product delivery, is just one manifestation of this change. In fact, many of the direct response marketing approaches may be conceptualized as the impersonal analog to the personal sales force, which traditionally provided customers with information, solicited orders, and guaranteed delivery.

Information technologies have been and are currently altering both communications channels and distribution channels and merging their functions. That this is the case is widely acknowledged. What has not yet been addressed are the implications of this merger. Distribution channels no longer need to be physical entities where consumers go to shop. Commu-

---

[2]There are, of course, products that are sold as commodities through various distribution channels. In such cases the firm either cannot or has chosen not to communicate information that differentiates its product from those of its competitors. These are not cases where the distribution channel has no communication function; rather, the firm has decided that expenditures on all forms of communication are unwarranted, whether through traditional media or through channels of distribution. In fact, in the case of commodity types of products, the distribution channel often assumes the role of the primary communication channel for the customer.

nication channels, even of the impersonal variety, no longer need to carry information in only one direction.

The need for greater integration of the distribution and communication functions has been made more manifest during the past decade as manufacturers have confronted increasingly powerful intermediaries (e.g., retailers, wholesalers) within their channels of distribution. The increasing power of these intermediaries has led to the need to devote greater financial and human resources to the development and maintenance of these channels. Attempts by manufacturers to enhance their power within the channel have become highly important (Stern & El-Ansary, 1992). At the same time, traditional channels of communication have become increasingly fragmented and potentially less effective and efficient than in the past. A result of these two trends has been an increasing frequency of trade-offs between expenditures in support of channels of distribution and those in support of traditional channels of communication. From a budgetary perspective, then, the distribution and communications decisions have become increasingly integrated.

Thus, from both a functional and a budgetary perspective, distribution and communication channels decisions are highly interrelated. Not well integrated is the organizational structure required to execute these decisions; although the functions are highly interdependent, the organizational forms utilized for managing these functions have frequently been largely independent. In those cases in which firms utilize intermediaries (e.g., distributors, sales representatives, retailers) in their channels of distribution, sales personnel who call on the distribution channels are often different from those who call on or meet with the customer or end user. In cases in which the firm owns its own channels of distribution, responsibility for the management of these channels is often independent of the management of the marketing communications function of the firm, except at the highest levels of the organization. Furthermore, the communications function itself has been fragmented, with the sales management function generally separated from the advertising and public relations functions of the organization.

The increasingly common need to make trade-offs among advertising, consumer promotions, trade promotions, and personal selling, to both the end user and channel members, frequently produces organizational conflict. This conflict reflects organizational and budgetary structures that are unsuited for making trade-offs among activities that have traditionally been managed independently.

Management structures that facilitate the integration of increasingly interdependent functions have been slow to develop. At the same time, there is not an established body of theory and empirical research that could guide decision making with respect to the trade-offs involved in integrated distribution and communication decisions. As we have already observed, the reasons for these deficiencies are largely historical.

There is no longer any good reason for separating the distribution and communications functions, and there are numerous reasons to move toward decision making that is more integrated. There is a compelling need to bring the distribution and communications decisions under a single organizational umbrella. There are few communications decisions exclusive of distribution decisions, and there are few distribution decisions that can be made in isolation of communications decisions. Rather, there are simply integrated channel decisions.

It seems more productive to view a channel of distribution as a mechanism through which a product or service can be selected, purchased/ ordered, and received by a segment of the firm's customers, and a channel of communication as a vechicle through which information of various forms and types are exchanged between sellers and buyers. The channel of distribution must involve some communication. Moreover, each channel of communication must be attached to or accompany in some fashion at least one channel of distribution.

Following this train of thought, integrated channels of distribution and communication are all media through which consumers (or potential consumers) gather information about products and obtain the products themselves. Integrated channels serve both communication and distribution functions, although they may vary with respect to the intensity with which they serve either or both functions. Traditional broadcast and print advertising play a greater communications role than distribution role, whereas certain types of distribution outlets play a greater role in providing the product to consumers than in offering information about the product (e.g., discount operations). Nevertheless, any particular medium could be scaled with respect to its efficiency and effectiveness as both a communications channel and a distribution channel.

SOME EXAMPLES OF
INTEGRATED CHANNELS

Consider the growth of so-called "event marketing" in recent years. Such "events" represent opportunities to attract the attention of a particular group of consumers in a relatively uncluttered environment. The event becomes the medium in which a product message is embedded. Such events may be exclusively sponsored by a single firm and can be matched with a particularly appropriate product, for example, a running shoe as sponsor of a 10-K race or a building materials manufacturer as sponsor of a home show.[3] At some such events, the sponsoring product may also be available for consumption or purchase, so that the event temporarily becomes both a ✳ communication channel and a distribution outlet.

Events need not be constructed, however. There are numerous events in the lives of consumers that include very natural links to products of various sorts. A trip to Disney World almost always includes the consumption of various foods and beverages. A trip to McDonalds with children almost always includes soft drinks. A professional baseball game without hotdogs is missing something. The link between product and the event experience is very strong in these instances. The distribution channel serves to make the product more salient for the consumer and, as such, serves the same role as "reminder" advertising in traditional media.

Consider that mundane channel of distribution, the grocery store. Shelf footage, in-store displays, shelf-talkers, and other merchandising and promotional tools serve as point-of-purchase communication tools. Shelf space 5-feet long and 3-feet high devoted to a product is very much akin to an outdoor billboard. The differences, of course, are that exposure to a billboard seldom occurs when the consumer's agenda is purchase, and consumers cannot reach into a billboard to obtain a product. Thus, shelf space is a far more powerful medium than billboards because it offers the same opportunity for communication, but at a time when consumers are most predisposed to purchase and in a manner that facilitates purchase of the product. This fact has not been lost on retailers, who are more than happy to explain why providing a manufacturer with shelf space is an appropriate use of the cooperative advertising budget.

Consider how important the placement of public telephones is for a telecommunications company. Certain locations, such as airports, are highly visible and tend to attract large numbers of potential customers, as well as persons who make decisions about telecommunications equipment (even if they do not happen to use a public telephone on a given trip to the airport). The placement of public telephones not only provides an outlet for distribution of telephone services at these locations, it also provides an opportunity to raise the salience of a particular service provider. This fact has not been lost on airport authorities, who frequently negotiate the price of public telephone placement based on the number of persons who pass through the airport, not the amount of telephone usage that occurs. Thus, the communications function of what is in effect a distribution outlet (the

---

[3]Not all event sponsorships represent a good match between product and event. This is probably due to the complexity of these types of decisions, as well as the current lack of understanding about the full impact of such events. Other things being equal, however, it is not clear that a life insurance company is a particularly good sponsor for a college football game. Fortunately, the irony of this pairing is probably lost on most consumers.

public telephone) is the primary driver of the cost to the service provider. The cost of the distribution channel is based on the number of exposure opportunities, not sales volume. It terms of the billing formula, this distribution channel more closely resembles an advertising medium.

It would not be difficult to identify many more such illustrations of the integration of the communications and distribution functions. The point is clear, however. Distribution and communication are inextricably linked, and decisions about the one cannot be made in isolation from the other. Distribution channels are, and always have been, modes of communication, at least in part. In some cases, perhaps in many, they are more powerful than traditional modes of communication. This leads to a very obvious conclusion: Distribution channels must be considered among the alternative media for use in communicating with consumers about a product.

The value of a channel of distribution cannot be measured exclusively in terms of the flow of revenue through it, although this facet of a channel of distribution should not be ignored. There may be circumstances, however, in which the value of a channel of distribution is better measured by its communications impact. In this latter circumstance, the typical approach to evaluating a channel of distribution is turned on its head. Revenue generated by the distribution function becomes a means for subsidizing the primary function of the channel, which is communication. This is in contrast to the more typical view that some communications funds, for example, funds for cooperative advertising and point-of-purchase displays, are used to subsidize and, hence, maintain a channel of distribution.

REDEFINING THE MEDIA AND THE CHANNEL

The concept of an integrated channel suggests a need to broaden the concepts of a medium and of a channel. Although advertisers have traditionally considered media within the context of marketing communications, points of distribution are also media in the sense that they have the potential to carry product information. Furthermore, like traditional advertising media, distribution channels differ along a wide range of dimensions. Some channels are better matches with the image of the company or brand, some channels are more involving and of higher salience for the consumer, and some channels are more ubiquitous than others. A consideration of the differences found across different types of retail outlets, such as convenience stores, grocery stores, department stores, specialty stores, mass merchandisers, and discount operations, certainly reinforces this viewpoint. Differences within each type of retail outlet based on store positioning efforts (e.g., low-end vs. high-end grocery stores) are are also very important.

When distribution channels are treated as communications media, and communication media as potential distribution channels, the task of coordination becomes quite complex. Not the least of the reasons for this increased complexity is the fact that what is already a very fragmented media environment must now be regarded as shattered.

THE SHATTERED MEDIA ENVIRONMENT

Even without consideration of distribution channels' role in marketing communication, it is quite clear that today's media environment has become highly fragmented. Statistics tell a part of this story. Twenty years ago, 90% of all households watched prime time television on any given night; today, it is only 68% (Russell, 1989). Similarly, 78% of all households regularly read the daily newspaper 20 years ago; today, it is only 64% (Russell, 1989). Additionally, it appears that only the leading edge of this fragmentation is currently visible. Each new technological advance seems to increase fragmentation. This appears to be particularly true for broadcast media, in which, until a few short years ago, three major networks and a few hundred local television stations dominated the broadcasting landscape; this is the case no more.

Cable television has vastly expanded the number of channels from which a household can select. Low-power television stations, which will have a broadcast radius of 15 miles or less, are already on the horizon. Television broadcasting increasingly resembles radio in terms of the availability of options. It is becoming a fragmented medium with increasingly specialized programming for smaller and more selective audiences. The fragmentation of such traditional media as television, radio, magazines, and newspapers has resulted in the coining of the term *narrowcasting* to refer to editorial content, broadcast programming, and marketing communications that are designed for highly specialized and selective audiences. Yet, events in the traditional media are only a portion of more profound changes. Whole new media have arisen in recent years, and more are on the horizon.

Consider for a moment the new technologies and formats of media that are now available. These technologies and formats, really new media, include such things as 900-telephone services, interactive television, computer bulletin boards, on-line information services — the list gets long. Table 10.1 provides a partial but representative list of new technologies and formats currently in existence, as well as high definition television, which is just on the horizon. Each of these new technologies and formats serve to reduce exposure to more traditional broadcast and print media. Almost all would be considered a type of broadcast medium, although it is not clear how much longer the classification of media as print or broadcast will be

TABLE 10.1
The New Media

Television	*Telephone*
High definition television	Information services
Interactive television	Entertainment services
Videocassette	Conversation lines
Pay per View	
Televised "magazines"	*Radio*
Shopping networks and video catalogs	
Televised yellow pages	Magazines
"Pocket" television	Conversation radio
Computer	
	Audio
Information services	
Bulletin boards	Customized recordings
Shopping services	
Messaging and electronic mail	
Conversation channels	

useful. In fact, it has been suggested that print is now little more than a hard copy of electronic broadcast media (Brand, 1988).

Many of these same media have also become modes of distribution as well. Services such as Compuserve and Prodigy not only provide information and entertainment, they also provide opportunities to shop for and order a wide array of products and services, ranging from groceries to travel services to fashion products. Culter (1990) called the new on-line interactive media the "fifth medium" (radio, television, newspapers, and magazines are the first four media). In contrast the other media, the fifth medium provides the opportunity to advertise, transact the sale, and collect payment at the same time and place. It also has one other important advantage—memory. What a customer has acquired, in terms of information, products, or services, can be captured for future use by either the consumer or the marketer. Thus, the consumer can automate grocery shopping by storing a shopping list that is automatically called from memory every week. Marketers can identify who inquired about what product or who bought what item.

More than 20 years ago, E. B. Parker (1970) described a new communications environment that has proven prescient:

This new communication medium can be described as looking like a combination of a television set and a typewriter, functioning like a combination of a newspaper and a library, and permitting a communication network that is something of a combination of a telephone and telegraph system. It has one radical new property that previous mass media lack: what is transmitted over the communication channel is controlled more directly by the receiver than the sender of the message. (p. 53)

The key to Parker's insight is not so much the technology he described, although clearly he was on target. Rather, it was the importance of self-selection on the part of the receiver. Technology has simply facilitated the development of a greater number of options for the consumer. Current opportunities for the self-selection of media are only the beginning; the future will bring far more options.

The increase in the number of options and concomitant growth in the importance of consumer self-selection among media alternatives has been accompanied by an increase in the number of distribution options that are available to consumers. It has long been recognized that consumers are active decision makers with respect to the selection of the distribution channels with which they deal. This self-selection process is guided not only by the types of goods and services provided by the channel, but also by such factors as atmosphere (Kotler, 1973–1974) and perceived congruency of self-image with store image (Stern, Bush, & Hair, 1977).

What we are only now beginning to see are far more options for self-selection than ever before. In the past, advertisers have largely been able to select audiences, because they could rather easily determine the characteristics of households who watched this or that program, or this or that commuter who tuned in to a particular radio station during drive time. Likewise, the demographics of a particular group of consumers could be readily profiled, and distribution strategies could be readily matched to these characteristics. What made this selection process practical, both for the scheduling of media and the selection of distribution strategies, was the relatively small number of options available to consumers.

In the past, marketers have largely been able to select audiences, because, as mentioned previously, we could rather easily determine the characteristics of households who watched this or that program, or this or that commuter who tuned in to a particular radio station during drive time. Increasingly, it is the individual who is doing the selecting. Individuals make selections among media, within media, and even within specific vehicles. They decide to shop by telephone, by mail, in person, by computer, and even by surrogate. Today, and certainly in the future, the options available to the individual for obtaining information and purchasing products will be more varied and individualized.

People choose to shop in some outlets and ignore others. People select certain places, events, and situations, but not others. Opportunities exist for communicating with those consumers who select a particular medium, whether it is a network television broadcast or a live professional basketball game, but other opportunities for communicating with different groups of

Variety has led to the change in advertising

consumers may be foregone. Even when a particular event is selected as a medium of communication, for example, through the use of large signs and exclusive distribution of a product at a football game, there is no guarantee that members of the audience will attend to the product message. Likewise, simply because an individual shops as a particular store, there is no guarantee that the individual will attend to the particular brand of product he or she is purchasing. This is analogous to the situation in broadcast or print advertising in which an opportunity to see an advertisement is not the same as an exposure, and in which exposure does not ensure that the message registers.

When individuals in an audience can be highly selective within a medium (or even vehicles within a medium), and this is increasingly an option, the link between media exposure and advertising exposure, which has always been tenuous, is weakened all the more. In the absence of technology that provides for the monitoring of exposures on a real-time basis (and for some media this will be possible), there will be a need some other surrogate or additional measures. Certainly, traditional media scheduling is going to be problematic. Determining who will be in a particular audience will be difficult enough, but coordination among media will become a nightmare. It is difficult enough to try account for the fact that regular viewers of a popular network television program also regularly read certain magazines. Add to this the need to account for the fact that these same viewers (or more likely a subset of these viewers) are also regular visitors to the zoo and patrons of professional basketball. The media scheduling task is now out of hand unless some means of simplification can be found. However, the task is even more complex yet.

The problem is more than one of auditing. Finding new ways to count and track audiences in a bewildering array of media is not enough. There is a need to measure the way audiences interact with media, including (perhaps especially) those that have intensive distribution functions. It is the nature of the interaction with media that increasingly determines its efficiency and effectiveness as a communications tool. It is also well established that interaction at the point of sale also determines the efficiency and effectiveness of an outlet as a distribution channel.

There are currently no systematic measures of the use of these media. Such tools are clearly needed and necessary. In the absence of technology that allows us to monitor exposures on a real-time basis (and for some media this will be possible), we will need some other surrogate or additional measures.

Several conferences and surveys of the advertising community have suggested the need for such measures as a means for making decisions among different media (Advertising Research Foundation, 1961, 1983; Schmalensee, 1983; Schultz, 1979). More than a decade ago, Raymond (1976) noted that "while acceptable methods exist for measuring target audience exposure to the vehicle, few equally acceptable measures permit valid comparisons of exposures in different media, and no acceptable measures of response to advertising exist for comparing vehicles in different media." Raymond was referring to only traditional advertising media, but his comment is even more valid when newer media forms are considered and when distribution channels are viewed as communication media.

This would be a significant problem even if there were but a few simple dimensions along which media differed. However, there are many. It would not be a problem if the effects of media could be captured through the judgment of experienced media professionals. Unfortunately, media differ on many dimensions, and the number of these dimensions is growing with the number of media. Furthermore, the form that a medium takes is increasing under the control of the individual member of the audience. For example, it has long been held that television is a passive medium. The advent of interactive television adds a more active element to this medium. Hence, we now have at least two types of broadcast media, passive and active. Or consider the case of an individual who views a sporting event on television versus the individual who attends the event in the stadium. In both cases, the event provides the background in which product messages are embedded. Yet, it is likely that those messages, even if identical, will be processed rather differently.

DIFFERENCES AMONG MEDIA

Research in communications and in media psychology has provided a rather large catalog of dimensions along which media may differ. For an Advertising Research Foundation (ARF) conference on intermedia comparisons, Chestnut (1983) reviewed some of this literature and concluded, "The literature on intermedia comparisons is small, but of respectable quality." In fact, he found 111 references to intermedia comparisons in the 1978 ARF bibliography *Evaluating Advertising*. A comprehensive review of the literature on media effects is obviously beyond the scope of this chapter. Some of the more useful treatments of media effects as they pertain to advertising are Schramm (1965), Klapper (1965), Corlett and Richardson (1969), Corlett (1971), Corlett, Lannon, and Richardson (1971), Richardson (1972), Nolan (1972), Clemens (1972), and Guggenheim (1984). In addition, there exists a growing body of academic research on media effects. This body of literature has identified a large and varied set of dimensions along which media may differ. Among the dimensions of media that have been identified and at least occasionally studied are those in Table 10.2.[4]

---

[4]The dimensions identified in Table 10.1 are restricted to only those factors related to the way people interact with and perceive media. There are obviously numerous audience,

TABLE 10.2
An Inventory of Media Factors

Active vs. passive	Prestige
Involvement	Arousal propensity
Imbeddedness	Duration of effect
Obtrusiveness/intrusiveness	Hot vs. cold
Informativeness	Identification
Mood	Expertise
Reality vs. fantasy orientation	Intimacy
Immediacy	Degree of interaction
Permanence	Entertainment value
Credibility	Utility
Complexity	Gratification
Vividness	Social context
Objectivity	Participation
Control	Relation to self

Channels of distribution have traditionally been evaluated primarily in terms of revenue generation, cost efficiency, control, and adaptability criteria (Stern & El-Ansary, 1992). No doubt, different channels also vary in terms of the dimensions in Table 10.2 as well (e.g., active vs. passive, duration). In fact, these media factors are likely to have a major bearing on the traditional indicators of channel performance. A complete appraisal of the channel of distribution would need to include consideration of these media factors.

SOME EXAMPLES

Consider the dimensions of intrusiveness and obtrusiveness. *Intrusive* refers to the extent to which something is an unwelcome interruption or disruption in routine. *Obtrusive* simply means how noticeable something is. One might suppose that advertising on television is highly intrusive, yet, aside from the occasional complaint, audiences seem perfectly accepting of the intrusions of advertising within a television program. In fact, there is evidence that people have so adapted their viewing routines to the presence of these intrusions that they feel uncomfortable when they are removed. On the other hand, the very nature of this adaptation to the intrusiveness of television advertising may have reduced the obtrusiveness of advertising. Television advertising now often blends into the background and receives scant attention. It is a welcome pause during which the viewer can remove

---

production, and delivery characteristics that differentiate media as well, but they are not the focus of the current discussion.

his or her attention from the screen. Advertising messages may still register with the viewer, but the advertiser has to work harder for a share of mind.

In contrast, consider the case of a different type of broadcast advertising, fax advertising. One might suppose that a paper message arriving on an unattended machine would not be regarded as terribly intrusive. However, recent experience shows very well that it is viewed as an intrusion, and an unwanted one at that. In fact, it is so unwanted that state legislatures all over the United States are considering legislation to restrict, if not completely ban, fax advertising.

Consider the social dimension in Table 10.2. Some media tend to be more likely to be used by a single individual, a book for example, whereas others, like cinema, tend to be used simultaneously by many individuals. One could add the dimension of interaction and the active–passive dimension to the social factor to arrive at an interesting categorization of media. Stanley & Steinberg (1976), in their book, *The Media Environment*, noted that both radio and television were originally promoted as social media that could be enjoyed by the entire family. Television would bring the family together again!

Today things are a bit different. Watching network television is often a solitary activity. On the other hand, videocassette use appears to be more of a social activity, that is, the average number of persons who participate in watching a videotape appears to be substantially higher than the average for watching network television programming. Recognition of this fact might suggest that some advertising could be targeted at single or multiple viewers with different results.

The change of traditional radio and television from more social to less social media is but one indication of how media use can change. Involvement is another dimension on which broadcast media have changed. Radio in particular has become a rather passive "background" medium for most individuals; it is not a particularly involving medium. However, this has not always been the case. In the early years of radio, the "Amos 'n' Andy" radio program was so popular and so involving that some movie theaters would stop the projector in mid-reel at 7:00 p.m. each weekday evening to broadcast the program to patrons that would otherwise have stayed home (Stanley & Steinberg, 1976, p. 114)—that is real audience involvement.

Today, some radio program formats deliberately seek greater audience involvement by soliciting on-air discussion and conversation. Although radio may be a low-involvement medium in general, there is variation on this dimension within the medium.

This example of changes in radio usage and involvement is simply an indication of the ability of individuals to shift from one usage mode to another within the same medium. Although this ability has always been present to some extent, it was restricted by the limitations of the media available. In fact, this is just one more manifestation of self-selection; individuals not only have greater options among media, they have options with respect to the way they will interact with the same medium. The consumer can watch the same movie in a theater, at home on a VCR, or at home via cable transmission. Some time later, but often not much later, the consumer might see the same movie on network television. It is not at all clear that the movie is experienced in the same way when the mode of presentation, or medium, is changed, and it is almost certain that advertising messages are perceived differently.

In the past there has been a tendency to characterize these modes of interaction more in terms of the medium than in terms of the audience behavior. The proliferation of media has suddenly made it clear that what is really at work are the ways in which individual members of audiences elect to interact with a given medium. People select particular media for use in very particular ways.

THE MEDIATING ROLE OF SELF-SELECTION

More than 20 years ago, Marshall McLuhan (McLuhan & Fiore, 1967) suggested that the medium is the message. Even if the medium is not the message, it is certain that the medium influences the way the message is perceived, processed, and stored. Empirical studies consistently reveal that more involving media are better vehicle for delivering product messages (Audits & Surveys, 1986; Lloyd & Clancy, 1989). This is the case regardless of whether the measure of performance is recall, persuasion, or message credibility. Numerous studies have shown that the medium in which a message is embedded can serve to prime responses to marketing communications (Herr, 1989; Higgins & King, 1981; Wyer & Srull, 1981; Yi, 1990a, 1990b). Still other media effects have been identified by researchers (see, e.g., Chook, 1985; Kennedy, 1971; Krugman, 1983; Singh & Churchill, 1987; 1989; Soldow & Principle, 1981). It is not at all clear that these effects are directly attributable to characteristics of the media; it is more likely that they are attributable to the way in which people interact with the media.

 The appropriate question is no longer what does media (or advertising) do to people, but what do people do with media (or advertising).[5] There is growing evidence of differential loyalty among consumers of media and media types. In addition, there are selective patterns of exposure or preferential attitudinal dispositions toward certain kinds of media and vehicles within media that are not constant across all viewers (Gunter,

---

[5]See Zillman and Bryant (1985) for a discussion of some of the implications of this change in perspective in the context of media.

1985). How people think and feel about various vehicles or the extent to which the audience flows toward or across certain programs varies between demographic divisions of the population. More significant, however, are findings that indicate differences in viewing patterns or attitudinal preferences for programs associated with enduring psychological characteristics of viewers (Gunter, 1985). There is also strong evidence that people selectively attend to information based on its relevance to them at a given point in time (Broadbent, 1977; Greenwald & Leavitt, 1984; Krugman, 1988; Pechmann & Stewart, 1990; Tolley & Bogart, 1994). There is a need to better understand why audiences behave as they do and to incorporate this information into the media selection decision.

Individuals who endorse information needs to watch more information programs. Those who endorse social and personal identity needs to watch more of those programs such as popular dramas and movies that can be seen to serve those needs related to vicarious social contact. However, there are no specific programs that particularly serve those with escapist needs — for the escapist, any program may do (Murray, 1980, p. 28). The effect of commercial messages will differ substantially depending on the use a particular consumer is making of a given medium. Some commercial messages will not even register, because they may be inconsistent with the consumer's purpose; they may spoil the mood, distract from the flow, and so on. Thus, in the future it will be important to identify those media, and the purposes for using them, that are consistent with the supportive of the commercial message.

The effects of self-selection also manifest themselves in the interaction of consumers with the channel of distribution. For one consumer, shopping may be a chore; for another, it may be a form of entertainment. Even for the same consumer, interaction with a given medium of distribution may vary with type of product, time, and purpose.

Greater selectivity exercised by consumers means, on the one hand, that consumers will be more difficult to reach through traditional mass media. On the other hand, the increase in the number of media vehicles available to consumers and consumers' selectivity in using these vehicles may also provide more opportunities for the marketer to reach consumers with the optimal message for the medium and medium use occasion. This is likely to be more expensive on a cost-per-thousand basis, but it may be far more efficient on an impact-per-thousand basis (Lloyd & Clancy, 1989). Realizing this possibility requires several things: (a) a better understanding of how and when people use and interact with various media, (b) a better understanding of how the mode of interaction with various media influences the processing of commercial messages, and (c) a better understanding of how to create commercial messages and distribution strategies that work within the context of specific media uses. Note that what is needed is not a better understanding of media, but a better understanding of how people interact with media and embedded commercial messages.

THE UNRELIABILITY OF MEDIA QUALITY JUDGMENTS

Although the dimensions along which interactions with media may differ, rather little is actually known about how people interact with different media. Very little is know about how these interactions differ across consumers, or how these interactions influence the effectiveness of communication and distribution strategies, however defined. This is not to suggest that marketers have totally ignored these dimensions. In the advertising profession such effects have been collectively referred to as *media quality, impact,* or *mood,* and media planners have tried to capture them through the use of subjective judgments. In the planning of distribution strategies, such factors are also important, but are equally subjective. Unfortunately, subjective media judgments are not reliable, even in simple cases.

For example, Haley (1985) reported a study on the agreement of 60 experienced media professionals from 10 agencies on the weights to assign the media impact of television vehicles. Even with a thorough briefing on the objectives of the advertising and a single standardized rating form, differences in weighting varied by 250%. In fact, there was not even good agreement within agencies. Among media professionals from the same agency, impact weights differed by 200%. Note that in this particular study the question revolved around the impact of vehicles within one particular medium, passive television. It is likely that enlarging the problem to include other media would very likely produce even larger variances.

Several recent studies (Blair, 1987/1988; Drane, 1988; Information Resources Inc., 1989) have suggested that a great deal of advertising simply does not work. If a message is not persuasive, spending more to ensure that consumers are exposed to it more often is unlikely to help — if an argument is not persuasive, shouting louder usually does no good.

Even the marginally effective advertisement may have difficulty breaking through the increasing media clutter. Given this increasing clutter and the fragmentation of media, it has become very expensive to make a marginally effective advertisement payout. Further reducing the effectiveness of advertising in traditional media is the fact that it must break through whatever mindset the consumer has brought to the media. The advertising may need to overcome the consumer's typical pattern of interaction with the media. Only the truly outstanding creative product (in the sense of having an impact on consumers) is likely to be an efficient use of advertising in these circumstances.

Greenberg (1988) suggested that in the present media context there are two competing views, the "drip" versus the "drench" hypotheses:

> The drench hypothesis, in its current, primitive form, asserts that critical images may contribute more to impression-formation and image-building than does the sheer frequency of television and behaviors that are viewed. The hypothesis provides an alternative to the no-effects hypothesis and to the view that the slow accretion of impressions cumulate across an indefinite time period. Finally, it also suggests that striking new images can make a difference—that a single character or collection of characters may cause substantial changes in beliefs, perceptions, or expectations about a group or a role, particularly among young viewers. (pp. 100–101)

What this means for both marketing communication and distribution strategies is that the creative dimensions of the business, which have been squeezed in recent years by escalating media costs and efforts by clients to economize, will become increasing important. Indeed, a shift in media expenditures to support greater creative effort is probably the only viable alternative to increasingly costly and less effective mass media.

THE NEED FOR MEDIA INDICATORS

The previous discussion suggested that marketers really do not have a good understanding of media effects, or of how these effects might influence the ultimate impact of advertising. It is certainly clear that there are differences among media, and members of media audiences confirm this. Surveys make it quite clear that audiences have different perceptions of different media. One example is given in Table 10.3.

Knowing that consumers of various media perceive them differently and have different attitudes about them is useful, but it is not enough. Such measures of perceptions and attitudes still do not tell use how people interact with a given medium or how this interaction influences response to products or other marketing stimuli. Chook (1983) made just this point when he stated that "the attitudinal approach is simple and relatively inexpensive, but at the same time is one that raises a number of critical questions. For one thing, measures of media interest, confidence, and enjoyment have no proven bearing on the performance of advertising. For another, such measures are too generalized for application to specific types of advertising" (p. 250). Spaeth (1983) made a similar point in stating that, "The only stage at which we can be confident that measures between media will be comparable is sales response. . . ."

A single measure of media quality is not enough—what is needed is a

TABLE 10.3
Comparison of Print Versus Televised Media

	Those Who Describe Advertisements As:	
	Press	*Television*
Useful	60	40
Entertaining	20	51
Truthful	40	18
Interesting	54	40
Informative	64	41
Helpful	59	29
Clever in approach	21	56
Trying to interfere with habits	6	26
Annoying	4	41
Stupid	4	38

Source: From *As Others See Us,* by Institute of Practitioners in Advertising, 1969. Occasional Paper No. 17. Reprinted by permission.

broad set of measures of media interaction. Moeller (1988), in a chapter in the book, *Beyond Media*, argued that a set of "Media Indicators" are need, much like we now have social indicators and economic indicators. This would require a comprehensive research program designed to transform qualitative channel characteristics into quantitative scales. In effect, what is needed is a matrix that includes media types on one axis and dimensions of interaction, like those in Table 10.2, on the other axis. Table 10.4 provides a stylistic example of such a matrix. It would probably also be necessary to include some type of measure of use occasion for some channels, because such "uses" are likely to establish the mode of interaction with media.

Although many of the dimensions that may need to be considered have been identified, there is little empirical research at this point in time to help us fill in the matrix suggested in Table 10.4. Even if the cells of the matrix could be filled, however, there would still not be sufficient information to make well-informed marketing decisions. What is required is a second

TABLE 10.4
Media By Dimensions of Interaction

Involvement Intrusiveness . . .
Medium 1
Medium 2
Medium 3
•
•
•
Medium *n*

TABLE 10.5
Measures of Advertising Effectiveness by Dimensions
of Media Interaction

Involvement Intrusiveness . . .		
Recall		
Comprehension		
Attitude change		
Persuasion		
Reinforcement		
•		
•		
•		

matrix, like the one illustrated in Table 10.5. This matrix would serve to link characteristics of channel interaction with specific measures of channel performance.

THE ROLE OF TRADITIONAL CHANNELS

New channels of communication and distribution are increasingly competing with existing channels. It is unlikely that these new channels will completely replace more traditional channels, but it is likely that each will have a more circumscribed role. To the extent that traditional mass media remain viable at all it is likely to be in context of delivering either simple and short product remainders or striking presentations that rivet attention and generate considerable word-of-mouth communication among consumers. Understanding this role for traditional communications media, as well as other types of media, requires careful consideration of the objectives of marketing communication.

Likewise, traditional channels of distribution will remain viable to the extent that consumers need to experience a product prior to purchase or when the shopping experience itself is attractive to the consumer. Thus, products like clothing, which the consumer may need to try on or have fitted, will continue to be sold through traditional distribution channels. Many products, however, will not require a visit to a "place" for purchase. These products include many frequently purchased consumer packaged goods. Thus, it is likely that for many consumers the local grocery store will become superfluous. This also means that the grocery store, which in recent years has become a very important medium for delivering marketing communications and incentives to consumers, will become a less important communications medium as it becomes a less important means of distribution. At minimum, the form of the distribution and communications functions of many retail outlets will be radically different in the future. The marketing objectives that are viable in these evolving media will require careful consideration. Thus, the role of channels in the marketing mix becomes a critical issue for planning and coordinating marketing programs.

WHAT ARE CHANNELS SUPPOSED TO DO?

There exist a number of assumptions about the role communication and distribution channels in the marketing mix. A great deal of advertising is carried out with the expectation that an increase in sales will follow. This may be a reasonable expectation for a new product, but it is likely to be an unreasonable expectation for many old products. Stewart (1989) recently called attention to this problem and suggested that for many mature products, the only way to determine whether advertising is working is to stop advertising. Ehrenberg (1983) also called attention to the tendency among advertisers and others to ignore the role of advertising for mature products. He argued that the role of advertising for mature products is to reinforce the existing attitudes and purchasing habits of loyal consumers. There exists an impressive body of empirical research and theory that supports such a view (see Stewart, Tellis, & Sanft, 1990, for a review).

Likewise, channels of distribution are expected to provide greater product availability, convenience, and, perhaps, an array of services to the consumer. In an era of increasing opportunities for the consumer to purchase products and services without leaving home, traditional channels of distribution may be less convenient and more troublesome than new channels.

An important facet of self-selection among consumers is that control of information flows are increasingly under the control of the consumer. Consumers can request information about products of interest and ignore information about products not of interest. Consumers can do this without revealing their identity or their purpose. They can obtain information and place an order while revealing little about themselves. In fact, the consumer can reverse roles by advertising an interest in a product.

Marketing communication and distribution channels will have different roles depending on who the consumer is, and the consumer's relationship to the product. For new products, marketing communications and distribution retains an important role in building awareness and stimulating trial for products. There may exist new and more varied types of channels to perform these functions, but the objectives for communication and distribution in the case of a new product will remain much as they have been in the past. For mature products this is unlikely to be the case in the future. For mature products, there are four distinct groups of consumers: (a) nonusers of the category, (b) brand loyal users, (c) brand switchers, and (d) emergent users. Marketing communications and distribution channels have, or should have, different objectives for each of these four groups.

Nonusers

Nonusers of a product category have rejected the need for the product and the benefit (s) it provides. Neither marketing communication nor distribution will change this circumstance. Short of the identification of new uses or benefits, communications or distribution directed at this group is a waste of money. Greater numbers of options for communication and consumer's own self-selection should enable marketing organizations to reduce the frequency with which unwanted and intrusive product information reaches these consumers. This should result in more efficient channels and less frequent irritation of consumers.

Loyals

Within any given product category there are individual consumers who are highly loyal to a particular brand or set of brands. The proportion of these individuals appears to vary from product category to product category (Ehrenberg, 1972); there are many such consumers in such categories as bleach and cigarettes and relatively few in categories like paper towels. These individuals are already persuaded that a given brand is best (or at least no worse than others), and they have high levels of brand awareness and positive brand attitudes. Marketing communications directed at these individuals is unlikely to raise awareness very much, particularly for well-known, frequently purchased brands. Neither is marketing communication likely to change attitude or the propensity to purchase. For these consumers, Ehrenberg's (1983) view of marketing communication as a reinforcer holds.

Loyal consumers simply need to be reminded that they have made a good choice and that they should remember to purchase their regular brand. A substantial body of research suggests that consumers are most likely to attend to information about their preferred brands and ignore information about other products (see Stewart, Tellis, & Sanft, 1990, for a review of this literature; see also Tolley & Bogart, 1993; Zillman & Bryant, 1985). This makes marketing communication a rather easy task, because the audience is attentive and a simple reminder, perhaps just the name, may be sufficient as a reinforcer.

The distribution decision is also somewhat easier, because loyal consumers are more likely to seek out their preferred product. In addition, the existence of significant numbers of consumers who are loyal to a given brand is a strong incentive for members of the distribution channel to stock it. As shopping for many product categories becomes more automated, brand loyalty is likely to become increasingly "programmed" for many products. For example, consumers may specify a preferred brand when ordering products through automated distribution channels that offer home delivery.

There are, of course, consumers who are loyal to competitive brands. Marketing communications that have any effect on loyal users of competitive products are particularly difficult to develop. These consumers are not disposed to pay attention to information about products they do not buy regularly, and such communications ask these consumers to change habitual behavior. To the extent that such habits have been "automated," change will be even more difficult to induce.

Consumers loyal to competitive brands may be induced to try another brand if the marketing communication is sufficiently creative and interesting that it gains their attention, and if it suggests something new and relevant to the consumer (whether a tangible benefit or an image association). Even this type of communication may be insufficient to induce trial of a nonpreferred product, however. In the case of traditional advertising, for example, there is almost always a lapse of time between advertising exposure and product purchase. This lapse of time provides an opportunity for the advertising message to be forgotten or countered by advertising for the consumer's preferred brand. On the other hand, channels of distribution that have strong communicative value offer an immediate opportunity for trial. Thus, the channel of distribution alone or in combination with more traditional channels of communication is likely to be the most effective means for changing behavior.[6] Evidence that marketers have recognized this fact is found in the growth of expenditures on point-of-purchase advertising and merchandising, including such recent innovations as frequent shopper programs (Lawmaster & Stewart, 1990).

As consumers "automate" more and more of their purchases, channels of distribution will assume an even more important role as reinforcers of behavior. Once a purchase decision is automated, the consumer will largely be removed from the role of decision maker. Switches based on impulse will be less common. This assumes that the channel will facilitate such purchasing automation. Alternative scenarios would place the channel in the role of decision maker, perhaps based on some rule offered by the

---

[6]There are instances in which promotions and merchandising activities may also play a key role as a bridge. In effect, they integrate the traditional channel of communication and the distribution channel. A good example is found in the Pepsi Challenge campaign. Pepsi did not merely tell people its product tasted better. If it had done so, the campaign probably would not have worked as well. Rather, the campaign facilitated trial through the use of Challenge Wagons and other events that provided additional points of consumer contact.

consumer. Such a rule might be "buy the least expensive" or "from among brands A, X, and Q, select the least expensive."

Still another scenario could place the distribution channel in a role that encourages switching. For example, an incentive (paid for by the manufacturer) might be offered to consumers who are willing to switch. This is not unlike current systems that offer automated coupons at the checkout counter based on what the consumer has just purchased.

These observations about how advertising and distribution may influence loyal users also has implications for defensive marketing. Insofar as a firm seeks to prevent loss of its own consumers, reducing opportunities for competitive product communication and trial at the point of distribution is important.

Switchers

Much of the research on marketing communications that has been carried out in both industry and academe has focused on this capricious group of consumers. Switchers have little or no brand loyalty. They most certainly make purchase decisions on the basis of something other than brand. Switching may be associated with price, availability, top-of-mind awareness, or any number of other factors. In cases in which price is the determinant characteristic, price promotions are likely to be the most effective vehicle for inducing switching. In cases in which the determinant factor is familiarity, top-of-mind awareness, image, or other communications-driven element, advertising may play an important role.

It is useful to note, however, that the effect of advertising on switchers is likely to be short lived and influenced more readily by the actions of competitors. Switchers are the most expensive group of consumers to attract and they are virtually impossible to hold. Unfortunately, this group cannot be ignored, because doing so leaves competitors with an unobstructed opportunity to reinforce a decision role favorable to its product.

Product availability is a key competitive tool in attracting switchers, because this group of consumers appears largely indifferent to product differences. Thus, other things being equal, a firm would want to maintain those distribution outlets that are very high in volume in order to ensure that it obtains a fair share of the business of these switchers. For this group of consumers, however, the lack of availability of a brand at a particular outlet is unlikely to have long-term consequences outside the context of this outlet.

The Emergent Market

The fourth group of consumers is the emergent market. Even in a mature market there are new consumers entering the market as others leave. The characteristics and composition of an emergent market will vary by product class, but there are two groups that are particularly important for a wide range of consumer markets, at least in the United States: young people (teens and young adults) and immigrants. Both groups are forming preferences for numerous products and both represent a market for products over a long time horizon.

Marketing communication and distribution targeted at the emergent market is closely akin to advertising and distribution for a new product. There is a need to create awareness, build brand image, and induce trial. There is a need to create within the consumer a sense of identity with the product, and to reinforce trial. An integrated channels approach, using traditional advertising (through appropriately targeted media), nontraditional advertising, promotion, and distribution channels, is essential for obtaining a share of the business of these emergent consumers, and, when possible, for moving them into the loyalist category.

The emergent market is most vulnerable to competitive activity, and at the same time, it is most important for the long-term viability of the firm. Marketing communications and distribution channels that specifically serve this market are particularly important to the firm. They represent tools for building a brand franchise and, by dominating channels that serve this market, the firm makes it more difficult for competitors to build a franchise of their own.

Thus, the objectives of marketing communication and distribution, and the media for achieving these objectives, will vary by customer segment. Traditional advertising, albeit in lesser amounts, will remain important for reinforcing purchase habits among brand loyal consumers. Distribution channels will play a strategic secondary and largely defensive role. For those consumers who are loyal to competitive brands, product modifications, blockbuster creative advertising, and distribution channel management may provide a means for inducing trial.

Dominance of large channels of distribution will remain the most effective means for obtaining the purchasing dollars of switchers. Blockbuster creative communication campaigns may play a secondary role in producing short-term increases in sales to this group. On occasion, such communication campaigns may also move some number of these consumers from the switcher segment to the loyal segment. Nevertheless, it is likely that the greatest effect on these consumers will be at the level of the distribution channel, where availability, relative shelf space, promotions, and other marketing activities can have their effect at the point of purchase.

Emergent markets represent an arena in which integrated channels management is likely to yield the greatest return. The synergistic effects of advertising, promotion, and distribution are greatest in this market, because all are necessary for creating a long-term, loyal customer. The emergent market also offers opportunity for efficient and effective targeting of both communications and distribution media.

SOME IMPLICATIONS

The discussion to this point has underscored the importance of developing an integrated channels approach to the management of the marketing communication and distribution functions. It has been argued that the increasing number of options for obtaining information and purchasing products is driving the merger of channels that have traditionally been dominant with respect to either the communications function or distribution function, but not both. It has also been argued that as a consequence of the increase in the number of communication and distribution channels available to them, consumers are increasingly taking control of the flow of information and products through a process of self-selection. This self-selection process is an important but infrequently studied mediator of efficiency and effectiveness of the distribution and communication functions.

In broadest sense, the world is a medium. There is a need to think of media more broadly, not just in terms of television, radio, and print. This is already recognized in outdoor advertising, in which the medium is the surrounding environment, and in event marketing. The distribution channel also serves as a medium through signage, packaging, and shelf space. Events of one type or another have increasingly become important media vehicles and often serve as temporary distribution channels. Interactive media expand the range of opportunities for direct response marketing by increasing the amount of the information that can be conveyed about any one product and by increasing the range of products that can be offered. Interactive media that allow consumers to select information and place orders are a prototypical example of the type of integrated channel that will be increasingly important in the future.

The linking pins between channels and marketing outcomes are the factors that influence the consumer's self-selection process and the dimensions of interaction with media. A better understanding of channel effects offers at least five advantages to marketers. The first and most obvious advantage is that it provides opportunities for more effective marketing by ensuring that the most effective and efficient channels are used. A second and related advantage is that new opportunities for coordinated marketing campaigns may be identified. Third, there may be increased opportunities for coordinated media buys. In fact, there already exist numerous diversified media organizations that have a whole portfolio of very different media offerings ranging from traditional print and broadcast to new media, such as computer information services. Creative "bundling" of media vehicles for specific audiences would be a natural product for such organizations, but such bundling requires a better understanding of media effects than is now possessed.

A fourth opportunity is the greater audience selectivity that is provided by the new media alternatives. There are two advantages associated with such selectivity. The first is that marketing can be made more efficient by reducing the number of persons in the audience who are not in the target. The second advantage is that marketing can be made more effective by doing more customization of messages for each medium. The final opportunity is that by examining the way people interact with media, and by identifying specific dimensions of that interaction, it becomes possible to work backward from these dimensions to construct new media. Information technology offers a great deal of flexibility and the opportunity for creativity.

The concept of an integrated channel has important implications for institutions other than the marketing organization. A broadened definition of media includes a wide array of channels that are not commissionable. Compensation for advertising agencies will have to be reconsidered if agencies are to contribute to the management of integrated channels. Likewise, the role of distribution channel members will need to be considered in light of their increasing role in marketing communications and a potentially diminished need to provide a physical location that consumers visit.

There is, perhaps, no better summary of the current status and needs than that provided by Sissors and Bumba (1989) in their most recent textbook on media planning:

> The 1990's will offer advertisers both opportunities and obstacles. A more fragmented media world results in greater audience selectivity, and greater selectivity results in less waste. In light of the increasing cost of media, the less waste in a media plan the better.
>
> More viewing, reading, and listening options should inevitably lead to higher interest, deeper involvement, and higher attentiveness—to both the media and the advertising within the media. There is a good chance that if advertisers react to this segmentation with personalized and localized messages, their media budgets can be used with greater discrimination and far more effectiveness. The key to all is research. (pp. 401–402)

REFERENCES

Advertising Research Foundation. (1983). *1983 Member representative questionnaire.* (Report 1R). New York: Author.

Advertising Research Foundation, Audience Concepts Committee. (1961). *Toward better media comparisons.* New York: Author.

Audits & Surveys, Inc. (1986). *A study of media involvement.* New York: Author.

Blair, M. H. (1987/1988, December/January). An empirical investigation of advertising wearin and wearout. *Journal of Advertising Research,* pp. 45–50.

Brand, S. (1988). *The media lab.* New York: Penguin.

Broadbent, D. (1977). The hidden pre-attentive processes. *American Psychologist, 32* (2), 109–118.

Chestnut, R. W. (1983). Many issues, few answers — A state of the art review of the intermedia literature. In *Advertising Research Foundation transcript proceedings of the intermedia Comparisons Workshop.* New York: Advertising Research Foundation.

Chook, P. H. (1983). ARF model for evaluating media, making the promise a reality. In *Advertising Research Foundation transcript proceedings of the Intermedia Comparisons Workshop.* New York: Advertising Research Foundation.

Chook, P. H. (1985). A continuing study of magazine environment, frequency, and advertising performance. *Journal of Advertising Research, 25* (4), 23–33.

Clemens, J. (1972). The effect of media on advertisement reception. In *Ten years of advertising media research, 1962–1971* (pp. 31–52). London: The Thomson Organization Ltd.

Corlett, T. (1971, March). Using media research — Perspectives from campaign planning. Media Research Group Seminar, January, 1970. *ADMAP,* pp. 1–3.

Corlett, T., Lannon, J., & Richardson, D. (1971, April). The use of media. *ADMAP World Advertising Workshop, 4.* 1–10.

Corlett, T., & Richardson, D. (1969). The inter-related effects of press and television advertising. *The Thomson medals and awards for advertising research 1969.* London: The Thomson Organization.

Cutler, B. (1990). The fifth medium. *American Demographics, 12,* 24–29.

Drane, R. (1988, June 8–10). *Boosting the odds of advertising success.* Paper presented to the Marketing Science Conference on Evaluating the Effects of Consumer Advertising on Market Position Over Time. Babson College Campus, Wellesley, MA.

Ehrenberg, A. S. C. (1972). *Repeat-buying: Theory and applications.* New York: American Elsevier.

Ehrenberg, A. S. C. (1983). Repetitive advertising and the consumer. *Journal of Advertising Research, 23,* 29–38.

Frazier, G., & Summers. J. (1985). Push and pull strategies in industrial markets: A normative framework. In G. Frazier & J. Sheth (Eds.), *Contemporary views on marketing practice.* Lexington, MA: Lexington.

Glazer, R. (1989). *Marketing and the changing information environment: Implications for strategy, structure, and the marketing mix* (Rep. No. 89–108). Cambridge, MA: Marketing Science Institute.

Greenberg, B. S. (1988). Some uncommon television images and the drench yypothesis. In S. Oskamp (Ed.), *Television as a social issue* (pp. 88–102). Newbury Park, CA: Sage.

Greenwald, A. C., & Leavitt, C. (1984). Audience involvement in advertising: Four levels. *Journal of Consumer Research, 11,* 581–592.

Guggenheim, B. (1984). Advertising media planning and evaluation: Current research issues. In *Current issues and research in advertising.* Ann Arbor: Mi University of Michigan Graduate School of Business Administration.

Gunter, B. (1985). Determinants of television viewing preferences. In D. Zillmann & J. Bryant (Eds.), *Selective exposure to communication* (pp. 93–112). Hillsdale, NJ: Lawrence Erlbaum Associates,

Haley, R. I. (1985). *Developing effective communications strategy.* New York: Wiley.

Herr, P. M. (1989). Priming price: Prior knowledge and context effects. *Journal of Consumer Research, 16,* 67–75.

Higgins, E. T., & King, G. (1981). Accessibility of social constructs: Information processing consequences of individual and contextual variability. In N. Cantor & J. Kihlstrom (Eds.), *Personality, cognition, and social interaction* (pp. 69–122). Hillsdale, NJ: Lawrence Erlbaum Associates.

Information Resources Inc. (1989). *Advertising works*. Chicago: Author.

Institute of Practitioners in Advertising. (1969). *As others see US* (Occasional Paper No. 17)

Kennedy, J. R. (1971). How program environment affects TV commercials. *Journal of Advertising Research, 11*, 33–38.

Klapper, J. T. (1965). The comparative effects of the various media. In W. Schramm (Ed.), *The process and effects of mass communication* (pp. 91–105). Urbana: University of Illinois Press.

Kotler, P. (1973–1974). Atmospherics as a marketing tool. *Journal of Retailing, 49*, 48–63.

Krugman, H. E. (1983). Television program interest and commercial interruption: Are commercials on interesting programs less effective? *Journal of Advertising Research, 23*(1), 21–23.

Krugman, H. E. (1988). Point of view: Limits of attention to advertising. *Journal of Advertising Research, 28*, 47–50.

Lawmaster, S., & Stewart, D. W. (1991). Frequent Shopper Programs: Supermarketers' new tool to stimulate store loyalty. *Journal of Promotion Management, 1*(1), 55–76.

Light, L. (1990). The changing advertising world. *Journal of Advertising Research, 30*, 30–35.

Lloyd, D. W., & Clancy, K. J. (1989). The effects of television program involvement on advertising response: Implications for media planning. In *Transcript proceedings of the First Annual Advertising Research Foundation Media Research Workshop*. New York: Advertising Research Foundation.

McLuhan, M., & Fiore, Q. (1967). *The medium is the message*. New York: Bantam.

Moeller, L. G. (1988). Untitled. In R. W. Budd & B. D. Ruben (Eds.), *Beyond media: New approaches to mass communication* (Rev. Ed.). New Brunswick, NJ: Transaction Books.

Murray, J. P. (1980). *Television and youth: 25 years of research and controversy*. Boys Town, NE: Boys Town Center for the Study of Youth Development.

Nolan, J. (1972), Combined media campaigns. In *Ten years of advertising media research, 1962–1971* (pp. 319–349). London: The Thomson Organization.

Parker, E. B. (1970). In H. Sackman & N. Nie (Eds.), *Information utility and social choice* (pp.). Montvale, NJ: AFIPS Press.

Pechmann, C., & Stewart, D. W. (1990). The effects of comparative advertising on attention, memory, and purchase intentions, *Journal of Consumer Research, 17*(2), 180–191.

Ray, M. L. (1985). An even more powerful consumer? In R. Buzzell (Ed.), *Marketing in an electronic age*. Cambridge, MA: Harvard University Press.

Raymond, C. (1976). *Advertising research: The state of the art* (pp. 57–58). New York: Association of National Advertisers.

Richardson, D. (1972). Measuring the role of media in people's lives. In *Ten years of advertising media research, 1962–1971* (pp. 443–464). London: The Thomson Organization.

Russell, C. (1989). People who lust after big numbers. *American Demographics, 11*, 2.

Schmalensee, D. H. (1983). Today's top priority advertising questions. *Journal of Advertising Research*, 49–60.

Schramm, W. (1965). 22, *The process and effects of mass communication*. Urbana: University of Illinois Press.

Schultz, D. E. (1979). Media research users want. *Journal of Advertising Research, 18*, 13–17.

Singh, S. N., & Churchill, G. A. (1987). Arousal and advertising effectiveness. *Journal of Advertising, 16*(1), 4–10.

Sissors, J. Z., & Bumba, L. (1989). *Advertising media planning* (3rd ed.). Lincolnwood, IL: NTC Business Books.

Soldow, G. F., & Principe, V. (1981). Response to commercials as a function of program context. *Journal of Advertising Research, 21*(2), 59–65.

Spaeth, J. (1983, December). Intermedia and intramedia comparisons, evaluations, and needs. *Communication Options*.

Stalk, G., Jr., & Hout, T. M. (1990). *Competing against time*. New York: The Free Press.

Stanley, R. H., & Steinberg, C. S. (1976). *The media environment*. New York: Hastings House.

Stern, B. L., Bush, R. F., & Hair, J. F., Jr. (1977). The self-image/store image matching process: An empirical test. *The Journal of Business, 50*, 63–69.

Stern, L., & El-Ansary, A. (1992). *Marketing channels* (4th ed.). Englewood Cliffs, NJ: Prentice-Hall.

Stewart, D. W. (1988). Advertising opportunities in a fragmented media environment. In *Transcript proceedings of the First Annual Advertising Research Foundation Media Research Workshop*. New York: Advertising Research Foundation.

Stewart, D. W. (1989). Measures, methods, and models of advertising response. *Journal of Advertising Research, 29*, 54–60.

Stewart, D. W., Tellis, G., & Sanft, H. (1990). *Advertising effects in the market place: What we know about how advertising does (and does not) work* (Working paper). Los Angeles: Department of Marketing, University of Southern California.

Tolley, B. S. & Bogart, L. (1994). How Readers Process Newspaper Advertising. In E. Clark, T. Brock, & D. W. Stewart (Eds.), *Attention, attitude, and affect in response to advertising* (pp. 69–78). Hillsdale, NJ: Lawrence Erlbaum Associates.

Webster, F. E., Jr. (1989). *It's 1990—Do you know where your marketing is?* (MSI White Paper). Cambridge, MA: Marketing Science Institute.

Wyer, R. S., & Srull, T. K. (1981). Category accessibility: Some theoretical and empirical issues concerning the processing of social stimulus information. In E. T. Higgins, C. P. Herman, & M. P. Zanna (Eds.), *Social cognition: The Ontario symposium* (pp. 161–197). Hillsdale, NJ: Lawrence Erlbaum Associates.

Yi, Y. (1990a). Cognitive and affective priming effects of the context for print advertisements. *Journal of Advertising, 19*(2), 40–48.

Yi, Y. (1990b). The effects of contextual priming in print advertisements. *Journal of Consumer Research, 17*, 215–222.

Zillmann, D., & Bryant, J. (1985). *Selective exposure to communication*. Hillsdale, NJ: Lawrence Erlbaum Associates.

11 Integrated Communication: Some Hidden Complications

John Philip Jones
Syracuse University

The concept of integrated communications has been talked about to an increasing degree during the past decade. There have been three reasons for this.

First, there has been a significant increase in manufacturers' expenditure on sales promotions, which accounted in 1991 for 75% of combined advertising and promotional budgets, up from 58% in 1978 (Jones, 1992). These estimates, by Donnelley Marketing, translate into increases in sales promotion expenditure amounting to tens of billions of dollars.

Such a growth in promotions should have lent great weight to the notion of linking advertising and promotions to improve synergism—in particular, by using promotions to reinforce the sales-building effects of advertising. Yet many manufacturers have paid nothing but lip service to this concept. The coordination of complicated marketing activities takes much time and trouble, and there are some additional difficulties. Promotions and advertising tend to have different effects (as will be apparent from the discussion later in this chapter).

The growth in promotions has been driven by marketplace trends that have been only to a limited degree within the control of individual manufacturers. Most consumer goods markets have reached maturity—a permanent plateau that set in, in most cases, at least a decade ago. It has been estimated that only 10% of consumer expenditure takes place at the moment in categories that are increasing strongly (Jones, 1992). Partly as a response to this category flattening, and in a desperate search for growth, manufacturers have fragmented their brands very extensively, under the guise of "line extension" and "brand stretching." Most manufacturers now offer for sale a bewildering collection of subbrands such as the 6 varieties of Tide, 15 of Crest, and 7 of Coca-Cola—all functionally different from one another (Jones, 1992). These trends—the flattening of category growth and splintering of brands—have led to a greater emphasis than ever before on a head-to-head conflict between competitors and a sharp concentration on a short-term fight for market share. This has inevitably led to an increasing use of trade and consumer promotions as key tactical weapons.

Added to these trends has been an increasing concentration of retail strength in the food and drug trades in important regions of the United States. This concentration, which has led to a growth in the bargaining power of retailers, has forced manufacturers to boost temporarily or even permanently the slotting allowances paid to the trade for stocking new brands, and, even more important, the retail margins on existing lines. This has been done mainly by increasing trade promotions. The manufacturer's own sales force, which operates at the "sharp end" of the competitive battle, often reinforces the retail demand for increased promotional discounts.

The second factor leading to the growth in businesspeople's interest in integrated communications has been a gradual but perceptible boosting of the importance of short-term measurability and accountability, something that has influenced virtually all aspects of business. This boosting has shifted the emphasis from all sales-generating activities that can be evaluated only with difficulty toward those that can be evaluated relatively easily. This has been a delayed effect of the inflation of the 1970s and early 1980s, compounded by the pressures of sluggish business conditions. In the words of one manufacturer in the food field:

> The real problem is the same one which pervades other aspects of corporate behavior today: an overemphasis on the short term with short term defined, at best, as "this year," "just as often "this quarter."
>
> Trade deals generate *measurable* volume *now*. . . . So when we need extra volume this quarter, or this year, whatever the reason, we do not increase advertising, we increase trade deals. (Jones, 1986, p. 171)

The author of these words need not have confined himself to trade deals. The same point applies equally relevantly to consumer promotions and to the various types of database marketing.

The third factor encouraging integrated communication has been the special position of advertising agencies. The increase in expenditure below the line has not benefited agency income at all. Agencies have consequently been attracted by integrated communications, as a device to increase their participation in their clients' marketing activities. Virtually all agencies have broadened their base, although the number of them that have been really successful in this has remained stubbornly small. This is for reasons connected with the average agency's culture, and is something that does not easily change.

Synergism between advertising and promotions is a desirable objective, but it is one that is not easy to achieve. Integrated communications must go much further than a simple cross-selling of services to agencies' clients. Integrated communications must embrace:

- A single overarching definition of marketing strategy, which means that all activities that result are planned together.
- a close co-operation between advertising and promotions at the tactical level.
- An exploration of sales-generating activities outside the traditional boundaries, for instance, database marketing for packaged goods.

Innovations on the lines described in the last paragraph are already taking place to some extent, but despite their undoubted attractions, such changes hold substantial concealed dangers. These are the main concern of this chapter.

The different tactical activities covered by integrated communications include traditional consumer advertising, direct marketing, trade promotions, retail display, consumer promotions, and public relations. A number of these are routinely evaluated according to their separate sales-generating capabilities. This is much easier with database marketing than with manufacturers' traditional advertising in which the sales stimulus is unconnected with the distributional pipeline. Evaluation of the sales effects of promotions is also easy; indeed, alluringly easy. However, there are two immediate complications, both concerned with measurement.

First, there is a difficulty related to sales results on their own. Evaluating the sales-generating effect of the different actions individually underestimates the value of synergism. Concentrating attention on individual activities diverts attention from their effectiveness in the aggregate. If synergism has any reality in the marketplace, and if, for illustration, we assume that the sales-generating value of each individual marketing activity is a magnitude of 2, then $2 + 2 + 2$ must add up to 7. This will not be clear if they are measured separately.

The second point concerns measurement at a more subtle level. In measuring the performance of different marketing programs, it is totally inadequate to judge then on their sales-generating effectiveness alone. Such activities must also be examined for their ability to generate net profit. The factor that makes profitability a criterion of major importance is that there is generally a huge disparity between the relative profitability of the two largest individual components of integrated communications: consumer advertising and sales promotions. Without taking profit into account, we are unable to compare these two activities with any accuracy, nor are we able to plan them to work cooperatively together.

PROMOTIONS — SALES AND PROFIT

It cannot be emphasized too strongly that most promotions yield an immediate sales return. This is because most of them are focused — sharply and occasionally dramatically — on the price that retailers or consumers pay for the manufacturer's product. Virtually all trade promotions are price related, and this goes for a substantial majority of (although not all) consumer promotions. The reality of most promotions is price reduction, yet this is disguised by manufacturers' terminology. Promotions are often described as "investments" when they are in reality income sacrificed; they should appear as that side of the ledger (as an income reduction), and not on the expenditure side (as money invested). This distinction acts as a reminder that promotions should not be expected to build for the future, but are intended to inject adrenaline, with its immediate but not prolonged effect. The effect of this adrenaline on sales can be evaluated.

As any student of microeconomics knows, the sales effect of any price change can be quantified — with a good deal of trouble and given enough data to allow a calculation of the coefficient of price elasticity. This is a number, and it means simply the percentage by which the sales of a brand will increase in the short run as a result of a 1 % reduction in price. The number is preceded by a minus sign, demonstrating that lower prices cause sales to go up, and vice versa. The calculation is made from a laborious examination of historical price and sales data that establish an average sales change associated with a price change, and this should ideally be arrived at from a range of prices. Time lags between price change and sales change have to be taken into account, as well as exogenous variables, including inflation.

The elasticity can be calculated for sales to the retail trade and also for sales to the consumer, and there are some interesting differences between the two. The main focus here is on the consumer, but it should be remembered that trade and consumer promotions can be connected; in particular, the profit from a trade promotion is not always retained by the retailer, but is sometimes passed on to the customer (e.g., by doubling the value of manufacturers' coupons). Incidentally, consumer promotions are all, to some extent, also directed at the retail trade insofar as they are intended to encourage retailers to display the merchandise promoted. Display is a major sales stimulus in its own right, and it can also reinforce other stimuli. It is an element in integrated communications.

Price elasticity is essentially a measure of how easily the consumer will accept a competitive brand as a substitute for the brand being examined. Low price elasticity means that substitution is difficult and that a change in price will not affect the demand for the brand very greatly. The opposite also holds: If elasticity is high, price change greatly affects demand. As the number of competitors grows (something that tends to happen over time even though markets do not grow much in absolute size), we would logically expect price elasticities in general to rise (Tellis, 1988).

Calculations of price elasticity are not simple, and manufacturers only rarely have on their staffs statisticians capable of making the estimates. However, the calculations have been made in hundreds of cases. They are almost invariably based on a relatively narrow range of price variations, so that they should not be extrapolated too far outside this range. They can, nevertheless, be used for sales optimization and profit maximization, a process in which I myself participated as long ago as the early 1960s.[1]

A number of estimates have been published of the average price elasticity of collections of brands. The most recent major study, by Tellis of the University of Southern California, summarizes the figures for 367 different brands that appeared in the academic literature published between 1961 and 1985 (Tellis, 1988). The most striking feature of Tellis's survey is the high level of the average price elasticity: -1.76. This means that, for an average brand, a 1% reduction in price would boost sales by 1.76%. Manufacturers do not, of course, vary their prices in 1% increments; a more realistic 10% price reduction would lift sales by 17.6%, an impressive figure.

Table 11.1 illustrates a number of calculations of the sales effect of a 10% price reduction, based on price elasticities of -1.6, -1.8, -2.0, and -2.2. Tellis (1989) argued that typical marketplace elasticities may be higher than the -1.76 average he worked out from his 367 cases. However, the empirical support for his hypothesis of higher elasticities is much more tenuous than that for his -1.76 average. Estimates based on European experience suggest that even Tellis's average of -1.76 may itself be too high (Broadbent, 1980; Roberts, 1980; Tellis, 1988). The calculations used in this chapter have, therefore, been limited to the range of coefficients listed previously, which cover elasticities on both sides of Tellis's average.

If we look solely at the sales projections in Table 11.1, these provide ample support for the view that promotions can shift merchandise. It is, therefore, perfectly easy to understand the attraction they hold for a brand manager, particularly one who finds him- or herself in the uncomfortable situation of running a brand whose shipments during the year have been

---

[1]This was when I was a young account executive at J. Walter Thompson, London. My client at the time was Chesebrough-Pond's (now part of Unilever); the brand on which we used price elasticity as an operational tool was Vaseline Petroleum Jelly.

TABLE 11.1
Effect of 10% Price Reduction

Variable Cost as Percentage of NSV	Price Elasticity	Effect on Sales (%)	Effect on Net Profit If 5% of NSV (%)	Effect on Net Profit If 10% of NSV (%)
40	− 2.2	+ 22	+ 20	+ 10
50	− 2.2	+ 22	− 24	− 12
60	− 2.2	+ 22	− 67	− 34
40	− 2.0	+ 20	No change	No change
50	− 2.0	+ 20	− 40	− 20
60	− 2.0	+ 20	− 80	− 40
40	− 1.8	+ 18	− 20	− 10
50	− 1.8	+ 18	− 56	− 28
60	− 1.8	+ 18	− 92	− 46
40	− 1.6	+ 16	− 40	− 20
50	− 1.6	+ 16	− 72	− 36
60	− 1.6	+ 16	− 104	− 52

slower than planned and whose sales target has to be met by December 31 — and, particularly, a brand manager whose career is on the line.

However, the attractive volume figures are not the whole story; we must look at how costs have been affected. In order to do this, we have to make certain assumptions about the cost structure of the brand that is being examined. In Table 11.1, alternatives have been worked out on the basis of ratios ("Advertising-to-Sales Ratios," 1989) that are reasonably typical for real brands:

- Variable cost representing 40%, 50%, and 60% of net sales value (NSV).
- Net profit representing 5% and 10% of NSV.

As has already been pointed out, the table examines four different levels of price elasticity, and a single price reduction, of 10%.

The most obvious feature of the profit calculations is that most of the sales increases provided by the price reductions yield a lower profit than before the sales rise. Indeed, some of the resulting profit reductions are disastrously large. The reasons for this unappealing outcome are an increase in variable costs (raw materials, packaging, labor, etc.) required by the extra sales volume, in conjunction with a deflation in the NSV that applies to all sales resulting from the lower consumer price (i.e., all sales of the brand offered on the promotional terms).

A certain amount of promotion is undertaken for defensive reasons, for instance, to maintain high distribution and display for brands in an increasingly concentrated retail trade (Wilson, 1982). This approach is understandable, although manufacturers should also be able to provide a countervailing force to retailers' strength, by the obvious method of ensuring that their consumer advertising will pull the merchandise through the retail pipeline, and, perhaps equally important, by ensuring that retail buyers will be aware of the effect of such advertising.

Although promotional actions are conducted from a mixture of offensive and defensive motives that cannot often be separated from one another, the former are generally the more important. Indeed, in the majority of circumstances, manufacturers who promote heavily are deliberately exchanging profit for volume; in other words, they are making less profit on greater sales or, to make the point more crudely, slicing into their own margins in order to dump their merchandise.

PROMOTIONS – LONG-TERM EFFECTS

The probability that most promotions will be unprofitable is a serious enough outcome, but there are three additional ill effects that are manifest only in the long term. The first of these stems from the strong emphasis of promotions on short-term sales. A price-off promotion generally causes sales to rise, but they then return to their original level once the promotion stops. (Peckham, 1981). The "blip" on the Nielsen consumer purchases graph looks like the silhouette of a top hat (B. Wilenkin, formerly of Unilever, personal communication). The reason is, very simply, that the strategy for such a promotion aims to move merchandise by bribing the retailer and the consumer. When the bribe stops, the extra sales also stop.

It has been argued by some commentators (e.g., Prentice, 1977) that a proportion of promotional money has a long-term franchise-building effect. There is a limited degree of truth in this argument when it relates to promotions that encourage repeat purchase. However, all trade promotions and the most important consumer promotions, temporary price reductions (TPRs) and coupons, have just about the smallest long-term effect of any below-the-line activity. With TPRs in particular, there is no stress on building a consumer franchise by emphasizing the competitive benefits of the brand or building warm nonrational associations with it, which might encourage the public to buy the goods on a more-or-less continuous basis. As a consequence, such promotions lead to volatile demand, in contrast to franchise building (e.g., by consumer advertising), which leads to relatively stable demand.

Most seriously, a promotion often results in what the A. C. Nielsen market-research company calls a "mortgaging" effect, by bringing forward sales from a later period; thus full-price sales in the period following the promotion may be even less than they would otherwise have been.

Mortgaging effectively prolongs the period during which the manufacturer is paying a heavy promotional subsidy to the consumer.

This all leads to a not insignificant weakening of the brand. A parallel point, for which there is patchy evidence, is that brands that are supported more by advertising than by promotions often carry, without too much trouble, a higher-than-average list price and tend, therefore, to be more profitable (e.g., Jones, 1989; Ogilvy Center, 1989). The consumer pays the premium price because the advertised brands have given more psychological added values than have heavily promoted brands (Jones, 1986). This point is related to the third legacy, to be discussed later.

The second long-term disadvantage of promotions is that they fuel the flames of competitive retaliation to a far greater degree than other marketing activities. As a result, diminishing returns set in with frightening rapidity (Peckham, 1981). When the competition is drawn into the promotional war, it can cause the sharp sales increases predicted by the original price elasticity coefficients to be significantly muted — with an even more disastrous effect on the profit outcome of the promotions.

The long-term result of such retaliation has sometimes been that all profit has been eliminated from total market categories. There is no shortage of examples of this self-destructive effect. Two dramatic instances from Europe are the market for laundry detergents in Denmark during the 1960s and the once-large market in Britain for fruit concentrates, which are mixed with water to make soft drinks. In both markets, heavy promotions eventually caused strong brands to degenerate into virtually unbranded (and unprofitable) commodities.

The third long-term legacy of promotions is the one that is most talked about, particularly by advertising agencies — promotions are said to devalue the image of the promoted brand in the eyes of the consumer. This theory accords with common sense, although there is no very extensive public evidence to support it. Indeed, the argument may not be quite as powerful as it appears, because once a brand has established a consumer franchise and a brand image, it takes a long time for these to decay, as the image is maintained more by people's personal familiarity with and usage of the brand than by external marketing stimuli. However, promotions have occasionally, but undoubtedly, had an unfavorable influence on consumers' brand perceptions. There is good (unpublished) evidence that this happened to Burger King in the late 1970s and early 1980s, when the brand was in a promotional war with McDonald's.

As a general rule, the image of a brand can never be improved by promotions — a matter directly related to the stability of the consumer franchise. In Unilever language, there is a vicious circle described as "promotion-commotion-demotion" (B. Wilenkin, personal communication).

The image can, on the other hand, be strengthened by consumer advertising. This strengthening represents a long-term effect in addition to short-term sales generation, and it leads to an increasing perceived differentiation of the advertised brand from rival brands. This differentiation, in turn, reduces consumers' ability to substitute other brands for the advertised brand, thus leading to greater stability (i.e., less elasticity) of consumer demand for the latter. This outcome can represent a significant advantage (although certain informed observers are skeptical about whether the low creative quality of present-day campaigns actually leads to as much image building as past advertising was capable of achieving).

ADVERTISING — SALES AND PROFIT

We now come to the very difficult matter of evaluating advertising investments, because readers will undoubtedly be asking themselves the following question: If promotions involve such massive short-term costs and bring about such worrisome long-term problems, can advertising investments promise anything better?

Setting to one side the potentially favorable long-term effect of advertising that provides something like an added bonus, we can on occasion quantify advertising's strictly short-term effect. This is based on a calculation of the advertising elasticity of a brand. This calculation is also a number, and it measures the percentage increase in sales that can be expected from a 1 % increase in advertising weight. The coefficient is preceded by a plus and not by a minus sign, because (it is hoped!) an increase in advertising will result in an increase in sales.

Estimating advertising elasticity involves complex regression calculations, but (as for price elasticity) the computation has been carried out in hundreds of cases. The spread of research based on single-source scanner data should make it easier to make such calculations in the future.

The most recently published examination of advertising elasticity was based on 128 cases, which provided an average short-term advertising elasticity of +0.22. This figure agrees well with earlier published studies (Assmus, Farlet, & Lehmann, 1984; Broadbent, 1980; Roberts, 1980). The reader will be struck by the large difference between this advertising elasticity coefficient of +0.22 and the average price elasticity of −1.76. It is, however, extremely dangerous to draw conclusions about the apparently much greater effectiveness of promotions. The key difference between promotions and advertising is that promotional price reductions cost the manufacturer much more money than advertising increases, so it is highly misleading to evaluate their relative effectiveness by their sales effect alone (Broadbent, 1989).

Table 11.2 looks at the sales and profit outcomes of a 50% advertising uplift. Table 11.2 (similar to Table 11.1) is concerned solely with the sorts of operational changes in marketing variables that a manufacturer is

TABLE 11.2
Effect of 50% Advertising Increase

Variable Cost as Percentage of NSV (%)	A:S Ratio (%)	Advertising Elasticity	Effect on Sales (%)	Effect on Net Profit if 5% of NSV (%)	Effect on Net Profit if 10% of NSV (%)
40	4	+0.1	+5	+20	+10
50	4	+0.1	+5	+10	+5
60	4	+0.1	+5	No change	No change
40	4	+0.2	+10	+80	+40
50	4	+0.2	+10	+60	+30
60	4	+0.2	+10	+40	+20
40	4	+0.3	+15	+140	+70
50	4	+0.3	+15	+110	+55
60	4	+0.3	+15	+80	+40
40	6	+0.1	+5	No change	No change
50	6	+0.1	+5	−10	−5
60	6	+0.1	+5	−20	−10
40	6	+0.2	+10	+60	+30
50	6	+0.2	+10	+40	+20
60	6	+0.2	+10	+20	+10
40	6	+0.3	+15	+120	+60
50	6	+0.3	+15	+90	+45
60	6	+0.3	+15	+60	+30
40	8	+0.1	+5	−20	−10
50	8	+0.1	+5	−30	−15
60	8	+0.1	+5	−40	−20
40	8	+0.2	+10	+40	+20
50	8	+0.2	+10	+20	+10
60	8	+0.2	+10	No change	No change
40	8	+0.3	+15	+100	+50
50	8	+0.3	+15	+70	+35
60	8	+0.3	+15	+40	+20

accustomed to making. Business does not operate with 1% advertising variations any more than it does with 1% price changes. From general experience of advertising pressure testing and the difficulties of measuring its effects, 50% is the minimum uplift in the advertising appropriation that will get the needle to swing. The profitability estimates in Table 11.2 are based on the following typical levels:

- Variable costs of 40%, 50%, and 60% of NSV.
- Advertising-to-sales (A:S) ratios of 4%, 6% and 8% of NSV.
- Advertising elasticity coefficients of +0.1, +0.2, and +0.3.
- Net profit representing 5% and 10% of NSV.

What is strikingly obvious in Table 11.2 is that, despite the relatively small sales effects of the extra advertising, these sales produce good profit increases in the majority of cases. This outcome is quite different from the effect of the price reductions analyzed in Table 11.1, in which the sales increases are all substantial but nearly all are accompanied by serious reductions in profit.

HOW DO WE RESOLVE THE DIFFICULTIES?

At the beginning of this chapter, the point was made that advertising and sales promotions have different effects. It should now be clear what these differences are. Advertising aims at a slow build of profitable sales through an even slower augmentation of a brand's user base. Promotions are aimed at shorter, sharper, temporary, and often highly unprofitable sales uplifts. Overpromotion is unattractive and even dangerous to the long-term health of brands, yet manufacturers are compelled to promote continuously, for reasons that are essentially competitive and defensive. Manufacturers should nevertheless keep the perils of exchanging sales volume for profit constantly in mind.

The lessons of this chapter point strongly to the danger of implementing promotions in anything but a carefully planned and well-disciplined fashion. In order to test the tightness of the planning for each brand's promotional program, manufacturers should estimate how much promotional activity is necessary for strictly defensive purposes, both to maintain competitive levels of display in supermarkets, and counter the more aggressive promotional activities of the largest and most direct competition. This is very much a judgment call. However, the projections of sales and profit from specific price reductions provide the best available data on which an evaluation of the probable results of the manufacturer's own actions can and should be based.

Only a small handful of manufacturers make any effort to improve by formal study their knowledge of the effects of promotions on sales of their brands. An old adage that is only too easily forgotten is that manufacturers should always strive to achieve a double benefit from their marketing programs: first, additional profit, and second, increased knowledge and expertise.

There is also, very importantly, the matter of interlocking the various components of integrated communications with the aim of increasing mutual support. This requires both combined planning and combined evaluation.

The best mechanism for the evaluation of multiple sales-generating activities is the difficult and laborious process of developing, testing and fine tuning mathematical models based on multivariate regressions. In these models, the relative weights of the different sales-generating activities can be individually computed with an acceptable degree of approximation. It is also possible to address the difficulty mentioned earlier in this chapter, the effect of synergism. With a model, an attempt can be made to quantify this "add on" of the total program to the effects of the different individual activities.

In the process of quantification, manufacturers must take into account not only short-run sales effects, but long-run ones as well, and they must measure the influence of their various activities on profitability as well as on sales.

The evaluation of profitability should lead to two specific courses of action: developing franchise-building (as opposed to merely sales-generating) promotions, and exercising great restraint about increasing promotional expenditures in response to marketplace pressures for increased sales volume.

The source of these pressures is not only consumer demand for price incentives in a competitive environment. The most important factor, and the one that operates the most directly, is the call for promotional price cutting by the retail trade and the manufacturer's own sales force. Yet, in the last analysis, the manufacturer's loyalty must be to the integrity and profitability of his or her brands. Promotions all too often act to undermine these core qualities.

REFERENCES

Advertising-to-sales ratios. (1989, November 13). *Advertising Age*, p. 32.

Assmus, G., Farlet, J. U., & Lehmann, D. R. (1984). How advertising affects sales: Meta-analysis of econometric results. *Journal of Marketing Research, 21,* 65–74.

Broadbent, S. (1980, November). Price and advertising: Volume and profit. *Admap*, p. 536.

Broadbent, S. (1989, August–September). Point of view: What is a "small" advertising elasticity? *Journal of Advertising Research*, pp. 37–39.

Jones, J. P. (1986). *What's in a name: Advertising and the concept of brands.* Lexington, MA: Lexington.

Jones, J. P. (1989). *Does it pay to advertise? Cases illustrating successful brand advertising.* Lexington, MA: Lexington.

Jones, J. P. (1992). *How much is enough? Getting the most from your advertising dollar.* New York: Lexington.

Ogilvy Center for Research and Development (1989). *Advertising, sales promotion and the bottom line.* San Francisco: Author.

Peckham, J. O., Sr. (1981). *The wheel of marketing.* Northbrook, IL: A. C. Nielsen.

Prentice, R. M. (1977, January 10). How to split your marketing funds between advertising and promotion. *Advertising Age*, pp. 41–44.

Roberts, A. (1980, December). The decision between above- and below-the-line. *Admap*, p. 590.

Tellis, G. J. (1988, November). The price elasticity of selective demand: A meta-analysis of econometric models of sales. *Journal of Marketing Research,* pp. 331–341.

Tellis, G. J. (1989, August–September). Point of view: Interpreting advertising and price elasticities. *Journal of Advertising Research*, pp. 40–43.

Wilson, T. W, Jr. (1982). *Achieving a sustainable competitive advantage.* New York: Association of National Advertisers New Product Marketing Research Workshop.

IV Integrated Campaigns: Case Studies

12

Integrated Marketing Communication in a Public Service Context: The Indiana Middle Grades Reading Program

Diana L. Haytko
University of Wisconsin–Madison

Most advertising practitioners would agree that the buzzword for the 1990s is "integrated marketing," also referred to as "the new advertising." There have been several definitions for this not-so-new concept, but primarily the concept's main focus is away from the use of traditional media vehicles as independent entities and toward a new synergy of all media voices in creating a coordinated communications effort.

Past integrated marketing campaigns have been primarily conducted in the for-profit sector, most often for consumer packaged goods companies, but also for service businesses. There are relatively few reported success stories regarding integrated marketing campaigns. However, efforts by Mr. Turkey, the Chelsea Inn of Toronto, Financial Security Assurance, Inc., Continental Banks, and the Genie Company have been well documented in the literature (Arab, 1991; Foster, 1990; Novosad, 1991; Rubin, 1991). Other campaigns that have been mentioned include Colgate's smile logo and theme line "Because your smile was meant to last a lifetime," Xerox's use of the theme line "Puttin' it together," and Pepsi's "Cool Can" summer promotion's link to the overall line "The choice of a new generation," (Kroll, 1991). However, these campaigns do not meet the criteria of an integrated marketing effort as well as those reported by Novosad, Arab, Foster, and Rubin. This is because integrated marketing involves much more than simply attaching the same logo and/or theme line to each media vehicle; it is the strategic coordination of all communication components of a marketing campaign.

The objective of this chapter is twofold: (a) to report on an integrated marketing campaign recently conducted in the nonprofit arena, and (b) to extract some basic principles to guide the planning of future integrated marketing programs. The campaign presented in this chapter was strategically designed and executed based on an integrated marketing strategy focused on a point of entry other than advertising. Although the campaign has several of the limitations inherent in public service campaigns, it does provide an example of the use of an integrated communications strategy in a nonprofit context.

THE INDIANA MIDDLE GRADES READING PROGRAM

Problem

In December 1989, Dr. Jack Humphrey (Director of Reading Services and Special Projects for the Evansville-Vanderburgh School Corporation in Evansville, In) came to the Keller-Crescent Company (a marketing communications company) with some alarming facts and a request. Dr. Humphrey provided statistics from the Indiana Department of Education that correlated the failure to read proficiently with several statistics of youth alienation, including leaving school, pregnancy, substance abuse, and crime. He also reported that the state of Indiana ranked in the lower half of the nation in terms of the number of library books circulated per capita, and the percentage of youth who enroll in college after high school. Dr. Humphrey requested the agency's help in developing a public service campaign to reinforce the importance of reading to children.

Objectives

Reading is at the heart of the educational process. Most children are engaged in reading in the primary grades, where much of the school day is spent on reading activities, many parents read to younger children, and children use school and public libraries. As children grow older, other interests — including television, video games, sports, and so on — involve much of their time. The result is that books may become less important in their lives.

Most children learn to read in school. Whether they will read depends on the opportunities afforded them, and the interest they have in reading. Those who do read will improve on the reading skills that they have learned in the classroom. Those who do not will probably have difficulty in the middle grades, where more reading is required.

The Indiana Middle Grades Reading Program was developed to combat the low reading scores reported by Indiana school districts. Fifty-three school districts were identified as having substandard reading scores in

Grades 6 through 9. These school districts were primarily in low-income, urban areas. The Lilly Endowment funded the program, through the Indiana Youth Institute (a nonprofit organization dedicated to meeting the needs of Indiana's youth) and the Evansville–Vanderburgh School Corporation.

Components

The Indiana Middle Grades Reading Program included several different components targeted to several different audiences. The following is a list of all the objectives of the program.

Indiana Middle Grades Reading Program

1. Market the umbrella concept through public service announcements featuring a logo and simple message using:
   a. Two 30-second television public service announcements (PSAs).
   b. Three 60-second radio PSAs.
   c. Three outdoor board designs.
   d. Six newspaper ads to fit a variety of size formats.
   e. A poster and a school year calendar, to reinforce the concept at schools, school libraries, public libraries, bookstores, public bulletin boards, and so on.
2. Continue creating student-operated bookstores in which recreational books are sold or traded.
3. Provide a reading leadership institute for teachers in Grades 6 through 9.
4. Develop an assessment for middle schools to determine ability to read and use a newspaper.
5. Fund new in-depth programs emphasizing a community focus on reading, parental involvement, and resources such as classroom libraries.

The focus of this chapter is on the first component of the program: the marketing campaign. The assignment was to develop a comprehensive advertising program utilizing several media vehicles to reach the following target audiences.

Target Audience

Primary: Indiana youth in Grades 6 through 9 who attend school in the 53 targeted school corporations.

Secondary: Teachers, parents, and all other residents who live in the area of the 53 school corporations.

Tertiary: Indiana youth in Grades 6 through 9 who attend school in areas other than the 53 targeted school corporations and their parents.

Creative Development

Initial brainstorming efforts on the part of Keller-Crescent (hereafter referred to as the agency) involved a project team whose members were drawn from the account service, creative, research, public relations, and production departments. Cooperation of members of the project team is very important in order to ensure that the ideas developed are feasible from a creative and production standpoint. Also, the account management team member must maintain focus on the client's objectives. Research team members were vital in monitoring how the program would be interpreted by the target audience. Originally, the assignment was viewed from a traditional advertising approach for a nonprofit client, in that the focus was on developing public service announcements for television and radio. Strategically, the choice of a spokesperson (or persons) was believed to be critical in reaching the children. The first group of potential spokespersons included Indiana celebrities and others tied to the state in some manner. The following is a list of the people initially considered:

- Susan Bayh, wife of Governor Evan Bayh
- Dean Evans, Indiana Commissioner of Education
- Chief Justice Randall Shepherd
- Indiana Basketball Coach Bobby Knight
- Notre Dame Football Coach Lou Holtz
- Yankee baseball player Don Mattingly
- Marilyn Quayle
- Clark Kellogg
- Purdue Basketball Coach Gene Keady
- Jane Pauley
- David Letterman
- Woody Harrelson
- Larry Bird

Several of the names on the list were recommended by the Indiana Youth Institute (hereafter referred to as the client) and other state officials. The problem that immediately arose is that many of these people do not appeal to children in Grades 6 through 9. Also, we were unsure if the children would recognize them.

The second brainstorming session resulted in the idea that was to be instrumental in developing and executing the campaign. One of the objectives was to avoid duplicating the efforts of the national literacy campaigns, which feature celebrities reading to children. In attempting to stay away from this type of effort, the suggestion was made to use "real" Indiana schoolchildren in the public service announcements. Once this suggestion was made, the entire focus of the assignment shifted from one of a traditional advertising campaign to a comprehensive communications effort that merely included an advertising campaign.

The theme for the campaign was based on the idea that reading will open doors to the imagination, and that a child's imagination is much more powerful than any video game. Hence, the notion of the "Theater of the Mind" was developed. All of the materials featured the following closing line: "Enter the Theater of the Mind. Read, Because Only Reading Makes It Real." The logo on all of the materials featured modern lettering of the words, "Only Reading Makes It Real." The visual components of the television execution were unique because only the children (as they read a book) were shown in color. The background scenery was black and white (drawn entirely from old movie footage) and designed to appear as if what the children were reading about was actually happening behind them. The print executions and the outdoor posters were also designed in the same manner. The radio executions utilized sound effects to give the feeling that the books had come to life.

All of the materials were coordinated in both visual and verbal components. The outdoor boards, poster, and calendar were also given the same "look," with the photograph of the child in color and the background illustrations in black and white. The newspaper ads (targeted to parents) did not include photographs or illustrations, but featured catchy lines from the other materials. All of the collateral materials utilized for the campaign (press releases, press kits, etc.) featured the logo and tag line, "Only Reading Makes It Real." In this way, the theme used in the advertising portion of the campaign was carried over to the public relations portion of the campaign. All materials were on display at the news conferences, and special logo boards were prominently featured on speaker podiums. This served to communicate consistency of the campaign theme for both controlled and uncontrolled media environments.

The Integrated Marketing Campaign

The point of entry to the campaign keyed on public relations activities. However, several other methods of communication were utilized, such as advertising, direct mail, and personal selling (phone conversations with media representatives, state officials, and programming directors).

The public relations portion of the marketing campaign had several objectives. The decision to use Indiana students as the "stars" of the campaign opened up many possibilities. One objective of the campaign was to generate a significant amount of interest among the students. As such, the first step was to organize and publicize the casting of the student actors.

A second objective of the campaign was to get the schools excited about the program. Thus, a direct mail campaign was launched to reach the principals of the 144 schools in the 53 targeted school corporations. These principals were invited to join in the program by sending three of the school's best readers to a casting session. The mailing was planned to meet two objectives. First, the letters to the principals would get the schools involved at the highest level. This was expected to have a "trickle down" effect in that principals would ask teachers and staff members to recommend students. Teachers would then choose students for the casting session. Thus, the entire school became involved in the process as a result of the letters to the principals. Second, although an open casting call would have generated an even greater response, it was not feasible given time and money constraints. Thus, the letters to the principals served as a means to limit the number of children at the casting sessions, thereby allowing the agency the time needed to work with each individual student.

The state of Indiana was divided into five regions for casting purposes. Casting sessions were held on consecutive weekends in May 1990, in Michigan City, Indianapolis, Evansville, Columbus, and Fort Wayne, In. Each event was heavily publicized in the host city and surrounding towns via to the use of the wire services and extensive distribution of press releases and press kits to 27 television stations, approximately 200 radio stations, and approximately 500 newspapers. Both the client and the agency received hundreds of calls from parents whose children were not selected by their principals to attend the casting.

From the casting sessions, 15 finalists were chosen (in mid-June 1990) from the approximately 400 who auditioned. This provided another public relations opportunity in that the names of the finalists were publicized around the state. As an award for their participation, the finalists received books. From a publicity standpoint, the finalists were chosen from around the state to make sure that the press coverage would be statewide and not confined to one area. The production department at the agency reviewed the auditions of the finalists and chose 10 students to participate in the campaign: 2 for the television spots, 3 for the radio spots, 3 for the outdoor posters, and 1 each for the poster and calendar. Again, the public relations department sent out press releases and kits to announce which students were chosen for which part of the campaign.

The next step was to film the television spots, record the radio spots, and photograph the remaining students. Keller-Crescent has the capability of producing all of the materials for the campaign in house. This was completed over a period of one week in mid-July 1990, during which media representatives were invited to all sessions. The production of the campaign was also well publicized. Concurrently, direct mail efforts continued to all of the media in the state requesting them to donate time and/or space to the program. The agency worked closely with the Hoosier State Press Association to ensure cooperation and coverage of the campaign.

In late August 1990, it was time for the public service portion of the campaign to air. Additional press kits and direct mail letters were sent with the materials to the broadcast general managers to encourage their participation. Two major kick-off press conferences were held: one in Evansville and one in Indianapolis, which included children featured in the campaign, and speeches by the head of the Lilly Endowment and several state officials. The kick-off press conferences were well covered by the state press.

The public service portion of the campaign ran for three months, August through October 1990 and again in August through October 1991. The entire program, from casting through air, ran from April through October of both years. As is often the problem with public service campaigns that rely on donated media time, it is very difficult to assess the success of the campaign. The traditional way to measure the success of this type of campaign is to determine the number of media impressions generated by the public service announcements. This was exceptionally difficult given this campaign, because much of the generated reach happened before the public service campaign even hit the air, in the form of the public relations efforts.

An attempt was made to evaluate the impressions generated by both the public service portions and the public relations portions of the campaign. The results showed that the campaign received coverage on the Associated Press wire, and all major Indiana newspapers; extensive television and radio coverage in Indianapolis, Fort Wayne, Terre Haute, South Bend, and Evansville, along with good coverage from stations in other areas of the state; and good coverage from the radio stations around the state. All Indiana television stations donated time; many radio stations followed suit — one station donated $19,000 worth of time. Indiana outdoor companies donated more than $250,000 worth of space to the program in its first year. The number of total impressions generated from the public service campaign and public relations activities exceeded 7,000,000 in the first year.

DISCUSSION AND IMPLICATIONS FOR FUTURE INTEGRATED MARKETING PROGRAMS

In evaluating the marketing component of the program, the key issue is in determining whether or not the campaign was a success. The program concluded in October 1991. The results are not yet in on the reading scores in the 53 targeted school districts, and the results from the media portion of the campaign are extremely difficult to analyze. However, initial awareness of the program was quite high given the focus on the schools and the students themselves. Also, public relations efforts were well planned from May through August in an attempt to maintain initial awareness levels. The use of students as the stars of the campaign was valuable in taking the Indiana Middle Grades Reading Program beyond the standard public service campaign to an integrated marketing communications program.

The main objective of an integrated marketing program is to communicate synergistically through a number of different channels. Based on the results of this campaign, three basic principles for the success of integrated marketing campaigns can be formulated: coordination, consistency, and complementarity.

Coordination

The first, and possibly most important, basic principle of integrated marketing campaign planning is coordination. This principle has two components. It all begins with the coordination of talent. This includes the assembly of representatives from various agency disciplines into a project team for the purposes of strategic campaign planning. Each project team member must be committed and cooperative with every other team member. This means that the selection of team members is extremely important to avoid possible ego or personality conflicts. One of the major criticisms of integrated marketing is that getting all of the agency disciplines to work together (given that they are often separate profit centers) is difficult, if not impossible (Snyder, 1991). However, the key to the future success of integrated marketing involves the coordination, commitment, and cooperation of all of those involved. This case history provides evidence that this goal can be achieved.

The second component of the coordination principle can be characterized as the coordination of ideas. This means that the project team must begin the planning process with a blank slate, that is, be open to any and all suggestions regarding the point of entry for the campaign. It is all too easy to assume that advertising is the best route and thereby ignore other options. Once the point of entry for the campaign has been determined and the general creative focus planned, the next basic principle should be considered.

Consistency

The second basic principle of integrated marketing campaign planning is consistency (see Park & Zaltman, 1987, for additional discussion). This principle has two components. The first is internal consistency within each communication vehicle. For example, each component of an advertising campaign should be consistent in terms of the message and its presentation. This means that the campaign should have an overall theme and that the theme should be communicated using similar audio and visual presentation within and across vehicles, such as television, radio, outdoor, newspaper, and promotional materials. This internal consistency will tie each individual component together, thereby creating positive synergy.

The second component of the consistency principle is external consistency among communication vehicles. The presentation of the message must be consistent across vehicles, that is, advertising, public relations, direct mail, sales promotion, personal selling, and so on. In the case study presented in this chapter, the consistency of message was achieved by displaying the creative materials from the advertising portion of the campaign at all of the activities in the public relations portion of the campaign. This included small efforts such as putting the logo and theme line on speaker podiums at press conferences, and utilizing the logo and theme line on all correspondence. The principle of consistency is important in maintaining the communication synergy of the entire integrated marketing program.

Complementarity

The third principle of integrated marketing campaign planning is complementarity. Each vehicle and each component within each vehicle must complement and reinforce one another. For the intended message to be conveyed, it is important that the total program be viewed as more than the sum of its parts. The principle of complementarity makes sure that each component builds and extends each other component to convey the desired message. It is also beneficial to use communication vehicles to build upon each other in an integrated campaign. For example, The Indiana Middle Grades Reading Program utilized public relations activities to build interest and awareness in the advertising campaign that was to follow.

In conclusion, an integrated marketing program should incorporate each of the three basic principles for success. Although the program presented in this paper is a not-for-profit, or social marketing, campaign, the principles set forth for effective development of integrated marketing campaigns are just as valuable in the for-profit arena. Coordination, consistency, and complementarity all impact on campaign development in different and unique ways. It is important to note that although the coordination of talent may be difficult, it is crucial to the development of a campaign based on an integrated strategy. This is because it is the first stage in the process and must be successfully completed before moving on to the principles of consistency and complementarity. In order for a campaign to truly communicate synergistically, both internal and external consistency must be maintained. Also, speaking to a target audience in one voice requires adherence to the principle of complementarity of media vehicles.

This chapter presented a case history of an integrated marketing program from a nonprofit perspective. Although public service campaigns are quite different from campaigns in the for-profit arena, the three basic principles are generalizable across marketing contexts. These principles should be helpful to marketing and advertising practitioners in guiding the strategic planning of integrated marketing programs.

ACKNOWLEDGMENTS

The author wishes to acknowledge the helpful assistance of Dan Smith, Peter Dacin, and the anonymous reviewers on a previous version of this manuscript.

REFERENCES

Arab, N. H. (1991, March). Integrated marketing repositions Toronto hotel; Occupancy soars. *Public Relations Journal*, pp. 22-24.
Foster, J. (1990, September). Working together: How companies are integrating their corporate communications. *Public Relations Journal*, pp. 18-24.
Kroll, A. (1991, August 5). New advertising fine, but; Y&R boss warns it calls for wealth of talent. *Advertising Age*, p. 15.
Novosad, R. (1991, September). Talking turkey through integrated communications. *Public Relations Journal*, pp. 40-42.
Park, C. W., & Zaltman, G. (1987). *Marketing management*. Hinsdale, IL: Dryden Press.
Rubin, B. (1991, February). Campaign opens door to safety issue. *Public Relations Journal*, pp. 28-31.
Snyder, M. (1991, October 28). Rethinking "integrated." *Advertising Age*, p. 32.

13 Features of Good Integration: Two Cases and Some Generalizations

John Deighton
Harvard Business School

Why would one not integrate a communications campaign? Integration is surely the natural condition, the simple and obvious way of doing things. Most marketing problems are solved with a combination of tools, even if the blending is no more complex than synchronizing advertising with trade promotion schedules. Unintegrated communication campaigns are aberrations, mistakes to be explained and avoided.

When a campaign is not integrated, the explanation can usually be found in the intensely specialized organization structure that manufacturers and their advertising agencies have built to manage their broad interests. Specialization is a good way to manage scale and to capture scale economies, but it is the enemy of integration. Failure to integrate is, thus, a problem of large firms and large economies. It reflects the eccentric behavior of managers whose natural inclinations have been distorted by bureaucratic incentives. Their simple concern to find the best solution to a communication problem has been replaced by considerations of turf, remuneration, and reputation. Although the problem is bureaucratic in origin, the solution is unlikely to be a matter of changing the organization's structure. Actions to reduce scale, such as breaking the organization into project teams, cost too much in lost scale economies.

THE CASE FOR CASES

The solution that I explore in this chapter is one that establishes integration as a matter of culture—that makes it a superordinate goal for every

specialist in the bureaucracy. Undoubtedly there are other actions needed —
attention to reward structures, reporting relationships, and so on — but it is
unlikely that an organization can integrate unless it first reaches an
intellectual consensus that integration is a good idea. This approach
depends, I contend, on the ability to tell good stories about integration.
Stories are a vehicle by which values may be transmitted (Bruner, 1986), and
if a principle does not make good stories it may not get disseminated.

The integrated marketing communications concept suffers from a dearth
of really impressive success stories. That may be because it does not have a
very long history, but alternatively it may be because the concept is
inherently mundane. No one, surely, would deny that integration is a
sensible idea, but sensible ideas, like sensible shoes, do not capture the
imagination. A skeptic might argue that integration does not make for good
stories because it does not deal with factors that can make a dramatic
difference — it is not a strategic activity. Can integration be done with flair,
or is it just a matter of diligence, a dull chore?

Advertising's exponents have always been great storytellers, able to
justify themselves to clients with tales in which brilliant advertising saved
the day. Our generalizations about how and when advertising works rest on
these concrete instances — the idea that the right advertising can take an
obscure product to great heights is memorialized, for example, in the story
of the lemon campaign for Volkswagen. But what would a story of the
power of integration look like? Are there vivid examples of business
problems solved because a campaign was skillfully integrated? My contention is that the integration concept does have the intrinsic capacity to be
dramatized. Two candidate stories follow: One is long and the other brief,
the second case serving to illustrate how the themes in the first repeat
themselves. In the conclusion to the chapter I summarize these repeated
themes, offering a list of the defining features of good integration.

THE TYLENOL POISONING RECOVERY

On September 30, 1982, news media announced an apparent link between
Tylenol and the deaths of several people in suburbs of Chicago. Within days
it became clear that seven people had died, killed by capsules of Tylenol that
had been contaminated with cyanide. Immediately the brand's share of the
U.S. analgesic market fell, from 37% to almost zero. Many observers felt
the brand was damaged beyond repair. Jerry Della Femina, chairman of a
prominent advertising agency, commented, "You'll not see the name
Tylenol in any form within a year" (Kleinfield, 1982).

Within four months, however, the brand was almost fully recovered. The
product had been relaunched in tamper-resistant packaging, and a couponing program had carried sales back to within 80% of their level before

the poisonings. The brand had been saved by the ingenious integration of advertising, public relations, couponing, sampling, trade promotion, and channel management. The program blocked competitors from exploiting Tylenol's weakness, and managed the unfolding pattern of consumer concerns.

Over the 4 months of the crisis, consumer involvement moved from low to very high and back to relatively low. Consumer attitudes moved from bewilderment and fear to an informed aversion to the brand and, ultimately, to a return to confidence and trust. Trade attitudes also moved sharply over the 3 months. Marketing tools were employed in a particular sequence. We speculate that the sequence was in part a response to, and in part a cause of, the patterns of involvement and attitude change, and the pattern was crucial to the brand's recovery.

Fig. 13.1 indicates how Tylenol's market share moved during this period, and highlights the important management actions. To describe the recovery process, I divide the period into seven episodes, as shown in Fig. 13.2. Each episode had its own constellation of beliefs, feelings, and behavior on the part of consumers and the distribution channels, as illustrated in Fig. 13.3. Each posed a discrete set of communication problems, and each transition had also to be managed. (The facts of the case are drawn from Blattberg &

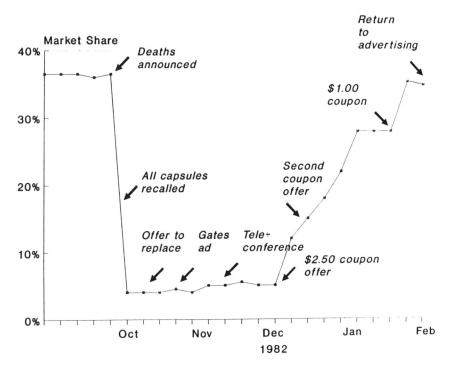

FIG. 13.1. Principal events of the crisis.

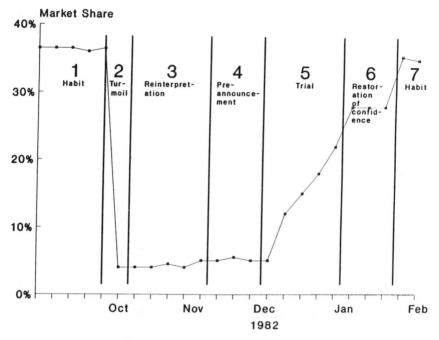

FIG. 13.2.   Evolution of consumer attitudes.

Wisniewski, 1982; Deighton, 1983; Greyser, 1982; Mitroff & Kilmann, 1984.)

1.   Habit

In 1982, Tylenol was the largest single brand in the U.S. health and beauty category. It was to be found in the homes and offices of 100 million Americans. Worldwide factory sales approached $500 million. Advertising support ran at $40 million that year, some 30% of all analgesic advertising. The brand's image rested on two claims: trust ("Trust Tylenol–hospitals do") and potency ("The most potent pain reliever you can buy without a prescription"). Perhaps the most important feature of consumers' beliefs was what they did not know–that the active ingredient in Tylenol was acetaminophen, available from competing brands, often at lower cost. The name Tylenol was the only name consumers knew for nonaspirin pain relief. They bought it routinely, the trade stocked it routinely, and no one had a strong incentive to behave differently.

2.   Turmoil

The week that followed the September 30 press reports of cyanide poisonings was a period of confusion and fear for consumers. Reports (later

Stage	1 Habit	→ Turmoil 2	→ Reinterpretation 3	→ Preannouncement 4	→ Trial 5	→ Restoration of Confidence 6	→ Habit 7
Consumer Communication Objective	Convey trust, potency of the brand	Reduce brand's visibility, increase J & J's visibility	Establish J & J as victim, present tablets as alternative, discourage consideration of competitors	Preannounce the new packaging plan	Induce trial, induce repeat purchase	Induce repeat purchase	Convey trust, potency of the brand
Tools	Advertising consumer promotions	PR, product recall	PR, consumer promotion	Teleconference	Consumer coupon promotion	Reduced-value coupon promotions	Advertising, consumer promotions
Trade Communication Objective	Maintain stock levels, share of facings	Announce recall	Hold tablet shelf space	Secure advance commitment to stock	Build displays and stock levels	Maintain stock levels, share of facings	Maintain stock levels, share of facings
Toos	Trade promotions	Sales force	Trade promotion	Forward ordering	Trade promotion	Trade promotions	Trade promotions

FIG. 13.3. Stages in the recovery.

proved false) implicated Tylenol in deaths in Texas, Pennsylvania, California, Tennessee, and Kansas. Eye drops contaminated with sulfuric acid
were reported in California. Many towns and suburbs called off Halloween
celebrations for fear of copycat poisoning of trick-or-treat candy.

Johnson & Johnson was active on many fronts in the first week. The
company issued a worldwide alert to the medical community, set up a
24-hour toll-free telephone service, recalled and analyzed sample batches of
the product from around the country, briefed the Food and Drug Administration, and publicized a $100,000 reward offer. All broadcast advertising
was immediately pulled, and all print advertising not already in production
was withdrawn. All Tylenol products were off the shelves of Chicago stores
by October 4, and on October 6 a telex message announced to 11,000
retailers and distributors a nationwide recall of capsules. Senior company
officers made themselves available to the media to explain what they knew
of the disaster and what they were planning to do. The company hired
Burke Marketing Research to track attitudes among consumers of analgesics. One thousand people were screened weekly, and in addition A.C.
Nielsen's Scantrack monitored supermarket sales in four U.S. markets.

During the first week, in summary, the company responded to consumer
horror and confusion by reducing the visibility of the Tylenol brand and
increasing the visibility of the firm. It mobilized public relations, the sales
force, telemarketing, market research, and advertising media services to
transform a low-involvement, brand-based media presence into a high-
involvement, personalized corporate presence. *Crisis comm response*

3.   Reinterpretation

By the second week, consumers understood the facts of the crisis relatively
clearly. The challenge to Johnson & Johnson for the next 6 weeks would be
to manage how consumers and the retail trade interpreted the hiatus that
would result from Tylenol's withdrawal from the market. Burke's research
showed that awareness of the poisonings was almost universal, that
consumers understood that the problem was confined to capsules, and that
no blame was attached to the marker. In terms of consumer beliefs and
emotions, therefore, recovery of the brand seemed worth attempting:

Knowledge of Tylenol tragedy	95%
Problem involves Tylenol capsules only	90%
Problem could occur for any capsules	93%
Maker not to blame	90%

The principal concern management faced was behavioral. Many capsule
users had disposed of their capsules in the week of the poisoning, and
Tylenol users had flocked to buy competitors' brands. Aspirin accounted

for most of the replacement purchases, with Bayer the main beneficiary. Unit sales of analgesics in Chicago rose 20% above normal for the three weeks following the poisoning, and then fell 12% below normal for several weeks thereafter in response to the replenished home inventories.

There was concern, too, about consumers' emotional interpretation of the events. Although consumers had accepted as a matter of fact that Johnson & Johnson was innocent of culpability in the disaster, the company could not be sure that the belief would inevitably evolve into a feeling of sympathy, and an appreciation of the company as a victim. There was concern, too, at how consumers would interpret their own actions in abandoning the Tylenol brand. When a purchase of a competitive brand had occurred, the consumer could choose to interpret it as a stopgap action, or as the start of a new pattern of loyalty. Would consumers start to look for nonaspirin brands, and decide that Tylenol was not materially different from its acetaminophen competitors?

Management's expressed aims during this interim period were to discourage consideration of competitive brands, encourage use of Tylenol in tablet form, and defend the Tylenol brand equity by convincing consumers they could continue to trust Tylenol. Management therefore mounted several initiatives.

The first element was a capsule exchange offer. On October 12, half-page press announcements appeared in 150 major markets: "We want you to replace your Tylenol capsules with Tylenol tablets. And we'll help you do it at our expense." They invited the public to mail in bottles of capsules and receive tablets in exchange.

The second component was a brief but intensive television announcement. It ran from October 24 to October 28, and reached 85% of the market four times in that period. It featured Dr. Thomas N. Gates, the company's medical director, as spokesperson because he rated well on credibility in pretesting. The form of this advertising was quite different to the two campaigns that had built the brand's reputation, but the theme of trust was reinforced. His message read:

> You're all aware of recent tragic events in which Extra Strength Tylenol capsules were criminally tampered with in limited areas after they left our factory. This act damages all of us. . . . We have voluntarily withdrawn all Tylenol Capsules . . . we urge all Tylenol capsule users to use the tablet form. . . . Tylenol has had the trust of the medical profession and 100 million Americans for over 20 years. We value that trust too much to let any individual tamper with it.

Burke's tracking studies indicated that intention to purchase Tylenol rose from 62% on October 22 to 74% on October 28. Although actual sales continued to languish, the company was reassured that the recovery was proceeding satisfactorily.

In a third component of the interim campaign, the company intensified the visibility of senior management on television. Chairman James Burke appeared on the *Donahue* show, *Good Morning America,* and other interview shows; on radio; and in newspaper interviews.

The fourth targeted the trade. Withdrawal of all capsule products had imperiled the brand's ability to command shelf space. The company used its sales force to keep the retail trade informed of developments and to maintain and, if possible, increase displays of its tablet form.

Competition, by this time, had begun to pursue share aggressively. Analgesic advertising expenditure rose 50% above normal in the final quarter of 1982, despite Tylenol's withdrawal. Acetaminophen brands increased unit sales from 5% share to 11% share in this period, although more of the share given up by Tylenol went to aspirin brands. Bayer sales rose 50% in October. American Home Products announced "unprecedented demand" for Anacin-3 and reported that production had increased from two shifts to three. Their advertising copy emphasized the product's likeness to Tylenol: "Like Tylenol, Anacin-3 is aspirin-free." Bristol-Myers began to recommend consumers to: "Ask your doctor about Datril." Aspirin pain relievers used copy that stressed safety. Bayer's television commercials said "At Bayer, we take care . . . and we've been doing that for over 25 years." The product was given a slick coating to make it as easy to swallow as a capsule.

4. Preannouncement

Six weeks after the poisonings, management was ready to commit to a plan for relaunching. The strategy shifted from managing a period of inactivity to building a climate of anticipation.

Although it needed four more weeks to complete manufacture and trade stocking, Johnson & Johnson chose an early preannouncement. On November 11, the chairman spoke live at a satellite-linked teleconference to 600 news reporters throughout the country. His announcement of the triple-sealed capsule pack was carried prominently in news media throughout the country. Burke monitored the effect of this announcement carefully. A phone survey over the next 5 days found that 79% of Tylenol users were aware of the new packaging and that 72% could name one or more specific elements of that packaging. Among former users, 95% expressed an intention to return to capsules in tamper-resistant packaging. Encouraged by this data, management called off plans to use a second commercial featuring Dr. Gates to announce the new tamper-proof packaging on television. The sales force carried this information to the retail trade and secured advance commitments to purchase capsules in the new pack.

5. Trial

By the end of November, stocks of the new pack were in stores. The goal now was to get consumers to try it. Management debated several methods of building trial: sampling in homes, sampling in stores, and couponing by mail or in magazines or newspapers. Coupons redeemable in stores were considerably more expensive than home-delivered samples, because a full retail margin was paid on each redemption. They did, however, ensure that retailers would carry shelf stocks and consumers would have to make some act of commitment to the brand to secure their sample.

Management, therefore, launched on November 28 the largest program of couponing in commercial history. The first wave on used Sunday newspapers nationwide to distribute 60 million coupons for a free Tylenol product to a limit of $2.50 each. Another 20 million coupons were offered the following Sunday. Samples distributed in this way began to appear in the company's audits of retail sales in four test cities. Share at retail rose by more than 10 share points, to within 6 points of predisaster levels. Management knew, however, that this performance needed support if it was to survive the end of couponing.

6. Restoration of Confidence

At the end of December 1982, sales promotion had worked well to return previous users of Tylenol to the brand, but it was extremely expensive. Redemption by December stood at 30% of all coupons issued, which generated a charge of $45 million to the brand's budget. A less expensive communications tool was needed to consolidate the recovery.

Although couponing had reestablished consumer purchase patterns, there was a need to restore consumer attitudes and emotions. Consumers could interpret their own behavior in buying the brand with a full-value coupon either as a return to loyalty or as mere opportunism. Here, as in Stage 3, management sought to suggest the interpretation most favorable to the brand. This task of influencing interpretations was one appropriate to advertising. The only television advertising for Tylenol in the three months since the poisonings had been the 4-day announcement featuring Dr. Gates. Although the coupon effort had been supported with newspaper feature advertising by retailers, management had suspended the low-involvement advertising themes that had been part of Tylenol's marketing program in the past, for the obvious reason that Tylenol had ceased to be a low-involvement issue. An implied message in the return to advertising would be that the situation had returned to normal.

In this phase, therefore, advertising was developed with the look and feel of precrisis advertising. The themes of trust and potency were reintroduced.

To encourage repurchase, coupons were distributed with face values first of 1 dollar and later 50 cents. Trade promotions were mounted with the objective of rebuilding stock levels and store displays. The character of marketing communications was almost indistinguishable from the precrisis blend.

7. Habit

By the start of February 1983, four months after the first report of the poisonings, Johnson & Johnson's management had effectively disposed of the threat to the brand. Tylenol's share of analgesic market revenues was 35%, 2 share points below precrisis levels. Sales of the capsule form were at 85%, and the tablet at 105% of previous levels. No competitive product had made any permanent share gain. Although the absolute level of marketing expenditures was higher than for the same period a year before, the marketing mix was not materially different.

Summary

The Tylenol recovery is a story of diverse actions administered so as to achieve an integrated impact. Consider the kinds of diversity that were managed. Many communication tools were used: advertising, press announcements, public forum appearances, trade promotions, consumer couponing, and teleconferencing. Several different audiences were addressed: users of the product, retailers, doctors, and the press. More than one audience decision process was managed: Consumers were navigated through an emotional rollercoaster from fear and turmoil through cautious reinterpretation of the events to tentative trial and culminating in a confident return to the franchise. At the same time, the retail trade was managed through a cycle that began with product rejection and delisting, led on to a period of exclusion from the shelves, and ended with restocking.

Some features of good integration are prominent in this account. There were overarching goals for each discrete phase of the crisis. The firm knew when a goal had been achieved and when it was time to negotiate a transition to a new goal because tracking research supplied the data to coordinate the transitions. A relatively close-knit team of communication specialists was available to management, because public relations consultant and sales promotion specialist were divisions of one firm, Young and Rubicam. Although many inputs had to be coordinated, the output was seamless in the eyes of the consumer. Fig. 13.4 presents the output as it might have been experienced by a hypothetical consumer. It shows that the consumer moves through successive stages, defined by beliefs, emotions, and behavior and tracked by market research, and at each transition

Wayne Doyle hears of seven Tylenol-related
deaths on CBS evening news, disposes of
his box of Tylenol.

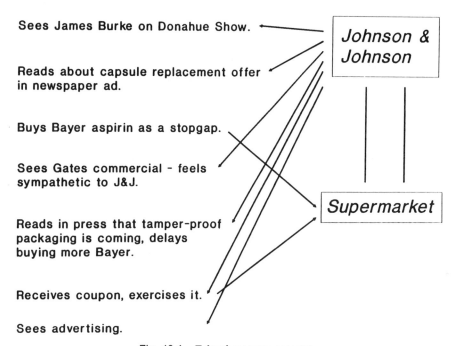

Sees James Burke on Donahue Show.

Reads about capsule replacement offer
in newspaper ad.

Buys Bayer aspirin as a stopgap.

Sees Gates commercial - feels
sympathetic to J&J.

Reads in press that tamper-proof
packaging is coming, delays
buying more Bayer.

Receives coupon, exercises it.

Sees advertising.

Johnson & Johnson

Supermarket

Fig. 13.4. Tylenol recovery program.

management anticipates problems and limits options by deploying the
appropriate marketing tools.

To isolate the defining features of good integration, however, it will help
to look for the common elements of this story and a second example of
impressive integration, — the launch of a disposable contact lens.

ACUVUE DISPOSABLE CONTACT LENS LAUNCH

The launch of Acuvue disposable contact lenses by Johnson & Johnson, like
the Tylenol recovery, illustrates communications integration as the phased
management of multiple communication tools. Unlike the first case,
coordination is achieved here with the use of an electronic customer
database.

Johnson & Johnson anticipated that entry into the contact lens market
would be difficult. The firm had no prior stake in the eyecare industry. In

particular, it had no relationship with optometrists and opticians. It knew that users of contact lenses would not switch to disposable lenses without the encouragement of an eye care professional. As a newcomer to the industry it would find it difficult to champion the diffusion of disposable lens technology. Competitors like Bausch and Lomb would follow, however, so the window of opportunity within which to establish a foothold would be narrow.

The program was managed by linking two databases: one a list of registered eye care professionals who had responded positively to a sales call promoting Acuvue, and the other the names of contact lens wearers. The second database was constructed of respondents to advertising describing the benefits of disposable lenses. These prospective customers were individually tracked as they moved from expressions of initial interest through a first appointment with an optometrist to successive purchases of lenses. Each step of the process of customer conversion was coordinated by the Johnson & Johnson computer: appointment making, delivery of collateral sales material, and delivery of purchase incentive coupons. What appeared to the customer as a seamlessly integrated flow of communications was, in fact, the product of a number of quite distinct communication disciplines — print advertising, direct mail, telemarketing, and sales promotion. Fig. 13.5 presents the management of the consumer adoption process from a similar perspective to that used to describe the Tylenol recovery in Figure 13.4.

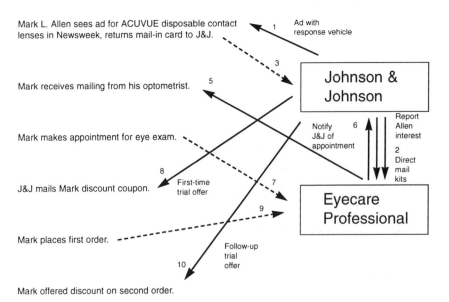

FIG. 13.5. Acuvue integrated communications program.

GENERALIZATIONS

These cases let us approach a definition of integration inductively. Four features occur in both cases:

Multiple Tools: Both cases used more than one of the traditional commu-nication tools, and used them to reinforce each other. This harmony among multiple modes of communication is integration in the most basic sense. The tools might span advertising, database marketing, sales promotion, sales force deployment, telemarketing, public relations, publishing, event marketing, and direct marketing, for example.

Multiple audiences: The communications program in each case targeted more than one audience. Consumer segments and members of the distribution channel were the audiences in these cases, but other targets, including opinion formers, could have been included.

Multiple stages: The audiences in each case were moved through several psychological and behavioral stages. When, as in the Acuvue case, the target was new customers, the stages corresponded to the standard sequence of awareness to interest to desire to action. As the Tylenol case illustrates, however, the stages can be idiosyncratic to the particular problem.

A coordination mechanism: In both cases, actions by the audience triggered the transition from one stage of the campaign to the next, using an explicit coordinating mechanism. In the Acuvue case, the mechanism was a database. A consumer used a reply card to respond to a print ad. On receipt of the card, the advertiser's database passed the consumer's name to a dealer and a coupon to the consumer. When the coupon was redeemed, the database signaled the manufacturer to recruit the customer into a retention program. Individual-level coordination is not mandatory: In the Tylenol case, aggregate market research results supplied the evidence that it was time for a transition to occur. As we argued elsewhere (Blattberg & Deighton, 1991), as databases become more available, so integration at the individual consumer level will become more common.

The cases also suggest some of the attributes that are not sufficient for integration. A program is not integrated just because it has one of the following features:

Thematic repetition: To be integrated, a campaign should do more than merely execute the same theme in different communication media, such as the use of the Energizer Bunny at point of purchase.

Consistent look and feel: It is not sufficient that all executions conform to a standard style. The fact that all presentations of IBM advertising use the same typeface does not alone make the program integrated. Indeed, it may be that executions should not look the same. The appearance of Tylenol's pre- and postcrisis advertising differed from the appearance of the mid-crisis Gates commercial.

Advertising with response vehicles: Including an 800-number in advertising does not ensure that the campaign is integrated. The program needs to consider how it will follow up on the lead, and to link the consumer program to actions of the distributor.

This chapter was concerned with defining integration as an outcome. A more important practical problem is to identify what it takes to achieve integration as a process. As a process, integration refers to the harmonious cooperation of bureaucratic specialties to solve a communications problem. On one hand, we have specialists in a variety of communications disciplines such as copywriters, art directors, media planners, database, technicians, and event marketing designers. On the other hand, we have management specialties such as sales force managers, sales promotion managers, advertising managers, and brand managers. These disparate interests must be made to work together.

To forge this partnership, it is necessary to instill a culture in which integration is understood and valued. That requires two kinds of learning: to come to know what an integrated product looks like, and to come to know what it can accomplish. On the first of these points, this chapter contended that integration is recognized by four features: multiple tools, both audiences and stages, and a coordinating mechanism. On the second point, the question of what good integration is capable of accomplishing, this chapter offers the view that this is a matter for stories.

REFERENCES

Blattberg, R. C., & Deighton, J. (1991). Interactive marketing: Exploiting the age of addressability. *Sloan Management Review, 33*, pp 5–14.

Blattberg, R. C., & Wisniewski, K. J. (1982). *Product tampering's effects on sales of analgesics in the Chicagoland Market.* (Working paper). Chicago: Center for Marketing Strategy Research, Graduate School of Business, University of Chicago.

Bruner, J. (1986). *Actual minds, possible worlds.* Cambridge, MA: Harvard University Press.

Deighton, J. (1983). *McNeil Consumer Products Company: Tylenol, a case study.* Unpublished manuscript, University of Chicago.

Greyser, S. A. (1982). *Johnson & Johnson: The Tylenol tragedy* (A). Boston: HBS Case Services, Harvard Business School.

Kleinfield, N. R. (1982). Long, Uphill odds for Tylenol. *New York Times*, p. D1.

Mitroff, I. I., & Kilmann, R. H. (1984). *Corporate tragedies: Product tampering. sabotage and other catastrophes* (pp. 3–16). New York: Praeger.

V Measuring the Impact of Integrated Campaigns

14
In Search of the Holy Grail: First Steps in Measuring Total Exposures of an Integrated Communications Program

Helen Katz
DDB Needham Worldwide

Jacques Lendrevie
Groupe HEC

In 1961, the Advertising Research Foundation published its six-stage model for evaluating media. Beginning with vehicle distribution, it posited that the evaluation must then consider vehicle exposure, advertising exposure, advertising perception, advertising communication, and finally sales response ("The ARF Model," 1989). If all six stages could be measured, one would gain a fairly good idea of how advertising works. However, since that time, although considerable research effort has been given to improving our knowledge of the first three stages, and experimental studies have been done on the last stage, more still remains to be learned on how best to evaluate the media messages themselves. Indeed, the focus tends to remain on media vehicle, as opposed to advertising exposure, and controversy persists on linking advertising exposures to sales effectiveness.

Yet as we more toward a new century, even bigger challenges are being presented. We are now seeing a shift away from thinking solely in terms of conveying brand messages through advertising, and are realizing more and more that all of the communications tools we have at our disposal can and should be used in a consistent, unified, and integrated marketing communications plan. That is, we must also take into account and plan for direct marketing, sales promotions, and publicity techniques as we work to define our communications goals and advertising objectives.

Having said that, the question remains of how to measure those disparate audiences. To some, this might seem overly ambitious, given the fairly limited knowledge we have regarding advertising effects, but unless we begin to consider the total marketing communications mix as we start to put such integrated plans together, we will end up with an incoherent and ad hoc mixture of vehicles that do little to further a brand's sales. Furthermore, by looking at how to evaluate all marketing communications, we may well also come up with new and better ways to evaluate traditional media vehicles.

This chapter presents an exploratory approach for evaluating and measuring all communications in an integrated marketing communications plan. The ability to measure all communications elements is a prerequisite for an effective integrated program. To be truly integrated, the advertiser's resources should be optimally distributed among the various voices, having evaluated various strategic alternatives available. Until now, although advertisers have been shifting their dollars away from traditional advertising media into sales promotions or direct marketing or public relations, little effort has been given to trying to evaluate all of the voices of an integrated strategy. Admittedly, the task is not an easy one, and in some cases it may well prove to be impossible. How, for example, does one measure the impact of word of mouth? Can trade promotions be measured?

Not to be deterred, we propose here one possible avenue to pursue in achieving the ultimate goal of complete measurement and evaluation of an integrated marketing communications program. The goal is not to provide the perfect solution, but rather to demonstrate the importance of this issue and suggest pathways down which future researchers may wish to embark.

HOW NOT TO EVALUATE AN INTEGRATED PROGRAM

There are three possible methods that could be utilized to measure an integrated communications program.

The Partial Approach

This might be considered the traditional method of presenting an integrated program. About 90% of the budget is dedicated to traditional advertising, and the remaining 10% is spent on other communications voices, such as a promotion or direct mail effort. Because most of the budget is given to advertising, most of the attention is paid here. The nonadvertising elements tend to be thrown in "for good measure," or because someone at the agency or client likes the idea. The prevailing attitude is "Well, it can't really hurt." Little or no effort is made to measure or evaluate any of the nonadvertising tools because the expenditures are relatively small and the task seems too difficult. At best, a plan might include the percentage of the total budget spent on the direct mailing or package design or sales brochures.

The Global Approach

The standard measures applied in evaluating an advertising campaign are transferred wholeheartedly to the nonadvertising tools. So for all communications, indicators such as gross rating points (GRPs), cost per thousand (CPM), reach, and frequency, are "adopted" for the measurement of a contest or bind-in cards or press release. Although this seems to make sense because it puts everything onto a level playing field, in reality it turns out to be highly impractical because the advertising measures do not necessarily apply elsewhere. For example, how does one measure the total number of rating points for a media tour? Or what is the reach of a trade deal?

The Specific Approach

With this measurement technique, each tool is evaluated according to the technique that is most appropriate for it. Thus a telemarketing campaign would be judged according to the number of calls received, whereas shelf-talkers would be assessed according to the number of those items sold. Again, this initially seems to make sense—except that there are well over 200 different, identifiable communications tools available, and the number continues to increase annually.

PROPOSED METHOD: SEGMENTING TOTAL EXPOSURES OF AN INTEGRATED PROGRAM

What we propose instead is to divide total exposures into one of three types: media exposures, product impressions, and personal contacts.

Media Exposures

These include all exposures to the brand's message that take place in traditional media. This not only encompasses advertising in traditional media such as TV, radio, newspapers, or magazines, but also embraces publicity generated in those media by public relations efforts (e.g,. press releases, video news releases). It also includes the media exposures in which sales promotions occur, such as coupons or rebates placed in the Sunday newspaper.

Product Impressions

As the name suggests, these are the target audience's exposures to the product itself. This occurs not only in the store but also in the home, at a dealership, or on the street, among others. For example, the French car maker, Citroen, released the first 1,000 vehicles of a new car model in red so that they would get more attention on the street. For a company such as McDonald's, product impressions include all consumer exposures to the fast food restaurant's logo, such as in front of the stores they drive by; the cartons, bags, and soft drink containers they use; or even discarded items seen on the streets or in trash cans.

Personal Contacts

Too often we underestimate how important dealings with individuals can be in influencing brand selections. Yet many of our decisions end up being based on our conversations with others. When we buy a car or a large appliance, we talk to several dealers. We might also talk to our friends and see what they think of the brands available. In some instances, we might listen to the advice or commentary of opinion leaders, such as our doctor in choosing an analgesic, or the veterinarian in selecting the right dog food.

IS THIS SEGMENTATION VALID?

Before adopting any kind of segmentation scheme it is first necessary to check on its validity. There are three elements we must test for:

Universality

In order to have a valid segmentation it must work in every instance. For our proposed scheme, that means it must apply to:

- Every communication tool we know (and those that come in the future).
- Every product or service a company wishes to promote (i.e., consumer goods, services, business to business).
- Every kind of target (consumer, trade, opinion leaders, government).

Measurability

The second quality to look for in a segmentation scheme is whether it can measure what we want to measure. That is, does this proposal in fact allow us to measure exposures in each of the three categories we have defined? Do we have the appropriate techniques and tools available in order to carry out this measurement? In our situation, that means being able to estimate the following:

* Number of planned exposures (contacts).
* Number of actual exposures (contacts) delivered.

Strategic Value

Last but not least, a truly valid segmentation scheme must help us define sound strategic alternatives. That is, the segmentation should provide a meaningful way to analyze the communication strategy and make appropriate decisions. There are two elements to consider here:

1. *Communication objectives.* At what stage in the communication (consumer decision making) process are we trying to reach consumers? Is the goal to make them aware of our product, or prefer it over competitors, or select it in the store, for example? Depending on this objective, we can then determine what the most effective and efficient mix of exposure types, and tools within those types, would be.

2. *Level of product involvement.* Although the concept of involvement is complex and difficult to deal with, it might be helpful for segmenting our communications tools. When consumers are highly involved with the product, such as cars or stereos, then personal contacts are likely to play a more important role. In contrast, media exposures are typically used for most low-involvement products, such as canned soup or detergents.

CHECKING THE EFFECTIVENESS
OF THIS SEGMENTATION SCHEME

Universality

1. Does This Segmentation Work for All Types of Exposures — Media, Product, and Personal?   See Fig. 14.1 for a complete listing of these types.

2. Does the Segmentation Work for All Communication Tools?   At DDB Needham, we have developed an integrated communications software program, InteComm™, which contains more than 200 different communications tools that might be employed in an integrated plan. As can be seen in the example in Table 14.1, these tools can be put into one of the three exposure types, regardless of the traditional discipline to which they belong. Thus, media exposures include spot television and cinema advertising, but also cover direct marketing in magazines and coupons in Sunday news-

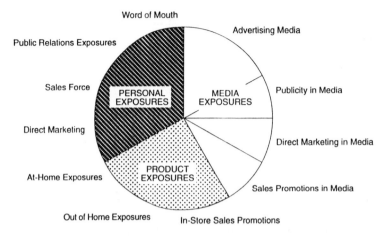

FIG. 14.1.   Types of exposure.

papers. Under product impressions we find package design, but also in-store vehicles, which might be thought traditionally to be categorized under promotions. And for personal contacts, we have dealerships, as well as the less expected telemarketing. Although only an excerpt is shown in Table 14.1, all of the 200 or so tools can in fact be classified into one of our three exposure types.

3. Does This Segmentation Work for All Products and Services?   Here, we must rely for now on our judgment and experience. In the case of consumer goods it is clear that media, product, and personal exposures all apply. We believe they also do for business-to-business products and services, although emphasis for such communications programs differs, with far more importance given to personal contacts and far fewer to advertising media. In the cases of services, personal contacts will often prove to be the most critical element in communicating with potential buyers or users. One problem here might be the use of the term *product impressions.* What exactly is an impression in the case of a service such as a hotel, a bank, or an insurance company, for example? We believe that in

TABLE 14.1
Examples of Vehicles by Exposure Type

Media Exposures	Personal Exposure	Product Exposures
Cinema advertising	Telemarketing	Container premiums
Directories	Lead-getting	Specialty advertising
Free-standing inserts	In-store sampling	Product in films
Magazine direct marketing	End-aisle display	Package logo
Spot television	Dealerships	Permanent merchandise holders

such instances, all of the target's exposures to that service constitute an impression. For the bank, for instance, the consumer forms his or her impression based on factors such as the location of its branches, the layout inside each office, or the quality and efficiency of the staff. Impressions can also be generated from external contacts with the bank, such as telephone access to one's account, the simplicity and user-friendliness of the bank statement, or corporate sponsorship of a local theater or ballet performance, for example.

4. Does This Segmentation Work for All Kinds of Targets? Again, based on our judgment we would answer affirmatively here. For consumer targets, the complete segmentation scheme can be readily applied regardless of the target type. In the case of the trade, such as retailers or manufacturers, media exposures are clearly meaningful as there are many trade media available. Personal contacts are equally important, through tools such as sales calls, seminars, training programs, and so on. Product impressions might pose a more difficult problem, although one can argue that the impact of the product or service on the trade is as important as it is for consumers. In order to get good distribution, shelf space, or favorable recommendations it is crucial to obtain solid trade support. Indeed, it is worth keeping in mind that the trade is going to be exposed to many of the same elements as consumers. In fact, they will often have considerable influence on which media or other communications tools are used. It should be noted here that in planning and executing an integrated communications strategy, a marketer would need to assess the exposures to be generated against each individual target. For example, for an athletic shoe manufacturer, there could be separate impression pies needed for the primary target of adults aged 25 to 54, the secondary target of teenagers, the retail trade, and the media.

Measurability

The second validation element is that of measurability—how can we measure the exposures in each category? Here, we provide a theoretical approach, realizing that this needs to be tested against actual brands in various categories.

Media exposures are the easiest to assess as the techniques are already familiar and well established. For established media, we can use standard measures such as reach, frequency, GRPs, and so on. For publicity, we would estimate the number of product or brand mentions picked up in the media and use these to calculate a "publicity GRP." There are some issues to consider here, however. Is it possible (or prudent) to mix our advertising GRPs with the publicity GRPs? And how do we account for negative publicity? We would also need to establish clear guidelines over what constitutes a "mention" in the media. Is it simply the name of the brand or must there be some kind of context given? Furthermore, it is difficult to estimate in advance the number of mentions that will be obtained when setting up the integrated plan. That would not preclude us from setting objectives for the number of mentions we would like to achieve, however. And perhaps over time ballpark figures could be established in a particular category or for a given product or service.

For direct marketing techniques, the primary measurement to use should be the number of potential contacts and, hence, impressions. This is relatively easy to calculate in advance because such techniques require this information up front. As with other forms of marketing communication, although every exposure will not result in a sale, there is likely to be some kind of impression made. It is worth pointing out that although some direct marketing techniques, such as direct response ads in magazines or newspapers, would be classified as media exposures, others, such as telemarketing, belong more appropriately in the personal contacts category.

The measurement of sales promotion tools varies depending on the type involved. Coupons, for example, would be considered media exposures and measured according to the newspaper or magazine circulation. Brochures or catalogs would, in contrast, be evaluated according to the number sent out or requested.

AN HYPOTHETICAL EXAMPLE

In order to show how this segmentation scheme might be applied to evaluate an integrated marketing program, the remainder of the chapter provides a hypothetical example.

For a brand of barbecue sauce, called Brand X, the marketing objective for the year is to maintain the brand's share by strengthening the price-value relationship. The target audience is adults aged 25 to 54 with children, a group that is 58 million in size. Efforts are designed to be national. Because barbecue sauce usage is highly seasonal, media and promotional activity occurs from mid-March through the summer. The focus is placed on three key sales and promotional periods: Memorial Day, July 4th, and Labor Day. Here are the communication (reach and frequency) goals for each of those periods:

	Memorial Day	July 4th	Labor Day
Reach	35%	45%	30%
Frequency	2+	3+	2+

Media Exposures

A total of 650 gross rating points is planned for the year, using a combination of television forms (network, spot, cable). With the target audience of 58 million, this means the television exposures generate 38,700,000 million impressions. Promotional expenditures should also be taken into account here. Brand X appears in free-standing inserts in the Sunday newspaper almost every month of the schedule. This generates an additional 68 million impressions.

Another type of promotion the brand uses is a special insert of recipes include in *Bon Appetit* and *Cooking Light* magazines. They have circulations of 1.2 million and 950,000, respectively. Assuming that the recipe insert is opened, on average, twice during the year, this would make the potential number of impressions 4.3 million over a 12-month period.

In addition, the brand receives promotional attention in the media when it sponsors summer golf tournaments. These include 30 announcements during live TV telecasts during the season. Assuming an average rating of 1.5 (against adults aged 25 to 54), this leads to an additional 75 GRPs. Multiplying the rating points by the target audience size generates an additional 4.4 million promotional media impressions.

Product Impressions

There are three types of product exposure to take into account: via distribution of the product, at home, and outside the home. The distribution of the product to stores probably provides the most important kind of product exposure. Every time a person walks into a store in which Brand X barbecue sauce is displayed and sees the bottle, even if he or she does not purchase one, an exposure to the brand occurs. In order to calculate the number of potential impressions, the number of store visits can be used. The rationale for this is that just as media vehicle exposures are assumed to be surrogate measures of advertising exposures, so one might argue that visiting the store where the product is sold offers a similar "opportunity to see" the brand. Advertising exposure in the media vehicle depends on factors such as product involvement, ad creativity, quality of readership or viewership, or ad size, among others. Similarly, whether the product exposure actually occurs depends on factors such as the size or location of the display, promotional activity in the store, and the package itself.

There are two elements to in-store product exposures – the size of the brand's distribution and the impact of sales promotions. Brand X is sold in 50,000 stores across the United States. If it is assumed that the target audience visits a store where the product is sold once a week, then that generates 2.9 million weekly in-store impressions. Taking the brand's selling season as lasting for 16 weeks during the summer, the product then accumulates 46.4 million in-store impressions throughout the year.

Product impressions in the home can be estimated through the use of syndicated research services of household panels that record their product usage and purchase frequency. Those usage and frequency numbers can then be used to estimate the number of times the householder is likely to take the product out of the cupboard or refrigerator and therefore be exposed to the brand name. For Brand X, which is typically used every other week during the 16-week summer season, the target would then be exposed to the product a total of 8 times. With the audience size of 58 million, a total potential number of in-home product impressions would be 464 million.

Outside exposures are, on the whole, very difficult to measure. There are some impressions of this kind that can be approximated. In the case of Brand X, exposures to the brand name are also obtained by promoting the product at food fairs across the country, such as "Taste of Chicago." The potential number of impressions can then be estimated based on attendance figures at those sites. This figure comes out to be 6.5 million, across 10 different festivals. Other outside exposures to the brand, such as at friends' homes or in other public places, are more difficult to gauge.

Personal Contacts

For Brand X, two kinds of personal contacts are used: trade calls and sponsorships. Sales calls to the trade are perhaps the most important. A total of 10,000 calls are made on 1,100 accounts across the country. Personal contacts with consumers are achieved by sponsoring participants in cooking contests. The number of such contacts can be estimated by knowing how many such events take place and how many people attend them. If 15 participants are sponsored at 25 different events, each of which is visited by 50,000 people, then there are a total of 1.25 million potential impressions available.

Looking at the overall marketing picture for Brand X barbecue sauce, one sees it has the potential to obtain a total of approximately 633 million exposures against its key target of adults aged 25 to 54. The breakdown between the three exposure types is as follows:

Media	18%
Product	81%
Personal	1%
Total	100%

Although this is clearly a gross estimate, it could be used to compare other combinations of marketing communications tools and/or strategies to see if improvements can be made or the effectiveness improved. In addition, by knowing the costs associated with each kind of impression, one can evaluate the efficiency of the total program.

SUGGESTIONS FOR FUTURE RESEARCH

As noted earlier, this segmentation scheme is intended to be merely the first, tentative step in trying to evaluate and measure all the elements of an integrated communications campaign. There are many areas that remain open for future research. In the following we list just a few of them.

Segmentation Validity

Before adopting this or any other segmentation scheme, it is critical that it be tested against a variety of cases and situations. Although we gave a brief example of Brand X barbecue sauce in this chapter, there is obviously a need to test the segmentation against other brands and products, in other categories. The service and business-to-business industries should be included as well.

Measuring Product Impressions

Until recently, most research efforts have been directed toward improving the measurement and evaluation of media exposures, both of traditional media such as television and magazines, and nontraditional alternatives, such as Channel One in high schools, or videocarts in supermarkets. Little is known at present about the impact and effectiveness of product impressions, or how we could best measure them. One possibility would be to try to measure in-store exposures. We suggested earlier using store visits as proxy measures for this, but such figures would fail to take into account many potentially important variables, such as the product location with the store, length and quality of the display, sales promotions, or package design, among others. In the case of services, we need to gain a better understanding of what the product impression really means.

Weighing the Exposures

In this measurement scheme, we propose looking at all three types of exposures evenly; that is, one media exposure is equivalent to one personal contact or product impression. In reality, however, some exposure types are probably a lot more influential and important than others. Indeed, we already know from our experiences with measuring traditional media that each type has a different kind of impact on the consumer, and those effects vary depending on the product, the message, and the timing and placement of the communication, among other variables. Therefore, it might be worth investigating whether certain kinds of integrated exposures should be weighted according to their impact within the total plan. Thus, for a business-to-business product, such as a fax machine, in-store visits could be given a weight of 1.0, whereas the trade magazine impressions might be discounted by .7 and telemarketing efforts considered only half as important, with those impressions weighted by .5. Again, more research would eventually be needed to validate the weights used, although judgment and experience are likely to play a large role here.

Other Issues

There are still several areas of the segmentation that are not readily measured at this time. These include trade promotions, special events, and word of mouth. Future research should examine procedures to quantify in some way each of these forms of communication.

As we move toward a new century, advertisers and agencies are looking for new and better ways of doing business. Integrated marketing communications, although not, strictly speaking, something "new," offers us the chance to improve the way we do business. By utilizing a coherent and integrated strategy that puts out a consistent and unified message across a variety of communications tools, marketers will find increased efficiency and effectiveness of their sales efforts. Consumers, in turn, will gain a better awareness and understanding of what those brands stand for and, we believe, be more responsive to the communications. If such an idyll is to be achieved, however, we must determine how best to measure and evaluate an integrated program so that we have measurable, valid, and strategically sound plans. Here, we have presented one potential path down which marketers may travel as they search for the holy grail of how marketing communication works.

REFERENCE

The ARF Model for Evaluating Media. (1989). *Journal of Media Planning, 4*(2), pp. 1–56.

15 Integrated Communication and Measurement: The Case for Multiple Measures

Allan L. Baldinger
Advertising Research Foundation

DEFINITION OF INTEGRATED COMMUNICATION

Caywood, Schultz, and Wang (1991), in their study of integrated communications, defined *integrated communication* as follows:

A concept of marketing communications planning that recognizes the added value of a comprehensive plan that evaluates the strategic roles of a variety of communications disciplines, example, General Advertising, Direct Response, Sales Promotion and Public Relations — and combines these disciplines to provide clarity, consistency, and maximum communications impact. This definition includes four basic types of communication: advertising, sales promotion, direct response, and public relations. The concept is, essentially, that the best way to build a brand franchise is to properly blend these four elements in a way that will most efficiently, and persuasively, communicate to the consumer.

I'm going to suggest to you that the best way to enter the dialogue on measuring across these four communication types is to start with the advertising component. This is because there has been more research done on advertising's communication values, and particularly TV advertising's communication value, than the other three. Second, not all of the shoes have yet dropped on the proper measures of advertising. It is important to get greater clarity regarding advertising effectiveness measures before we move to the more difficult task of measuring the impact of integrated campaigns.

Once upon a time, in TV copy-testing land, life was simple. There were three primary types of evaluative measures — brand name recall, communications of sales points, and some kind of persuasion measure. There was a fourth class, vaguely called "diagnostics," but this measure was not considered evaluative. It was an "all other" category, a place in which brand managers' strange questions went to die. It merely served to help explain, or maybe even rationalize, the results of the other three.

Everyone, at least in packaged goods research, agreed on this basic model, and it was well grounded in the accepted industry models. For example, the ARF model for media evaluations, shown in Fig. 15.1, followed this basic model. The six stages in the model included vehicle distribution, vehicle exposure, advertising exposure, perception, communication, and sales response. The last three, which take place after the consumer becomes actively involved in the process, roughly parallel the three copy-testing measures (Fig. 15.2).

The ARF model is a sequental model. It assumed that consumers went through certain orderly stages. Once they saw an ad, they must have understood which brand was being advertised, and then gained some information about the brand. That information would then lead to an attitude change, which would logically lead to a sale.

The new product models follow the same logic. These models suggest that brand awareness is followed by positive purchase intent (Fig. 15.3). If you

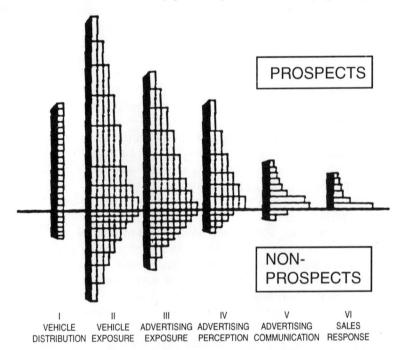

FIG. 15.1. A model for evaluating media.

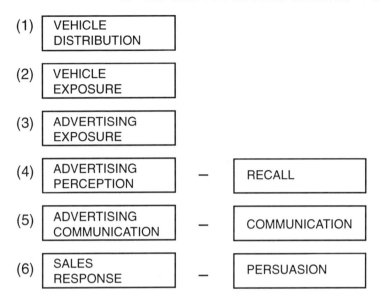

FIG. 15.2.   Parallels between ARF model and copy-testing measures.

FIG. 15.3.   New product models.

mix in a dollop of information and product distribution, you will motivate trial of product. A good product and a continuous flow of product news then encourage repeat purchase, and a successful brand is the result.

A problem with this model, however, concerns the relative weight of the three basic measures. For a new product, it is not possible to obtain a sale without trial, and trial is not possible without brand awareness; hence, the importance of recall is high. In contrast, for an established brand, the copy-testing industry seems to have moved in the direction of persuasion as the key measure. The relative emphases for new and established products are represented in Fig. 15.4).

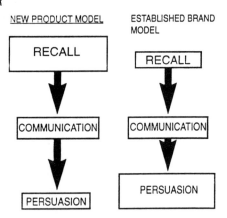

FIG. 15.4.   Relative emphases for new and established products.

After all, in a sequential model of human behavior, persuasion is the measure that is closest to the actual sale of the product. All else being equal it is likely to make more sense to go with a commercial that persuades those who see it, rather than one that is seen by lots of people but persuades no one. I remain impressed by the validation evidence, provided by the providers of new product simulated test markets models on the one hand, and those with persuasion-oriented copy-testing systems on the other. For many circumstances, a strong persuasion score means the advertiser is on the right strategy, or that the ads have something meaningful to say about the brand. Having the right strategy must sell more product than having the wrong strategy.

An additional concern, however, is whether this logic is true for all new products and all established brands. Actually, I submit to you that, to the consumer, there's no such thing as a new product or an established brand; there are only brands they have heard of, and those they have not. The terms *new products* and *established brands* are the manufacturer's terms, not the consumer's. The manufacturer has either been making the product for a while, meaning it has been established on the factory floor, or has just introduced it.

I submit to you that measures of brand recall (read "awareness") and communication must be related to sales if the brand's ingoing awareness is low, regardless of how long the brand has been on the market. If a consumer has never heard of Heinz ketchup, Heinz is a new product to that consumer.

The first time the consumer sees a commercial for Heinz, the new product model of awareness and communication is in effect, not the persuasion-based system. Persuasion is only likely to be the predominately important measure when awareness of the brand is already recognized by everyone. Logically, then, a persuasion-based system is likely to be more appropriate for a dominant well-known brand than for an established brand, ranked 3 or 4, or one that has historically received less widespread support. In other words, an established brand should be thought as a new product, if its ingoing level of awareness is low (Fig. 15.5). Basically, what I am suggesting here is that the relative importance of the critical measures of recall, communication, and persuasion are rarely likely to be black and white. Their relative importance are very likely to be brand–situation dependent.

In 1991, the ARF and Russ Haley, published a report called the *ARF Copy Research Validity Project* (Haley & Baldinger, 1991). It was a $400,000 industry-supported study of copy-testing measures in common use, tied to the BehaviorScan split-cable sales measurement system. To the surprise of many, measures of ad likability, or what many might call "affect," emerged as a strong predictor of sales.

But how might likability fit into the theory I have been describing? Well, I think likability deserves a place as a fourth measure, right up there next to communication, recall, and persuasion (Fig. 15.6). Although the ARF Copy Research Validity Project certainly hinted at likability's potential, that is not, in fact, why I think it deserves to be recognized as a fourth class of measure. There are actually three reasons.

First, there are many categories in which the simple reminder value of an established brand's existence can motivate a sale. A recent article (Moran, 1990) made a strong case in this area and I refer it to your attention. I believe that likability can affect this salience. Put another way, the salience of TV advertising can have a synergistic effect with the other types of communication measures, such as the sales promotion events employed in stores. A likable campaign can improve the effects of your in-store promotions when the in-store media successfully brings to mind the likable advertising seen at home.

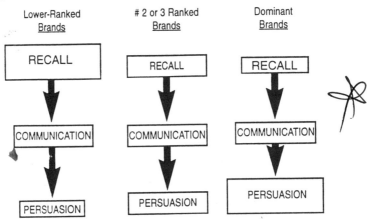

FIG. 15.5.   Established brand models.

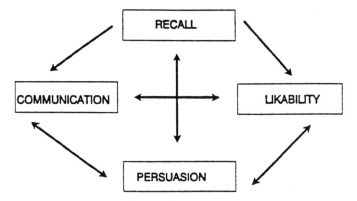

FIG. 15.6.   The likability factor.

Second, there are many categories in which logical product benefits play almost no role, emotion reigns supreme, and consumer perceptions of brands greatly exceed any ability to differentiate based on actual product performance. Jeans, beer, cigarettes, and fragrances are examples of product categories in which this is likely true.

Third is the emergence of consumers' active control of their advertising consumption, most recently being greatly increased by the use of remote control devises. The passive commercial watcher of yesteryear is a fond and quickly fading copy effectiveness memory. For many brands, and certainly after the first several TV exposures, making your commercial likable may be the only way to guarantee its exposure.

The Foote, Cone & Belding grid (Fig. 15.7) suggests that there is a thinking/feeling map. I prefer to think of it as describing categories that are

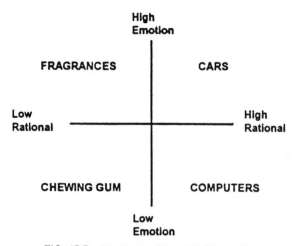

FIG. 15.7.   The Foote, Cone & Belding grid.

rational by nature, versus those that are likely to be driven by emotion. Cars are probably high on both dimensions (the upper-right quadrant). Fragrances are largely emotion driven (in the upper-left quadrant). Computers are probably largely rational (the lower-right box), and impulse categories, such as chewing gum, might be relatively low on both dimensions (the lower-left box).

It is likely that the more your category is rational, the more your brand sales are likely to vary with measures of persuasion (see Fig. 15.8). The more your category is emotionally driven, the more your brand is image-driven and the higher the likelihood that likability will be important. In a category in which both reason and emotion play a role, such as buying a car, both likability and persuasion are likely to play a role. At the other end of the spectrum, such as a low-impulse product like chewing gum, it is possible that in-store variables and sales promotions, such as displays, may be of much greater relevance. Simple brand salience and recall might be the key copy-testing measures.

An important caveat about existing persuasion measures concerns the issue of whether persuasive advertising should get the brand a new user or simply get an existing user to use more product. Campaigns to put Arm and Hammer Baking soda in your refrigerator, or using Steak Sauce on hamburgers, might be some appropriate examples of that approach. However, most copy-testing systems measure how many people are persuaded before and after the advertising, and then measure the difference. Somebody who already uses the brand is in the "pre" and the "post" groups. More usage among your current users might not show up in a pre–post question, but would show up in long-term sales impact.

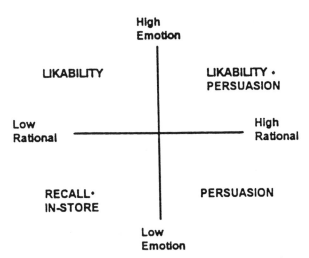

FIG. 15.8. How categories vary with measures of persuasion.

The importance of use-up rates among existing buyers received dramatic support with the 1991 release of the IRI "How Advertising Works" project. As Josh McQueen of Leo Burnett pointed out, the IRI study indicated that when established brand TV advertising was effective, 70% of the growth came from increased sales from existing brand buyers, whereas only 30% came from increased penetration, or attracting new users to the brand. This finding has clear and dramatic implications for most existing brand communication strategies. A strategy attracting new buyers versus a strategy of increasing the purchase rate among existing buyers may call for completely different mixes of investment in product improvement versus advertising versus sales promotion. Even more important, perhaps, is the hypothesis that most copy strategies that exist today are penetration-based strategies. Shifting to buying-rate strategies for many brands will almost require a revolution in culture.

There is also, however, at least one important caveat that concerns measures of likability. It must be constantly reinforced that likability is a means, not an end in itself. The purpose of advertising is to sell products. Everyone enjoys watching enjoyable advertising, but it is possible to make advertising that is so enjoyable that it distracts from, or even overwhelms, the brand's intended message. It should also be noted that creative award shows are judged by people, seldom by difficult-to-come-by sales evidence.

The ARF Copy Research Validity Project should never be interpreted to mean that likability is the sole measure by which advertising copy should be judged. In fact, it is my belief that the most effective advertising is likely to be that advertising in which all four types of measures are the most highly intercorrelated. It is when a likable execution is directly tied to a persuasive brand strategy that effectiveness is maximized. A commercial that scores high on measures of likability, but low on recall, communication values, or persuasion, is one about which to be particularly careful.

A second major caveat about likability is the fact that there is more than one type of consumer response to advertising that might be called a likability response. As Biel (1990) pointed out so convincingly, likability does not mean just humor, music, or entertainment; there is a strong information component to the best likability-oriented copy. Again, the goal is creating a positive feeling toward the brand and its advertising, not to entertain for the sake of entertainment alone.

It is now possible to return to see how this advertising-based theory fits with the new world of integrated communication. Let us look again at the four types of communications in Caywood, Shultz, and Wang's (1991) list—advertising, sales promotion, direct response, and public relations.

The first thing I want to do is simplify this list a little bit. My focus is on marketing for packaged goods brands. I believe that public relations is an infrequent communications option for packaged goods. After all, when was the last time you got a reporter for the *Chicago Tribune* or the *New York Times* to write a nice positive article on the merits of your brand? If your answer is "not lately," you will agree with me that public relations can be laid aside for now (for an alternative view, see Hallahan, chap. 17, this volume).

The next category in this list is direct response. My view of the successful applications of direct response might be exemplified by L.L. Bean catalogs, or the Home Shopping Network, or maybe my compact disc club. They work best when the convenience of shopping by mail, and the cost efficiencies of eliminating the retail middleman, make for a happy marketing marriage.

However, I would argue that, for most packaged goods, eliminating the retail middleman is not a realistic or even desirable alternative in the foreseeable future. It is unlikely that consumers will be buying soup, coffee, or shampoo by mail anytime soon.

After eliminating public relations and direct marketing, we are left with two important categories: advertising and sales promotion. We consider first where the actual exposure to those two forms of communication takes place. For most advertising, for most brands, and most of the time, the advertising exposure takes place in home. At the same time, most forms of sales promotion have their effects in stores. If we then think of that as comparable to the sequential model I described earlier, perhaps we can start thinking about integrated communications in a new way.

In an earlier study (Smith, 1987), the focus was on advertising and promotional variables and their perceived effects. About 60 marketing people were interviewed. Smith produced some interesting correspondence maps based on those data (Fig.15.9).

Oversimplifying a little, there were essentially four clusters. There was an advertising cluster in the upper-right quadrant. There were also three separate promotion clusters. In the middle of the chart is the couponing cluster. These were the coupons distributed in home to the consumer, either in newspapers or directly to the consumer. Number 3, at the bottom, are the price-oriented in-store promotions (largely controlled by manufacturers), such as cents-off packages. And Number 4, in the upper left, are the trade promotion allowances, oriented toward and largely controlled by the retailer.

Notice that Clusters 1 and 2 take place largely in home, whereas Clusters 3 and 4 largely take place in the store. It can also be noticed that the two in-home clusters are the closest to one another, and that the two in-store clusters are furthest away from the advertising cluster. The two in-store clusters seem to be separated by the issue of who controls the variables, the manufacturer, in Cluster 3, or the retailer, the "bad guy" trade promotion cluster, in the upper left.

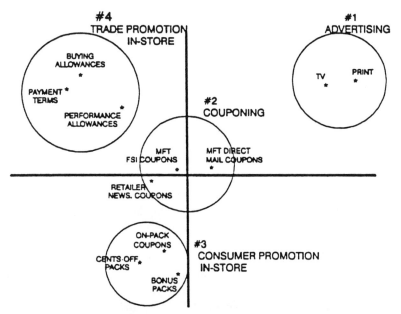

FIG. 15.9. Correspondence map.

If we then superimpose the marketers' perceptions of effects from this same study, another interesting pattern emerges (Fig. 15.10). As can be seen in Fig. 15.10, advertising's role has been largely perceived as oriented toward the functions of awareness and communicating a favorable image, the first two stages of the traditional model. But product trial, the direct result of effective persuasion, lies squarely between the two in-home clusters, advertising and couponing. Clearly, couponing now takes on the role of an in-home communications vehicle, not just a carrier for price reductions. Communicating a synergistic message across the in-home and the in-store variables will be the challenge.

I believe we are at the dawn of a new age of marketing. It is the same idea coming at us from different angles, and with different names, but it is all the same idea. It is called *value marketing* by some, and *everyday low pricing* by others. I know it is a trend, and not just a fad, because the marketing press is actually starting to use the letters EDLP to describe it. (As we at the ARF know full well, you are not really a player until your organization has been abbreviated.)

Further, EDLP is being led by the leaders in various industries. From Sam Walton's successful use of the strategy at Wal-Mart, to Procter & Gamble's apparently successful experiment with it for their major brands, the message is the same.

All consumers want a reasonable price, but they do not want to wait for

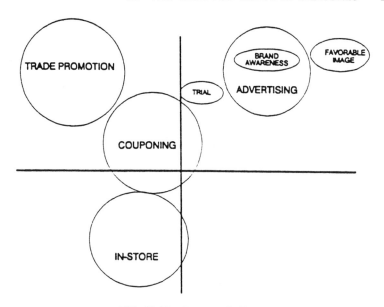

FIG. 15.10.   Pattern of effects.

it, and they do not want to hunt for it. To do so contradicts the trends toward convenience—the need to simplify life, not complicate it. Proliferation of meaningful product choice is good. Proliferation of arbitrary price choice, is bad.

As that begins to happen, sales promotion should no longer be viewed as simple price manipulation. If the store becomes a new form of media (for further elaboration of this concept, see Stewart, Frazier, & Martin, chap. 10, this volume), a new place where the variables of recall and communication and persuasion can be enhanced rather than disrupted, advertising and sales promotion can become partners instead of enemies. And that, after all, is what integrated communications is all about.

What does this mean for measurement? If in-store pricing declines as a factor, the store can be used to enhance the brand's image, not to cause a last-minute persuasion shift (or brand switch) based on a special price break. The real issue then becomes what is a brand's proper value positioning? There are only three possibilities.

A first possibility is that the brand has superior quality at a reasonable price (the Lexus/Infiniti strategy). A second possibility is that the brand has superior quality at a premium price (the Tide Liquid or Gillette Sensor strategy). The third possibility is offering the leaders' quality at a lower price. This is the retailer's private label strategy, successful if the retailer is able to match the leading brand's product quality. All three will work, and individual category and brand characteristics will dictate relative probabilities of success. The measurement of an integrated campaign will then entail three basic steps.

Step 1 will be to pick a brand's value strategy, based on a careful analysis of the category's emotional as opposed to its cognitive components and the brand's particular dimensions. Step 2 will be to select the brand's communications strategy, the extent to which the communications should be oriented toward advertising-based or promotion-based vehicles. Step Number 3 will be the choice of measurement strategy, the extent to which measurement should be oriented toward the in-home-oriented measures of recall, communications, and likability, or the in-store-oriented measures of persuasion, trial, and actual sales.

In-store scanners, the rapid growth of single-source household panels, as well as some of the new and growing linkages to households by household measurement of media consumption will make these measurements, both in home and in store, both possible and, eventually, mandatory. I view the future as a place where the barriers between advertising and promotion will break down, and ineffective advertising and promotion will be slowly but surely driven from the system. Manufacturers will start talking about brand equity in measurable terms. They will find ways to drive the inefficiencies from the existing trade promotion system, and to work within a truly positive trade partnership. Retailers will start to realize that in-store vehicles can build store traffic and brands, that the existing price-based promotion system just eats away at everybody's profit margins and efficiencies. ad agencies will start thinking of themselves as communications agencies, not just producers of traditional media advertising.

Building the right kind of measurement system will be a true organizational challenge. It represents a tremendous opportunity for the marketing research community. New models will need to be built, and the effects across tools will need to be much better understood.

REFERENCES

Biel, A. L. (1990). Serious thoughts about likable advertising. In T. X. Lockwood & S. Xenakis (Eds.), *The copy research agenda for the 1990s. The Seventh Annual ARF Copy Research Workshop* (pp. 201–209). New York: Advertising Research Foundation.

Caywood, C. L., Schultz, D. E., & Wang, P. (1991). *A survey of consumer goods manufacturers.* New York: American Association of Advertising Agencies.

Haley, R. I. (1990). The ARF Copy Research Validity Project. In T. X. Lockwood & S. Xenakis (Eds.), *The copy research agenda for the 1990s. The Seventh Annual ARF Copy Research Workshop* (pp. 29–68). New York: Advertising Research Foundation.

Haley, R. I., & Baldinger, A. L. (1991, April–May). The ARF Copy Research Validity Project. *Journal of Advertising Research*, (pp. 11–31).

McQueen, J. (1991). Important learning about how advertising works in stimulating long-term growth. *ARF Marketplace Advertising Research Workshop* (pp. 53–73). New York: Advertising Research Foundation.

Moran, W. T. (1990). Brand presence and perceptual frame. *Journal of Advertising Research*, (pp. 8–16).

Smith, W. (1987). Thinking about marketing: Perceptions of the market process in theeighties. *ARF Promotion Effectiveness Workshop* (pp. 19–41). New York: Advertising Research Foundation.

VI   The Role of Public Relations in Integrated Marketing Communication

16 Integrating Marketing Communication and Public Relations: A Stakeholder Relations Model

Anders Gronstedt
University of Colorado at Boulder
Kreab/Strategy XXI

> If you can only deal with yolks or whites,
> it's pretty hard to make an omelette.
>
> —Gene Amdahl (cited in Kanter, 1983, p. 156)

The purpose of this chapter is to bring public relations and marketing communications into a common conceptual framework. I am arguing that the divisionalizing of the communications responsibility into narrow disciplines has created communication technocrats. Marketers and public relations practitioners are both preoccupied with the technicalities of their tools, distracting them from the joint communicative purpose they serve. They ask myopic questions for which the answers are confined to a particular discipline—how can we increase the awareness of our magazine ads, or how can we increase the attendance on our next press conference—rather than asking fundamental questions like who are our key stakeholders and how can we communicate more effectively with them.

This chapter discusses the areas of overlap between marketing communications and public relations, suggests an integrated approach to these communications functions, and applies the model of integrated communications to a case study. This chapter is occasionally polemical; opening up a door will let wind in as well as light. The purpose here is to stimulate thinking about integrated communications, rather than to provide a set of axioms.

THE BLURRING OF BOUNDARIES

To create a context for a synthesis of marketing communications and public relations, it is appropriate to review and critique how the two functions traditionally have been defined and distinguished. Fig. 16.1 offers a schematic depiction of distinctions between public relations and marketing communications.

Two defining traits of public relations are, first, that it addresses publics by using, second, public relations tools, such as news releases, annual reports, and newsletters. Traditionally, public relations practitioners have relied largely on publicity or uncontrolled media in their communication to publics. Hard-sell marketing methods are normally considered inappropriate in public relations.

Marketing communications is conventionally defined in similar sender–receiver terms: A few monolithic audiences are being addressed with a limited set of communication tools. The audiences of marketing communications consist of markets, and the tools are paid mass media outlets, sales promotion, and personal selling.

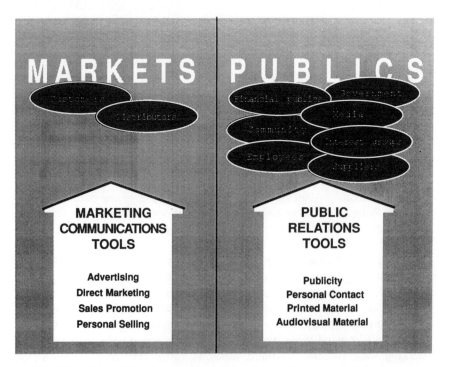

FIG. 16.1.   The traditional models of marketing communications and public relations.

Critique 1: Publics and Markets Overlap

Indeed, publics and markets are not as insular as the top of Fig. 16.1 indicate. Marketing lore contains numerous instances in which publics are the target of marketing activities. An example of publics being addressed as markets is the area of "cause-related marketing," in which the company supports a cause that appeals to their customers. American Express, for instance, promised its customers that 1% of the bill would be given to the Statue of Liberty restoration campaign. Other instances in which publics are being treated as market segments are green marketing and sponsorship of events.

Marketers are not only addressing publics as markets, they are also targeting publics that block the entrance to a market. This argument was put forth by Kotler (1986) in an article entitled "Megamarketing." Kotler argued that numerous markets are being blocked by publics such as government, labor unions, banks, or interest groups. Marketers have traditionally regarded these environmental factors as extraneous forces that are out of their control. Kotler points out, however, that there are ways to attract the support or at least neutralize opposition of these parties. Entering a blocked or protected market demands two additional Ps to the four Ps of marketing strategy: power and public relations. Other marketing literature has elaborated on the same idea that marketing activities should move from reactive accommodation to charges from various publics (or "environmental forces," as marketers prefer to call them) to proactive formation of publics (Achrol, 1991; Webster, 1992; Zeithaml & Zeithaml, 1984).

Contrary to the traditional view, illustrated by Fig. 16.1, markets and publics are interacting and overlapping systems that cannot be treated in splendid isolation.

Critique 2: Marketing and Public Relations' Tools Overlap

Along with the blurring of publics and markets, there is a crossover between the communicative tools of marketing and public relations. The strategies and tools of marketing communications are entering into public relations. Public relations practitioners are, in the words of Kotler and Mindak (1978), realizing that "the best way to solve a public relations problem might be through the disciplined orientation that marketing provides" (p. 19). Advertising, for instance, is no longer the sole province of marketing. There are numerous examples of so-called "corporate advertising" successfully used in public relations campaigns. For years, Mobil has featured "advertorials," ads in the format of an editorial, on the op-ed page of a few major newspapers and magazines (Heath & Nelson, 1986; Schmertz & Novak, 1986).

A number of studies have found corporate advertising to benefit marketing as well as public relations. Yankelovich, Skelly, and White (cited in Garbett, 1981, p. 92) found that managers perceived companies with higher spending on corporate advertising to have more competent managers, attractive stocks, quality products, and better financial conditions and social responsibility. Brouillard Communications (1988) found a positive correlation among managers between spending on corporate advertising and the corporation's ability to attract investors and skilled employees, as well as to succeed in plant siting and to find companies willing to engage in joint ventures. These are goals traditionally associated with public relations. The public relations departments are not only the principal originators of the concept and themes of most corporate advertising, they are increasingly taking over the responsibility of media selection and placement of the ads from the advertising departments (Grunig & Hunt, 1984).

Public relations practitioners are finding themselves addressing markets as well as using marketing strategies and marketing tools. Recent textbooks in public relations are incorporating a variety of marketing tools such as print advertisement, TV and radio commercials, and direct mail (e.g., Cutlip, Center, & Broom, 1985; Grunig & Hunt, 1984; Wilcox, Ault, & Agee, 1992;).

Similarly, marketers are resorting to PR tools. The Walt Disney Company has, for instance, relied exclusively on PR activities in their marketing up until the mid-1980s (Grover, 1991). Still, most marketing textbooks mention *publicity* only briefly and note that the expertise on these tools is usually found in public relations departments. Marketing textbooks treat public relations as a set of tactical tools rather than as a strategy.

There is, however, a recent surge of literature explicitly dealing with the usage of public relations tools for marketing purposes. Goldman (1990) offered advice from a practitioner's perspective on the utilization of public relations tools in marketing. McKenna (1986) bore witness to the crucial role of public relations tools in the introduction of the Macintosh computer. Harris (1991) distinguished marketing public relations (MPR) from corporate public relations (CPR). He defined MPR as public relations tools used to promote products, making it synonymous with product publicity. CPR was defined as public relations in traditional terms: a management function concerned with the relations to stakeholders other than the customers.

Clearly, the boundaries between marketing communications and public relations are eroding. Public relations is evolving from a press-agentry/publicity role into a managerial communications function. In a like manner, marketing is evolving from a sales function to a strategic marketing management discipline. Because the definitions of the two disciplines are broadening, the distinction between them is blurring. Public relations practitioners are addressing markets, and marketers are addressing publics. Marketing communications tools have become a subset of PR, and PR tools have become a subset of marketing communications. The strictly demarcated division of marketing communications and public relations has more historic than operational value.

AN INTEGRATED MODEL

The eclectic view of communications proposed in this chapter requires an overarching theory of organizational communication. Fig. 16.2 presents one approach to integrated communications. The model explains and unites the main dimensions of public relations and marketing communications disciplines identified in this chapter:

1. The circle on top of Fig. 16.2 illustrates the merger of the public relations' target audiences of publics and the marketing audiences of markets.

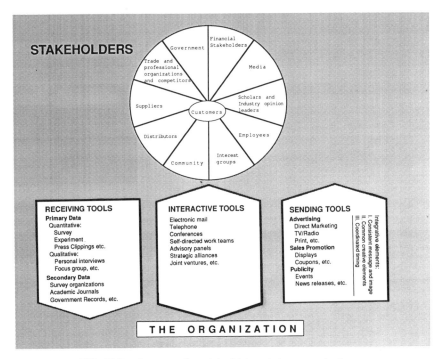

FIG. 16.2. A proposed model of integrated communications.

2. The right arrow of Fig. 16.2 joins the public relations tools and the marketing communications tools in a single communications tool box. The left arrow joins the research, or receiving tools, from marketing with those of public relations, and the middle arrow joins the interactive tools.

The model is applicable to nonprofit entities as well as to corporations, which will be referred to collectively as *organizations*. This integrated communications model is represented by the following working definition:

> Integrated communications uses an appropriate combination of sending, receiving, and interactive tools drawn from a wide range of communication disciplines to create and maintain mutually beneficial relations between the organization and its key stakeholders, including the customers.

The component parts of the model consist of stakeholders, receiving tools, interactive tools, and sending tools.

The Stakeholders

The circle on top of Fig. 16.2 illustrates the fact that every organization is linked to a complex system of interrelated individuals and organizations who have a stake in the organization's deeds. I will refer to them as *stakeholders*, defined as "any group or individual who can affect, or is affected, by the achievement of a corporation's purpose" (Freeman, 1984, p. VI). This label avoids the term *audiences*, with its connotation of a homogeneous passive mass, and the terms *markets* and *publics*, whose ambiguities were discussed earlier.

The groups and individuals who most affect the achievement of an organization's purpose are the customers, shown at the center of the stakeholder system in Fig. 16.2. Good relationships with the customers are the essence of a successful performance by any organization. In the words of Levitt (1991, p. 131), "A business is an organized system of activities whose existence and level of success are based entirely on its ability to attract and hold a necessary number of solvent customers in some econom- ically effective way." For nonprofit organizations, the definition of cus- tomers is more complex — it might include clients, volunteers, and donors.

Organizations' relationships to their customers are affected in various ways by a number of other stakeholders. Most stakeholders fall into the 10 categories depicted in the outer circle of Fig. 16.2: government, financial stakeholders, media, scholars and industry opinion leaders, employees, interest groups, communities, distributors, suppliers, and trade and profes- sional organizations and competitors. These groups are not monolithic entities, but broad generic categories. Most organizations can identify a number of specific stakeholder groups and individuals under each of the 10 categories. For example, the category labeled "media" might contain trade magazines, local newspapers, radio and TV stations, and national media. The configuration of specific stakeholders is highly situational: It changes from organization to organization and from time to time.

In the model, these stakeholders are all attached to the inner circle of customers, illustrating the point that all the stakeholder groups have consequences for the customers in the center. The integrated communications approach treats the communication with each stakeholder in the outer circle as an integral part of the customer communication. The customer can be addressed through communication with the other stakeholders, as the following brief case studies illustrate:

- An example of communicating to customers through *industry opinion leaders* is when Apple gave key computer industry opinion leaders 7-hour demonstrations of the Macintosh computer several months before its introduction. Most of them fell in love with the Mac and spread the good word about it to potential customers (McKenna, 1986).

- An example of communicating to customers through *employees* is when Scandinavian Airline Systems reminded its employees, through seminars, booklets, events, and other communications tools, that a passenger's impression of the airline company results from the sum of the "moments of truths": the moments when the passengers interact with an employee at the company (Carlzon, 1989).

- An example of getting access to customers through *government* and *interest groups*, offered by Kotler (1986), is when Pepsi-Cola struck a deal with the Indian government to gain entry to India's huge consumer market by satisfying various special interests. Pepsi offered to bring new food processing, packaging, and water technology to India. They promised to focus their selling efforts on rural areas, and to help India export its agri-based products. Pepsi orchestrated a set of benefits that was designed to please various interest groups in order to win government approval to sell in the Indian market.

- Communicating with *distributors* is crucial for consumer goods manufacturers because of the increasing power of a few retail giants. The tried and trite "push strategy" of trade shows, personal selling, and retail trade press advertising is no longer sufficient; manufacturers and distributors need to develop close relationships. Black & Decker involves retail chains in every step of the development process of new product lines. Procter & Gamble set up an office with 70 employees right next to Wal-Mart's Arkansas headquarters that works in close collaboration with Wal-Mart on improving quality and minimizing cost of every detail of the delivery, down to how the diapers are stacked on the trucks (Schiller et al., 1992).

• Japanese companies have demonstrated that long-lasting relationships with *suppliers* is one of the keys to creating quality products for a low cost. Their *kanban*, or just-in-time, systems rely on a few suppliers that deliver quality products frequently and in small quantities to keep inventory down. American companies are also now beginning to treat suppliers as long-term partners. Ford exchanged security passes with key suppliers so they can go to each other's facilities and find ideas for improvements.

• Japanese companies also provide examples of how customers benefit from solid relations with the *financial community*. The patience and trust from shareholders and lenders allow Japanese firms to cut prices below production cost in anticipation of higher demand in the future. Many American companies cannot pursue such long-term strategies because of shareholders' demands for quarterly earnings and because American banks will not allow companies to operate on the huge debt levels — over 80% — of Japanese companies(Abegglen & Rapp, 1974).

• An example of communicating to customers through *competitors and trade organizations* is Florida Citrus Commission's advertising campaigns that push orange juice as "not just for breakfast anymore." Since this program began more than 50 years ago, Florida orange consumption has grown over 1,000%. Competing citrus companies in Florida have success-fully integrated their marketing efforts to increase their total market (Harris, 1991; Kinnear & Bernhardt, 1986).

• An example of communicating to customers through the *local community* is the newsletter published by the First State Bank of Northern California, San Leandro in which local nonpolitical groups mention their meetings, events, drives, and sales. The community benefits because the newsletter is read by a larger number of potential customers (California Bankers Association, cited in Cutlip, Center, & Broom, 1985, p. 401).

• An example of communicating to customers through *media* is when a British Petroleum (BP) tanker spilled oil two miles off the Southern California coast. The chairman of BP immediately flew to the scene and took charge. Media headquarters were set up next to the cleanup command center, BP officials appeared on TV and radio, and the media were provided underwater pictures of the hole. BP emerged from the accident with enhanced credibility among customers (Wilcox, Ault, & Agee, 1992).

These cases exemplify that the stakeholders are all interdependent; their action or inaction has consequences on other stakeholders. Changes in one group of stakeholders tend to trigger changes in others. As systems theory reminds us, "The output of one system is the input to another system" (Cleland & King 1972). The integrated communications approach builds on this interdependency by coordinating communication activities with the entire web of stakeholders.

Stakeholders are not only interacting, they are also overlapping. Most of the Walt Disney Company's shareholders are, for instance, customers as well. Disney always holds its shareholders meetings close to Disney World or Disneyland on either a Thursday or a Tuesday, to encourage the 5,000 stock owners to spend a 3-day weekend at the parks (Grover, 1991). Another instance in which the same individual has different stakes in an organization occurred when Ralph Nader bought two GM stocks to wage a proxy fight on such issues as product safety and the rights of minorities employed by GM (Freeman, 1984). Nader was acting in the roles of shareholder, consumer activist, consumer, and on the behalf of GM employees. Multiple stakeholder roles are becoming more common along with the emergence of such phenomena as shareholder activism (like the Nader case), employee shareholdership, and consumer environmental concern.

The fact that stakeholders interact and overlap requires a reconceptualization of the traditional notions of a target market. The responsibility of a communicator goes far beyond just addressing a target audience defined by some sterile demographic data, such as "bisexual female motorcycle drivers, with a household income of $25,000 to $40,000." The integrated communicator is also responsible for building relationships with opinion leaders who legitimize the product, with the government that might legislate against it, with media that critique the product, with activist groups that might condemn it, with the financial community that invests in the production of the product, and with employees who create it.

Boulding (1981) noted that organizational ecology does not involve survival of the fittest, but "survival of the fitting." The survival of organizations is not dependent on the ability to compete as much as on an ability to collaborate with the environment. Contrary to the marketing textbook notion of the corporate world as a competitive arena of combatting forces, free enterprise builds on mutually beneficial relations. Integrated communications is replacing the old warfare metaphors in marketing, such as *target audience, campaign*, and *impact*, with a new vernacular of terms like *alliances, joint ventures, networking, vertical and horizontal integration, keiretsus*, and *partnerships*.

Integration of the Receiving Tools

Integrating communications activities with the entire system of stakeholders requires a dialogue approach by which the stakeholders are recognized as receivers as well as senders of information. The stakeholders can be treated as senders of information through the use of receiving tools drawn from marketing and public relations. The left arrow of Fig. 16.2 gives examples of the receiving tools at the integrated communicator's disposal. The receiving toolbox consists of marketing research tools such as experiments, focus groups, perceptual mapping, and store audits. The integrated communicator may also bring PR research tools to bear, such as readership surveys and content analysis of the clippings about an organization, community case studies, opinion polls, and the monitoring of key news outlets. The list of tools in Fig. 16.2 serves to illustrate the range of tools rather than to offer a comprehensive list.

The diversity of audiences and sending tools employed in integrated communications calls for multimethodological research tools. These tools can be used in continual cycles for formative research to monitor stakeholders' perceptions and to plan communication activities, and for evaluative research to determine the success of the communication efforts.

The starting point of formative stakeholder research, suggested by Freeman (1984), is to identify the generic categories of stakeholders and to rank their relative importance to the organization. The next step would be to identify the specific groups and individuals that have a stake in the organization's purpose. A continual monitoring of a wide range of stakeholders with a wide range of receiving tools will enable the communicator to anticipate and prepare for events that are likely to affect the organization in the future, such as evolving debates over political issues or changes of customer preferences. Such a proactive approach will enable organizations to see opportunities rather than to react to *faits accomplis*. Organizations that enter a communication process at an early stage are more likely to manage issues in a win–win mode (Heath & Nelson, 1986).

Furthermore, the integrated communicator uses research to evaluate stakeholders' perception of the organization. It is important to note that an integrated stakeholder approach calls for pretest and postevaluation of all stakeholders that will encounter a communication activity, including stakeholders that do not constitute the primary target audience. If Coca-Cola had pretested their "New Coke" concept in 1987 with their brewers, the conflict it stirred might been avoided.

Research is traditionally used by advertising or public relations specialists to fine tune their single communicative tool's ability to manipulate a single target audience. The integrative communicator, however, is concerned with *insights* into the thoughts and behaviors of various stakeholders.

Interactive Tools

There are tools from both marketing communications and public relations that facilitate a two-way dialogue between the organization and its stakeholders, such as personal selling, self-directed work teams, and advisory panels consisting of in-house and advocacy group representatives that address issues of mutual concern. Additional tools that ought to be included in the interactive tool box, suggested by Stewart, Frazier, and Martin (chapter 10, this volume), are the emerging tools that combine communication and distribution functions, such as telemarketing, home shopping networks, video catalogs, and future interactive high-definition TVs (HDTVs).

The integrated use of receiving tools and interactive tools marks a departure from the linear stimulus/response view of communication from which marketing and public relations stem. Public relations originates from press agents transmitting a one-way flow of information. Similarly, marketers are heirs of salespersons who simply distribute the products to the customers. (In fact, when this author took his first introductory marketing course as late as in 1988, in Sweden the class was still called "Distribution.") The receivers were, according to these traditional views of marketing communications and public relations, presumed to absorb and react to the information given them. The communication process was perceived in the simplistic terms of a doctor injecting the patient with an hypodermic needle (Heath & Nelson, 1986). The division between marketing communications and public relations is motivated by this outdated view of the audiences being "injected" with a message; the marketing and public relations departments are perceived as operating on different patients (target audiences) with different injection solutions (media tools).

In contrast, the integrated use of the receiving, interactive, and sending tools will facilitate a dialogue in which the stakeholders are active, interactive, and equal participants of an ongoing communication process. The purpose of such communication processes is to build lasting relationships that, in the words of Levitt (1986), are treated as a marriage rather than a date.

Integration of the Sending Tools

Once the integrated communicator has identified the key stakeholders and set communication objectives for each group of stakeholders, it is possible to select the appropriate sending tools. Effective communications requires an optimal mix of sending tools for each identified group of stakeholders. The tools may be drawn from any communication discipline. The right arrow of Fig. 16.2 gives examples of the range of sending tools that the integrated communicator's tool box could contain. It holds marketing tools such as advertising, sales promotion, and personal selling, and PR tools such as media kits, events, and conferences. The box also contains tools that don't readily fit into any discipline, such as infomercials, documercials, product placement in movies, and place-based media (i.e., advertising-supported television programing in supermarkets, health clubs, airplanes, salons, doctors' offices, and even in public schools). The advertising agency Leo Burnett has identified 600 discrete media vehicles to reach a stakeholder. If none of the existing 600 vehicles seems appropriate, there is always the option to invent new ones. For instance, Columbia Pictures featured the logo of a 1993 summer movie release on an unmanned space ship. Not discipline boundaries, but imagination now sets the limit for possible combinations of tools.

One approach to finding an optimal combination of sending tools that the advertising agency DDB Needham is in the process of exploring is the organization of a database of marketing communications and public relations tools. Integrating media selection and scheduling methods of marketing communications and public relations will require a reconceptualization of the concepts of media selection. Marketing communicators and public relations practitioners both have methods of media selection that are based on information about audience media habits and cost-effectiveness data. The selection of advertising media is conventionally guided by reach and frequency comparisons. Because publicity space is not bought, PR practitioners maximize the *probability* of getting exposure in the most appropriate media (Alcalay & Taplin, 1989). As if developing comparative media selection methods between paid mass media outlets and editorial publicity will not be hard enough, comparing mass mediated messages with interpersonal communication channels provides an even larger challenge. How do reach and frequency figures compare between a print ad in *The Wall Street Journal* and a seminar for investors? The integrated communications approach will have to develop processes of "communication tools selection" to replace current "media selection."

When an eclectic mix of sending tools has been selected it remains to make them work together according to three key integrated elements: consistent message and image, common creative elements, and coordinated timing (found vertically on the upward arrow of Fig. 16.2).

Integrating the sending tools involves harmonizing the messages they contain and the image of the organization they convey. For instance, the exclusive image created around a product by the advertising department might be undermined by the free samples handed out by the sales promotion department. Likewise, the advertising department might hype the company's size and stability in the advertisements, whereas the PR department may announce cutbacks and layoffs. As the CEO of British Airways, Sir Colin Marshall (1990) put it:

> Have you as a company clearly articulated a statement of what image you are seeking to achieve? Precisely what image do you want? How do you want to be perceived by your key audiences? What are the characteristics you want

them to feel your company possesses? Is there a consensus view on these issues which is understood and accepted, or would you get 10 different answers if you asked 10 directors of the same company what the company's image is and what it should strive to be?

That is to say, the communicators need to share a common understanding of how the corporation should be portrayed.

Another integrated element of the model is time sequencing. For example, if the customers of an airline company get the news about the new low rates to Rome through an ad before the booking agents are informed, there is a problem of employee morale as well as customer confidence. Stakeholders interact, overlap, and run across sending tools intended for other stakeholders. To ensure that most stakeholders get the word from the horse's mouth, the timing of all communication has to be meticulously coordinated.

Integrating message, creative elements, and timing will cause the sending tools to enforce each other synergistically. The totality will have a better effect than the sum of the discrete events.

A CASE STUDY: INTEGRATED TURTLES

A case study of the Teenage Mutant Ninja Turtles illustrates integrated communications in practice. The study is intended to give an example of ingenious ways in which a number of stakeholders can be addressed with a multitude of integrated tools.

The subject of the case study should be familiar to anyone who has opened a magazine, turned on the television, or talked to a child during the last several years: Teenage Mutant Ninja Turtles. These four green reptiles are being featured in an ubiquitous network of media and products. Tony Marsiglia, whose agency coordinates the marketing of the Turtles, puts it: "Marketing isn't one activity, nor is it really the sum of many activities. Rather, it is the result of the interaction of many activities" ("Marketer of the Month," 1990).

The story of the Teenage Mutant Ninja Turtles originated in 1983 in an obscure black and white comic book with a modest circulation. Most people have heard the original story: A quartet of turtles were dropped as babies into some radioactive nastiness in a New York sewer. Transformed into semi-human beings, they met Splinter, a mutant rat, who taught them the martial arts. Since then they have been practicing their martial arts skills on Splinter's archenemy, Shredder.

The integrated communication of the Turtles began when licensing agent Mark Freeman's Surge Licensing, Inc. bought the exclusive licensing rights of the Turtles in 1986 (Hammer & Miller, 1990). Mr. Freeman convinced Playmates Toys to invest $2.5 million in an animated television show and to launch a line of 10 Turtle figures (Robie, 1991). A marketing agency, Responsive Marketing Communication, was hired by Mark Freeman to handle the marketing and licensing of the Turtles.

The Turtle goods came to the market during a few months in 1988. Later that same year the stores were flooded with Turtle packaged frozen pizza, Turtle cereal, Turtle pajamas, Turtle toothbrushes, Turtle underwear, Turtle sheets, and Turtle shampoo. More than 600 Turtle products were on the market before the end of 1988 (Schneider, 1990). Each product was promoted with various sending tools.

After the success of these products and the television series, the Turtles were ready to go on to the big screen. The release of the first Teenage Mutant Ninja Turtles movie was preceded by a very intricate integrated communications campaign. The Turtles were already a quarter-billion dollar business before the movie was released (Harris, 1991). Movie trailers and television advertising ran for months before the release of the movie. Research indicated that the movie was not only appreciated by its core audience of children, but also by parents and college students (Kelleher, 1990). Based on this research, the customers were segmented into young males, young females, and families. Different television spots were aimed at these segments ("Ninja Turtle Power," 1990). Another stakeholder segment, parents, were targeted with newspaper ads. Still another segment, college students, were addressed through advanced midnight screenings at 27 colleges. The screenings were intended to attract college opinion leaders who would spread the word of mouth to make the movie a "campy cult thing" ("Ninja Turtle Power," 1990).

The licensing agent Mark Freeman and the film distributor New Line staged a number of cross-promotions between the movie and other products. The designated "Official Turtlemania Center," KMart, ran $72 million worth of newspaper ads and showed trailers of the movie in the stores ("Ninja Turtle Power," 1990). Burger King sold 7 million Turtles cartoon videos and gave away $15 million in Turtle buttons ("Don't Believe the Hype," 1990). Light 'N' Lively Yogurt awarded Turtle Weekends at Universal Studios, where the actual costumes used in the movie were on display. Toys 'R' Us created separate Teenage Mutant Ninja Turtles sections in their stores. A million copies of a novelization of the movie appeared in the stores during the opening week of the movie. Pizza Hut was sponsoring the year-long, 40-city "Coming Out of Their Shells" live rock concert tour soon after the release of the first movie (Harris, 1991). The Turtles' debut album went gold in one week — selling only at Pizza Hut locations ("Don't Believe the Hype," 1990).

The release of the first movie on videocassette was backed by a $20 million marketing effort that included a tie in with Pizza Hut. The video carried a 60-second Pizza Hut commercial and a Pizza Hut coupon book. The video distributor, Live Home Video, and Pizza Hut each developed television and print ads to promote the release. In addition, Live Home Video aired radio spots, whereas Pizza Hut's efforts included direct mail. Their campaigns were closely coordinated and carried the same theme: "Turtle Power To Go" (Magiera, 1990).

This huge range of sending tools had been carefully integrated. The message, image, and creative elements were designed to be easily transferred to any media while still being unified. The Teenage Mutant Ninja Turtles are a postmodern composite of Asian ninjas in a New York setting with Italian renaissance names, talking California surfer jargon, in *Three Musketeers*- and *Star Wars*-inspired plots. This ambiguous state of race, nationality, species, and time makes them ideal for transmedia integration. Willis (1987, p. 415) captured this characteristic of the Turtles: "Everything transfers but nothing changes." The Teenage Mutant Ninja Turtles are being featured as a transmedia network. A Turtle music video is not a discrete event, but a component of this network. Every component of the web mutually supports the other components.

The results of the Turtle integration are quite remarkable. The toy versions of the Turtles grossed over $600 million in retail sales in 1990 ("Marketer of the Month," 1990), grabbing 60% of the U.S. market of action figure toys, and making Playmate the most profitable toy company in history (Tanzer, 1991). In 1991, there were over 200 companies marketing more than 1,000 products with the Turtle's logo. The average 3- to 8-year-old boy in the United States has more than five Turtles in his bedroom (Tanzer, 1991).

Teenage Mutant Ninja Turtles are communicated by a stakeholder network of 200 companies—with the licening agent as the coordinating nucleus. This virtual organization has used every conceivable way to reach a 10-year-old in a highly coordinated fashion. Admittedly, movies and television series are high-involvement products and easily transferable to other media. Nevertheless, the case illustrates the possibilities available for communicators who do not hesitate to transgress marketing communications and public relations boundaries.

CONCLUSION

The word *department* originates from the French word *departir*, which means "to separate." Marketing and public relations departments have traditionally used separate tools to communicate with separate audiences, rather than addressing the larger network of stakeholders with a variety of appropriate tools. The traditional advertising department is likely to cast any problem as an advertising problem, and the PR department will turn the same problem into a PR problem. The different communications guilds have the answers before they know the problem. It is like the carpenter who only has a hammer and thinks any problem can be fixed with a nail: Marketers and PR practitioners are in charge of great communication tools, but do not always realize that the tools are not all purpose. The rapid changes that are taking place in the media and business environment are, however, necessitating new conceptual approaches to corporate communication.

The business environment is growing increasingly complex. The stakes of the stakeholders have never been higher. An integrated stakeholder perspective is required because the government is more intrusive than ever, the stock market is more active than ever, the employees are more important than ever, the media are more scrutinizing than ever, and the competition is more innovative than ever. The organization is not being surrounded by isolated enclaves of monolithic audiences that can be "injected" with information; it is serving customers and other interacting and overlapping stakeholders. An organizational communicator cannot understand one group of stakeholders without relating them to all other groups and individuals that have a stake in the organization's activities.

The job of integrating the communication to various stakeholders is becoming increasingly complex because of media's new world disorder. More information has been produced on the earth since the Kennedy administration than in the previous 5,000 years (since the King Tut administration). A person from the preindustrialist era would experience more images while watching contemporary television for 1 hour than he or she would have during a 19th-century lifetime. Denver will soon get access to 500 cable channels. We are not newspaper readers or television viewers anymore, but browsers and zippers. It is not so much a matter of filtering out what does not appear to be interesting, but to tune in what seems attractive. As media proliferates and becomes fragmented, effective communicators are required to orchestrate an eclectic combination of sending, interactive, and receiving communicative tools.

Integrated communications is not about inventing a new theory with catchy buzzwords and esoteric acronyms; it is a theory that draws from, rather than substitutes for, previous research and experience with marketing communications and public relations. The theory of integrated communications recognizes that organizational communication is too complex and interactive to be fractionalized into insular disciplines. This interdisciplinary theory inserts the various communication disciplines into a holistic perspective, drawing from the concepts, methodologies, crafts, experiences, and artistries of marketing communications and public relations. Specialists in certain communicative tools will still be in demand, but instead of being solo performers, they will find themselves being instrumentalists in an orchestra, under the conductorship of the integrated communicator.

REFERENCES

Abegglen, J. C., & Rapp, W. V. (1974). Japanese managerial behavior and 'excessive competition. *International business 1973 — a selection of current readings*, pp. 65-82.

Achrol, R. S. (1991, October). Evolution of the marketing organization: New forms for turbulent environments. *Journal of Marketing*, pp. 77-93.

Alcalay R., & Taplin, S. (1989). Community health campaigns: From theory to action. In R. E. Rice & C. K. Atkin (Eds.), *Public communication campaigns* (2nd ed., pp. 105-130). Newbury Park CA: Sage

Boulding, K. E. (1981). *Evolutionary economics*. Beverly Hills, CA: Sage.

Brouillard Communications. (1988). *The Winning Edge*. New York.

Carlzon, J. (1989). *Moments of truth*. New York: Harper & Row.

Cleland D. I., & King, W. R. (1972). *Management: A systems approach*. New York: McGraw-Hill.

Cutlip, S. M., Center, A. H., & Broom, G. M., (1985). *Effective public relations* (6th ed.). Englewood Cliffs, NJ: Prentice-Hall.

Don't believe the hype. (1990, December 13-27). *Rolling Stone*, p. 70.

Freeman R. E. (1984). *Strategic management: A stakeholder approach*. Boston: Pitman.

Garbett, T. F. (1981). *Corporate advertising*. New York: McGraw-Hill.

Goldman, J. (1990). *Public relations in the marketing mix*. Lincolnwood, IL: NTC Business Books.

Grover, R. (1991). *The Disney touch: How a daring management team revived an entertainment empire*. Homewood, IL: Business One-Irwin.

Grunig, J. E., & Hunt, T. (1984). *Managing public relations*. New York: Holt, Rinehart and Winston.

Hammer, J., & Miller, A. (1990, April 16). Ninja Turtle power adds a record-grossing movie to the toy industry's latest craze. *Newsweek*, pp. 60-61.

Harris, T. L. (1991). *The marketer's guide to public relations*. New York: Wiley.

Heath, R. L., & Nelson, R. A. (1986). *Issues management: Corporate public policymaking in an information society*, Beverly Hills, CA: Sage.

Kanter, R. M. (1983). *The change masters*. New York: Simon & Schuster.

Kelleher, E. (1990, March). New Line readies Ninja market blitz. *Film Journal*, p. 8.

Kinnear, T. C., & Bernhardt, K. L. (1986). *Principles of marketing* (2nd ed.). Glenview, IL: Scott, Foresman.

Kotler, P. (1986, March–April). Megamarketing. *Harvard Business Review*, pp. 117-124.

Kotler, P., & Mindak, W. (1978, October). Marketing and public relations, should they be partners or rivals? *Journal of Marketing*, pp. 13-20.

Levitt, T. (1986). *The marketing imagination* (2nd ed.). New York: The Free Press.

Levitt, T. (1991). *Thinking about management*. New York: The Free Press.

Magiera, M. (1990, July 30). Pizza Hut ties in with Turtles video. *Advertising Age*, p. 14.

Marketer of the month—Tony Marsiglia: Out of his shell. (1990, August). *Sales & Marketing Management*, pp. 28-29.

Marshall, C. Sir. (1990). *What are a CEO's expectations of his PR advisors?* Speech delivered at the International PR Association Conference, London.

McKenna, R. (1986). *The Regis touch*. Reading, MA: Addison-Wesley.

Ninja Turtle power — or how to ride out a runaway. (1990, June, 13). *Variety*, p. 48.

Robie, J. H. (1991). *Teenage Mutant Ninja Turtles exposed*. Lancaster, PA: Starburst & Publishers.

Schiller, Z., Zellner, W., Stodghill, R., & Maremont, M. (1992, December 21). Clout! More and more retail giants rule the market place. *Business Week*, pp. 66–73.

Schmertz, H., & Novak, W. (1986). *Goodbye to the low profile*. Boston: Little, Brown.

Schneider, K. S. (1990, April 23). Cowabunga! Unshelled, these Teenage Mutant Ninja actors kick off the 1990 silly season. *People Weekly*, pp. 44–47.

Tanzer, A. (1991, Oct. 28). Heroes in a half shell. *Forbes*, pp. 49–55.

Webster, F. E. (1992). The changing role of marketing in the corporation. *Journal of Marketing, 56*, 1–17.

Wilcox, D. L., Ault, P. H., & Agee, W. K. (1992). *Public relations, strategies and tactics* (3rd ed.). New York: HarperCollins.

Willis, S. (1987). Gender as a commodity. *South Atlantic Quarterly, 86* (4), 403–421.

Zeithaml, C. P., & Zeithaml, V.A. (1984). Environmental management: Revising the marketing perspective. *Journal of Marketing, 48*, 46–52.

17 Product Publicity: An Orphan of Marketing Research

Kirk Hallahan
University of North Dakota

Merims (1972) described product publicity as "marketing's stepchild." From a marketing theory and research perspective, this fourth element in the promotion mix might better be described as an orphan.

Despite the millions of dollars spent by marketers and publicists to gain exposure for products and services in the editorial (nonadvertising) portions of the mass media, little theoretical literature exists about product publicity or how it works together with other marketing elements. This gap exists at a time when marketing professionals are calling for integrated marketing programs that combine all of the promotion mix elements.

The purpose of this chapter is to outline a research agenda in this neglected area. It begins with an analysis of why product publicity has been so ignored by practitioners and academicians, reviews recent pertinent marketing literature, summarizes important characteristics of product publicity that impact its study, and then briefly suggests, in capsule form, avenues for original research in four broad areas.

PRODUCT PUBLICITY AS A MARKETING TOOL

Product publicity is defined here as the dissemination of product news and information in the editorial (nonadvertising) portions of the mass media—

newspapers, magazines, radio, and television. This definition excludes hybrid messages (such as product placements in movies and books, advertorials, infomercials, and music videos) for which a fee is paid by the brand maker (Balasubramanian, 1991; Sandler & Secunda, 1993).

The major media are interested in covering product news because they have found that product information attracts audiences. This trend received a boost in the mid-1960s with recognition of consumerism, when media responded by adding consumer reports and features such as Action Lines. Today, consumer newspaper sections, magazines features, and even whole television shows are devoted to such diverse categories as food, fashion, entertainment and leisure, books, autos, real estate, home furnishings, and travel. Many business sections and publications are full of product-related information, whereas sports and entertainment sections in publications and comparable segments in the broadcast media are the ultimate examples of product publicity at work.

Media personnel actively seek out product information, and are dependent on marketing sources. More than one third of all material in the mass media is provided by public relations sources (Cutlip, 1962, 1989). For product publicity, this figure is probably higher. News from product publicists serves as an information subsidy that facilitates news gathering and reduces the costs of obtaining material (Gandy, 1982).

Marketers use product publicity to reach a variety of audiences. These include consumer-related audiences (purchasers, specifiers, approvers, end users), channels-related audiences (sales forces, distributors, retail managers and buyers, and retail sales staffs), and external audiences (suppliers, competitors, legislators and regulators, activist groups, and others).

Marketers use product publicity for various reasons: to build awareness, to enhance product knowledge, to demonstrate or dramatize how a product works or has been accepted, to take advantage of the inherent news value of a product, to identify the product or service with current or historic events, and to test market ideas. Strategically, marketers also can use publicity to "heavy up" communications directed to primary targets, to reach secondary or tertiary markets that cannot be reached with advertising due to budget limitations, to penetrate audiences that would otherwise avoid or react negatively to advertising, or to pinch hit when other marketing communications tools cannot be used (Rotman, 1973; Wilcox & Nolte, 1990).

Marketers and PR practitioners ascribe a variety of strengths to publicity (Cushman, 1988; Rotman, 1973; Softness, 1976). Kotler suggested that publicity is most notable for three distinct qualities vis-à-vis advertising: its high credibility, its ability to catch people off guard (i.e., they are not expecting a promotional message), and its ability to dramatize a product (Kotler, 1984, p. 605). Elsewhere he suggested the publicity is most useful for products that have an interesting story, as a stimulus for the sales force, when credibility is needed, and in cases of a small budget (Kotler, 1984, pp. 670–671). Goodrich, Gildea, and Cavanaugh (1979) proffered a similar set of benefits. They stress that publicity is inexpensive, can cut through advertising noise, has more credibility, and may be the only way to get to some publics. They add that publicity can generate sales leads.

Marketers have acknowledged publicity since the initial conceptualization of the 4Ps of the marketing mix (McCarthy, 1960), and publicity has been preserved as a separate element of the communication mix in subsequent models (van Waterschoot & Van de Bulte, 1992). Most marketing textbooks include obligatory summaries about product publicity in sections dealing with promotional strategy. However, such discussions are often short and superficial.

ROOTS OF PRODUCT PUBLICITY'S ABANDONMENT

The orphan status of product publicity as a marketing research concept results, in part, from the fact that publicity is often considered to be a function of public relations, not marketing or advertising. In fact, publicity is one of many tools used in public relations; product publicity is the application of the tool in a marketing context.

Public relations, as a management function, concerns itself with managing an organization's relationships with key stakeholders or constituencies (Grunig & Hunt, 1984). Cutlip, Center, and Broom (1994) defined *public relations* more specifically as the "management function that establishes and maintains mutually beneficial relationships between an organization and the publics on whom its success or failure depends" (p. 1). The practice's roots are largely in journalism, due to its early emphasis on media relations and its ongoing involvement in communications (cf. Cutlip, 1994; Olasky, 1987; Raucher, 1968). Customers, dealers, distributors, and sales forces—the principal audiences for product publicity—are only some of the many publics of concern to public relations practitioners.

Despite attempts to differentiate marketing public relations from corporate public relations (T. Harris, 1991), and the recognition of the role of public relations in times of marketing crisis or vulnerability (Deighton, chapter 13, this volume; Goldman, 1984; Sherrell, Reidenbach, Moore, Wagle, & Spratlin, 1985), product publicity is frequently regarded as a rather prosaic component of the practice. PR practitioners often accord it a low priority compared to more pressing challenges posed by employees, investors, community groups, and governmental officials.

Three characteristics of product publicity programs further explain why marketing practitioners and academicians have paid so little attention. First, most marketers have little experience in product publicity. Their roots usually are in product management, advertising and promotion, sales, or market research. Product publicity production and evaluation is delegated to specialists. As Kotler (1984, p. 673) also noted, publicity is the least utilized of the major promotion tools.

Second, expenditures in other marketing areas, especially advertising, far outstrip product publicity. Marketers naturally tend to focus on those areas with big budgets and high levels of financial risk. In advertising, where expenditures commonly range from 10 to 30 times more than product publicity, an "effective" strategy is generally believed to involve a single, highly focused, albeit well-researched campaign that is funded at the highest available dollar level. Few product publicity campaigns concentrate their effort in a similar way, although it could be argued that the potential risk to a company's reputation or a brand's equity is just as high.

Third, the evaluation of product publicity is difficult, especially when programs are undertaken as part of an integrated program that combines other promotional tools. Because product publicity represents the least costly — and most ephemeral — element of the promotion mix, measuring its impact relative to other elements is nearly impossible with any level of confidence. The relative cost of evaluative research is also high compared to the low cost, which dissuades many firms from believing they can get an sufficient return from research related to publicity.

Measurement of product publicity's effectiveness is confounded by the comparatively low level of control that marketers (or their publicists) have over whether items actually are run, and over the final content and context of stories. Publicity items that are rewritten or even run verbatim are subject to factual errors and omissions, misinterpretations, and deliberate or inadvertent "slanting" by media personnel. Thus, a story might appear in a hundred different newspapers, but with different headlines, leads, localizations, and page positions, which makes the field measurement of cumulative effects difficult. Advertising, by comparison, involves guaranteed insertions on predetermined dates, pretested and tamper-resistant creative, and negotiated positions. Measuring publicity impact is also made difficult by the fact that most product news stories only run once in a publication, whereas advertisers depend on frequency of insertions.

Marketers often cope with the difficulties of measuring product publicity by ignoring evaluation altogether, relying on anecdotal reports (particulary whether management or the client liked the effort), not efforts to quantify either the output or impact (Cutlip, Center, & Broom, 1994; Hendrix, 1992).

SCANT CONSIDERATION BY MARKETING RESEARCHERS

With the comparatively low level of practitioner involvement, and the measurement problems specified earlier, it is not surprising that marketing academicians have ignored the topic.

A review of scholarly journals covering a 15-year period, from 1976 to 1991, revealed no empirical studies focusing on product publicity per se.[1] Moran (1990) summed up the situation well by noting that marketers traditionally have equated publicity effects with brand presence. Publicity effects generally have been considered "declasse among earnest minded researchers, not intellectually elegant enough to be treated seriously." He added (1990):

> Advertising we were told, is a more sophisticated communication technique, principally concerned with what is stated or deliberately implied about the brand with words, music, pictures, casting, etc. Publicity, by contrast, was characterized by the old-fashioned publicity agent's credo: "I don't care what you say about me as long you mention me by name." (p. 10)

Kotler has recognized the value of public relations and publicity as marketing tools more than any other marketing scholar, in part due to his interest in social marketing and marketing for not-for-profit organizations—two areas in which public relations traditionally has played a greater role than either advertising or sales promotion (Broom & Tucker, 1992; Kotler & Andreasen, 1991; Kotler & Levy, 1969).

Kotler and Mindak (1978) addressed marketing's relationship to public relations in the only major marketing journal article dealing with public relations during this period. They noted marketing people were increasingly interested in incorporating publicity as a tool within the marketing mix and described marketing and public relations as the two major external functions of the firm. However, their primary focus was on the relationship between the two functions, not product publicity per se. (For an update and discussion of organizational relationship issues, see Hallahan, 1992; Holmes, 1991; Public Relations Review, 1991.)

When marketing and consumer researchers have addressed product news, they have done so only incidentally. In a majority of these studies, particularly in the information search literature, media habits are used as

---

[1]Among journals surveyed were: *Journal of Advertising, Journal of Advertising Research, Journal of Consumer Marketing, Journal of Consumer Research, Journal of Marketing, Journal of Marketing Research, Journal of Public Policy and Marketing,* and *Psychology & Marketing.* The topic also is absent from the two principal public relations journals, the *Journal of Public Relations Research* and *Public Relations Review.*

scale items to operationalize broader theoretical constructs. Descriptive data are rarely reported.

Notable research that touches on the use of media containing product news content are studies dealing with the role of public relations within consumer goods companies in Britain (Kitchen & Procter, 1991), the relationship between news coverage and sales of caffeine-free colas (Fan & Shaffer, 1990), and simulated searches for new car information from various sources, including news articles (Hauser, Urban, & Weinberg, 1993). Other research includes the impact of information sources on industrial buying (Moriarty & Spekman, 1984), information seeking and the reduction of consumer purchasing anxiety (Locander & Hermann, 1979), purchase information sources of the elderly (Lumpkin & Festevald, 1988), media understanding and learning deficiencies among the elderly (Cole & Houston, 1987), preannouncing activity prior to the introduction of new products (Eliashberg & Robertson, 1988), diffusion of product information among individuals identified as "market mavens" (Feick & Price, 1987), and the impact of the publication of quality ratings on advertising practices and product pricing (Archibald, Haulman, & Moody, 1983).

TOWARD A THEORETICAL FRAMEWORK

Marketing researchers and practitioners need to better understand product publicity. As a foundation, it is useful to summarize some key characteristics of product publicity.

Publicity Involves Intermediaries. Product publicity is a form of public communication that always involves three parties: marketers, who must understand and gain access to the media; media employees, who judge, process and often present the information; and target audiences, who are the ultimate receivers. The intermediary role of media personnel is probably the most distinguishing difference between publicity and advertising. It explains the lack-of-control problem, but also provides an important set of variables for examination: the beliefs, values, attitudes, and practices of media personnel. Product publicity thus bridges traditional marketing/advertising research and mass communication research.

Product Publicity, Like Advertising, Generally is Intended to Persuade but Is Not Necessarily Persuasive. The intention of most marketers and publicists is to encourage buyer behavior, that is, consideration, inquiry, store visits, or purchase.

Because product publicity is largely controlled by media personnel, the tone and approach of product publicity generally must be more subtle and less commercial than the approach taken in advertising. This fact does not negate the influence of publicity vis-à-vis advertising, but suggests that the techniques are different and that researchers face a particular problem in measuring its power. Similar to the function of the advertiser, the role of the publicist is to enhance the motivation, ability, and opportunity of the audience to process product news and information (Batra & Ray, 1986a; MacInnis & Jaworski, 1989; MacInnis, Moorman, & Jaworski, 1991).

Product Publicity is Disseminated and Consumed in a Highly Competitive Environment. Marketers compete against marketers, but media also compete against media, using their editorial content (not their advertising) to attract an audience. Competition also characterizes product publicity messages: Stories must contend against all other product publicity stories seeking coverage in the media due to the limited channel capacity.

As a result, perceived news value is an essential ingredient in determining story use. A major strategy of marketers is to increase the likelihood that a story will be appealing. This often involves tailoring a story to be more newsworthy, in a way that is consistent with a product's core positioning (Geltzer & Ries, 1975). A key to success is balancing desired positioning for a product with the realities of news operations, to create messages that speak in the brand's single voice, and to understand the conventions and routines for successful publicity (cf. Daubert, 1973; Elsberry, 1988; Hart, 1974; E. C. Williams, 1988; J. Williams, 1983).

The Source is a Critical Element in Product Publicity. Product publicity, like advertising, always involves a source. This might be the marketer or another provider of information about the marketer's product, or the person who actually delivers the message as a spokesperson. However, the source often can be perceived by the audience as being the channel of communication itself. Characteristics of the source, and which of these is perceived to be the source, thus play a central role in product publicity research. (For an early discussion of source credibility in marketing communications, see Levitt, 1967.)

Product Publicity Generally is Proactive and Most Often Involves Positive News Generated by the Brand Maker—but not Always. Whereas the brand maker is almost always the only source of advertising for a product, and usually presents product information in an accurate and consistently positive light, such is not the case with product publicity.

Brand makers are not the only source of news about their products. Sometimes positive news can be generated by an unsolicited outside source, such as when a product receives a positive product rating, or when a reporter has a positive experience with a product, or when readers or listeners share experiences with the media.

However, product publicity can also involve negative news generated by the marketer (such as an announcement of a voluntary recall, warning, or price increase) or by external sources (such as competitors, government, or activist groups, who typically make claims about issues such as safety, pollution, or labor practices). In the case of negative news, the intention of the message might be to exhort the audience to exercise caution, avoid purchase, or return the item (such as in the case of a recall), whereas the response of the brand maker might be to mitigate the impact of such claims by others. This potential for negative valence is a distinguishing characteristic, although the majority of product information in the media is unabashedly positive.

PRODUCT PUBLICITY RESEARCH AGENDA

The dearth of research on how product publicity works suggests the opportunity for a programmatic study of an otherwise unresearched facet of marketing. I have identified two dozen questions worthy of examination. These are drawn from existing theories, models, and metaphors found in the marketing, mass media, and public relations literature. These can be grouped into four broad areas discussed next.

Product Publicity in Marketing Strategy

One fundamental area for study is to better understand how marketers evaluate product publicity as tool and, more specifically, their success in using product publicity vis-à-vis other tools in the promotion mix. These questions principally deal with managerial issues.

Product Publicity as an Alternative to Advertising. Hastings (1990) argued that the assumption advertising is the *sine qua non* of promotion is being challenged, and suggests that new product introductions can be promotion-, distribution-, or PR-driven. Such an assumption is consistent with practitioners' calls for greater use of integrated marketing, as well as Kotler's observation that publicity can be especially effective for clients with small budgets.

Among key questions meriting study are whether marketers actually consider publicity a viable alternative marketing tool. Separate from the perceptions of marketers, which influence their decision making, how can researchers develop empirical evidence of the superiority (or inferiority) of publicity vis-à-vis advertising to encourage inquiries or trial use of a product? Anecdotal evidence suggests that certain product categories lend themselves to receiving considerable publicity treatment, whereas others do not. The likelihood of success is mediated by circumstances that have yet to enumerated in any theoretical scheme.

Cost Trade-Offs.   A specific approach for considering publicity vis-à-vis advertising is to develop a model comparing returns on investment of the two techniques. Some marketers attempt to assess placements by calculating the value if the same amount of space had been purchased as advertising (Bolland, 1990). Many PR practitioners vehemently object to this approach, arguing that a 6-inch story in the *New York Times* is not comparable to a similar story in another daily newspaper, either in terms of circulation or prestige. However, other approaches might be possible, such as analyses of aggregate spending and results (such as inquiries obtained). Such a model would be useful in better understanding the claim made by many PR professionals that publicity both costs less and is more efficient (Rubinstein, 1992).

Market Signaling.   Some work in marketing channels arena has drawn on economic game theory to examine the way that formal and informal announcements by companies are intended to influence the behavior of others, whether competitors or distributors (Burke, Cho, DeSarbo, & Mahajian, 1990; Eliashberg & Robertson, 1988). Product publicity can be conceptualized as one of many signaling devices used by marketers to alert or condition the marketplace, frequently prior to more extensive promotional activities, such as advertising. A worthy extension of this research would be to examine strategies used by marketers in making press announcements about forthcoming products and how they view publicity vis-à-vis other potential communications forms.

Pioneering.   It is generally accepted that the first entrants in a product category enjoy larger market share and greater profitability over time (Carpenter & Nakamoto, 1989; Robinson & Fornell, 1985). Several researchers have extended the implications of pioneering, using schema research, to suggest that pioneers set up consumer expectations for a particular product category (Ratnewshwar & Shocker, 1988; Sujan & Bettman, 1989). Because publicity is frequently the first communications element deployed in the rollout of a new product, product publicity can be used by pioneers to capture substantial press visibility, opinion leader support, and favorable word of mouth. Specifically, it would be beneficial to understand the advantages enjoyed by pioneers in the publicity process and how successful pioneers employ product publicity as part of a first-in-the-category strategy.

Accessing Media

A second area deals with analyzing how marketers (and their publicists) access both consumer and trade media, and how media personnel process product information. Topics in this area revolve primarily around institutional characteristics of mass media work.

Functions of Media in a Marketing Context.   Lasswell (1948) suggested that media perform three functions in at the macrosociological level: surveillance, correlation, and transmission of culture. Within a marketing context, it would be potentially useful to analyze more fully how these functions are perceived by marketers, the media, and consumers. Beyond the general press, two specialty categories of media merit special exploration: consumerist publications and the trade press.

Consumer publications and certain broadcast shows position themselves as friends and protectors of the consumer. *Consumer Reports*, the best-known example, has been the focus of several studies (Anderson, Engledow, & Becker, 1978; Beales, Mazis, & Staelin, 1981; Thorelli & Engledow, 1980), but virtually no research has been done to relate their content to consumer confidence or to examine whether consumerist media are any more influential than general media.

The trade press is probably the single largest outlet for the dissemination of product news, justifying special attention in understanding how mediated communications work in tandem with interpersonal communications within a marketing channel. Hallahan (forthcoming) suggests that the trade press perform three distinct roles: as an external source of information, as a contributor to channel climate, and as a conduit of influence. However, as Webster (1968) noted, little is known about how noncommercial sources of information are used.

Conflicting Perceptions of News; Commercialism.   Marketers and news media often have divergent opinions about the newsworthiness of publicity materials. Some research has been done in public relations to develop predictors of success in placing press releases and matching the news values of publicists and editors (Aronoff, 1976; D. Harris, 1961; Knodell, 1976; Martin & Singletary, 1981; Morton & Warren, 1992). Much more needs to be done in terms of understanding the interactions between media and commercial news sources.

A central question in this area deals with the acceptable level of commercialism or brand identification in product materials. Marketers seek maximum brand name identification, whereas many media personnel are wary of excessive "product plugs" (Karp, 1971; Knopf, 1977; Sesser, 1970;

Surface, 1972; Williams, 1976; Zinman, 1970). Many marketers with large market shares can afford to forego brand identification if generic publicity exposure will lead to greater demand for the category as a whole. For example, Eastman Kodak, with a lion's share of the consumer photo market, stands to gain simply by promoting consumer interest in photography. However, for most marketers, obtaining brand mention is an imperative.

Commercial names appear regularly in media of all types. Of special interest is determining the decision-making process and news values of media personnel who permit and often condone blatant product promotion in certain instances, but not others. This would include how media personnel's own brand loyalty or personal product experiences affect news judgments.

Influence of Advertising on Publicity Coverage.   Although major media claim to differentiate the two functions, various media researchers have noted the influence that advertisers have on the editorial content of the press (Bagdikian, 1983; Gans, 1979). The 1991–93 recession sparked examples of outright interventions (Agins, 1992; Helliker, 1992; Hwang, 1992; Rykker, 1992), which prompted the American Society of Newspaper Editors to sponsor a study (Zachary, 1992).

Soley and Craig (1992) provided a useful summary of empirical research, as well as findings from the ASNE survey of daily newspapers, which showed that just under 90% of editors have experienced attempts to influence content. Marketers and media researchers alike would benefit from a better understanding of these cross-currents, particularly as to how they affect story selection and treatment. Beyond overt efforts by advertisers to shape content, past research on social influences in news operations, dating back to Breed (1955), suggests that such influence is often indirect and unconscious on the part of news personnel.

Product Portrayals and Framing.   Stories carried by the news media invariably carry a point of view. The "spin" given a particular story often follows journalistic conventions and cliches and might not necessarily be liked by the marketer, nor be consistent with the positioning developed for the product. Framing theory (Gamson, 1989; Gitlin, 1980; Goffman, 1974; Ryan, 1991) suggests the media portray stories in persistent, routine patterns that affect the selection, emphasis, and exclusion of news.

Frame labels that might be applied to products or services include "revolutionary" or "money-saver," and "unsafe" or "environmental threat." Useful research would involve identifying common product "frames" and segregating factors (including the routines of news work) that lead to this media "typing" of product publicity stories.

Product Agenda Setting.   Similarly, it is useful to study the product publicity process in terms of how the media focus attention on specific issues in the public discourse. As popularized by McCombs and Shaw (1972; see also McCombs, 1973; Rogers & Dearing, 1986; Shaw and McCombs, 1977), the agenda-setting metaphor says that the media perform an important function by telling people what to think about, not what to think. Advertising researchers have acknowledged the relevance of the concept to promotion (Fan & Shaffer, 1990; Ghorpade, 1986; Sutherland & Galloway, 1981). Product publicists are integrally involved in agenda setting by focusing the attention of media personnel on particular product categories and brands. Conversely, a strategy of publicists is to tap existing media interest, when particular product categories are in the news, in order to obtain access. Agenda-setting research provides a technique for comparing media content to audience awareness levels, as well as for publicists to evaluate the newsworthiness of their client's product.

Sampling and Media Ethics.   Sampling is a standard technique used by marketers to promote trial of a new product. The distribution of product samples to media is used by product publicists to encourage coverage, but has been the criticized sharply. Many organizations prohibit "freebies" (Long, 1973) and junkets (Wylie, 1975), believing that the receipt of products or services of value jeopardize the journalistic integrity of reporters. An interesting ancillary question is to examine the effectiveness of this type of operant conditioning (Nord & Peter, 1980) in media relations and whether receipt of samples actually results in more favorable stories.

Uses of Product Publicity

A third area involves the dissemination and use of product publicity material by the end user or audience. This area represents largely a social-psychological approach.

Information Search.   A basic assumption in much product publicity is that people actively seek out information to help them make buying decisions. Although marketing researchers have a substantial body of knowledge on information seeking, few studies have distinguished between how individuals use the editorial versus advertising portions of the press. (e.g., Cole & Houston, 1987; Locander & Hermann, 1979). Most studies omit making the distinction because their primary focus involves measuring the influence of personal versus nonpersonal sources (e.g., Armstrong & Feldman, 1976; Dash, Schiffman, & Berenson, 1976; Kiel & Layton, 1981).
   A specific application of search deals with the use of marketing information by industrial buyers. Robinson and Stidsen (1967, cited in Kotler,

1984) suggested that the importance of product publicity is relatively small, although consistent across the continuum of industrial and consumer goods (with personal selling dominant in industrial goods and advertising the prevalent tool used in promoting consumer goods). However, Moriarty and Spekman (1984) analyzed 14 sources of information among industrial buyers and found that news in trade publications was a significant source of information, outranking both trade shows and trade publication advertising as sources of information.

Product News Diffusion.   Opinion leadership (Katz & Lazarsfeld, 1955) and diffusion theories (Rogers, 1962) have been studied exhaustively by marketers (Mahajan, Muller, & Bass, 1990; see also Armstrong & Feldman, 1976; Feick & Price, 1987; Richins, 1983). Despite the extensive examination, virtually no studies have focused on diffusion of product publicity messages.

Beyond the general issue of how publicity combines with word of mouth and interpersonal communication is the special case of fads — products that achieve high attention and sales during a short lifespan. Faber and O'Guinn (1988) pointed out that trends and fads are accelerated by the mass media. An interesting study of product publicity deals with the life cycle of fads and how media coverage contributes to a fad's promotion and mystique, particularly if the use of other promotional tools is limited or absent, as was the case with Cabbage Patch Kids dolls in the mid-1980s (Blyskal & Blyskal, 1985).

Another useful context in which to study the dissemination of product publicity is to analyze how one company's publicity is used by competitors. Organizations routinely scan media as one method of environmental monitoring. Although many firms hear about competitors' products before-hand, media reports emanating from publicity sources can provide confirmation and details not previously obtainable. Such research might analyze the reconnaissance process and apply the emerging literature and methodology on marketing networks (Reingen & Kernan, 1986).

Secondary Uses of Publicity.   News coverage confers status on a product, which might be interpreted as a reason either for attention, or greater credibility, or both. References to products in the news are widely used by marketers. Reprints of favorable articles are often distributed (Maher, 1991), banners referencing publicity exposure appear on point-of-sale displays, and sales forces frequently reference favorable mentions in the press in presentations and negotiations.

Consumer Gratifications.   Finally, product publicity can be studied in the context of how consumers use information separate from the intended purpose of influencing behavior. McQuail, Blumler, and Brown (1972) suggested that media provide gratifications to individuals in at least four categories: diversion (escape), personal relationships (social utility of information), personal identity (value reinforcement), and surveillance. The value of this "uses and gratifications" approach has been acknowledged by marketers (Holbrook & Hirschman, 1982; Hornick & Schlinger, 1981). Many product publicity genres—food recipes, travel features, sports stories, book reviews, self-help segments, and personality features on celebrities in upcoming entertainment productions—can be seen as providing lifestyle gratifications only tangentially related to intent of the marketer. The principal question here is not what product publicity does to people, but to understand what people do with product publicity. The answer might provide insights as to why consumers are willing to expose themselves to marketers' publicity messages at all.

Product Publicity and Message Processing

The final arena for examination—and the one potentially of most interest to consumer researchers and practitioners concerned with integrated communications—deals with how individuals process product publicity. The level of analysis here is the individual; the paradigm is principally psychological.

Differentiation Between Advertising and Publicity. The ability of individuals to discern between (paid) advertising and (nonpaid) publicity is generally accepted, despite the lack of any extensive empirical research. Indeed, the question has been addressed only in the limited policy context of the potentially adverse effects of advertising on children (Faber, Brown, & McLeod, 1979; Ward 1974; Ward, Wackman, & Wartella, 1977).

Conventional wisdom suggests that people tend to avoid, resist or discount advertising because they believe the sponsor is trying to sell them something—phenomena that have been explained in terms of dissonance, reactance, and attribution theories. Publicity, on the other hand, is less obvious and provides less forewarning. As Lesly (1959) noted, public relations techniques are "especially selected and used to impact ideas so that the recipient comes to feel they are his own" (p 5).

Researchers have found that individuals respond differently to advertising and publicity messages, but the results are fragmentary at best. Salmon, Reid, Pokrywcznski, and Willet (1985) and Schwarz, Kumpf, and Bussman (1986) provided partial evidence for the belief that publicity is more credible, but found contradictory results in terms of purchase intent. Cameron (1994) found publicity to be more memorable than advertising. McLeod, Pan, and Rucinski (1988) suggested that message processing patterns might be different between advertising and news, but admitted that their research was inconclusive and limited in scope.

Hallahan (1995) suggested that individuals engage in a process of content class categorization, that is, audiences identify messages as either news or advertising and apply alternative rules and strategies depending on content class heuristics. Work needs to be pursued to understand if and precisely how consumers differentiate between news and advertising. In a similar way, more needs to be known about how consumers and others respond to the kind of hybrid messages that have become commonplace (Balasubramian, 1991; Sandler & Secunda, 1993) and how they respond to messages found in nontraditional media, such as interactive computerized bulletin boards, which are being used for both informational and promotional purposes.

Product Publicity, Purchase Decision Models, and Involvement. Early marketing theorists believed that publicity's primary benefit was creating awareness (Cash & Crissy, 1965; Kotler, 1984). This assumed that consumers were logical and objective processors of product information.

Early hierarchy of effects models suggested that purchase decisions involve a series of cognitive→affective→conative steps (Lavidge & Steiner, 1961; Strong, 1925). Ray et al. (1973) described this approach as a learning hierarchy, in which the role of publicity can be seen essentially as educational. However, at least two other alternate approaches can be seen operating. Under Ray et al.'s low-involvement hierarchy, which is rooted in Herbert Krugman's work on television's ability to generate learning without involvement, extensive education is not necessary. Instead, product publicity can be seen as performing primarily a reminder function. Under the alternative dissonance-attribution hierarchy, based on the separate work of psychologists Elliot Aronson, Daryl Bem, and Harold Kelley, there are situations in which behaviors occur first, then attitude change, and finally learning: a conative→affective→cognitive relationship. In this situation, product publicity can be viewed as primarily a reinforcement vehicle.

These alternative functions — education, reminding, and reinforcement — represent potentially different objectives and time-order relationships with other integrated marketing communications components. Publicity can either precede or follow other campaign elements, and can be examined from either a pretransaction or posttransaction perspective. In the pretransaction situation, useful research would more thoroughly examine how consumers use publicity to reduce risk or uncertainty. Posttransaction research could also shed light on why consumers attend so much to media stories on products already purchased (presumably to validate previous consumer decisions).

These alternative approaches underscore the potential role of involvement as a variable for researchers in product publicity (see Salmon 1986 for a valuable review of the role of involvement). Presumably, individuals for which a publicity message is highly relevant are willing to effortfully or systematically attend to publicity messages (Chaiken, 1980; Petty & Cacioppo, 1981, 1986). On the other hand, individuals with low involvement in a topic might be willing to use a variety of peripheral cues (including but not limited to the source, prominence in the media, the number of mentions, etc.) as heuristics or peripheral cues to make a summary judgment about product news.

Cognitive Processing of Marketing Messages.   Perhaps the most critical question for marketers concerned with integrated communications is how publicity might facilitate the processing of subsequent campaign elements. Marketing communications generally suffers from the failure of researchers to address communications from an integrative perspective, for example, to conduct studies that test theories in more than one medium or that involve more than one communications technique. This failure is due to higher costs, control problems, and the lack of researcher interest discussed previously.

Major work awaits to be undertaken about how publicity operates from a cognitive point of view. The most prevalent scenario in integrated communications campaigns is to maximize product publicity in the kickoff of a new product introduction, after which intensive advertising begins. Under this regimen, publicity can be conceptualized as facilitating the processing of communications that follow. However, researchers have not yet begun to understand how this integregation works. At least five explanations are possible:

- Repetition effects: Publicity can be viewed merely as another exposure opportunity for the basic message in integrated campaign message, and might facilitate the "wearin" of advertising (Pechmann & Stewart, 1988).
- Retrieval cue effects: Publicity could be considered as a generator of memory traces that are stimulated through association in subsequent advertising, point-of-purchase messages, and other cues (Edell & Keller, 1989; Keller, 1987, 1991a, 1991b).
- Multiple sources effects: Hearing about a subject from two or more independent sources, or hearing slightly inconsistent messages, has been demonstrated to result in greater cognitive effort, resulting in more elaboration and learning (Harkin & Petty, 1987; Moore, Reardon, & Mowen, 1989; Wyer & Srull, 1989).
- Schema effects: Publicity, like all other sources of information, can

be seen as a contributor to the creation of cognitive structures — categories, prototypes, or scripts — under which product information is organized (see especially Alba, 1983; Cohen & Basu, 1987; Sujan, & Bettmann, 1989; Sujan & Deklava, 1987).

• Priming effects: Finally, publicity can be seen as a priming mechanism (i.e., it highlights particular attributes of products), thus increasing the likelihood that the audience subsequently will inspect product information or broaden their memory traces in terms of these attributes. Priming can also be examined in contextual terms, underscoring the potential role of publicity in creating a "favorable editorial environment" for advertising (Chook, 1985; Gardner, 1983; Soldow & Principe, 1981; Wilder & Buell, 1923; Yi, 1990).

Affective Processing of Publicity. Separate from cognitive processing, researchers have devoted increased attention to the role of affect in marketing communications. The trend began with Zajonc's (1980) work showing that repeated mere exposure can lead to greater liking of a message (Zajonc & Markus, 1982). Since then, various content and context elements of advertising have been examined (see especially Batra & Ray, 1986b; Stayman & Batra, 1991).

Affect has been operationalized various ways. Among these, researchers have demonstrated that a consumer's attitude toward the ad (Aad), which combines cognition with affect, can mediate the processing of the message (see especially Mackenzie & Lutz, 1989; Mackenzie, Lutz, & Belch, 1986). Hallahan (1995) suggested that a more general construct, attitude toward the message (Amessage), would permit the same approach to be applied to publicity research. In keeping with Moran (1990), it could be argued that many content and contextual affective factors can be seen at work in publicity as in advertising — with a notable difference being that publicists have less control over them.

Impact of Negative Publicity. A question of special interest in today's era of heightened reporting of product news is understanding of the impact of negative news on consumer knowledge, attitudes, and purchase intent. Stated more generally, negative publicity involves information that is incongruent with a consumer's expectations or experience.

Various psychological studies have shown that individuals assign relatively more value, importance, and weight to events that have negative versus positive implications (Kahneman & Tversky, 1979, 1984; Pratto & John, 1991).

The effects of negative news reports have been documented in terms of their effects on financial markets (Klein & Prestbo, 1974), and various examples can be cited as to how negative news reports have adversely impacted products (Tanouye, 1992). Sherrell, Reidenbach, Moore, Wagle, and Spratlin (1985) provided a cogent review of recent research. Also of special note are Weinberger & Dillon's (1981) work on the effects of unfavorable product rating information, Mowen's (1980) study on consumer perceptions of product recalls, Iyer and Debevec's (1991) empirical research on product rumors, and Deighton's study (chapter 13, this volume) of responses to a product tampering.

Much more needs to be known as to why and how consumers respond to negative product information in media. Mizerski (1982) suggested attribution theory as an explanation of the disproportionate influence of unfavorable information. Alternatively, involvement and the nature of the elaborative processing engaged in might provide insight (Petty & Cacioppo, 1981, 1986). Negative news reports, despite their pervasiveness, are often discounted or criticized by high-involvement audiences. On the other hand, individuals with low levels of involvement can be oblivious to negative news that is of of no concern to them, whereas many others with relatively little stake in the issue can be keenly aware of the problem. Marketers and publicists alike would benefit from understanding the differential impact of negative news in both pretransaction and posttransaction contexts.

Media Credibility. Probably the single most important issue to be examined in product publicity research centers around the higher credibility generally attributed to news (Levitt, 1969; McGuire, 1973; Reeves, Chaffee, & Tims, 1982). Many publicists ascribe the superiority of publicity over advertising to a third-party endorsement effect. Rotman (1973, p. 13) explained that publicity in the media carries "an implied endorsement by the editor, who [the reader or viewer feels] sure would not allow anything unverified or incomplete to occupy editorial space or time in the media." However, Detwiler (1974) noted such a concept is largely an article of faith.

Although researchers have addressed aspects of the issue (Cameron, 1994; Hallahan, 1995; Salmon et al., 1985; Schwarz et al., 1986) no comprehensive work has been completed within the general population on implied product endorsement, or the idea that news is any more credible than advertising. Similarly, although self-proclaimed consumerist publications strive toward high levels of credence, media credibility has been shown to be highly dependent on the specific medium (Appel, 1987).

The assumption that news is necessarily more credible than advertising runs counter to popular complaints about media bias. Many argue that there is a media credibility gap (Gannett Center for Media Studies, 1985), whereas critics have charged that public relations' undue influence has created cynicism (Cutlip, Center, & Broom, 1994). These are charges not unlike those lodged against advertising. Recent studies have demonstrated that claims about media bias are related to characteristics of the audience involved, not the medium (Gunther, 1992; Robinson & Kohut, 1988; Roper Organization, 1991; Whitney, 1985). If news is more credible than advertising, the evidence is yet to be substantiated.

CONCLUSION

This chapter has outlined research areas that seem particularly interesting and worthwhile to pursue in the area of product publicity, in light of today's emphasis on integrated communications. It has attempted to weave together conventional wisdom about product publicity with research drawn from the marketing, public relations, and mass communications literature.

Each of these areas merit further elaboration and examination. The implication is inescapable: There is no reason that product publicity should be neglected as a research interest by marketers. Not only has the subject been overlooked, but many of these questions represent thought-provoking issues with broad implications that go far beyond the product publicity practice.

REFERENCES

Agins, T. (1992, October 10). Editorial plugs for apparel are in style. *The Wall Street Journal,* pp. B1, B7.

Alba, J. W. (1981). The effects of product knowledge on the comprehension, attention and evaluation of product information. In A. M. Tybout & R. P. Bagozzi (Eds.), *Advances in consumer research* (Vol. 10, pp. 577–580). Provo, UT: Association for Consumer Research.

Anderson, R., Engledow, J., & Becker, H. (1978). How consumer reports subscribers see advertising. *Journal of Advertising Research, 18*(6), 29–34.

Appel, V. (1987). Editorial environment and advertising effectiveness. *Journal of Advertising Research, 27*(6), 11–16.

Archibald, R. B., Haulman, C., & Moody, C. E., Jr. (1983). Quality, price, advertising and published quality ratings. *Journal of Consumer Research, 9,* 347–356.

Armstrong, G., & Feldman, L. P. (1976). Exposure and sources of opinion leaders. *Journal of Advertising Research, 16*(4), 21–30.

Aronoff, C. E. (1976). Predictors of success in placing releases in newspapers. *Public Relations Review, 2*(3), 43–57.

Bagdikian, B. H. (1983). *The media monopoly.* Boston: Beacon Press.

Balasubramanian, S. K. (1991). *Beyond advertising and publicity: The domain of hybrid messages* (Rep. No. 91-131). Cambridge, MA: Marketing Science Institute.

Batra, R., & Ray, M. L. (1986a). Situational effects of advertising repetition: The moderating influence of motivation, ability and opportunity to respond. *Journal of Consumer Research, 12,* 432–445.

Batra, R., & Ray, M. L. (1986b). Affective responses mediating acceptance of advertising. *Journal of Consumer Research, 13,* 234–249.

Beales, H., Mazis, M., Salop, S. C., & Staelin, R. (1981). Consumer research and public policy. *Journal of Consumer Research, 8,* 11–22.

Blyskal, J., & Blyskal, M. (1985). Media doll: Born in a cabbage patch and reared by a PR man. *The Quill, 73,* 28–32.

Bolland, E. J. (1989). Advertising versus public relations: A comparison using cost-per-thousand for print ads and PR placements. *Public Relations Quarterly, 34*(2), 10–11.

Breed, W. (1955). Social control in the newsroom: A functional analysis. *Social Forces, 33,* 326–355.

Broom, G. M., & Tucker, K. (1989). An essential double helix. *Public Relations Journal, 45,* 40ff.

Burke, R. R., Cho, J., DeSarbo, W. S., & Mahajan, V. (1990). The impact of product-related announcements on product intentions. In M. E. Goldberg, G. Gorn, & R. W. Pollay (Eds.), *Advances in consumer research* (Vol. 17, pp. 342–350). Provo, UT: Association for Consumer Research.

Cameron, G. (1994). Does publicity outperform advertising: An experimental test of the third-party endorsement. *Journal of Public Relations Research, 6,* 185–207.

Carpenter, G., & Nakamoto, K. (1989). Consumer preference formation and pioneering advantage. *Journal of Marketing Research, XXVI,* 285–298.

Cash, H. C., & Crissy, W. J. (1965). Comparison of advertising and selling. In *The psychology of selling.* Flushing, NY: Personnel Development Associates.

Chaiken, S. (1980). Heuristic versus systematic information processing and the use of source versus message cues in persuasion. *Journal of Personality and Social Psychology, 39*(5), 752–766.

Chook, P. H. (1985). A continuing study of magazine environment, frequency and advertising performance. *Journal of Advertising Research, 25*(4), 23–33.

Cohen, J. B., & Basu, K. (1987). Alternative models of categorization: Toward a contingent processing framework. *Journal of Consumer Research, 13,* 455–471.

Cole, C. A., & Houston, M. J. (1987). Encoding and media effects on consumer learning deficiencies in the elderly. *Journal of Marketing Research, XXIV,* 55–63.

Cushman, A. D. (1988). "New" element in marketing mix makes budget headway. *Marketing News, 22*(26), 10, 17.

Cutlip, S. M. (1962, May 26). Third of newspapers' content PR-inspired. *Editor & Publisher, 95,* 68.

Cutlip, S. M. (1989). Public relations: The manufacture of consent. *Gannett Center Journal, 4*(2), 105–116.

Cutlip, S. M. (1994). *Public relations: The unseen power.* Hillsdale, NJ: Lawrence Erlbaum Associates.

Cutlip, S. M., Center, H., & Broom, G. M. (1994). *Effective public relations* (7th ed.,). Englewood Cliffs, NJ: Prentice-Hall.

Dash, J. F., Schiffman, L. G., & Berenson, C. (1976). Information search and store choice. *Journal of Advertising Research, 16*(3), 35–42.

Daubert, H. E. (1974). *Industrial publicity.* New York: John Wiley.

Detwiler, R. M. (1974, May). Yes, Virginia, it's all true—what they say about third-party endorsement. *Public Relations Journal, 30,* 10–11.

Edell, J. A., & Keller, K. L. (1989). The information processing of coordinated media campaigns. *Journal of Marketing Research, XXVI,* 149–163.

Ehling, W. P., White, J., & Grunig, J. E. (1992). Public relations and marketing practices. In J. E. Grunig et al. (Eds.), *Excellence in public relations and communication management* (pp. 357–394). Hillsdale, NJ: Lawrence Erlbaum Associates.

Eliashberg, J., & Robertson, T. S. (1988). New product preannouncing behavior: A marketing signaling study. *Journal of Marketing Research, XXV,* 282–292.

Elsberry, R. B. (1988). It doesn't have to be a dud: Your news product press conference.

Business Marketing, 73, 96–101.

Faber, R. J., Brown, J. D., & McLeod, J. M. (1979). Coming of age in the global village. In E. Wartella (Ed.), *Children and communication* (pp. 215–249). Beverly Hills, CA: Sage.

Faber, R. J., & O'Guinn, T. C. (1988). Expanding the view of consumer socialization. In J. N. Sheth & E. R. Hirschman (Eds.), *Research in consumer behavior* (Vol. 3, pp. 49–77). Greenwich, CT: JAI.

Fan, D. P., & Shaffer, C. L. (1990). Effects of mass media news on trends in the consumption of caffeine-free colas. In M. E. Goldberg, G. Gorn, & R. W. Pollay (Eds.). *Advances in consumer research* (Vol. 17, pp. 406–414). Provo, UT: Association for Consumer Research.

Feick, L. F., & Price, L. L. (1987). The market maven: A diffuser of marketplace information. *Journal of Marketing, 51,* 83–97.

Gamson, W. A. (1989). News as framing. *American Behavioral Scientist, 33*(2) 157–161.

Gandy, O. H., Jr. (1982). *Beyond agenda-setting: Information subsidies and public policy.* Norwood, NJ: Ablex.

Gannett Center for Media Studies. (1985). *The Media and the people: Americans' experience with the news media: A fifty-year review.* New York: Gannett Center for Media Studies, Columbia University.

Gans, H. J. (1979). *Deciding what's news.* New York: Pantheon.

Gardner, M. P. (1983). Advertising effects on attributes recalled and criteria used for brand evaluations. *Journal of Consumer Research, 10,* 310–318.

Geltzer, H., & Ries, A. (1975, November). Positioning. *Public Relations Journal, 31,* 40–43.

Gitlin, T. (1980). *The whole world is watching.* Berkeley: University of California Press.

Ghorpade, S. (1986). Agenda setting: A test of advertising's neglected function. *Journal of Advertising Research, 26*(4), 23–27.

Goffman, E. (1974). *Frame analysis: An essay on the organization of experience.* New York: Harper & Row.

Goldman, J. (1984). *Public relations in the marketing mix.* Chicago: Crain Books.

Goodrich, J., Gildea, R. L., & Cavanaugh, K. (1979). A place for public relations in the marketing mix. *MSU Business Topics, 27,* 53–57.

Grunig, J. E., & Hunt, T. (1984). *Managing public relations.* New York: Holt, Rinehart & Winston.

Gunther, A. C. (1992). Biased press or biased public? Audience assessments of media news coverage. *Public Opinion Quarterly 56*(2), 147–167.

Hallahan, K. (1992, August). *A typology of organizational relationships between marketing and public relations.* Paper presented to Public Relations Division, Association for Education in Journalism and Mass Communication, Montreal, Canada.

Hallahan, K. (1995). *Product publicity versus advertising: An investigation of third-party endorsement effects.* Unpublished doctoral dissertation, University of Wisconsin–Madison School of Journalism and Mass Communication.

Hallahan, K. (forthcoming). *Three roles of the trade press in marketing channels.* (Working paper). Grand Forks: University of North Dakota Communication Research Center.

Harkin, S., & Petty, R. E. (1987). Information utility and the multiple source effect. *Journal of Personality and Social Psycholkogy, 52*(2), 260–268.

Harris, D. H. (1961). Publicity releases: Why they end up in the wastebasket. *Industrial Marketing, 46,* 98–100.

Harris, T. L. (1991). *The marketer's guide to public relations.* New York: Wiley.

Hart, N. A. (1973). *Industrial publicity.* New York: Halsted Press.

Hastings, H. (1991). Introducing new products without advertising. *Journal of Consumer Marketing, 7*(3), 19–25.

Hauser, J. R., Urban, G. L., & Weinberg, B. D., (1993). How consumers allocate their use of time searching for information. *Journal of Marketing Research, XXX,* 452–466.

Helliker, K. (1992), October 14). Wal-Mart cuts ads, papers cut coverage. *The Wall Street*

Journal, p. B8.

Hendrix, J. A. (1992). *Public relations cases* (2nd ed.). Belmont, CA: Wadsworth.

Holbrook, M. B., & Hirschman, E. C. (1982). The experiential aspects of consumption: Consumer fantasies, feelings and fun. *Journal of Consumer Research, 9,* 132–140.

Holmes, P. (1991, January). 1991 and the death of marketing. *inside PR, 2,* 5–7.

Hornik, J., & Schlinger, M. J. (1981). Allocation of time to mass media. *Journal of Consumer Research, 7,* 343–355.

Hwang, S. L. (1992, September 1). Consumers Digest mines its best-buy list. *The Wall Street Journal,* p. B1.

Iyer, E. S., & Debevec, K. (1991). Origin of rumor and tone of message in rumor quelling strategies. *Psychology & Marketing, 8*(3), 161–175.

Kahneman, D., & Tversky, A. (1979). Prospect theory: An analysis of decision under risk. *Econometrica, 47,* 263–391.

Kahneman, D., & Tversky, A. (1984). Choices, values and frames. *American Psychologist, 39,* 341–350.

Karp, R. (1971, November/December). Newspaper food pages: Credibility for sale. *Columbia Journalism Review, X,* 36–43.

Katz, E., & Lazarsfeld, P. F. (1955). *Personal influence: The part played by people in mass communications.* Glencoe, IL: The Free Press.

Keller, K. L. (1987). Memory factors in advertising: The effect of advertising retrieval cues on brand evaluations. *Journal of Consumer Research, 14,* 316–333.

Keller, K. L. (1991a). Memory and evaluation effects in competitive advertising environments. *Journal of Consumer Research, 17,* 463–476.

Keller, K. L. (1991b). Cue compatibility and framing in advertising. *Journal of Marketing Research, XXVIII,* 42–57.

Kiel, G. C., & Layton, R. A. (1981). Dimensions of information seeking behavior. *Journal of Marketing Research, XVIII,* 233–239.

Kitchen, P. J., & Proctor, R. A. (1991). The increasing importance of public relations in fast moving consumer goods firms. *Journal of Marketing Management, 7,* 357–370.

Klein, F. C., & Prestbo, J. A. (1974). *News and the market.* Chicago: Henry Regnery.

Knodell, J. E. (1976). Matching perceptions of food editors, writers and readers. *Public Relations Review, 2*(3), 37–56.

Knopf, T. A. (1977, January/February). Plugola: What the talk shows don't talk about. *Columbia Journalism Review, XV,* 44–46.

Kotler, P. (1984). *Marketing management: Analysis, planning, control.* Englewood Cliffs, NJ: Prentice-Hall.

Kotler, P., & Andreasen, A. (1991). *Strategic marketing for nonprofit organizations* (4th ed.). Englewood Cliffs, NJ: Prentice-Hall.

Kotler, P., & Levy, S. J. (1969). Broadening the concept of marketing. *Journal of Marketing, 33,* 10–15.

Kotler, P., & Mindak, W. (1978). Marketing and public relations. *Journal of Marketing, 42,* 13–20.

Lasswell, H. (1948). The structure and function of communication in society. In L. Bryson (Ed.), *The communication of ideas.* New York: Institute for Religious and Social Studies. Reprinted in Schramm, W. (Ed.). (1960). *Mass communications* (2nd ed., pp. 117–130). Urbana: University of Illinois Press.

Lavidge, R. J., & Steiner, G. A. (1961). A model of predictive measurements of advertising effectiveness. *Journal of Marketing, 26,* 55–62.

Lesly, P. (1959). Public relations and the challenge of the marketing revolution. *Journal of Marketing, 24*(2), 1–6.

Levitt, T. (1967). Communications and industrial selling. *Journal of Marketing, 32,* 15–21.

Levitt, T. (1969). *The marketing mode.* New York: McGraw-Hill.

Locander, W. B., & Hermann, P. W. (1979). The effect of self-confidence and anxiety on information seeking in consumer risk reduction. *Journal of Marketing Research, XVI,* 268–274.

Long, C. (1973, August). Games newspeople play: The freebies game. *The Quill, 61,* 15–18.

Lumpkin, J. R., & Festevald, T. A. (1988). Purchase information sources of the elderly. *Journal of Advertising Research, 27*(6), 31–43.

MacInnis, D. J., & Jaworski, B. (1989). Information processing from advertisements: Toward an integrative framework. *Journal of Marketing, 53,* 1–23.

MacInnis, D. J., Moorman, C., & Jaworski, B. J. (1991). Enhancing and measuring consumers' motivation, opportunity and ability to process brand information from ads. *Journal of Marketing, 55,* 32–51.

Mackenzie, S. B., & Lutz, R. J. (1989). An empirical examination of the structural antecedents of attitude toward the ad in an advertising pretesting context. *Journal of Marketing, 53,* 48–65.

Mackenzie, S. B., Lutz, R. J., & Belch, G. E. (1986). The role of attitude toward the ad as a mediator of advertising effectiveness: A test of competing explanations. *Journal of Marketing Research, XXIII,* 130–143.

Mahajan, V., Muller, E., & Bass, F. M. (1990). New product diffusion models in marketing: A review and direction for research. *Journal of Marketing, 54,* 1–26.

Maher, T. (1991). Why PR? Publicizing public relations. *National Underwriter* (Life/Health/Financial Services), 95(42), 13–14.

Martin, W. P., & Singletary, M. (1981). Newspaper treatment of state government releases. *Journalism Quarterly, 58,* 93–96.

McCarthy, E. J. (1960). *Basic marketing: A managerial approach.* Homewood, IL: Irwin.

McCombs, M. E. (1977). Agenda setting function of mass media. *Public Relations Review, 3*(4), 89–95.

McCombs, M. E., & Shaw, D. L. (1972). The agenda-setting function of the mass media. *Public Opinion Quarterly, 36*(2), 176–284.

McGuire, W. J. (1973). Persuasion, resistance and attitude change. In I. Poole, F. W. Frey, W. Schramm, N. Maccoby, & E. B. Parker (Eds.), *Handbook of communication* (pp. 216–253). Chicago: Rand-McNally College.

McLeod, J. M., Pan, Z., & Rucinski, D. M. (1988, August). *Processing news and advertising: Same strategies and same effects?.* Paper presented to Communication Theory and Methodology Division, Association for Education in Journalism and Mass Communication, Portland, OR.

McQuail, D., Blumler, J. G., & Brown, J. R. (1972). The television audience: A revised perspective. In D. McQuail (Ed.), *Sociology of Mass Communications* (pp. 135–165). Harmondsworth, England: Penguin.

Merims, A. M. (1972, December). Marketing's stepchild: Product publicity. *Harvard Business Review, 50,* 107–113.

Mizerski, R. N. (1982). An attribution explanation of the disproportionate influence of unfavorable information. *Journal of Consumer Research, 9,* 301–310.

Moore, D. J., Reardon, R., & Mowen, J. C. (1989). Source independence in multiple source advertising appeals: The confederate effect. In T. Srull (Ed.) *Advances in Consumer Research* (Vol. 16, pp. 719–722). Provo, UT: Association for Consumer Research.

Moran, W. T. (1990). Brand presence and perceptual frame. *Journal of Advertising Research, 30,* 9–16.

Moriarty, R. T., Jr., & Spekman, R. E. (1984). An empirical investigation of the information sources used during the industrial buying process. *Journal of Marketing Research, XXI,* 137–147.

Morton, L. P., & Warren, J. (1992). Proximity: localization vs. distance in PR releases. *Journalism Quarterly 69*(4), 1023-1026.

Mowen, J. C. (1980). Further information on consumer perceptions of product recalls. In J. C. Olson (Ed.), *Advances in consumer research* (Vol. VII, pp. 519-523). Ann Arbor, MI: Association for Consumer Research.

Nord, W. B., & Peter, J. P. (1980). A behavior modification perspective on marketing. *Journal of Marketing, 44,* 36-47.

Olasky, M. (1987). *Corporate public relations: A new historical perspective.* Hillsdale, NJ: Lawrence Erlbaum Associates.

Pechmann, C., & Stewart, D. W. (1988). Advertising repetition: A critical review of wearin and wearout. In C. H. Leigh, Jr. & C. R. Martin, Jr. (Eds)., *Current issues and research in advertising* (Vol. 11, pp. 285-329). Ann Arbor: University of Michigan Graduate School of Business Administration.

Petty, R. E., & Cacioppo. J. T. (1981). *Attitudes and persuasion: Classic and contemporary approaches.* Dubuque, IA: Brown.

Petty, R. E., & Cacioppo, J. T. (1986). *Communication and persuasion: Central and peripheral routes to persuasion.* New York: Springer-Verlag.

Pratto, F., & John, O. (1991). Automatic vigilance: The attention-grabbing power of negative social information. *Journal of Personality and Social Psychology, 61*(3), 380-391.

Public Relations Review. (1991, Fall). [Special issue on Public Relations and Marketing], *17*(3).

Ratnewshwar, S., & Shocker, A. D. (1988). The application of prototypes and categorization theory in marketing: Some problems and alternative perspectives. In M. J. Houston (Ed.), *Advances in consumer research* (Vol. 15, pp. 280-285). Provo, VT: Association for Consumer Research.

Raucher, A. (1968). *Public relations and business, 1900-1929.* Baltimore: Johns Hopkins University Press.

Ray, M., Sawyer, A. G., Rothschild, M. L., Heller, R. M., Strong, E. C., & Reed, J. (1973). Marketing communication and the hierarchy of effects. In P. Clarke (Ed.), *New models for communication research* (pp. 147-173). Beverly Hills, CA: Sage.

Reeves, B., Chaffee, S. H., & Tims, A. R. (1982). Social cognition and mass communication research. In M. E. Roloff & C. R. Berger (Eds.), *Social cognition and communication* (pp. 287-326). Beverly Hills, CA: Sage.

Reingen, P. H., & Kernan, B. (1986). Analysis of referral networks in marketing. *Journal of Marketing Research, XXVI,* 370-378.

Richins, M. L. (1983). Negative word of mouth by dissatisfied consumers: A pilot study. *Journal of Marketing, 47,* 68-78.

Robinson, M. J., & Kohut, M. J. (1988). Believability and the press. *Public Opinion Quarterly, 52*(2), 154-189.

Robinson, W. T., & Fornell, C. (1985). Sources of market pioneer advantages in consumer goods industries. *Journal of Marketing Research, XXII,* 305-317.

Rogers, E. M. (1962). *Diffusion of innovations* (2nd ed.). New York: The Free Press.

Rogers, E. M., & Dearing, J. W. (1986). Agenda-setting research: Where has it been: Where is it going? In J. A. Anderson (Ed.), *Communication yearbook* (Vol. 11, pp. 553-594). Newbury Park, CA: Sage.

Roper Organization (1991). *America's watching: Public attitudes toward television 1991.* Washington, DC: National Assaociation of Broadcasters.

Rotman, M. B. (1973). Public relations is still a necessary adjunct to marketing today. *Advertising and Sales Promotion, 21,* 13-16.

Rubinstein, M. (1992). Effective industrial marketing with a piggy bank budget. *Industrial Marketing Management, 21,* 203-214.

Ryan, C. (1991). *Prime time activism*. Boston: South End.

Rykker, R. (1992). Is real estate news for sale? *Presstime, 14*(8), 19–21.

Salmon, C. T. (1986). Perspectives on involvement in communication research. In B. Dervin & M. Voigt (Eds.), *Progress in communication sciences* (Vol. 7, pp. 243–268). New York: Ablex.

Salmon, C. T., Reid, L. N., Pokrywcznski, J., & Willet, R. W. (1985). The effectiveness of advocacy advertising relative to news coverage. *Comunication Research, 12*(4), 546–567.

Sandler, D. M., & Secunda, E. (1993). Point of view: Blurred boundaries – Where does editorial end and advertising begin? *Journal of Advertising Research, 34,* 73–80.

Schwarz, N., Kumpf, M., & Bussmann, W. (1986). Resistance to persuasion as a consequence of influence attempts to advertising and non-advertising communications. *Psychology, A Quarterly Journal of Human Behavior, 23*(2/3), 72–76.

Sesser, S. N. (1970, Spring). The fantasy world of travel sections. *Columbia Journalism Review, IX,* 44–47.

Shaw, D. T., & McCombs, M. E. (1977). *The emergence of American political issues: The agenda-setting function of the press*. St. Paul, MN: West.

Sherrell, D., Reidenbach, R. E., Moore, E., Wagle, J., & Spratlin, T. (1985). Exploring consumer response to negative publicity. *Public Relations Review, 11*(1), 13–28.

Softness, D. G. (1976, August 2). What product PR can do for you in today's advertising world. *Advertising Age*, pp. 19–20.

Soldow, G. F., & Principe, V. (1981). Response to commercials as a function of program context. *Journal of Advertising Research, 21*(2), 59–65.

Soley, L. C., & Craig, R. L. (1992). Advertising pressures on newspapers: A survey. *Journal of Advertising, XXI*(4), 1–10.

Stayman, D. M., & Batra, R. (1991). Encoding and retrieval of ad affect in memory. *Journal of Marketing Research, XXVIII,* 232–239.

Strong E. K. (1925). *The psychology of selling*. New York: McGraw-Hill.

Sujan, M. (1985). Consumer knowledge: Effects on evaluation strategies mediating consumer judgments. *Journal of Consumer Research, 12,* 31–46.

Sujan, M., & Bettman, J. R. (1989). The effects of brand positioning strategies on consumers' brand and category perceptions: Some insights from schema research. *Journal of Marketing Research, XXVI,* 454–467.

Sujan, M.,, & Dekleva, C. (1987). Product categorization and inference making: Some implications for comparative advertising. *Journal of Consumer Research, 14,* 372–378.

Surface, B. (1972, January/February). The shame of the sports beat. *Columbia Journalism Review, X,* 48–55.

Sutherland, M., & Galloway, J. (1981). Role of advertising: Persuasion or agenda setting? *Journal of Advertising Research, 21*(5), 25–30.

Tanouye, E. (1992, October 21). Medical article raises doubts on Merck drug. *The Wall Street Journal*, p. B1.

Thorelli, H. B., & Engledow, J. I. (1990). Information seekers and information systems: A policy perspective. *Journal of Marketing, 44,* 9–27.

van Waterschoot, W., & Van den Bulte, C. (1992). The 4Ps classification of the marketing mix revisited. *Journal of Marketing, 56,* 83–93.

Ward, S. (1974).   Consumer socialization. *Journal of Consumer Research, 2,* 1–14.

Ward, S., Wackman, D. B., & Wartella, E. (1977). *How children learn to buy: The development of consumer information processing skills*. Beverly Hills, CA: Sage.

Webster, F. E., Jr. (1968). On the applicability of communication theory to industrial markets. *Journal of Marketing Research, V,* 426–428.

Weinberger, M., & Dillon, W. (1981). The effcts of unfavorable rating information. In J. C. Olson (Ed.), *Advances in Consumer Research* (Vol. VII, pp. 528–532). Ann Arbor, MI:

Association for Consumer Research.

Whitney, C. D. (1985). *Attitudes toward the news media: Three publics.* Paper presented to the American Association for Public Opinion Research, Delavan, WI.

Wilcox, D. L., & Nolte, L. N. (1990). *Public relations writing and media techniques.* New York: HarperCollins.

Wilder, R. H., & Buell, K. L. (1923). *Publicity: A manual for the use of business, civic or social organizations.* New York: The Ronald Press.

Williams, E. C. (1988). Product publicity: Low cost and high credibility. *Industrial Marketing Management, 17,* 355–359.

Williams, J. D. (1983). Industrial publicity: one of the best promotional tools. *Industrial Marketing Management, 12,* 107–211.

Williams, M. (1976, June 26). Deleting product identification. *Editor & Publisher, 109,* 33.

Wyer, R., & Srull, T. (1989). Person memory and judgment. *Psychology Review, 96,* 58–83.

Wylie, F. W. (1975, March). Junkets and the public's right to know. *The Quill, 63,* 30.

Yi, Y. (1990). The effects of contextual priming on print advertisements. *Journal of Consumer Research, 17,* 215–222.

Zachary, G. P. (1992, April 27). Editors to study news coverage and advertisers. *The Wall Street Journal,* p. B10.

Zajonc, R. B. (1980). Feeling and thinking/preferences need no inferences. *American Psychologist, 35*(2), 151–175.

Zajonc, R. B., & Markus, H. (1982). Affective and cognitive factors in preferences. *Journal of Consumer Research, 9,* 123–131.

Zinman, D. (1970, Spring). Should newsmen accept PR prizes? *Columbia Journalism Review, IX,* 37–42.

VII

Theoretical Summary,
A Research Agenda,
and Conclusions

18

The Circle of Synergy: Theoretical Perspectives and an Evolving IMC Research Agenda

Sandra E. Moriarty
University of Colorado

The idea behind integrated marketing communication (IMC) is coordination of messages for maximum impact. This impact is created through synergy — linkages created in a receiver's mind as a result of messages that connect. Synergy suggests that an entire structure of messages — with its links and repetition — creates impact beyond the power of any one message on its own and this happens even in situations where there might be little attention paid to conventional advertising. Integration occurs at several levels — in strategy and planning, in conceptually linked executions, and in coordinated uses of traditional and nontraditional communication channels. Communication synergy can be best maximized by extending message encounters beyond the traditional advertising media into every possible situation where a receiver might have contact with a message from a company.

To investigate this concept of message synergy as created by multidimensional IMC programs, a review of theory and research from marketing, consumer behavior, communication, education, and psychology will be analyzed, looking for trends of theory that might help explicate the various concepts embedded in the idea of message integration.

Synergy exists through the function of memory — messages that are conceptually integrated and that repeat essential units of meaning over time through different channels and from different sources come together to create coherent knowledge and attitude structures in the receiver. As expressed through a *circle of synergy* — concept or message, channel, and audience response — they are contained within a field of repetition and coordination to establish message impact. The circle provides the structure for the following analysis of theoretical foundations and the IMC research opportunities that derive from them (see Fig. 18.1).

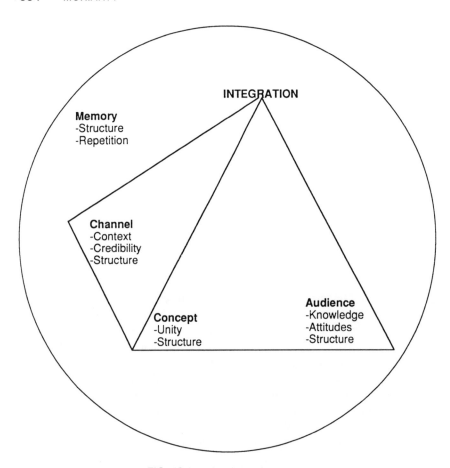

FIG. 18.1.   The circle of synergy.

CONCEPT

The word *concept* appears often in marketing communication literature and practice. Manufacturers conduct concept tests as part of product development and advertisers do concept tests to evaluate big ideas on which they hang advertising campaigns. In the latter sense, a concept is the central idea of an advertisement. In IMC, a concept is the central factor around which a company, product, or brand image is built.

The idea of a company or a brand as a concept that needs to be formed — established over time and reinforced in the consumer's mind — is not well developed in marketing communication literature. *Concept development* is a phrase that is rarely seen in scholarly work. *Concept formation,* however, is an area with a large body of literature in educational psychology.

Borrowing from that and other streams of related literature, we need to learn more about how these types of concepts are developed through IMC message design.

Structure

Concepts are presented in messages and developed in peoples' minds as discrete bits of information that are bundled together and linked in patterns of similarities and differences, as well as routinized experiences. Message elements— primarily words and pictures—are the creative tools to mold and shape the concept that evolves through a variety of exposures and impressions built up over time. Like an artist working on a canvas, an image begins to appear from a variety of brush strokes and colors that are applied at different times in different places.

Concept formation happens when the same stimuli elicit a similar pattern of meaning construction when repeated over time. We need to know much more about marketing communication ideas as concepts— about how they are shaped, developed, maintained, and changed. In particular, we need to know how these patterns can be better formed and managed through strategically designed and integrated communication.

Analysis of the concept is intertwined with analysis of the receiver's response. Many of the conceptual threads supporting message integration are to be found in theories based on knowledge and cognitive processing, as well as in noncognitive structures such as those identified with associations and emotions. These processes will be addressed in more detail in the discussion of audience response theories.

Unity: Seeing Similarities and Differences

Although marketing communication has not focused much on the psychology behind how the process of building conceptual coherence occurs in a complex arena like brand or product image development, one related aspect of message design that has received attention is product differentiation. Although concepts are based on patterns of similarities and differences, product differentiation relies on establishing lines of difference, as well as connecting unifying features that make the linkages work. In other words, in order for a brand to stand on its own as a concept, it must be conceptualized in the receivers' minds as having attributes that link up to form a unified perceptual structure and this structure must be different from the structure of other concepts (brands) that might compete or be confused with it.

Clearly seeing differences and similarities is important to understanding how concept development works and how marketing communication creates coherent images of companies, products, and brands. However, recognizing that concepts are developed from myriad pieces of messages and complex patterns of relationships suggests intuitively that coordination and strategic planning are essential in marketing communication if the varied message impressions are to have any cohesion.

AUDIENCE

Concepts are developed in the minds of people, thus to analyze the structure of concepts inevitably means moving to some form of audience analysis focusing on the way people acquire and make sense of knowledge. Cognitive structure, for example, is an important dimension of message integration that derives its theoretical base from gestalt psychology. Cognitive processing theorists posit a model of knowledge based on mental structures that organize perceived information into maps, networks, or schemas of connected and interrelated categories. Consumer responses, then, are governed by the interaction of new information with the complex structure of previously acquired information.

A concept and its structure as presented in a communication program will have a parallel structure that evolves in the receiver's mind. Sometimes the perception is similar to the intention, sometimes the intention and the perception are far apart. The distance is a measure of communication effectiveness. The challenge, however, is how to analyze the structure of the concept as it has evolved in the receiver's mind.

Cognitive Structures

One of the earliest theorists in this area is Tolman (Burgoon, Burgoon, & Miller, 1981), who proposed that people develop cognitive maps of the various worlds they inhabit and that these maps are used in goal seeking. In other words, people develop expectations about their world based on the way they have organized information about it and past experiences with it in their minds. Advertising uses the related concept of perceptual maps to identify the location of product, brand, and corporate images and attributes in relation to competitors. This technique could also be used in IMC planning to analyze the attributes and image contributions of various messages in various media to map out the dimensions of a product, brand, or corporate concept.

Scripts and Schemas.   Script and schema theory is one approach that is being adapted to communication research. A schema is a mental map of a generalized routine or pattern of thinking, whereas a script is an outline of a routinized sequence of behaviors. Abelson (1981) described a schema as a hypothesized cognitive structure that, when activated, organizes behaviors encountered in event-based situations. In other words, it maps an individual's expectations and routines that operate in particular situations such as getting up in the morning, getting to work, going to a restaurant, or attending a cocktail party. Schemas are stereotypical knowledge structures based on the principle of parsimony that let us deal with a complex but familiar situation or event sequence by routinizing our behavior so we do not have to think about it.

Rittenburg and Laczniak (1990) proposed using script theory to analyze viewers' decision processes that operate when they encounter an advertising message on television, an idea that was followed up by Moriarty (1991). Along the same line, script or schema theory could be used to analyze how people deal with various types of message encounters involving various types of channels and message strategies. This would be useful in mapping creative strategies for integrated communication situations.

An example of how schema theory can be used in building advertising strategies was reported by Camden, Verba, and Sapin (1990) in a study of the perceptions of General Dynamics. The market assessment study, which involved eight focus groups with a variety of opinion leaders, investment officers, government bureaucrats, and the military, examined critical values and current symbology for the various audiences. It discovered four dominant schema that affected perceptions of defense contractors. The schema were then tested with 275 telephone surveys to establish quantitative benchmarks, perceptual maps of the company's current and desired position, and the critical decision rules driving the image campaign. The schemas were then translated into instructions for the creative department for its work on a multitargeted corporate image campaign for General Dynamics to overcome the existing negative image.

Conditioning and Association.   Other theories about knowledge propose a system of linkages that are learned through conditioned responses. As Burgoon et al. (1981) explained in a review of learning theory and persuasion, once a stimulus evokes a particular response, a similar pattern of stimulus and response is more likely in the future. In particular, this is how associational thinking is learned. Attitudes, with their potential for negative–positive polarity, are also thought to be subject to development through conditioned response. Recognizing the importance of this concept, Preston and Thorson's (Preston, 1982; Preston & Thorson, 1984) *associative model* of advertising posits this process as a general theory for understanding how advertising works.

There are other important approaches that help explain how concept formation works. *Contiguity theory,* as proposed by Guthrie (1959), focuses on the complexity of the processing situation. He postulated that a combination of stimuli leading to a response will, when repeated, lead to that same response again. As Burgoon et al. (1981) explained in analyzing persuasive communication, "the communication pattern that preceded a particular desired behavior should, upon its repetition, elicit the behavior again: the same arguments should touch the same responsive chord" (p. 164).

Guthrie's second contiguity "postulate" is that a stimulus has its most striking image when it is first paired with the response. However, when applying this idea of persuasion, Burgoon et al. noted that not all stimuli are attended to by everyone on any one occasion, therefore to ensure that the behavior is repeated by a range of people, the message should be repeated under varying circumstances—an important concept, of course, in IMC planning. Furthermore, the greater the similarity of language and arguments, the more likely it is that the same response will be elicited again, which provides support for the notion of conceptually integrated messages.

Conditioned learning, however, is not a magic wand and IMC planners need to be aware of the many problems faced in concept development as well as associative learning when messages are competing. Underwood's *interference theory,* for example, suggests how competing messages may interfere with one another and inhibit learning (Burgoon et al., 1981). In practice inhibition, that which is learned first inhibits learning of what comes later; in retroactive inhibition, that which is learned last inhibits the recall of previously learned information. Given the clutter in the marketing communication environment, IMC message researchers might want to investigate how interference can hinder the presentation of messages and the formation of concepts, particularly those that are not effectively integrated.

Cognitive Response Theory.   More recently, researchers have been developing theories of cognitive response that suggest that persuasive messages are mediated by the thoughts generated by the receiver as the communication is processed. This reflects the interest in more individual-istic cognitive theories based on a receiver-oriented model, rather than the mechanistic sender-oriented perspectives associated with traditional com-munication models and the effects research tradition. Mendelsohn (1990) described this paradigm change from behaviorist to constructivist ap-proaches as requiring "message recipients to treat 'stimuli' as problems to be understood and solved rather than as overpowering shots from a cannon against which no defense but surrender was possible" (p. 42).

Construction theories propose that receivers are not passive processors; in fact, they bring thoughts based on previous experiences to the encounter that are used to elaborate on or, in some cases, counterargue with the new information. In other words, people are not cognitively passive because they have a reservoir of prior knowledge and experiences that are activated by cues in a new message and this prior information serves as a sounding board for the evaluation of the new information.

Thoughts and feelings, labeled cognitive responses, are thought to affect attitude formation and change (Mehta & Davis, 1990; Ostrom, Petty, & Brock, 1981). The mediating thoughts may or may not be reflected in the material itself because everything that has registered in the past about a company or brand, however idiosyncratic, comes to the surface in a communication encounter. New messages are integrated with the old in order to build a coherent and consistent image, attitude, or impression. Actually, recent research in schema theory has found that these cognitive structures may not be as coherent or as consistent as was once thought (Graber, 1988).

That is another reason why integration of message concepts is not only important but essential in order to avoid unnecessary and counterproductive cognitive responses. Olson, Toy, and Dover (1982) argued that a commercial message can stimulate people to remember or infer brand-relevant information — even that which is not contained in the ad itself — as well as by providing such information directly or explicitly. Monitoring cognitive responses generated by people exposed to one or a variety of messages with varying degrees of integration by a methodology referred to as *thought listing* should allow some understanding of how people do or do not process integrated messages.

Cognitive response, of course, is influenced by cognitive style — that is, different people approach information processing in different ways, so this methodology can also be used to focus on individual, and even idiosyncratic interpretation, as well as streams of common responses. Methodologically cognitive response involves coding open-ended responses into total number (which gives a measure of level of attention), and three other general categories: polarity (favorable, neutral, unfavorable), target (response to message topic vs. response to message format elements), and origin (restatement of message, reactions to or elaborations of the message, or the issue unrelated to message content; Cacioppo, Harkins, & Petty, 1981).

IMC planners can gain insight from such a model. For example, as Slater, Auld, Keefe, and Kendall (1991) explained, knowing which audiences are primarily concerned with message content and which are concerned with message characteristics could influence the selection of message channels and the investment of resources in message production. Furthermore, combining this information with polarity data would make it possible to know who is likely to like or dislike the topic or the presentation of a message, and who is likely to respond favorably or unfavorably to the issue after being exposed to different types of messages.

Attitude Formation

Knowledge structures are not the only form of audience response to communication messages; equally important are attitude structures. In contrast to concept formation, attitude formation is an area of research that has long intrigued marketing communication scholars. Much of the research and theory in this area parallels the work in cognitive processing because it hypothesizes a network of linked attitudes forming an attitudinal structure. According to Fishbein and Ajzen's (1975) *multiattribute model of attitude formation,* people perceive brands (or companies) as bundles of attributes and, given what we know about how people perceive and process information, these bundles are built up over time from bits and pieces of accumulated information and experiences. Information from advertisements, as well as from other sources, is integrated into an attitude structure and this structure determines both intention to purchase – the attitude – and the actual purchase behavior.

Fishbein's model is based on the idea of concept integration. A set of beliefs about a concept becomes organized in the mind as a cognitive structure – a complex network of integrated beliefs that makes up an attitude. Fishbein's theory hypothesizes that beliefs lead to attitudes although he does not locate the belief/attitude structure in terms of a more complex information-processing model. His familiar algebraic model that specifies the relationship between this set of salient beliefs and a concept provides, however, as Mitchell and Olson (1981) observed, a "theoretically integrated set of measures of the cognitive effects of marketing variables." As they explained, "This formula can be used to measure the multiple effects of a particular communication message on cognitive structure variables" (p. 329). It should be noted here that cognitive processing is clearly a mediating factor in attitude formation.

Although Fishbein's theory has been used to explain the development of attitudes regarding advertising, the model is a complex structure built on a variety of communication encounters, which is clearly in line with the way IMC works. Logic suggests that the more encounters and the more consistent they are, the stronger the attitude. Thus, conceptually integrated messages are likely to be the most effective approach to attitude as well as concept development. The notion of integrated messages in a multichannel environment offers an area for the logical extension of Fishbein's work.

Dimensions of Attributes.   There are a number of dimensions to attributes including strength (salience), direction (positive or negative), and breadth (degree of involvement). According to Fishbein's attitude theory, salient beliefs are those activated from memory to become a consideration in a particular situation. If such beliefs are anchored in a person's memory, then that means the person must have heard something relating to it previously. In other words, saliency is built up over time through repetition as stored knowledge. This relationship of saliency to repetition is also fundamental to understanding the process of communication on which the concept of IMC is built.

In addition to a variety of dimensions, theorists working with mathematical models of attitude development and change suggest that there is an important element of variation that enters into cognitive structures. A person may have a variety of beliefs associated with an object and the best measure of that person's attitude comes from averaging across this set of beliefs (Burgoon et al., 1981). Anderson (1983) described this process as *information integration theory,* and predicted that attitudes develop and change as a result of the weight of their initial position in relationship to the weight of the new position communicated by the incoming information. More recent work has lead researchers to conclude that the more messages the person receives, the more stable the attitude. Attitude "massiveness" then, is a factor in cognitive processing.

Consistency.   Attitudes are built on the integration of cognitive and affective responses to information. They represent complex thoughts made up of likes and dislikes, as well as knowledge, considerations, and ideas organized as an attitudinal structure. Because these complex thoughts contain pieces of attitudes that are interdependent, change in one attitude can affect other parts of the attitudinal structure. Modern analyses of cognitive integration, the *consistency theories*— Rosenberg's Consistency theory, Heider's Equilibrium theory, and Festinger's Theory of Cognitive Dissonance—based largely on Lewin's work on cognitive structures, were developed to explain these connections and interactions.

More importantly, the need for cognitive consistency drives the selective perception process and therefore impacts on message exposure. As a result, concept integration in a message may be a factor in determining its exposure. All of these theories are relevant to IMC message design because of its need for repetition and, likewise, consistency in message presentation. Consistency theories, in particular, are relevant because they address the need for integration without conflict when a variety of messages are presented.

Involvement and Motivation.   More recently the *elaboration likelihood model* (ELM; Petty, Cacioppo, & Schumann, 1983) and the *heuristic-systematic model* (HSM; Chaiken, 1980) have been developed to explain situations in which people's primary motivational concern is to attain attitudes that square with relevant facts (Ratneshwar & Chaiken, 1991). Systematic processing reflects an analytical orientation in which people take

account of relevant information and judge accordingly. Rational arguments, similar to the ELM model's "central route," elicit cognitive elaboration of incoming information. In contrast, heuristic processing uses less
cognitive effort and fewer cognitive resources and, like the ELM's "peripheral route," people rely on simple decision rules and obvious cues to form
judgments. Source expertise and emotional appeals, for example, are relied
on in heuristic processing.

In contrast to the traditional assumption that people make rational and
intentional responses to advertising, Thorson (1991) identified heuristic, or
noncognitive, processing as the type of processing that occurs in natural
situations and under that natural motivation to process. She observed that,
"Occasionally the consumer desires and is motivated to find and thoroughly
process the information in advertising, but that situation is probably more
the exception than the rule" (p. 200).

Both systematic and heuristic processing rely on previous knowledge and
experience, although for different reasons. With systematic processing a
learning curve may be operating that demands considered judgment based
on information that usually is acquired over time; with heuristic processing
repetition of impressionistic appeals builds images over time. The synergistic phenomenon associated with effectively integrated messages can be
created using either strategy, however the executional tactics are entirely
different. These differences and their impact on IMC strategy need to be
investigated and defined using either the ELM or HSM models.

CHANNEL

The word *channel* is used in communication to refer to any physical means
of transmitting a message—speech organs, ear drum, retina, telephone
wires, and fiber optics, for example. It derives from the original information-
processing model developed by Shannon (1949). The term *medium* is used
to refer to a channel that has certain distinguishable characteristics in terms
of content presentation, such as the television medium or the newspaper
medium. Advertising, of course, has adopted the concept of medium—as in
media planning and media mix—but rarely discusses communication channels. In IMC, given the variety and complexity of message sources, channel
may be more appropriate for describing the means by which the message is
carried.

Multichannel Processing

The body of channel research of interest to IMC considers such issues as
channel capacity and multichannel processing. In a complex communication situation, either one channel must carry several messages simul-

taneously or several channels are involved simultaneously. How does this work and what does it say for complex multichannel communication programs?

In terms of the most basic processing of visual information, the different cues in the message are analyzed simultaneously in order to establish recognition. In perceptual psychology each cue is thought to elicit a system of analyzing information and, therefore, each one is considered to be a separate channel operating in parallel with all the other sets of cue analyzers (Travers, 1970). That suggests the complexity of the simple perceptual task of recognizing a visual object. Consider how the level of complexity increases when auditory stimuli, as well as motion, are added to the channel, as is the case with television and how many different sets of parallel processing operations may be occurring simultaneously. Clearly this calls for a model of complex multichannel information processing.

Single-Channel Models. Broadbent's (1957, 1958) early model of human perception suggests that an individual's perceptual system is restricted and that it can only process sensory information selectively due to limited capacity. In other words, when information is presented simultaneously via two different channels — such as verbal and visual — the perceptual system can only attend to one at a time, switching back and forth. His work suggests the need for integration to minimize confusion as this switching process operates.

Confusion is a problem for information delivered simultaneously that is not conceptually integrated. According to Broadbent, when people process two different and competing (or unrelated) pieces of information presented at the same time, typically one message will dominate and only that message will receive attention. In other words, in a complex or cluttered message environment, the system generally handles only one channel at a time, switching back and forth in a scanning procedure to piece together a message. Based on this concept of limited capacity, he posited a *single-channel model* of information processing. The other messages will either be processed by memory afterward, ignored, or the competing messages may create so much "noise" that neither is processed. Depending on the nature and extent of the synchronicity, this may pose a problem for commercial messages from the same source that are not conceptually integrated.

More recently, other psychologists have modified Broadbent's theories and their work has found that people have a rather impressive ability to pay attention to what they need to attend to and at the same time monitor other less well-attended sources of information at some minimum level of meaning (Deutsch & Deutsch, 1963; Snodgrass, Levy-Berger, & Haydon, 1985; Triesman, 1964). In other words, people have some ability for synchronous processing although our understanding of this processing ability is inexact. How does information reception differ when people are just scanning information as opposed to when they are concentrating and analyzing it? Is there a difference in channel capacity and processing mode for low-involvement as opposed to high-involvement information situations? Certainly IMC researchers should be interested in investigating the nature of multichannel processing, both simultaneous and switching, to better understand perceptual limits and how much variation and complexity can be included before confusion sets in.

Instructional communicators and learning theorists extol the value of information reinforcement through multimedia communication. The idea is that people learn better when they hear and see the same message at the same time, a theoretical perspective that informs and confirms the notion of integrated communication. This is an idea that needs to be tested in the arena of integrated marketing messages.

Channel Capacity. An area of research that seeks to determine how much information an individual can process given the physiological or psychological limits on the person or the situation is called *channel capacity* (Travers, 1970). Although there are a number of uses of the term *channel capacity,* the most relevant approach for IMC theory is the approach that refers to the amount of information that a person can process simultaneously. In a classic work called "The Magical Number 7, Plus or Minus Two: Some Limits on Our Capacity for Processing Information," Miller (1956) presented the theory that the perceptual system has a limited capacity for processing information. Miller's idea is that we process information by assigning it to appropriate categories and we can only handle a limited number of categories in our minds. The more complex the information, the more it draws on overlapping and competing sets of categories. The channel capacity may increase somewhat as additional dimensions are added, but people become less accurate as they have to confront more than one concept at the same time.

Dual Encoding. Another dimension of multichannel communication that has been investigated by advertising researchers is the relationship between the visual and verbal elements in messages. Although there is a tendency to focus on the words as the carrier of meaning, research in advertising has found that visuals can have an effect on brand attitudes and that visuals apparently enhance memory for ad content (Edell & Staelin, 1983; Lutz & Lutz, 1977). Furthermore, this research has also found that when the visual and verbal content are interactive, that is, the brand name is integrated into the visual, then recall is intensified. The opposite is also true: If the visual and verbal elements are not integrated, then recall is lower.

Researchers have long known that framing a visual with reinforcing verbal content significantly increases message effectiveness; however, this can be a problem in advertising where pictures seldom run with captions and the visual–verbal integration is dependent on other forms such as headlines, which may or may not serve effectively as picture captions. Furthermore, dual coding is seldom considered in corporate message campaigns that cross media, some of which are more intensely visual than others. This suggests an area of research into cross-channel communication that would be useful for the development of IMC theory.

Paivio's (1969, 1971) *dual-coding hypothesis* suggests that although pictures are coded with more variation than are words, pictorial elements are easier to retrieve from memory. The dual-coding theory suggests that visual elements are coded into memory twice — once with a verbal label and a second time with a pictorial code — which explains why it is easier to recall pictures. In effect, there are twice as many memory units operating for pictorial elements, which is why picture-dominant advertising tends to get higher recall scores.

Although deconstructing visual and verbal processing in research is usually done with one message, it makes sense that the same approach might apply to combinations of media that are variously more visual or more verbal and that appear within the same time frame although at different locations — logos on t-shirts and newspaper articles, for example. Whereas such studies would investigate the extremes of the dual-coding theory, they might also prove useful in investigating the cognitive and noncognitive links between various message elements. Clearly most marketing communication channels use messages that involve both visual and verbal processing — broadcast, print, and outdoor ads, as well as editorial material in magazines, annual reports, and sale literature. Marketing communication researchers have conducted some research into the nature of the perceptual problems, but IMC introduces new levels of complexity to the problems created by cross-channel communication.

Signal Detection. The *theory of signal detection* is another research approach that might be useful in analyzing breakdowns in complex communication situations. Signal detection has been used to investigate cross-channel decision making where signals are in conflict. Usually this involves measuring responses to competing audio stimuli that are emitted close to the threshold of hearing. This methodology is used by perceptual psychologists to analyze memory strength and has been proposed as a useful advertising methodology to evaluate the impact of clutter (Singh & Churchill, 1986; Tashchian, White, & Pak, 1988). It could also be used with messages that are not conceptually linked to determine which ones, or which elements, are more likely to be perceived. In other words, signal detection methodology might help sort out the nature of the conflict, as well as patterns of dominance, in messages about a company from different channels and sources.

Channel and Source Credibility

An important goal of integrated communication is to create a higher level of impact and one way that can be obtained is by enhancing the credibility of the message. Not every marketing communication message, of course, relies on credibility for impact and there are different types and levels of credibility operating in message reception. The product category, as well as message content, for example, have different credibility levels.

Credibility is situational for both source presenters in a message as well as for the channel or medium carrying the message. *The New York Times,* for example, is a highly credible source for most information of record — although not for information about rock music. *Rolling Stone,* on the other hand, would not be seen as a highly credible source for information about cancer breakthroughs or the national budget.

Credibility is also a function of repetition — the "everyone is saying it" phenomenon. The strategy is to intensify believability by spreading credibility among a variety of sources. Learning theory suggests that learners seem positively affected when persuasive messages are presented in as credible a manner as possible (Simonson, 1984). In other words, they learn more easily from credible sources. Furthermore, *attribution theory* suggests that messages lacking in credibility will be discounted and will not be very persuasive (Gotlieb & Sarel, 1991; Jones et al., 1972). Attribution theory looks at how receivers of messages perceive the communicator's objective; in other words, why a communicator takes a particular position and how that impacts on the receiver's acceptance or rejection of the message.

Person perception theories look at the effect of physically attractive communicators and models and has consistently found that attractive (vs. unattractive) communicators are liked more and have a more positive impact on the products with which they are associated (Joseph, 1982). Wackman (1973) also noted that little is known about how meanings are assigned to cues or configurations of cues that a person presents and he called for more research to identify the "vocabulary" for identifying the meanings of communicators in terms of the palette of cues that suggest such qualities as expertise, aggressiveness, trustworthiness, and so on. Given the variety of message sources used in integrated communications, it might be particularly useful to have more information about how person perception can be managed in a complex communication program to best coordinate source credibility.

Context

Another dimension of channel impact is context or the environment in which the communication is conveyed or confronted by the receiver. For IMC designers to effectively deliver their program of messages, they must understand the situational constraints that complicate their efforts. Bandura (1976) found that certain types of message strategies rely on social learning for impact, such as authority and bandwagon appeals. His work on modeling and social learning ties repetition to contiguity, although primarily in vicarious learning situations. However, vicarious learning is relevant to the situation in which much marketing communication occurs. The importance of his work is that it opens up a debate about whether message persuasiveness is more a function of repetition, with a gradual building up of attitudinal structures, or of situational conditions, where imitation and modeling are engaged — or both (Burgoon et al., 1981).

Approaching the idea of context from another angle, the work of Sherif and Cantril (1945, 1946) emphasizes a receiver's frame of reference as a factor in selective perception. The total perceptual field determines what people are exposed to and can select from. Likewise, an attitude that is formed as a result of this exposure and selection process then determines future selective perception in other fields of perception. The field of perception, however, is always limited by a complex of environmental and personal factors — selection being only one. Sherif's *field of perception, concept* suggests an interesting way to analyze the environmental context within which various IMC messages are conveyed and constrained.

Situation Theory. Contextual considerations are also related to motivation and involvement. Grunig and Hunt's (1984) *situation theory* suggests that the audience uses different types of processing for different types of message encounters. Situation theory, for example, distinguishes between two means of encountering a campaign message: the deliberate search for information and the unplanned encounter with an unsought after message; this is analogous to the situations hypothesized in both the ELM and HSM models. The importance of situation theory is that it distinguishes attention to a message from mere exposure to that message (Slater et al., 1991).

The question for IMC planners is what the connection is between context and message impact. Obviously there will be different levels of attention and what does attention contribute to impact? It makes sense to presume that a message encountered as part of a search is likely to affect attitudes, knowledge, and behavior in a different way than will a message encountered unexpectedly and at random. What exactly is the nature of the varied patterns of impact? With Grunig's Situational Theory as a model, is it possible to plan the use of various message channels for strategic reasons in terms of their presumed contributions to the overall message impact?

MEMORY

The key to synergistic message effects is memory. Memory is often discussed in terms of learning theory and the various types of conditioning models. As Thorson (1991) pointed out, although there is some question about how much people can really be conditioned to respond under the classical conditioning model, there is reason to believe that people do link things together that have previously occurred together and, in particular, use this process of connection to make associations. This is a largely unconscious, nonrational form of mental activity described by Thorson as "the most parsimonious model of memory" (p. 220). Through associative conditioning, fragments of information are linked to one another and, as one fragment is sued, it in turn activates the other unit or units. This is how the cognitive network or attitude structure is built over time in memory. Certainly this process would only be strengthened by multichannel messages that reinforce one another over time by building on the same associational structure.

Structure

The *spreading activation model* of memory is another way to explain how the process of developing connections works (Anderson, 1983; Cameron, 1990). Building on neural physiology, this model posits that concepts are linked in memory by pathways among the concepts built up of neurons or sets of neurons. The pathways are activated by a stimulus that then spreads to relate networks in long-term memory. Neural net research approaches are based on this concept.

As Thorson explained, memory is the system that allows consumers to carry the effect of ad exposure over to the purchase opportunity. Likewise, memory is the system that allows consumers to carry over one piece of a previously processed message and link it to another similar or related message. Without memory, the accumulated impact of repetition is impossible. Research by Zinkhan and Muderissoglu (1985) has also found that prior knowledge results in extensive long-term memory networks and activation of these more complex networks can also lead to processing at higher levels of involvement.

Thorson pointed out that even attitudes must be remembered. She also stated that emotions produced by the experience of encountering a communication will affect subsequent processing of memory and attitudes, regardless of whether it is produced in a high- or low-involvement situation. Furthermore she related evidence that the dual-state ELM model may be inadequate because emotional impact seems to operate continuously in both involvement states, not just in low-involvement processing as the ELM model suggests. This is in line with the research of Pechmann and Stewart (1989) who note that it is not possible to classify commercials as either rational or emotional because most commercials contain heterogeneous or mixed stimuli. In other words, planning for message integration must also consider the contingent nature of cognitive and emotional responses and establish objectives and strategies that are complementary because both types of responses are operating to some degree simultaneously.

Repetition

The primary objective of repetition is to expose the audience members to a message enough times so that they understand, learn, and file it away in memory. Repetition also contributes to positive evaluation. Frequency-of-exposure research has consistently found that mere exposure to stimuli such as words or visual elements produced increasingly positive affect toward those stimuli (Burgoon et al., 1981). Guthrie's (1950) *law of associative inhibition* suggests that unfamiliar stimuli evoke a wide range of responses, many of them competitive or incompatible, but that through repetition some of the responses become more dominant, and thus relieve the tension generated by the competing messages. In other words, habituated responses to familiar messages are more "comfortable" and reduce the stress of dealing with inconsistency, an idea that is in line with theories of selective exposure.

Novelty, Complexity, Familiarity. In his research into novelty and complexity, Berlyne (1970) found that increased familiarity with complex stimuli produces more positive responses, although increased familiarity with simple stimuli can produce boredom. Media planners in advertising deal with the boredom question and frame questions on repetition levels in terms of message wearout. Additional IMC research needs to be done on the repetition and wearout question using Berlyne's ideas of complexity and novelty.

Carryover Effects. The *carryover effects* of message repetition are also important to IMC. By carryover we mean the residual or cumulative effects of prior message exposures. As media planners have long known, after advertising is discontinued, brand sales may remain at the same level for an extended period of time. That is the carryover effect. What is difficult to estimate is what level of repetition is necessary for effective carryover and how carryover effects are maintained or built over time. Unfortunately relatively little is known about how advertising carryover effects work and clearly this concept is even more important to an understanding of how synergy is managed in IMC message planning.

Other important related dimensions of carryover effects are *wearin* and *wearout*. As Pechmann and Stewart reported, research into advertising media frequency and repetition has found that, in general, wearout probably will not occur until after three massed exposures. (Wearout means that the ad message no longer has any significant effect on its audience; wearin determines what level of repetition is necessary for a message to have a significant positive effect on the audience.) In spite of this commonly recognized rule of three, Pechmann and Stewart also made the point that in order to maximize carryover effects, it may be advantageous to expose consumers to a purportedly "worn out" ad again and again. The exposures beyond the "significant effect" level may not increase recall or understanding; however, it may prolong recall, and that, of course, is how carryover impact is maximized.

Although advertising has developed a body of literature relating to wearout and wearin that will be useful to IMC planners who are trying to gauge the value of multichannel repetition, it is an inexact science. That problem, in addition to the lack of knowledge about how carryover works, will only be compounded in the IMC situation with its opportunities for complex patterns of multichannel repetition.

SUMMARY

The notion of IMC makes sense only if the concept of integration has something to offer to the effectiveness of marketing communication. What are the benefits of integration and, in particular, can integration be used to create synergy—messages that interconnect and create impact beyond the power of any one message on its own? A review of the literature in related fields suggests that there are certain key dimensions to integration that can be summarized as a *circle of synergy*— concept, audience, and channel surrounded by repetition and coordination to lock a message concept in memory. These factors must be manipulated by IMC strategic planners to create and enhance message effectiveness.

REFERENCES

Abelson, R. P. (1981). Psychological status of the script concept. *American Psychologist, 36*(7), 715–729.

Anderson, J. R. (1983). A spreading activation theory of memory. *Journal of Verbal Learning and Verbal Behavior, 22,* 261–295.

Bandura, A. (1976). *Social learning theory.* Englewood Cliffs, NJ: Prentice-Hall.

Berlyne, D. E. (1970). Novelty, complexity and hedonic value. *Perception and Psychophysics, 8,* 279–281.

Broadbent, D. E. (1957). A mechanical model for human attention and immediate memory. *Psychological Review, 64*(3), 205–215.

Broadbent, D. E. (1958). *Perception and communication.* New York: Pergamon.

Burgoon, J. K., Burgoon, M., & Miller, G. R. (1981). Learning theory approaches to persuasion. *Human Communication Research, 7*(2), 161–179.

Cacioppo, J. T., Harkins, S. G., & Petty, R. E. (1981). The nature of attitudes, cognitive responses, and their relationships to behavior. In R. Petty, T. Ostrom, & T. Brock (Eds.), *Cognitive responses in persuasion* (pp. 31–54). Hillsdale, NJ: Lawrence Erlbaum Associates.

Camden, C., Verba, S., & Sapin, G. (1990). Corporate image advertising and the federal government: A case study of the application of information-processing models. In S. Kraus (Ed.), *Mass communication and political information processing* (pp. 171–204). Hillsdale, NJ: Lawrence Erlbaum Associates.

Cameron, G. T. (1990). Involvement, arousal, attention, salience and so forth: The location of involvement and related variables in the spreading activation model of memory. In P. Stout (Ed.), *Proceedings of the AAA Conference* (pp. 117–123). Austin: University of Texas.

Chaiken, S. (1980). Heuristic versus systematic information processing and the use of source versus message cues in persuasion. *Journal of Personality and Social Psychology, 39*(5), 752–756.

Deutsch, J. A., & Deutsch, D. (1963). Attention: Some theoretical considerations. *Psychological Review, 70,* 80–90.

Edell, J. A., & Staelin, R. E. (1983). The information processing of pictures in print advertisements. *Journal of Consumer Research, 19,* 45–61.

Finn, A. (1988). Print ad recognition readership scores: An information processing perspective. *Journal of Marketing Research, 25,* 168–177.

Fishbein, M., & Ajzen, I. (1975). *Belief, attitude, intention and behavior: An introduction to theory and research.* Reading, MA: Addison-Wesley.

Gotlieb, J. B., & Sarel, D. (1991). Comparative advertising effectiveness: The role of involvement and source credibility. *Journal of Advertising, 20,* 38–45.

Graber, D. A. (1988). *Processing the news* (2nd ed.). New York: Longman.

Grunig, J. E., & Hunt, T. (1984). *Managing public relations.* New York: Holt, Rinehart & Winston.

Guthrie, E. R. (1959). Association by contiguity. In S. Koch (Ed.), *Psychology: A study of a science.* New York: McGraw-Hill.

Jones, E. E., Kanouse, D. E., Kelly, H. H., Nisbett, R. E., Valins, S., & Weiner, B. (Eds.). (1972). *Attribution: Perceiving the causes of behavior.* Morristown, NJ: General Learning Press.

Joseph, W. B. (1982). The credibility of physically attractive communicators: A review. *Journal of Advertising, 11*(3), 15–24.

Lutz, K. A., & Lutz, R. J. (1977). The effects of interactive imagery on learning: Application to advertising. *The Journal of Applied Psychology, 62*(3), 493–498.

Mehta, A., & Davis, C. M. (1990). *Celebrity advertising: Perception, persuasion and processing.* Paper presented at the AEJMC Annual Conference, Minneapolis, MN.

Mendelsohn, H. (1990). Mind, affect, and action: Construction theory and the media effects dialectic. In S. Kraus (Ed.), *Mass communication and political information processing* (pp. 37–45). Hillsdale, NJ: Lawrence Erlbaum Associates.

Miller, G. A. (1956). The magic number 7, plus or minus two: Some limits on our capacity for processing information. *Psychological Review, 63,* 81–97.

Mitchell, A. A., & Olson, J. C. (1981). Are product attribute beliefs the only mediator of advertising effects on brand attitude? *Journal of Marketing Research, 18,* 318–332.

Moriarty, S. (1991). Explorations into the commercial encounter. In R. Holman (Ed.), *Proceedings of the 1991 Conference of the American Academy of Advertising* (pp. 215–222).

Olson, J. C., Toy, D. R., & Dover, P. A. (1982). Do cognitive responses mediate the effects of advertising content on cognitive structure? *Journal of Consumer Research, 9,* 245–262.

Ostrom, T. M., Petty, R. E., & Brock, T. C. (1981). *Cognitive responses in persuasion.* Hillsdale, NJ: Lawrence Erlbaum Associates.

Paivio, A. (1969). Mental imagery in associative learning and memory. *Psychological Review, 76,* 241–263.

Paivio, A. (1971). *Imagery and verbal processes.* New York: Holt.

Pechmann, C., & Stewart, D. W. (1988). Advertising repetition: A critical review of wearin and wearout. *Current Issues & Research in Advertising, 11,* 285–329.

Pechmann, C., & Stewart, D. W. (1989). The multidimensionality of persuasive communications: Theoretical and empirical foundations. In P. Cafferata & A. Tybolt (Eds.), *Cognitive and affective responses to advertising* (pp. 00–00). Lexington, MA: Lexington Books.

Petty, R. E., Cacioppo, J. T., & Schumann, D. (1983). Central and peripheral routes to advertising effectiveness: The moderating role of involvement. *Journal of Consumer Research, 10,* 135–146.

Preston, I. (1982). The association model of the advertising communication process. *Journal of Advertising, 11*(2), 3–15.

Preston, I., & Thorson, E. (1984). The expanded association model: Keeping the hierarchy concept alive. *Journal of Advertising Research, 24*(1), 59–66.

Ratneshwar, S., & Chaiken, S. (1991). Comprehension's role in persuasion: The case of its moderating effect on the persuasive impact of source cues. *Journal of Consumer Research, 18,* 52–62.

Rittenburg, T. L., & Laczniak, R. N. (1990). Future research in television advertising: The commercial break, not the commercial. In P. A. Stout (Ed.), *Proceedings of the 1990 Conference of the American Academy of Advertising* (pp. 87–92).

Rosenberg, M. J. (1956). Cognitive structure and attitudinal affect. *Journal of Abnormal and Social Psychology, 53,* 367–372.

Shannon, C. E. (1949). A mathematical theory of communication. *Bell System Technical Journal, 27,* 379–423, 623–656.

Sherif, M., & Cantril, H. (1945). The psychology of attitudes: I. *Psychological Review, 52,* 295–319.

Sherif, M., & Cantril, H. (1946). The psychology of attitudes: II. *Psychological Review, 53,* 1–24.

Simonson, M. R. (1984, February). Media & persuasive messages. *Instructional Innovator,* pp. 23–24.

Singh, S. N., & Churchill, G. A. (1986). Using the theory of signal detection to improve ad recognition testing. *Journal of Marketing Research, 23,* 327–336.

Slater, M. D., Auld, G., Keefe, T., & Kendall, P. (1991, August). *Information processing and situational theory: A cognitive response analysis.* Paper presented at the AEJMC Annual Conference, Boston, MA.

Snodgrass, J. G., Levy-Berger, G., & Haydon, M. (1985). *Human experimental psychology.* New York: Oxford University Press.

Tashchian, A., White, J. D., & Pak, S. (1988). Signal detection analysis and advertising recognition: An introduction to measurement and interpretation issues. *Journal of Marketing Research, 25,* 397–404.

Thorson, E. (1991). Consumer processing of advertising. *Current Issues and Research in Advertising, 12,* 197–230.

Travers, R. M. W. (1970). *Man's information system.* Scranton, PA: Chandler.

Triesman, A. M. (1964). Verbal cues, language and meaning in selective attention. *American Journal of Psychology, 77,* 206–219.

Wackman, D. B. (1973). Theories of interpersonal perception. In S. Ward & T. S. Robertson (Eds.), *Consumer behavior: Theoretical sources.* Englewood Cliffs, NJ: Prentice-Hall.

Zinkham, G. M., & Muderisoglu, A. (1985). Involvement, familiarity, cognitive differentiation, and advertising recall: A test of convergent and discriminant validity. *Advances in Consumer Research, 132,* 356–361.

19 Some General Observations About Research on Integrated Marketing Communications

Richard J. Lutz
University of Florida

The purpose of this chapter is to provide a summary reaction to the chapters presented during the second day of the conference. Rather than discuss my reactions to each individual chapter, I have attempted to organize my thoughts into some general themes that run through the entire set of chapters. In so doing, I have on occasion overstepped my bounds, so to speak, by incorporating a few particularly pertinent chapters from the first day of the conference. Additionally, I have taken the liberty of going beyond the chapters in several instances, using the many good ideas expressed in them as springboards for my own thoughts about integrated marketing communications (IMC).

Three distinct IMC themes emerged from the collection of chapters at this conference: organizational issues, that is, the implementational barriers to effective integration both within and across organizations; consumer psychology issues, that is, understanding consumer response to the increasingly complex and cluttered communications environment; and measurement issues, that is, the new approaches and tools needed to monitor and evaluate a variegated IMC program. The measurement issue obviously hinges a great deal on the nature of consumer response, whereas the organizational issue is largely a separate matter. As the latter is rather far removed from my area of (claimed) expertise, I discuss it only briefly, concentrating my remarks on the consumer response to IMC and attendant measurement implications.

ORGANIZING FOR IMC

In organizing for effective IMC programs, both intraorganizational and interorganizational concerns rise to the forefront. The interface between the client organization (e.g., a manufacturer) and its IMC supplier (e.g., a full-service advertising agency) has been a traditional source of concern. However, that relationship typically was limited to that between the client's brand management team and the agency's account management team, with dominant or even exclusive focus on the advertising portion of the client's total promotional mix. For effective IMC to occur, increased coordination is implied within both the client and its agency (or agencies). The advertising and public relations and sales promotion and product placement and direct mail and even sales force functions need to be carefully orchestrated to accomplish IMC objectives.

The chapters by Prensky, McCarty, and Lucas[1] (chapter 9) and by Petrison and Wang (chapter 8) highlight these important organizational issues. Prensky et al. referred to a content versus process distinction, whereas Petrison and Wang contrasted execution versus planning. In each case, the latter term applied to the organizational processes and mechanisms through which IMC programs are produced. The barriers to implementation noted in these chapters are reminiscent of classic channel management issues in the marketing literature. Indeed, perhaps the single most interesting chapter presented here, in my judgment, was the one by Stewart, Frazier, and Martin (chapter 10). In it they introduce the concept of integrated channel management (i.e., ICM instead of IMC), wherein the channel serves to integrate the distribution and communication functions of the firm (effectively reducing the famous "4 Ps" to only 3). This strikes me as potentially a very fundamental change in the way we think about marketing, let alone communications. Obviously, even more institutional barriers exist that may hamper implementation of ICM, but it may represent the most appropriate organizational response to the contemporary consumer and competitive environment.

In her paper Chapter (chapter 12), Haytko identified three "principles" of IMC: coordination (of people and ideas), consistency (within and across media), and complementarity. Of these, the former two are neither novel nor exclusive to IMC. This is not meant as a criticism, but rather as a way of signifying complementarity as the hallmark of IMC. Coordination and consistency are necessary but not sufficient for a "true" IMC program. Another way to say it (as have many of the authors in this text) is *synergy*. When all is said and done, successful IMC contributes something over and above the mere sum of its parts.

Above all, integration does not equate to uniformity. This comes through quite clearly in Gronstedt's identification of the organization's many stakeholders, as well as Stern's rhetorical analysis of the organization's "voice" as being comprised of multiple "personas." The combination of all

---

[1]Except as otherwise noted, all works cited in this discussion appear in this volume.

the many persona–stakeholder communication linkages, if properly organized around the organization's intended voice (i.e., "distinctive authorial presence," Abrams, 1988, cited in Stern, chapter 5, this volume), serve to envelop the consumer and other key audiences in a richly textured and interlocking web of meanings.

The key point underlying the potential synergy of IMC is the recognition that different media (broadly construed) have very different strengths. IMC attempts to capitalize on those differential strengths. By way of an example, let me briefly describe a project I have just completed with a former doctoral student, Alice Wright (Wright & Lutz, 1992). We contrasted new product advertising with product sampling, two different IMC media. We first constructed, through careful pretesting, a full-page four-color print ad for a candy bar. The ad was designed to communicate information about the product attributes that were most salient to those actually tasting the candy bar (e.g., sweetness, crunchiness), as well as ingredient information available on the package. Comparing two groups, one that saw the ad and the other that received the candy bar itself, we found that their attribute ratings of the candy were identical; both the ad and the sample had conveyed the same basic information. However, there was a dramatic difference in the confidence the subjects placed on their attribute ratings, particularly for so-called "experience attributes" (Nelson, 1970) like sweet and crunchy; here, those receiving the sample were much more confident. Importantly, those holding more confident attribute beliefs also formed more confident brand attitudes, which Fazio and Zanna (1978) and others showed are more predictive of subsequent behavior. The key for IMC planning that can be inferred from our result is that various media (and their combinations) can be compared on their ability to create confidently held attribute beliefs. In a sense, confidence serves as sort of a metric for comparing the value of an expensive sample exposure with a relatively inexpensive advertising exposure. If one selects the right measure, apples and oranges *can* be compared.

Coordinating advertising and sampling is trivial in the experimental laboratory, but formidable in a real-world IMC program. Let me return to the Stewart et al. chapter (chapter 10) for a moment, which, despite its many virtues, neglected the crucial organizational implementation issue. In the marketing channels literature increasing attention is being given to the notion of strategic alliances, that is, partnerships among manufacturers, their vendors, and their distributors that are bonded by the common goal of customer satisfaction. One of the keys to forming a successful strategic alliance is the fostering of trust among the allies. Trust, in turn, can be built by the sharing of "transaction-specific assets" (Heide & John, 1988). For example, some allies go so far as to disclose to each other proprietary information like income statements and balance sheets. Thinking like this,

I believe, militates against continuation of the 15% commission rate that is still the dominant compensation model in the agency business. If an ad agency is to become a strategic ally, it needs to accept some real responsibility for the client's marketplace performance; agency profits should be tied to sales revenue.

If IMC becomes a major force in the promotional landscape, I predict that thinking of a strategic alliance nature will become the norm. Manufacturers are learning the ropes with their distributors and raw materials suppliers. It is only a matter of time until the same relationships will be forged with their ad agencies and sales promotion houses. Indeed, the most significant barriers to successful IMC implementation may well lie within the manufacturer's own organization rather than between it and its communications partners. External partners can be incentivized to cooperate, or the relationship will be severed. It is not that simple to force coordination among internal factions.

In sum, although the organizational challenges to successful IMC efforts are many and varied, they will be met. IMC content is most likely less problematic than is the IMC process, but the content domain and its effects on consumer response are far from being understood.

THE PSYCHOLOGY OF CONSUMER RESPONSE TO IMC

In attempting to tackle the task of understanding consumer response to IMC, let's begin by using the Foote, Cone Belding matrix (see Fig. 19.1) as modified by Baldinger in chapter 15. Baldinger did a nice job of integrating

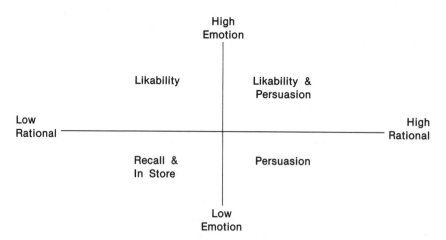

FIG. 19.1. Modified Foote/Cone/Belding matrix.

probable communications mediators into the four quadrants of matrix. In particular, he extended past accounts by incorporating the recent ARF study (Haley & Baldinger, 1991) findings regarding ad likability ("attitude-toward-the-ad" in current academic parlance). There can be no doubt that the nature of consumer response varies with the degree of emotional and rational intensity invested by the consumer in the category. On that the record is clear. However, the matrix as presented may have the unintended consequence of distorting the nature of "typical" consumer response. By creating four quadrants, the matrix may lead to the inference that these are somehow of equal importance. My contention is that they are equal only in the *Animal Farm* sense: Just as the animals were all equal but the pigs were more equal, the quadrants are all equal but the low rational/low emotion quadrant is more equal. We tend to forget that most products for most consumers are simply not all that important. Consumers save their thought and emotion for other things in life.

Failure to recognize this leads to unwanted skewness in the nature of research on communications effects. For instance, in his chapter on product publicity (chapter 17), Hallahan posited that an axiom of publicity is that people seek information about products. I don't think so—I think that consumers tend to "scan" the environment. Consider the ubiquitous TV channel changer that has become standard fare for comedians; the viewer scans through the channels until something interrupts the process by capturing his or her attention, at least momentarily. Not very often will that attention grabber be an ad for a consumer product. This basic fact is even more important when considering the impact of IMC. The "new" media that fall under the IMC rubric may often represent an even lower involvement stimulus exposure than the typical television commercial (e.g., publicity releases, coupons, shelf facings, product placements in movies, etc.).

When one considers the overwhelming number of IMC stimuli to which the typical consumer is exposed each day, the "clutter" that TV advertisers fret about compounds itself exponentially. How many of these potential exposures become "real?" How many do we attend to at a conscious level? How many register at a nonconscious level? One of my colleagues at the University of Florida, Chris Janiszewski, has an impressive program of research documenting the persuasive impact of unattended (in a conscious sense) advertising stimuli (Janiszewski, 1990a, 1990b). It may well be that unorthodox conceptual and methodological approaches hold the key to understanding the effects of much IMC activity.

The vast preponderance of published research, however, continues to focus on advertising at the expense of other forms of communication. Recently, researchers have begun to recognize that response to advertising often does not entail vast amounts of elaborated cognitive activity, as represented by the righthand side of Fig. 19.1. Instead, attention has been directed to more affective (often mislabeled "emotional") response to ads, as represented by the upper-left quadrant. In essence, this viewpoint argues that advertising works by engendering emotional reactions that somehow rub off onto the brand.

Fig. 19.2 portrays my critique of both the hypercognitive and the newly emerging hyperemotive views of advertising response. The vertical axis represents the degree and valence of both cognition and emotion in response to a stream of ad stimuli encountered by the consumer over time (horizontal axis). Using zero as a baseline, the question of interest becomes one of the percentage of ads that exceed either threshold (most often the upper, we hope, unless we are of the Ted Bates school). My contention is that most ads, for most people, most of the time, fall within the threshold levels and, hence, spawn very little mental activity of either kind. It is only the rare commercial that manages to poke its head up out of the churning sea of the everyday clutter. This might be characterized as the "flying fish hypothesis" of advertising effects. The problem is that ad responses, like fish, don't fly very often, at least not nearly as often as implied by our obsession first with cognition and now with emotion.

If the consumer is both hypocognitive and hypoemotional with respect to the vast preponderance of IMC stimuli, where does that leave us in the way of explanatory models? One preliminary answer to this question is provided by the relevance–accessibility model, or RAM (Baker & Lutz, 1988), which Bill Baker developed in his dissertation research. A key premise of RAM, and a point of departure from other accounts of advertising effects, is its separation of the ad exposure occasion and the brand response occasion. Whereas most advertising research implicitly assumes that advertising exerts its impact at contact, RAM explicitly posits that advertising can work only

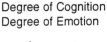

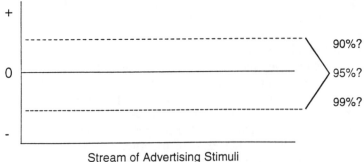

FIG. 19.2. Arousal potential of advertising.

at the purchase occasion, which is separated from the exposure occasion by time, space, and intervening clutter. RAM thus places a premium on memory and retrieval factors. This approach is consistent with Keller's work on retrieval cues in the purchase situation. Another way to improve memory performance, and a direct implication of RAM, is to reduce the separation between ad exposure and brand response. Displaying an ad in store, even in the appropriate aisle as permitted by videocarts, is responsive to that charge; time, space, and clutter separation are minimized.

RAM asserts that the efficacy of advertising rests, in part, on a matching of consumer involvement at the time of ad exposure and the time of brand choice. Furthermore, the type of information that will be attended and retrieved, respectively, differs with involvement. When involvement is high, relative brand performance information is prepotent; under more moderate involvement, heuristic quality cues move to the forefront (consistent with the elaboration likelihood model's "peripheral route" to persuasion). However, when involvement is low, as I have argued is most often the case for both ad exposure and brand choice, the task of advertising is to foster brand salience and familiarity and/or to leave a mild affective trace in memory. Initial empirical findings (Baker, 1991) support RAM's predictions, which are quite consistent with the state-dependent learning literature (e.g. Blaxton, 1989). The simple message is that in order to influence an inherently low-involvement purchase decision, the most effective approach is low-involvement advertising that is relatively free of cognitive and affective content, instead emphasizing brand salience. This finding is in need of replication, but it at least offers hope for IMC's low involvement media.

Another dissertation conducted recently at the University of Florida (Holden & Lutz, 1992) extended the RAM logic by modeling the ad exposure and brand response occasions in more phenomenological terms. As shown in Fig. 19.3, both occasions can be characterized using a spreading activation representation of memory. At ad exposure the brand is in the center of the network, and the advertiser attempts to associate the brand with certain positive benefits and/or consumption occasions (e.g., "Heinz Ketchup is thick," "Weekends are made for Michelob"). Parenthetically, it should be noted that ad effectiveness (i.e., Baldinger's "communications" variable) is most often assessed by presenting the consumer with the brand name and asking what associates come to mind. If "Heinz" prompts "thick," then the ad has done its job. However, Holden and Lutz (1992) argued that the "Heinz-to-thick" linkage is not as instrumental as the reverse, that is, the "thick-to-Heinz" link. As depicted in Fig. 19.3, at the center of the network at the purchase occasion is a desired consumption benefit. The key to ad effectiveness, then, is the degree to which the brand (e.g., Michelob) becomes salient given the operant situational cue (e.g., beer

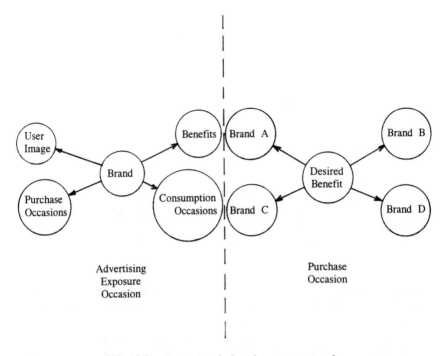

FIG. 19.3.   Asymmetry in brand memory networks.

for the weekend). Holden and Lutz (1992) argued that asymmetry exists between the brand–benefit and benefit–brand links in memory, with the latter being the critical one for brand performance. This model of communications effects is reflective of the notion of goal-derived categories (Barsalou, 1991).

In sum, the psychology of consumer response to IMC dictates a less cognitive, less emotional portrayal of the consumer. Instead, lower involvement and situationally driven accounts are needed.

IMC MEASUREMENT

As if the measurement of advertising effects weren't controversial and troublesome enough, the challenges of measuring IMC effects seem almost insurmountable. Whereas so-called "qualitative" media factors (e.g., the difference between a television and print exposure) have never been fully understood or adequately modeled, consider the complexity of incorporating in-store exposures, coupons, free samples, news releases, ad infinitum. We've gone from comparing apples and oranges (which are both spherical at least!) to comparing apples, oranges, bananas, grapes, watermelon, blueberries, guavas, and kiwi fruit! Where to begin? On what dimensions to compare? Katz and Lendrevie correctly employed the metaphor of the Holy Grail in their innovative and intriguing approach to IMC measurement (chapter 14, this volume). Their classification of media exposures, product impressions (e.g., in store, consumption at home), and personal contacts (e.g., sales force, telemarketing) is a very useful starting point for addressing the problem. Upon some further reflection, at least four general priorities seem clear for IMC measurement to proceed fruitfully: more attention to "natural" exposure settings, a contingency approach to the selection of appropriate dependent variables, the use of multiple methods, and a "metric" for comparing the value of an exposure across IMC media. I consider each of these briefly.

Far too much advertising research is conducted in the laboratory. IMC demands movement into the field, both for exploratory purposes and for greater ecological validity. In a brilliant but largely obscure 1966 paper in the *Journal of Business*, Steiner had his undergraduate students surreptitiously observe their families watching television in the evening, recording what happened when commercials were aired. To perhaps no one's surprise, during commercials people read, conversed, or even left the room. We don't need a complex cognitive model to explain advertising ineffectiveness in that instance; we simply need to get out there *in situ* and observe what's really happening when real consumers are confronted with real ads. As someone once said, find out what people do with communications rather than what communications do to people.

Observing consumers at the purchase occasion is similarly important and similarly neglected. Hoyer (1984) found that consumers averaged 13 seconds in making their detergent selection in the supermarket, and this included the time it took to push the cart down the aisle. Dickson and Sawyer (1990) obtained similar findings across a wider array of product categories. This is not indicative of a lot of in-store cognitive machination and deliberation.

A contingency approach to the selection of appropriate dependent variables is essential. Bill Wells has advocated this for years in his writings; the type of product (i.e., approach or avoidance) and the type of advertising (i.e., lecture or drama) dictate the type of litmus paper we need to detect the effect. Both the Baldinger (chap. 15) and Katz and Lendrevie (chap. 14) chapters emphasize that basic fact. Although most of the action will of necessity be at the low-involvement end of the continuum (e.g., brand salience, consideration sets, etc.), let me depart from that theme for a moment to represent the other end of the involvement continuum. Spurred by the recent reemergence of anthropological thinking in the field of consumer research, brand "meaning"—in a symbolic sense—has become more prominent. What does a Teenage Mutant Ninja Turtle mean to a small boy? What does a Barbie doll mean to a young girl? McCracken (1986, 1989) developed a cultural account of how advertising imbues products with meaning, which, in turn, can be procured and internalized by the consumer. This general approach seems quite promising for understanding the effects of communications on behalf of products and brands about which consumers do care.

The use of multiple methods is closely related to the contingency approach to measurement. As noted previously, we have been too wedded to the lab and, perhaps, to the results of scanner panel data analyses. For example, in trying to measure product exposures, Katz and Lendrevie advocated the use of purchase frequency and promotion frequency data (both available from scanner databases); however, they had no suggestions regarding the measurement of in-home, postpurchase product exposure. One simple approach is to measure via survey self-report the consumption frequency of the product/brand. However, consumption does not necessarily imply brand name exposure. One of my students, Betsy Moore-Shay, and I have been researching intergenerational carryover of brand preferences, that is, the tendency of adult children to prefer the same brands as their parents (Moore-Shay & Lutz, 1987). Not only have we found a significant intergenerational carryover effect, but we have also found that it is strongly moderated by the visibility of the brand in consumption. For example, in most families the mayonnaise jar is placed on the family dinner table, whereas canned vegetables usually are removed from their containers before serving. Intergenerational carryover is much greater for the former than the latter, even after adjusting for the number of brands in the two categories. Thus, brand visibility in the consumption situation translates into IMC exposures.

Finally, the "value" of various IMC media exposures must be calibrated somehow. My earlier description of the advertising versus sampling research with Alice Wright pointed to the concept of benefit belief confidence, but that measure would appear to be limited to more deliberative purchase decisions. Recent work by Fazio and his colleagues (e.g., Fazio, Powell, & Williams, 1989) implicated brand accessibility (as measured by response latencies), which may be a promising approach for more spontaneous purchases and for more low-involvement communications exposures.

CONCLUSIONS

Table 19.1 is my attempt at summarizing the points I have made in this chapter, as well as those offered by the authors of the various chapters I have cited. I have organized my lists of "what's hot" and "what's not" into

TABLE 19.1
What's Hot And What's Not In IMC Research

What's Hot	*What's Not*
Input variables	
IMC media (especially interactions!)	Advertising (especially insolation)
Process variables	
"Seepage"	Cognition
Priming	Emotion
Framing	
State-dependent learning	
Goal-derived categories	
Incidental learning	
Unconscious processes	
Outcome Variables	
Recognition	Recall
Brand salience	Brand beliefs
Consideration sets	Brand attitude
Brand meaning	Attitude toward the ad
Moderator Variables	
Occasions	Need for cognition
Exposure	Self-monitoring
Purchase	
Consumption	
Distance	
Temporal	
Spatial	
Motives	
Methods	
Naturalistic observation	Laboratory experiments
Multiple methods	

five categories: input variables, process variables, outcome variables, moderator variables, and methods.

My characterization of "what's hot" is more often a plea for change in emphasis than an accurate assessment of the current state of the art. As well, my label of "what's not" is not intended to imply that entries in this column should be jettisoned altogether, but rather that they need less but more judicious attention. Movement from a focus on advertising to the broader-based and multifaceted IMC necessitates concomitant movements along all dimensions of the research enterprise. Of most far-reaching significance, in my opinion, is the need to study interactive or synergistic effects of IMC media; isolated main effects are relics of the past.

Of equal importance is the need to go "back to the future" in our conceptualization of the processes through which IMC exerts its effects. Herb Krugman introduced us to "learning without involvement" in 1965, and it is time to revisit that idea with the tools of the 1990s. I use the term *seepage* as a metaphor for the effect of IMC. Like the unseen leak in the basement during a spring rain, IMC leaves a puddle in the corner, but we don't know how it got there. But it is there! I am increasingly of the opinion that higher order cognition and emotion are not the answer; instead, some of the lower involvement, incidental, perhaps even unconscious processes listed in Table 19.1 may hold the key. As Thorson (1990) put it so vividly, much of the past 20 years of advertising research can be viewed as resting on the assumption that consumers process product information [in ads] as they would learn the capitals of Europe" (p. 198). It is high time that we eschew that assumption, once and for all.

REFERENCES

Baker, W. E. (1991). *The relevance-accessibility model of advertising effectiveness.* Unpublished doctoral dissertation, University of Florida.

Baker, W. E., & Lutz, R. J. (1988). The relevance-accessibility model of advertising effectiveness. In S. Hecker & D. W. Stewart (Eds.), *Nonverbal communication in advertising*, pp. 59–84). Lexington, MA: Lexington.

Barsalou, L. W. (1991). Deriving categories to achieve goals. in G. H. Bower (Ed.), *The psychology of learning and motivation* (Vol. 27, pp. 1–64). New York: Academic.

Blaxton, T. A. (1989). Investigating dissociations among memory measures: Support for a transfer-appropriate processing framework. *Journal of Experimental Psychology: Learning, Memory, and Cognition, 15* (4), 657–668.

Dickson, P. R., & Sawyer, A. G. (1990). The price knowledge and search of supermarket shoppers. *Journal of Marketing, 54* (3), 42–53.

Fazio, R. H., Powell, M. C., & Williams, C. J. (1989). The role of attitude accessibility in the attitude-to-behavior process. *Journal of Consumer Research, 16,* 280–288.

Fazio, R. H., & Zanna, M. P. (1978). Attitudinal qualities relating to the strength of the attitude-behavior relationship. *Journal of Experimental Social Psychology, 14,* 398–408.

Haley, R. I., & Baldinger, A. L. (1991). The ARF copy research validity project. *Journal of Advertising Research, 31,* 11–32.

Heide, J. B., & John, G. (1988). The role of dependence balancing in safeguarding transaction-specific assets in conventional channels. *Journal of Marketing, 52*(1), 20–35.

Holden, S. J. S., & Lutz, R. J. (1992). Ask not what the brand can evoke; ask what can evoke the brand? In J. F. Sherry, Jr. & B. Sternthal (Eds.), *Advances in consumer research* (Vol. 19, pp. 101–107). Provo, UT: Association for Consumer Research.

Hoyer, W. D. (1984). An examination of consumer decision making for a common repeat purchase product. *Journal of Consumer Research, 11,* 822–829.

Janiszewski, C. (1990a). The influence of nonattended material on the processing of advertising claims. *Journal of Marketing Research, 27,* 263–278.

Janiszewski, C. (1990b). The influence of print advertisement organization on affect toward a brand name. *Journal of Consumer Research, 17,* 53–65.

Krugman, H. E. (1965). The impact of television advertising: Learning without involvement. *Public Opinion Quarterly, 29*(3), 349–356.

McCracken, G. (1986). Culture and consumption: A theoretical account of the structure and movement of the cultural meaning of consumer goods. *Journal of Consumer Research, 13,* 71–84.

McCracken, G. (1989). Who is the celebrity endorser? Cultural foundations of the endorsement process. *Journal of Consumer Research, 16*, 310–324.

Moore-Shay, E. S., & Lutz, R. J. (1987). Intergenerational influences in the formation of consumer attitudes and beliefs about the marketplace: Mothers and daughters. In M. J. Houston (Ed.), *Advances in consumer research*, (Vol. 15, pp. 461–467). Provo, UT: Association for Consumer Research.

Nelson, P. (1970). Information and consumer behavior. *Journal of Political Economy, 78*, 311–329.

Steiner, G. A. (1966). The people look at commercials: A study of audience behavior. *Journal of Business, 29*, 272–304.

Thorson, E. (1990). Consumer processing of advertising. *Current Issues and Research in Advertising, 12*(2), 197–230.

Wright, A. A., & Lutz, R. (1992). Effects of advertising and experience on brand judgments: A rose by any other frame. . . . In L. McAlister & M. L. Rothschild (Eds.), *Advances in consumer research* (Vol. 20, pp. 165–169). Provo, UT: Association for Consumer Research.

Author Index

Subject Index